BETWEEN
TWO
ARMIES

in the Ixil Towns
of Guatemala

BETWEEN TWO ARMIES

in the Ixil Towns of Guatemala

DAVID STOLL

Columbia
University Press

NEW YORK

Columbia University Press
New York   Chichester, West Sussex

Copyright © 1993 Columbia University Press
All rights reserved

Library of Congress Cataloging-in-Publication Data

Stoll, David, 1952–
    Between two armies in the Ixil towns of Guatemala / David Stoll.
        p.   cm.
    Includes bibliographical references and index.
    ISBN 0-231-08182-0 (cl.)
    ISBN 0-231-08183-9 (pa.)
    1. Guatemala—Politics and government—1945–1985.
    2. Guatemala—Politics andgovernment—1985–
    3. Ejército Guerrillero de los Pobres (Guatemala)
    4. Government, Resistance to—Guatemala—History.
    5. Ixil Indians—Social conditions.
    6. Ladino (Latin American people)—Social conditions.
    7. Indians of Central America—Guatemala—Social conditions.
    I. Title.
    F1466.5.S76   1993   320.97281—dc20   93—22046
                                                              CIP

Casebound editions of Columbia University Press books are printed
on permanent and durable acid-free paper.

Printed in the United States of America

c 10 9 8 7 6 5 4 3 2 1

Contents

List of Tables

Preface

This book is intended to challenge how the human rights and solidarity movements think about Guatemala. It is not that activists have been
hopelessly wrong, only that it is time to start thinking about the situation in new ways. I do so through a case study of an area reputed to
have been a guerrilla stronghold—the so-called Ixil Triangle. From my
first visits to Ixil country, at the end of 1982, I sensed that its experience
of a failed revolution differed greatly from the claims being made by
the left as well as the right. There was a third side not being reported.
It was that of most of the population, who were being taken for grant-
ed in a grand contest between armies, ideologies, and presumed social
classes. True, hundreds of thousands of Mayan Indians supported the
guerrilla movement of the early 1980s. But judging from my interviewing in Ixil country, the movement was not a spontaneous uprising
in the sense of a French jacquerie, nor was it a highly organized Long
March, nor was it "popular" in any but a transitory and coerced way.
Instead, most of the people of Ixil country were rebels against their will,
and they were coerced by the guerrillas as well as the army.

Scholars are already of two minds about the popular roots of the
guerrilla war in the western highlands. I am far from alone in sensing
that Mayan support for guerrilla warfare was very localized, often
forced, and generally fleeting. We have been slow to draw out the

implications, however. One reason is that confronting the role of the guerrillas in bringing on the violence punctures a good deal of left-wing mythology. That, in turn, can be interpreted to justify the human rights violations of the Guatemalan army. After some hesitation, I decided that I would have to proceed anyway, and on three levels. On the level of scholarship, I would have to question the Vietnam-era assumption that guerrilla insurgencies are popular. On the level of the solidarity movement, that is, the international support network for the Guatemalan Left, I would have to question specific claims about the guerrilla movement in the western highlands. And on the level of the closely related but distinct human rights movement, I would have to question how it defines the problems of ordinary Guatemalans and seeks to address these.

Such an agenda set me against prevailing forms of interpretation in ways that were not easy to sort out. If the guerrilla movement represented the popular will in the western highlands, then the most pertinent explanation for its failure should be the apparatus of repression set up by the Guatemalan army, for which the Ixil region has become well known. It would also be logical to study the popular response in terms of "resistance," a catch-all category that became as fashionable in the cultural anthropology of the 1980s as "acculturation" was in the 1950s. Resistance certainly can be found in Ixil country. Guerrillas roam the mountains, and refugees shelter there from army bombardments. Even under army control there is plenty of passive resistance, of the foot-dragging kind that James Scott has called the "weapons of the weak."

But if the revolutionary movement did not grow out of popular aspirations, then framing events in terms of oppression, rebellion, and repression is not going to capture local experience, not even if we add apologetic categories like "accommodation." If we listen to what Ixils say in public and private—accompanied by refrains like "we were deceived," "we're in between," "the land doesn't give anymore," and "there's no work"—their experience can hardly be summed up with an all-purpose concept like "resistance." "Resistance" does not describe why a man battling addiction to alcohol joins an evangelical church. Or why, after population growth has shrunk his inheritance to less than a hectare of land, he wants to go to the United States to work.

My purpose, it finally became clear, was to reinterpret the recent history of Ixil country in a way more in accord with how the inhabitants talk about it. At center stage I wanted to place all the people who were as likely to damn one side as the other, who denied any commitment to either, and whose behavior was consistent with those denials. How to do so is no small problem: in a repressive atmosphere like Guatemala, any statement of neutrality may be simply a tactical defense to ward off punishment. Aside from the problem of how frank Ixils are with a foreign anthropologist, what about all the people with whom I could not talk? Those who had joined the revolutionary movement in the early 1980s and were now dead? The survivors who were still in the mountains, in exile, or silently biding their time? There is no fully satisfactory answer to these objections: they are legitimate challenges to what is possible to conclude about a war that shows little sign of ending. But without being able to prove the interpretation which follows, I hope to convince readers that it is more plausible than the alternative, to assume that the guerrillas represent Ixil aspirations.

The first chapter introduces Ixil country, particularly the largest of the three *municipios* there, the town and hinterland of Nebaj, on which I will focus. The second chapter provides a brief social history of the area, particularly colonization since the late nineteenth century and how Ixils responded to it. Ladino (non-Indian) plantation owners and labor contractors came to weigh heavily in local politics, adding to the opportunities for revolutionary organizers. Yet various imported institutions—a Catholic Action movement led by Spanish priests, government schools taught by non-Indians, and political parties—helped Ixils assert themselves in new ways, prior to and quite independently of the guerrilla movement.

The next three chapters look at the origin of military violence in Ixil country, how the Guatemalan army gained the upper hand, and how Ixils view the conflict. Chapter 3 plays previous accounts against my interviews with Ixils. According to the solidarity perspective, the guerrilla movement grew out of the army's reprisals against peaceful social activists. What this ignores is how the Guerrilla Army of the Poor (EGP) provoked the army's arrival by implanting itself in the area and staging attacks: hence the sequence of EGP blows and army counterblows that Ixils describe as coercing them from both sides. The result appeared to be a popular revolutionary movement in the early 1980s, but only because of what I will call "dual violence," a double-bind situation that Ixils describe as "living between two fires."

Chapter 4 examines how revolutionary organizing was broken by the army's conscription of all the men under its control into antiguerrilla civil patrols. According to the army, the patrols protected the population from subversion. For the beleaguered participants, the objective was also to protect themselves and their families from the army. "If we obey," one patroller said in 1985, "they don't kill us anymore."[1] The cruel paradox was that, even as the civil patrols violated international definitions of human rights, they buffered civilians against both sides.

Chapter 5, "From Montaña to Model Village," follows the path of refugees from life with the guerrillas to life with the army, from the EGP-administered "communities of population in resistance" to the army's model villages or concentrated resettlements. Because of how the revolutionary movement unraveled, I will argue that Ixil support for the guerrillas was mainly a reaction to government repression, not the result of a peasantry pregnant with revolutionary impulses, or seeking to restore a lost moral community, or calculating how to assert its land claims. If so, then the familiar narrative of popular frustration giving rise to a revolutionary movement, to be followed by repression and continuing resistance, imposes an agenda most Ixils do not share.

The next four chapters describe how Ixils have responded to military violence by using the civil patrol, religious congregations, and other seemingly subordinate, conformist institutions to reconstruct civil society, that is, political space to make their own decisions. Chapter 6 describes the persecution of the Catholic Church in the early 1980s and how this gave rise to the interpretation of events propagated by the Guatemalan Church in Exile and the solidarity movement. If we accept their narrative of impending liberation, then religious reform culminated in Ixil country with the revolutionary movement. Yet around the three army-controlled towns, among the majority of the population, what was most evident was the growth of new, pentecostal-style congregations, Catholic as well as Protestant. The persecution of the Catholic Church was the most obvious stimulus for these groups, but they also grew out of contradictions in the Catholic structure of authority before the war. During the height of the violence, the new reformed groups became political sanctuaries. The language of personal salvation they employ may seem oblique, but I argue that they carry the same aspirations for equality embodied in Catholic social activism and the revolutionary movement.

Chapter 7, "The Ixil Recovery of Nebaj," describes how Ixils have continued the prewar trend of recovering control of the town hall and local commerce from ladinos.* Contrary to revolutionary depictions of Nebaj as a detention and torture center, the army has permitted a definite space for independent organization and dissent. But while a minority of Ixils have prospered from the war, out in the resettlements nearly everyone is worse off than before. The concentration of population has aggravated a preexisting crisis of land scarcity, ecological degradation, and poverty which, now that the violence has subsided, is once again the most pressing problem Ixils face.

Consequently, chapter 8 focuses on the ecology of Ixil country. Popular history blames the shortage of land facing Mayas on losses to plantations, but among Ixils population growth has taken over as the main cause of dwindling per capita holdings. Indeed, the war has forced many plantation owners to put their land on the market, but the Ixil population is growing so rapidly that, even if all large properties are redistributed, the net gain for each family will be small. Anthropologists have often defended the survival value of subsistence peasant agriculture, but here population growth has made maize farmers structurally dependent on seasonal migration to plantations for pitiful wages.

Now that we have looked at the gradual Ixil recuperation of their homeland and the ecological crisis making this a hollow victory, chapter 9 explores how Nebajeños are making peace with one another. Scholars have paid much attention to ethnic conflict between Indians and ladinos in the western Guatemalan highlands, but the violence in Nebaj had the paradoxical effect of improving relations between the two. Even though Ixils have taken refuge in a language of neutralism and personal salvation, this has not prevented them from renegotiating

---

*Ladinos can be of white, mestizo, or even indigenous heritage but identify themselves as non-Indians.

power relations in their town, nor from using new institutions to reestablish the parameters of civil society. Now that human rights discourse is reaching the Ixil area, it is important to assess the implications for a population that decided to curtail bloodshed by aligning itself with the army. Hence, the concluding chapter, "Let the Dead Bury the Dead?," questions current forms of human rights activism in a context such as Nebaj.

An earlier version of this work was submitted to Stanford University as a Ph.D. dissertation, under the title "Between Two Fires: Dual Violence and the Reassertion of Civil Society in Nebaj, Guatemala." My research was supported by the Inter-American Foundation, the Organization of American States, the National Science Foundation, the Center for Latin American Studies at Stanford, and the Morrison Institute for Population and Resource Studies, also at Stanford. To each of these institutions I am greatly indebted. In Antigua, the staff and visiting scholars of the Centro de Investigaciones Regionales de Mesoamerica (CIRMA) provided interregnums from fieldwork in Nebaj. I would especially like to remember Bill Swezey, the founding director of CIRMA, who passed away during our stay; his old-fashioned conviviality will always be missed. At the Stanford Department of Anthropology, my adviser William Durham, committee members George Collier and James Fox, and counselor emeritus Benjamin Paul provided help whenever I needed it. Their patience and understanding has been considerable.

I would also like to thank several more experienced Guatemala scholars, including Duncan Earle, Erica Verrillo, Carol Smith, and David McCreery, who encouraged me to follow my intuitions wherever they led. An essential collaborator in the final months of my 1988––89 fieldwork was Sarah Gates. She helped organize a household survey, then entered all the data and did a great deal of preliminary analysis; none of it would have happened without her. Thomas Lengyel shared his experience in Ixil country in the crucial period before the violence, as did Pierre van den Berghe. James Loucky directed me to scholarship on fertility and child labor. Joel Simon, who was conducting parallel research north of Ixil country in the Ixcán, was very helpful in explaining the situation there.

My life in Nebaj would have been much harder without my family.

Indeed, without Susan and Benjamin, it is unclear whether the town would have put up with me for long. Foreign visitors and residents, the latter mainly aid workers, provided many fresh observations and occasional medical assistance. I will not mention any by name, but they know who they are and they have my thanks. In Antigua, Stephen Elliott figured out how to make my encounters with the Departamento de Migración as painless as possible. I owe another special debt to Elaine Elliott. Her unpublished archival research clarified the history of land tenure, including agrarian reform in the early 1950s, in ways that might never have emerged from field interviews. Paul Goepfert, Mary Jo McConahay, Victor Perera, Bruce Calder, George Lovell, and Sarah Hill provided moral support and hospitality, as did Michael Shawcross, who in addition always made himself available for a frank airing of our disagreements.

With Robert Carlsen, Linda Green, and Judith Zur I will remember doing fieldwork during the same period. Jo-Marie Burt showed up from Peru at the right moment to remind me of the concept of civil society. At home in Davis, California, Norman Stoltzoff provided valuable insights from his studies with René Girard. During the revision from dissertation to book, Richard N. Adams, Robert Carlsen, Peter Hatch, Fred Harder, Linda Green, Pierre van den Berghe, Timothy Wickham-Crowley, Paul Goepfert, Jake Bernstein, Phil Berryman, and an anonymous reviewer for Columbia University Press gave me valuable comments, while Mike Shawcross provided help with cross-cultural spelling. For the computer-generated maps I would like to thank Peter Powers of Terragraphics in Eugene, Oregon. At Columbia University Press I am grateful to Gioia Stevens, Rita Bernhard, Teresa Bonner, Anne McCoy, Eve Bayrock and Sara Cahill for a commitment to prompt publication that outmatched my own.

Since I was not always able to accommodate the larger objections of collaborators and readers, none of the people mentioned above should be assumed to hold the positions that follow. My greatest debt is to the Nebajeños, Cotzaleños, and Chajuleños who have been so forthcoming in sharing their experiences and explaining their towns. What follows is little more than my interpretation of theirs. Regrettably, in a situation like that which exists in Guatemala, the people who are most important to an anthropologist's work cannot be named, either here or in the notes. Hence, living persons will not appear under their real names nor will their words be attributed to them: if a quotation is unattributed, it can be assumed to derive from my interviews and conversations in Ixil country between 1987 and 1992.

The people who made my research possible include Ixils and ladinos, church leaders, town officials and village representatives, farmers, artisans and shopkeepers, civil patrollers, ex-soldiers and ex-guerrillas. Hundreds of people patiently explained their affairs at my unexpected arrival. Many went beyond that to share their hopes, fears, and anger. They are on every page, and the book is dedicated to them in the hope that it is worthy of their trust.

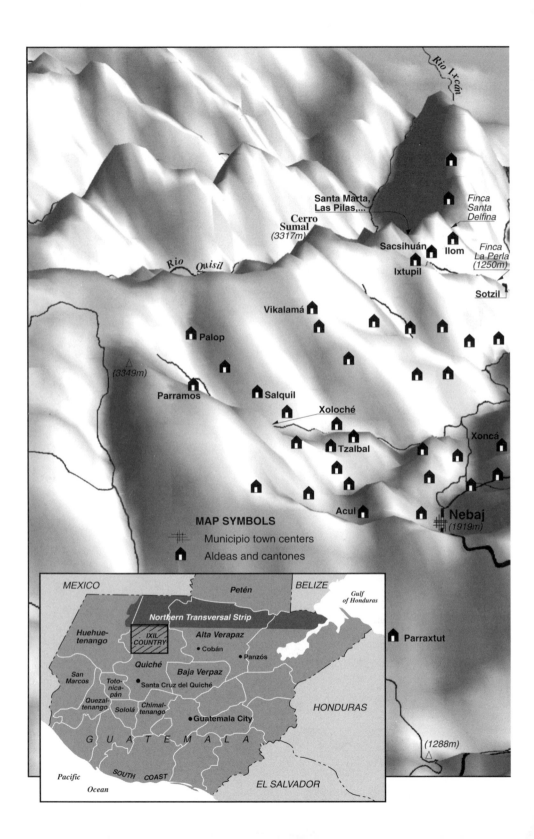

MAP SYMBOLS

Municipio town centers

Aldeas and cantones

Santa Marta,
Las Pilas,...

Cerro
Sumal
(3317m)

Río Ouisil

Río Ixcán

*Finca
Santa
Delfina*

Sacsihuán

Ilom

*Finca
La Perla
(1250m)*

Ixtupil

Sotzil

Vikalamá

Palop

△
(3349m)

Parramos

Salquil

Xoloché

Tzalbal

Xoncá

Acul

Nebaj
(1919m)

Parraxtut

MEXICO

Petén

BELIZE

*Gulf
of Honduras*

*Huehue-
tenango*

Northern Transversal Strip

IXIL
COUNTRY

Alta Verapaz

• Cobán

• Panzós

Quiché

Baja Verpaz

*San
Marcos*

• Santa Cruz del Quiché

*Toto-
nica-
pán*

HONDURAS

*Quezal-
tenango*

Sololá

*Chimal-
tenango*

• Guatemala City

G U A T E M A L A

△
(1288m)

*Pacific

Ocean*

SOUTH   COAST

EL SALVADOR

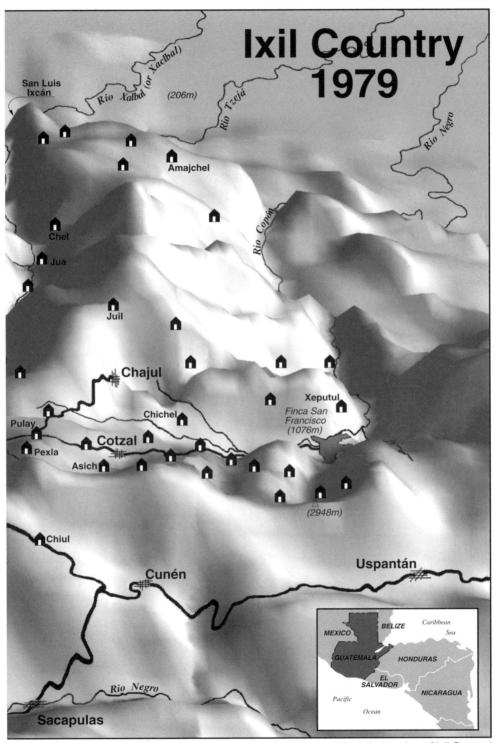

Ixil Country
1979

San Luis
Ixcán

Rio Xalbá (or Xaclbal) (206m)

Rio Tzejá

Rio Copón

Rio Negro

Amajchel

Chel

Juá

Juil

Chajul

Chichel

Xeputul
Finca San Francisco
(1076m)

Pulay

Cotzal

Pexla

Asich

(2948m)

Chiul

Cunén

Uspantán

Rio Negro

Sacapulas

MEXICO

BELIZE

Caribbean Sea

GUATEMALA

HONDURAS

EL SALVADOR

NICARAGUA

Pacific Ocean

(North-facing view of Ixil Country)

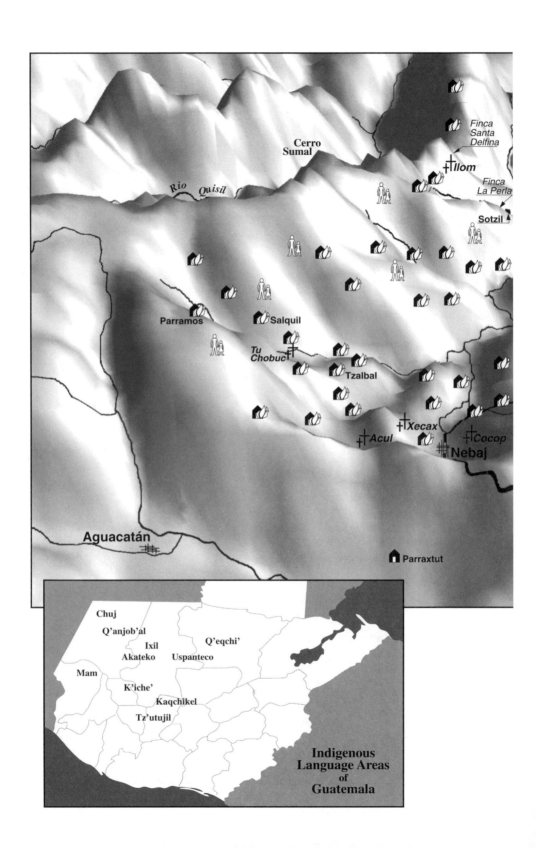

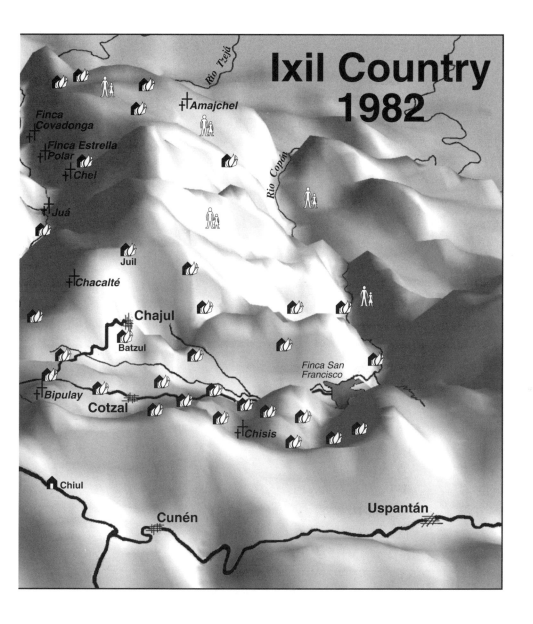

Ixil Country 1982

Finca Covadonga
Finca Estrella
Polar
Chel
Amajchel
Juá
Juil
Chacalté
Chajul
Batzul
Bipulay
Cotzal
Finca San Francisco
Chisis
Chiul
Cunén
Uspantán

Río Tzejá
Río Copón

MAP SYMBOLS

✝Xecax .... Major Rural Massacres, 1980-82

.... Other Burned Settlements

.... Refugees beyond Army Control, 1983-87

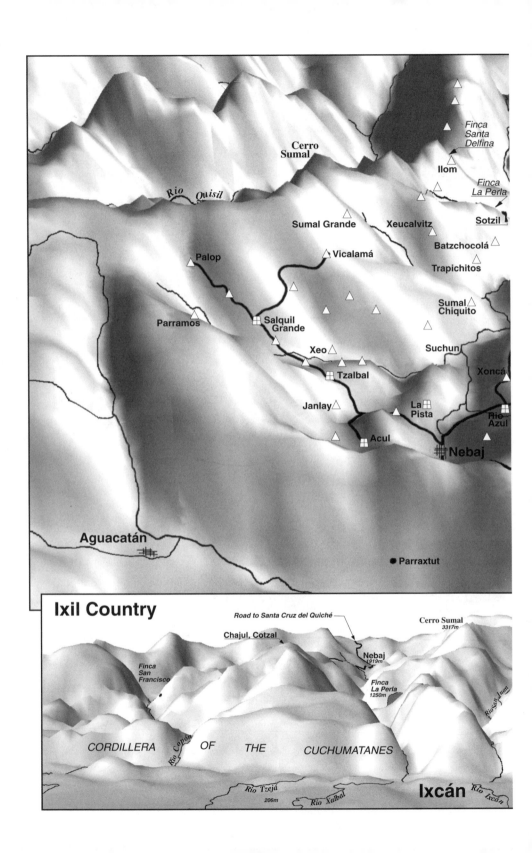

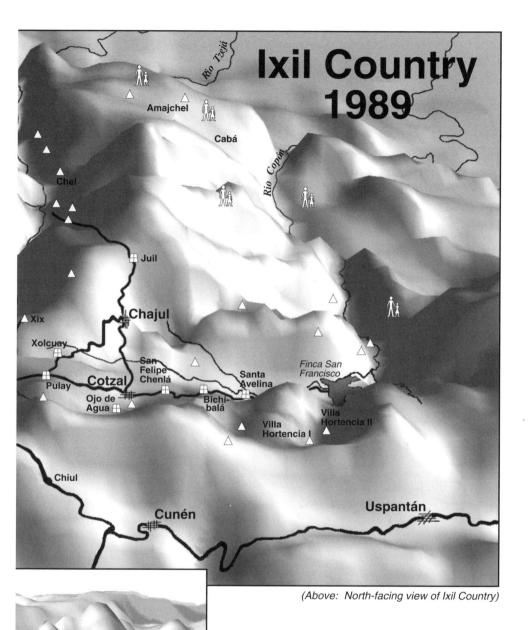

Ixil Country
1989

Río Tzejá

Río Copón

Amajchel

Cabá

Chel

Juil

Xix

Chajul

Xolcuay

San
Felipe
Chenlá

Santa
Avelina

Finca San
Francisco

Pulay

Cotzal

Ojo de
Agua

Bichí-
balá

Villa
Hortencia II

Villa
Hortencia I

Chiul

Cunén

Uspantán

(Above: North-facing view of Ixil Country)

MAP SYMBOLS

⊞ .... Model Villages 1983-85

△ .... Other Resettlements 1984-90

𝕚 .... Communities of Population in
Resistance as of 1989

(Left: South-facing view of Ixil Country)

BETWEEN
TWO
ARMIES

in the Ixil Towns
of Guatemala

ONE

La Situación

The annual pilgrimage to the Christ of Chajul, 1989

Nebaj has Las Tres Hermanas (friendly, very basic), good food available for about US$0.50. . . . There is also an army camp. . . . There are magnificent walks from Nebaj along the river or in the surrounding hills. Although the weather is not very good at this altitude, the views of the Cuchumatanes mountains are spectacular. . . . 2 hours' walk from Nebaj is Acul, one of the new villages settled by the government to control guerrilla activity. —South American Handbook, 1988 edition

IN 1988–89 my wife, our toddler, and I spent a year in a counterinsurgency zone of Guatemala. Living in Nebaj was not as risky as it might seem, at least for researchers enjoying the usual gringo immunities and careful not to test the sensibilities of the Guatemalan army. Backpacking tourists arrived daily, many on sociopolitical tours of Central America. In our conversations it became apparent that they were coming to Guatemala to find oppression, and to Nicaragua (still ruled by the Sandinistas) to find liberation. Of oppression there was plenty in Nebaj, but we found something else as well. Just as revolutions that win usher in staggering new problems, revolutions that lose can accomplish some of their purposes anyway.

Nebaj is one of three *municipios* (municipalities) in the Cuchumatanes mountains inhabited by speakers of Ixil Maya. The Ixils have lived in the northernmost outcrop of the Guatemalan Highlands for at least fourteen hundred years,[1] their Mayan ancestors having built the temples and tombs whose remains dot the area. The three towns still carry the names of patron saints dating from the Spanish conquest in the sixteenth century: Santa María Nebaj, San Gaspar Chajul, San Juan Cotzal. Each is laid out around an imposing colonial church whose whitewashed facade is visible for miles. Visitors invariably note the self-contained quality of Ixil country, ethnically homogenous and enclosed by high ridges. Even after being conquered by the Spanish empire in 1530, it was not settled by outsiders in any number until the start of the twentieth century.

The homeland of the Ixils occupies the waist of one of Guatemala's poorest and most Mayan departments, El Quiché, whose infertile mountains have become a stronghold of peasant smallholders and their minifundia. Before the recent troubles, Ixils were known to the outside world chiefly for the spectacular red dress worn by the women of Nebaj and Chajul. Anthropologists came to consult with Ixil prayer-makers, native priests who preserve part of the ancient Mayan calen-dar.[2] Most of the population lived in dispersed settlements (*aldeas*) that carpeted the broken-floored valleys surrounding the three towns. Except for periodic departures to labor on plantations, most Ixils con-tinued a traditional Mayan existence of growing maize, raising ani-mals, and weaving with backstrap looms.

Then, in the late 1970s, news of government assassinations and mas-sacres began to filter out of the area, along with reports of a Guerrilla Army of the Poor (EGP) that was occupying villages and tearing down jails. Suddenly, the Ixils appeared in the pronouncements of the EGP as a revolutionary people in arms. Ten years later, the survivors were a showcase for the pacification programs of the Guatemalan army.

Asked what happened, Nebajeños respond with vague references to *la situación, el problema,* or *la bulla* ("the uproar"). Then, after a bit of hes-itation, they corroborate human rights reports. When the Army of the Poor appeared in the area, the reaction from government security forces was so furious that it drove much of the population into the rev-olutionary movement. The scenario repeated itself elsewhere, to the point that the guerrillas seemed on the verge of seizing the western highlands. In 1981–82 the Guatemalan army lashed back with an offen-sive that devastated entire departments and displaced a million or more people.[3] Because Ixil country was one of the first areas organized by the Army of the Poor, it was considered a "solid heartland of sup-port"[4] and suffered accordingly.

To discourage Ixil farmers from helping the guerrillas, the army burned down all hamlets and homesteads outside the three towns. At first in reaction to guerrilla ambushes, then by plan, army units shot, hacked, or burned to death thousands of unarmed men, women, and children. As refugees fell under the army's control, it drafted all the males into "civil patrols" which it then sent out against the insurgents, who retaliated with massacres of their own. So sweeping was the destruction that it gave credence to the accusation that the Guatemalan army was committing genocide. Startling drops in population figures dramatized the tragedy: while the national census projected a population of ninety-six thousand for the three Ixil municipalities in 1987, that same year local government health centers could account for only about fifty thousand—a 48 percent shortfall (see table 8.3 in chapter 8).

Presiding over key episodes in this demographic mystery was Efraín Ríos Montt, a Protestant general who seized power in the capital, announced a series of reforms and, while the army continued to massacre villagers, admonished Guatemalans to save themselves and their country by reforming their personal lives. The general's preaching was not very convincing on the international level, where his name became a byword for human rights violations. But in Nebaj, he is remembered almost fondly because, part way through his seventeen months in the national palace, the mass killing around the three Ixil towns came to an end. As Ríos addressed the nation every Sunday over the radio, Ixil peasants interpreted his admonitions as a new dispensation and, by the thousand, declared themselves *evangélicos*. The Catholic Church, driven underground after the army killed three Spanish priests and hundreds of local leaders, reported that parishioners were turning Protestant to save their lives.

From a reputed stronghold of the guerrilla movement, Ixil country was refashioned into a network of "model villages" and "development poles." These were resettlements that the Guatemalan army intended to show how well it was treating refugees, and that critics denounced as concentration camps. Rebuilt along counterinsurgency lines, Nebaj became a regular stop in the geography of Central American war reporting, a place where journalists collected war stories and tried to take the pulse of an entire country.[5] With the insurgents popping up again after every counteroffensive, Quiché became a symbol for guerrilla warfare in Guatemala, like Chalatenango in El Salvador and Ayacucho in Peru. But by the late 1980s it was clear who had won. The army controlled most of the population in a typical counterinsurgency scheme of closely watched, concentrated resettlements, compulsory military service for the male inhabitants, and periodic offensives against the remaining guerrillas and refugees in the mountains. While the guerrillas could not be defeated militarily, they were unable to protect their supporters, which discredited them in the eyes of most Ixils. Revolutionaries who claimed to give primacy to political over military struggle had been defeated on their chosen terrain.

In the town of Nebaj, where my family and I lived from October 1988 to September 1989, the climate was—despite occupation by the Guatemalan army and regular probes by two columns of the EGP—almost *tranquilo*. Life out in the army's resettlements was less tranquil, with villagers feeling trapped between the two forces demanding their cooperation. Other parts of Quiché Department were definitely not relaxed. In the Ixcán rain forest to the north, there was heavy fighting, with the army trying to cut off the EGP's supply routes to the Mexican border. In southern Quiché, a struggle of a different sort was underway. Now that guerrilla columns had disappeared from the vicinity, so had the army's rationale for its mandatory civil patrols. Thousands of Mayan *campesinos* were insisting on their constitutional right not to serve. Widows asked civil authorities to exhume the remains of their husbands from the clandestine cemeteries where they had been dumped by government killers. The army retaliated the way it usually does, with thinly veiled threats, kidnappings, and assassinations, as international human rights organizations made ineffective denunciations. In Nebaj, in contrast, no one openly defied the army and—despite the active presence of the guerrillas—there were no kidnappings during our stay.[6]

Little of the foregoing will be new to readers who follow Guatemala, and documenting a well-known picture was not my reason for doing a study. What most impressed me about the destruction was how Nebajeños seemed to be overcoming it. Central America was exhausted at the end of the 1980s, with terms of reconciliation being debated in peace talks. I wanted to know how Nebajeños were working for reconciliation at the local level.

Coming to terms with life in an impoverished garrison town, so emblematic of the wider situation in Latin America, forced me to adopt a different perspective than that of the many human rights reports on the region. Such reports focus on violations of a universal conception of rights, but I was face to face with a modus vivendi which Nebajeños had worked out with the "army of the rich" and the "army of the poor," in which they did not assert rights in the ways visualized by human rights activists. Despite continuing abuses, Nebajeños were working out ways, not just to survive the continuing confrontations between guerrillas and soldiers, but to take advantage of a miserable situation. Ever so carefully, they were putting their own agenda back on the table.

Living Between Two Armies

The guerrilla doesn't take our maize and we don't take theirs. We don't know why there's a war.
—*Civil patrol leader on duty with his squad in Nebaj, 1987*

My first visits to Nebaj were brief, in November and December 1982. I was working as a journalist and wanted to assess the claims being made for Guatemala's new evangelical dictator, General Efraín Ríos Montt. Soldiers occupied the center of town around the Catholic church. Every evening, long lines of civil patrollers cradling antique rifles filed into the surrounding hills where much of the population was still hiding from army reprisals. Fourteen hundred refugees who had come into the army's hands were camped in crude stick shelters at the airstrip north of town. Here they were visited regularly by North American missionaries who, despite their admiration of the born-again general, wanted to make sure that his subordinates stopped killing noncombatants. In town, hundreds of widows lined up to receive rations of maize. The army commander summoned the town's orphans to the plaza for a Christmas party.

El problema had been worst around the start of the year, Nebajeños told me. Now it was quieter, they were heaving a collective sigh of relief, and fervently hoping that the five-month lull in kidnappings and massacres in their vicinity would become permanent. My assessment of Ríos Montt and the evangelical contribution to his counterinsurgency drive was eventually published in *Harvest of Violence*, a collection of reports from anthropologists edited by Robert Carmack.

When I returned to Nebaj five years later, the curfew had been lifted, electricity was restored, and many checkpoints went unmanned.

Long lines of civil patrollers still filed out of town, but now the countryside was dotted with resettlements. Their metal roofs glinted in the afternoon sun, and they were controlled by the army. Around the edge of town, the wooden shacks of refugees climbed up hillsides that were now stripped of trees. Between the houses every square meter was buried in maize plants, a sign that the peasant farmers were running out of land.

Now I was in graduate school, at the Stanford Department of Anthropology, and looking for a place to do fieldwork. Like many a foreigner before me, I was fascinated by Nebaj for all the wrong reasons. My motives for going there were inadmissibly romantic, of the kind that get shot down in seminars. The Ixils fit the nostalgic image of a people apart, holed up in their mountains against the twentieth century. The narrow road into Ixil country switchbacked up the massive wall of the Cuchumatanes, then wound through afternoon cloud banks and over the pass, to the lip of a wet, green valley. Far below lay a town of whitewashed walls and red-tile roofs, which could be from centuries ago. There were religious processions out of the Middle Ages, the faces of men who had never become modern consumers, and the spellbinding effect of masses of Ixil women with their bright red skirts, richly woven *huipiles* (blouses), and defiant hair bindings.[7] Fortunately I was married, saving me from the fate of foreigners who courted Nebaj women with a conspicuous lack of success. No matter the burned-out homesteads dotting ridge lines, the horrifying stories to be heard at every turn, the evident feelings of deprivation with which Nebajeños greeted gringos on safari, or their eagerness to go to the United States to earn dollars. This was the nearest I would get to Shangri-la.

In choosing a topic, the model dissertation writer selects an issue in anthropological theory, frames a hypothesis, and finds a suitable place to test it. My procedure was the reverse, to start with the place. Besides my vague dissatisfaction with received understandings of the violence, Nebaj was the only country town in my experience where enough was happening that I could spend a year without going mad from impatience. Unlike the misnamed model villages surrounding it, Nebaj would also be a relatively comfortable billet for my little family. It would be safer than Guatemala's baby-snatching, murder-wracked capital, and healthier than the humid, disease-ridden south coast, even though both coast and capital were higher research priorities judging from the many anthropological studies of quaint Indian towns.

I also calculated that, despite its status as a war zone, Nebaj would be safer politically than many other areas. There were a number of reasons for this, the most important being the army's confidence that it controlled the population. Not only was the army relatively restrained in and around the town: it regarded Ixil country as a showcase for its pacification efforts, to the point of tolerating North Americans and Europeans taking up residence there. The gringo colony in Nebaj was nothing new: it dated back half a century, starting with evangelical missionaries from the United States and reinforced in the 1970s by hippies. All were forced to leave by the violence, the last being a homesteader who manufactured claymore mines for the guerrillas until the army turned him over to the U.S. embassy. During my visits to Nebaj at the end of 1982, I was greeted like the first goose honking northward in spring. I was a sign that foreigners were coming back, of returning peace and stability.

By the late 1980s, Nebaj was again a popular stop for backpack tourists. Other foreigners had a larger sense of purpose. There were evangelical missionaries and wholesale weaving buyers; graduate students looking for research sites; journalists taking a break from the war in El Salvador or filing an easy story; and couples looking for orphans to adopt. Those residing in Nebaj were mainly volunteers starting aid projects. The majority worked for Refugee Children of the World, a French-based agency connected to the well-known Doctors Without Borders, and the Shawcross Aid Programme for Highland Indians, a small organization run by an English businessman in Antigua. A mysterious group calling itself the Air Commando Association occasionally sent a small medical team but no longer had anyone in residence. It used to be represented by a nurse from Texas who operated out of army bases and was known for dispensing ideology as well as medicine. She was riding in an army helicopter when her legs were hit by groundfire, crippling her for life.[8]

In 1966 my predecessors Benjamin Colby and Pierre van den Berghe were received in the manner befitting a scientific expedition. But anthropologists no longer carried much weight in Nebaj unless they showed up in a Land Rover and had something concrete to offer. What impressed contemporary Nebajeños was *ayuda* (aid), customarily spoken in the plural (*ayudas*) with a certain raw hunger. Even though the avalanche of refugee programs was administered by Guatemalans, gringos were considered the source of the bounty. As a church leader observed, no one flocked around him when he got off the bus like they did around me. "The gringos have more opportunity here than any other group," a K'iche' Maya truck owner noted enviously of our respective ethnic identities. Doing in Rome as the Romans, I explained that I was, besides studying the social changes that had occurred since Colby and van den Berghe twenty years before, assessing development needs. It was true: I filed reports faithfully. But they were my pact with the devil. Talking to people about their immediate needs meant that, despite my denials, I was regularly interpreted as a collector of aid requests.

Another reason Nebaj seemed a safe place to do fieldwork were the three sisters who operated one of the town's more enduring institutions, a pensión where gringos customarily stayed, in a walled compound just off the town square. Even though their Spanish father had pioneered the plantation district to the north, the sisters were, judging from their low prices and simple life-style, holdovers from a precapitalist economy. They spoke some Ixil and, unlike many other ladinos, never left town at the height of violence. They were there operating by candlelight in 1982, and when I showed up in 1988 with my wife and child they took care of us. We moved into an adobe room, took our meals on the covered porch, and waited out the downpours there. When the flow of temporary visitors became distracting, we took rooms elsewhere for sleeping but continued to eat and pass the day at the pensión.

Besides doing so much for us, the sisters provided a special kind of listening chamber on the town. From the kitchen, where they and their assistants cooked over a wood stove, came a perennial flow of exclamations, death stories, and scandals in the soft, resigned Spanish of the Nebajeños. In a town that had seen bloody political warfare, the sisters seemed beyond politics. Their establishment was within earshot of unexpected events in the center of town, an intersection for gossip of all kinds, and a theater where small dramas were acted out daily.

Ixil villagers coming into town seemed to feel relatively comfortable at the pensión, hence I ended up conducting many interviews there.

But it was a ladino and gringo-controlled environment, not an Ixil one. Living there distanced us from intimate details of Ixil life, particularly at the family level. It was also dominated linguistically by Spanish and English rather than Ixil. Owing to Ixil bilingualism, especially in town, it was so easy to communicate in Spanish that, after two months, I gave up trying to learn Ixil. Abandoning language study freed up the time to interview many more people, with a translator providing help where necessary, but at the obvious cost of not working in the native tongue of most of the population.

Owing to the vast changes in Ixil country and the ease of finding interlocutors, I chose an extensive rather than intensive approach to fieldwork, spreading my time through the three Ixil municipios. Of the three Ixil centers, San Juan Cotzal had the most obvious air of repression. Military control was stricter than in the other two towns, and it was easy to find people who looked and acted as if they had been traumatized by violence. Cotzaleños were more likely than Nebajeños and Chajuleños to blame themselves for the violence. Their town seems to have been more sophisticated than Nebaj in the nineteenth century, and in the 1920s and 1930s visitors described it as prosperous. There was a small but active colony of ladino settlers, and Cotzaleños seem to have been more commercial, literate, and fluent in Spanish than Ixils of the other two towns. But after the motor road came to Nebaj in 1942, Cotzaleños found themselves in its shadow, marginalized by the new commercial circuit. The ladino colony declined, but in the meantime Cotzal had lost far more of its land base—at least a third—to plantation owners than Chajul and Nebaj. The town hall was given over to bitter struggles between Ixil factions, who eventually called in guerrillas and soldiers to eliminate each other.

Six years after the height of the violence, Cotzal had a stagnant air. Even the town's physical location, in a narrow valley unlike Nebaj and Chajul, suggested a more constricted horizon. Unlike in the other two towns, no one in Cotzal had ever started a volunteer fire company that in rural Guatemala handles medical emergencies and retrieves the dead. The only motor vehicle that spent the night in Cotzal was a Dodge pickup belonging to the town hall. It sat on flat tires because there was no mechanic to fix it. "Before they were very pleasant and friendly, would invite you in to eat and spend the night," one of the few remaining ladinos remarked, "but because of the violence they were mistreated, beaten, killed, and now they don't confide in anyone. In every family there are two or three who will never appear. Bodies were left in the street by the military. There were families where only the women were left to carry home the dead."

San Gaspar Chajul was the least bilingual of the three towns, the only one where my lack of Ixil was a regular embarrassment. Chajul was supposed to be the most conservative of the three municipios: certainly outsiders made the fewest inroads there. While Chajuleños lost valuable coffee-growing terrain to ladinos around Finca La Perla, closer to town most land stayed in Indian hands. Thanks to their relatively ample land base, Chajuleños also remain more absorbed in subsistence maize agriculture and are less dependent on seasonal labor migration than other Ixils. But during the violence Chajul was swept by a new religious movement called the charismatic renewal. With subsequent defections to evangelical Protestantism, the town now boasted approximately twelve electronically amplified church bands. Children could be heard singing Negro hymns of emancipation like "When the Saints Come Marching In." Three new evangelical temples ringed the massive Catholic church on the plaza.

After spending a few days in Chajul, Cotzal, or out on a trail, returning to Nebaj was a cosmopolitan experience. Toward evening the streets filled with people and were illuminated by electric lights. It was the Paris of the zone. Superficially, Nebaj was the least Ixil of the three towns, the only one that still had a substantial ladino population, as much as 25 to 30 percent of the ten thousand people within an hour's walk. It was easy to communicate in Spanish. Yet, it was the only one of the three towns where the traditional religious system, with its distinctively Mayan saint cults, still flourished.

Having chosen to do fieldwork in Nebaj for emotional reasons, I was left with the problem of how to define my research. The war was an obvious subject, and would intrude on any other theme, but I wanted to avoid focusing on it. Even though Nebaj seemed calm and friendly, dredging for information about recent homicides would make it less so. I could stir up animosities that would endanger myself, my family, and—more important, given the kid-glove treatment North Americans usually enjoy in Guatemala—local people helping with my research.

Aside from the risks involved, I was fatigued by the subject of violence and doubted my ability to tell the world anything new about it. Human rights groups had already publicized the crimes of the Guatemalan army sufficiently that I might end up focusing on the Guerrilla Army of the Poor, whose human rights record was not as bad as its adversary's but not as good as often supposed. Were I to drag guerrilla violence against civilians into the light, my work could bolster the propaganda claims of the Guatemalan army, which was not a contribution I wanted to make.

Hence my decision to study reconstruction. This was a subject in which Nebajeños could see a certain value, which could be explained to the Guatemalan army as the need arose, and which encompassed a topic of great interest: how Nebajeños had responded to the violence by manufacturing a new kind of neutralism for themselves and recreating institutional space to make their own choices.

My main research technique was the guided interview, different versions of which were conducted with aldea (village) representatives, religious leaders, labor contractors, and other groups of interest. Toward the end of my year of fieldwork in 1988–89, I employed another North American and four Ixil teachers and students to help me do a survey. We asked a wide range of questions concerning household composition and economy, labor migration, religious affiliation, ethnicity, and tradition. I chose to survey two rather different levels of the Ixil population in Nebaj. The first consisted of 164 Ixils in leadership or entrepreneurial roles. They included teachers and bilingual promoters, evangelical pastors, Catholic catechists and saint society heads, labor contractors, and merchants. The second sample consisted of virtually all the household heads (ninety-eight of them) in Cantón Xemamatze, an outlying neighborhood of the town which had absorbed many refugees from destroyed aldeas. While neither group is a representative sample of the larger Ixil population, the first provides a sampling of better-off Ixils in the town center and the second of the Ixils most heavily impacted by the war. Because of the quantity of data I collected and priorities imposed by the situation, only a few of the most salient results of the survey are reported in this book. After returning to the United States for my write-up, I was able to visit Nebaj on four occasions—in August 1990, December 1990, July 1991, and June 1992—for two months of follow-up interviewing.

As with any local study, my picture of Nebaj should not be generalized to other towns without great care. Nebaj is not a microcosm of
Guatemala or even a typical community. The Ixil area is economically
marginal, even by the standards of the western highlands. Ixils have
long had a reputation for uniqueness and, despite their recent fame as
guerrilla supporters, are not paragons of ethnic or class consciousness
as debated by academics and activists. Compared to the rest of the
country, they were hit unusually hard by the violence. Since then, they
have received an unusual amount of help from refugee agencies.
Hence, the politics of Ixil country may seem backward, especially in
comparison with areas where the human rights movement emerged
earlier. But because Ixil country was a core area for the largest guerrilla organization in the early 1980s, an analysis of why it failed here
should tell us something about why the revolutionary movement
failed in other parts of the western highlands. I also suspect that the
experiences of Nebajeños speak to broader realities, in Guatemala and
other parts of the world, about how outsiders project their agendas into
peasant populations, how political violence emerges, and how noncombatants respond to it.

A Revisionist Account of the Violence

*There were lots of ambushes there, then the army would take vengeance
against the people. They would just be passing along with their burdens
and had to pay with their blood.*
> —*A 1992 account of what followed EGP ambushes
> around Pulay at the start of the violence*

To explain the political terror for which Guatemala is so well known,
analysts typically begin with the country's plantation-based social
order and the national security state that protects it. Despite periodic
changes of regime and announcements of reform, political life has been
dominated by plantation owners and military officers since the nineteenth century. The only exception was a fractious decade of reform
from 1944 to 1954, which ended when a civilian government redistributing land was overthrown by the U.S. Central Intelligence Agency.

Soldiers posing for a photograph, 1988

Guerrilla movements emerged in the following decade. Ironically, they were started by dissident army lieutenants who, probably without intending to, gave their former military cohorts an enduring rationale for militarizing the Guatemalan state.

Army-controlled regimes not only suppressed the first guerrilla movements but made political opposition so dangerous that, by the late 1970s and early 1980s, even a centrist Christian Democratic party was losing hundreds of its leaders to death squads coordinated from an annex to the presidential palace. Meanwhile, survivors of the first guerrilla movements were moving west into the homeland of the Mayas, about half the country's population, in search of the geographical and social terrain they needed for a prolonged revolutionary war.

The reaction of the Guatemalan army was so brutal that it helped the insurgents in various ways. Not only did the army's reprisals force thousands of local people to defend themselves by joining the guerrillas, the army's response also discredited it nationally and internationally. Every clumsy attempt to cover up an atrocity seemed to corroborate the contrasting version of events put out by the Left.

To appreciate the international response, we must distinguish between "human rights work" and the "solidarity movement." Strictly speaking, human rights organizations like Americas Watch and

Amnesty International hold governments accountable to international law, while solidarity organizations like the Network in Solidarity with the People of Guatemala (NISGUA) provide political and humanitarian support to opposition movements. For people like myself involved with both kinds of organization, there may seem little contradiction between the two. But their objectives can and do collide: while a human rights organization expects a government to carry out due process, a solidarity organization may support an insurgency that disrupts the last vestiges of due process.

In practice, moreover, human rights work and solidarity activism can be hard to distinguish. Solidarity activists find that human rights appeals to a broader audience than any other theme, and they provide one of the most important constituencies for human rights organizations. Indeed, the latter can reinforce solidarity biases by focusing exclusively on government abuses and ignoring the violence of opponents. When international human rights organizations set up alliances with local organizations, the groups they sponsor are oppositional. In the case of Guatemala these groups are on the Left, more or less sympathetic to the guerrilla movement and clearly "solidarity" in their ideology and rhetoric. Hence, a fuzzy line between human rights work and solidarity organizing may be inevitable because of the overlapping objectives of the two. Both set themselves against state regimes in the name of "the people." Solidarity activists go on to assume that "the people" achieve their fullest representation in a revolutionary movement, an identification that human rights organizations have often preferred not to challenge.

In Latin America, various situations have forced members of the overlapping human rights and solidarity communities to sort out their priorities. The Contra war against the Sandinistas was one of several U.S. efforts to turn revolutionary tactics against leftist governments by supporting "freedom fighters." Imitating the Left, the administration of President Ronald Reagan (1981–89) used the language of human rights to promote insurgents who terrorized civilians. In putting down the Contra rebellion, meanwhile, the Sandinista government became implicated in human rights violations of its own, to the embarrassment of solidarity backers abroad.

Another telling situation has been Peru. The terrorism of the Shining Path revolutionaries has been so flagrant that human rights organizations have been forced to take it into account, side-by-side with government crimes. Other bloodbaths like El Salvador and Colombia have not polarized human rights and solidarity activists to the same degree. Nor has Guatemala. Its guerrillas have never become infamous for killing noncombatants like Shining Path in Peru. Meanwhile, thinly disguised official kidnappings and murders have kept up Guatemala's status as an institutionalized terror state. With the army a clear human rights violator, and guerrillas who have refrained from flagrant killing of civilians, the solidarity interpretation continues to be a popular way of understanding the situation, especially in universities.

The most well-known statement of the solidarity position on Guatemala—and also the most popular way of trying to look at the violence through Mayan eyes—is *I, Rigoberta Menchú*, the story of a K'iche'[10] Maya survivor from the same Cuchumatanes range inhabited by the Ixils. Rigoberta's testimony was taped by an anthropologist in January 1982, just as the Guatemalan army was gaining the upper hand against the guerrillas. Forced into exile by the assassination of her parents and brother, she believed that the army's massacres were galvanizing her people to revolutionary militancy. Due in no small measure to Rigoberta's powerful account, many human rights activists have continued to assume that the Guatemalan National Revolutionary Union (URNG)[11] has widespread popular support and is getting that support because it represents popular aspirations.[12]

Certainly, there are Mayan campesinos who fit Rigoberta's description, especially with the guerrillas in the mountains and among the refugees in Mexico. But among the large majority of the Ixil population who are under army control, to say nothing of most of the population of the western highlands, the expectations raised by *I, Rigoberta Menchú* were sure to be disappointed. Since the terrible massacres of the early 1980s, Nebaj had become a law-and-order town. It harbored deep resentments against the army but, insofar as the guerrillas were concerned, was firmly on the army's side. When former dictator Ríos Montt ran for president in 1990, his local supporters nearly won all three Ixil town halls, even though it was under his command eight years earlier that soldiers burned many Ixil villages to the ground.

Ríos Montt's popularity was difficult to comprehend for most scholars and journalists because they have been so deeply influenced by human rights and solidarity work. Indeed, scholarship can be as hard to distinguish from solidarity and human rights work as the latter two are from each other. The most influential literature on Guatemala has been written by activists, the majority of whom are also academics. Generally, this literature has been slow to admit the defeat of the guerrillas in 1982, their subsequent lack of popular support, and contradictions in the human rights movement. In the specific case of anthropologists, our personal ties with communities led to accepting human rights and solidarity assumptions in varying degrees. Yet our ability to communicate with victims of the violence has also put us in an unusual position to question those assumptions.

Identifying revolutionary movements with popular aspirations has been a widespread premise of dissent against U.S. foreign policy. Guatemala happens to be a classic case of the U.S. government's use of force in the Third World: when the Eisenhower administration overthrew an elected government in 1954, the counterrevolutionary state it established spun out of control. For North American universities, meanwhile, the issue of revolution became urgent with the Vietnam War. To build a case for military intervention, U.S. policymakers and their academic consultants emphasized the manipulation and coercion involved in revolutionary movements, as dramatized by the role of external agents. The Viet Cong (and insurgents in general) became infiltrators and terrorists. To make the case against U.S. intervention, university critics explained the conflict in social terms. Revolution was the result of colonialism and exploitation. The Viet Cong (and insurgents in general) became popular movements.

Since then, social scientists have produced considerable literature debating the structural causes of peasant-based revolutions and the motivations of participants, hence Theda Skocpol's question, "Which peasants are most prone to revolution?"[13] If Eric Wolf pointed toward a threatened "middle peasantry" with enough "tactical mobility" to join a revolutionary movement, Jeffrey Paige argued in favor of rural proletarians displaced by agribusiness and state terrorism.[14] When Guatemala scholars applied the tradition to our own area in the early 1980s, we emphasized the social roots of the violence and the revolutionary movement. Among other things, we inherited the assumption of a unitary revolutionary subject, a social class (or fraction or coalition of same) that was responding to social conditions as a recognizable group and driving the insurgency.

Guatemala scholars also inherited the assumption that the revolutionary movement was "popular." If we followed the lead of James Scott, Guatemalan campesinos joined the guerrillas after capitalist penetration disrupted their "moral economy" of subsistence agriculture. Were we to follow Samuel Popkin, on the other hand, the Ixils were "rational peasants" who joined the insurgency after weighing its costs and benefits. But whether participation is explained in terms of the logic of maximization (a lá Popkin), or the attempt to recover an endangered vision of the collective good (per James Scott), the assumption is that insurgents represent popular aspirations.[15]

How do they do so? Solidarity organizations take revolutionaries at their word. They assume that a revolutionary movement represents "the people" in terms of revolutionary ideology. But scholars must reckon with substantial ideological gaps between revolutionary intellectuals, cadre, and followers, as well as wide variation in local support for insurgents. Hence Popkin stressed that the revolutionary movement would have to provide peasants with immediate, tangible benefits to win their support, such as freeing them from the exactions of landlords.[16]

Theda Skocpol agreed that a successful revolutionary organization must "address peasant needs successfully" and "provid[e] . . . benefits."[17] The same point was made by Joel Migdal, who argued that peasants join a political organization not for ideology[18] but for "immediate material trade-offs . . . that overcome some of the shortcomings of the institutional network." It is only when revolutionaries manage to institutionalize mutually beneficial exchanges with a peasantry that the latter becomes revolutionary in Migdal's view.[19]

Perhaps this explains why, in Guatemala, the revolutionary movement that appeared so popular at the start of the 1980s no longer appeared so at the end of the decade. Except for a holdout population of about twenty-three thousand in the communities of population in resistance, the Guerrilla Army of the Poor failed to institutionalize mutually beneficial exchanges. Indeed, running through the scholarly literature is the proviso that, to be successful, revolutionaries must defend their peasant supporters from state repression. In this the

Guatemalan guerrillas failed. Indeed, the only benefit that the EGP provided most Ixils was to protect them from the army, but not very effectively or for very long.

Being protected from the army becomes even more paradoxical if, as will be argued in chapter 3, the only reason the army attacked Ixils was to get at the EGP. This raises the question of what Ixils saw in the guerrilla movement in the first place. Certainly, conflicts over land, labor contracting, and local elections provided grievances for the guerrillas to address. But I will argue that class and ethnic conflicts do not explain why so many Ixils sided with the revolutionary movement at least briefly, let alone why political violence erupted. Judging from their stories, the main reason Ixils cast their lot with the guerrillas were the coercive pressures created by the blows and counterblows of two military forces, a dilemma Nebajeños typically describe as being *entre dos fuegos* ("between two fires").[20]

The popularity of this expression corroborates a point made by Timothy Wickham-Crowley in a comparative analysis of state and guerrilla terror. Once an armed conflict is under way, the violence exercised by both sides can easily become the most important factor in recruitment. People may join the revolutionary movement less because they share its ideals than to save their lives, because of a set of coercive pressures emanating from both sides that I will refer to as "dual violence."[21] Hence, just because an insurgency grows rapidly does not mean that it represents popular aspirations and has broad popular support, a point being increasingly noted by Guatemalanists.[22]

Obviously, repression limited the testimony I could collect. Ixils who had taken leading roles in the revolutionary movement were dead, in the mountains, or in exile in Mexico. I was interviewing survivors who had decided to submit to the army in the early 1980s, been seized in army offensives since then, or been pressured into surrendering by those same offensives. Doubtless, Ixils were measuring their words with care. Even in less extreme situations, James Scott has underlined the importance of distinguishing between "public" and "hidden" transcripts, between what subordinates say to those in power and what they say to each other.[23] How do I know that Ixils are sharing their real feelings when they claim to be neutral?

I do not know for certain. But the willingness of Ixils to condemn the army that had so much power over them seemed to validate their simultaneous repudiation of the guerrillas. So many Ixils seemed open about their feelings[24] that it convinced me to take their express condemnation of both sides at face value.[25] To not take their statements at face value seemed even more problematic. Compared with what Ixils tell an army officer, I was hearing the hidden transcript or at least much of it. But how much of the spectrum of Ixil opinion was I hearing? A broad range of people in Ixil country, including recently arrived refugees and ex-combatants, told me they had been deceived by the guerrillas. Nor were such sentiments heard only inside the government-controlled perimeter. In 1991 visitors to the displaced population in the mountains picked up the same expressions of neutralism that refugees expressed after removal to Nebaj.[26]

Revolution in the Counterrevolution?

This is what we want, that the world be free for everyone. That everyone does what they want but that there is peace. Why have fights over religion? Only when the Judge comes are we going to know who is right.
—*Evangelical pastor in Cotzal, 1989*

Despite the victory of the Guatemalan army, Nebaj has experienced a revolution of sorts. Usually we think of counterinsurgency as a defense of the status quo, but counterrevolution may require some of the same changes as revolution. In the case of Ixil country, some of the plantation land owned by outsiders is returning to the hands of local cultivators, a new class of indigenous professionals has taken over the town hall, and Ixils are expanding into commercial roles previously dominated by outsiders, including permanent market stalls, labor contracting, and ownership of heavy transport. The most abusive labor contractors and plantation administrators have left the scene; their successors tread more warily. But most of the paradoxical gains of war have gone to the more educated and advantageously placed Ixils living in town, continuing trends that were underway before the violence. Class relations in Nebaj have not changed in any fundamental sense. If some Ixils have extracted advantages from the last decade of destruction, such as more education for their children or a government job, out in the resettlements nearly everyone is worse off than before.

This brings us to the cruelest issue Ixils face in their struggle to reconstruct their lives, one that dates to well before the violence, stares them in the face every day, and will never be resolved by political negotiations. I refer to their relation with their beloved mountains. Like contemporary Mayas elsewhere in Guatemala and Mexico, Ixils continue to prize the growing of maize, their precious *milpa*, which has been the material basis of their culture for millennia. Even in the 1960s it was obvious that Ixils faced a deep-seated crisis in peasant ecology, because their rapid growth in numbers was outstripping the carrying capacity of the land. The shortfall was made up by massive seasonal migration to coffee and sugar plantations, where Ixils worked for the equivalent of a dollar a day or less. Carrying capacity can always be expanded, of course, and in this case the level of technology employed by Ixils—mainly hoes and maize monoculture—would seem open to vast improvement. In the early 1970s, just such an escalation of productivity appeared in the making with the spread of chemical-based fertilizers, until a rise in petroleum prices jerked them out of reach of most peasant farmers. Now technological innovation is impeded by the fragmentation of land holdings and the pauperization of the population, even as Ixils continue to produce large numbers of children for whom the land will have to be subdivided even further.

There is little sign that Ixils are coming to grips with their ecological crisis, but *la situación* could have the paradoxical result of giving them more political space to do so. If there was anything the Indians of Guatemala clearly wanted at the start of the 1990s, it was the maneuvering room to make their own decisions. In southern Quiché, Mayan peasants organized into the Runujel Junam Council of Ethnic Communities (CERJ) refused to serve in the army's civil patrols, for which more than a few gave their lives.[27] Around Lake Atitlán, various towns expelled abusive police detachments and, in the case of Santiago Atitlán, shut down an army base that had kidnapped and murdered hundreds of people.[28] But the struggle for political space was not just directed against Guatemala's security state, even if this was the principal target. In the case of Santiago Atitlán, the people made a point of asking the guerrillas to stay away too. In the case of northern Quiché,

Ixils trying to reestablish space for their own decisions could, with great reluctance, support the army's civil patrols as a way of protecting themselves from both sides.

One way to understand the struggle to open up political space is in terms of "civil society," an amorphous, almost residual category defined by what it is not.[29] Civil society exists above the level of kinship groupings but is not the state or an economic organization: it does include religious organizations and other forms of association even if these are not completely autonomous. In Mayan communities, David McCreery points out, civil society used to be defined primarily by *costumbre* (custom), the moral basis for civil-religious hierarchies that revolve around the worship of Catholic saints.[30] But times have changed. With the arrival of ladino settlers and a disruptive new plantation economy, civil-religious hierarchies have broken down, many Mayas have repudiated costumbre, and new kinds of social organizations have proliferated. As a result, civil society in Mayan towns must be interpreted in terms of more voluntaristic forms of association.

In Ixil country, the first of these was Catholic Action (AC), a pastoral movement started by Spanish priests to turn Mayan Indians into orthodox Catholics. Its catechists organized village *centros* (centers), quasi-congregational groups who took on wider social goals, such as building schools and potable water systems. When the Guatemalan army destroyed the villages and disrupted the AC network in the early 1980s, two other kinds of group proliferated, often led by former catechists. Evangelical Protestant churches had, until the violence, been small islands in a Catholic sea. Now they swelled with Ixils fleeing from the army's persecution of the Catholic Church. Many other Ixils joined the charismatic renewal, a movement led by ex-catechists who continued to identify themselves as Catholic yet clearly had been influenced by Protestantism.

Together with remaining catechists, the evangelicals and charismatics represent a religious reformation in Ixil Maya tradition. All repudiate costumbre, appeal to the Bible to one or another degree, and have a more or less congregational form of organization. By 1989, about half the population claimed to belong to these groups. Most were led by Ixils, employed pentecostal forms of worship and, in a notable departure from traditional norms, advocated strict abstention from alcohol.

Their leadership was prominent in development projects, active in electoral politics, and achieving upward mobility into commerce and professions.

But they were only part of a wider change in the civil society of Ixil country. A system of authority that used to be dominated by *principales* (elders) was being supplanted by a more fluid, competitive field of catechists, pastors, and *promotores*. The "promoter" was a figure being encouraged by government schools and private development agencies to educate and organize Ixils in new ways. The obligations of community service in the civil-religious hierarchy were being supplanted by congregations, civic committees, cooperatives, and political parties. In a repressed society, these were all obviously constrained and subordinate forms of social organization, to the point—in the case of civil patrols and development committees—of appearing mere instruments of the state. Yet, even the most subordinate, the civil patrols denounced in human rights reports, were serving to open up the space between the two armies. Deploying an ambiguous language of neutralism and salvation, Ixils were engaged in a low-key struggle to reestablish room to make their own decisions.

TWO

Ixils and Ladinos

*Nebaj town officials surrendering their staffs of office for
blessing by an Ixil priest, 1989*

*If there's an Old Testament and a New Testament," the Ixil elder asked,
"who is writing the history of now? The pope, the bishops, the journalists?" I explained that the Old Testament and the New Testament were
already finished; that people like myself—historians, anthropologists,
journalists—write the history of now; but that it depended upon old men
like him. "Upon the death of this world, this epoch, this century," he
answered, "let something be written."*
> —*Elderly catechist in Nebaj, 1989*

IN a century of nationalism, the history of Ixil country is easy to interpret as a confrontation between ethnic groups. The conquest of
Mayan chiefdoms by the Spanish in the sixteenth century, the influx
of ladino colonists early in the twentieth century, finally the war of
the Guerrilla Army of the Poor against the "army of the rich," all had
strong ethnic markers. Yet the drama of ethnic conflict has often
diverted attention from the conflicts within ethnic groups that are
essential to understand how a society changes. To find the contradictions that drove Nebajeños to act as they did and change the way their
town operates, we must delve into conflicts among Ixils and among
ladinos. To members of both groups, internal conflicts over authority
have often mattered as much as the inequalities between the two.
Change has proceeded through, not just ethnic competition between
Ixils and ladinos, but internal reformations that change how the two
groups relate to each other. If we look at those internal reformations,
moreover, we will find that cross-ethnic alliances play a major role in
them.

What follows is a brief social history of Nebaj before the war. It
draws on the field notes of Jackson Steward Lincoln (1939–40), Benjamin Colby and Pierre van den Berghe's *Ixil Country: A Plural Society
in Highland Guatemala* (1969), David McCreery's *Rural Guatemala, 1760–
1940* (forthcoming), Elaine Elliott's unpublished archival research, and

oral history gathered in my own fieldwork, to describe the colonization of Ixil country since the late nineteenth century.

To summarize the argument, only after Ixils lost much of their best land and control over local government did new kinds of leaders appear, more capable of competing with ladinos in an expanding market economy. Such leaders emerged through conflicts between Ixils over religion, hierarchy, and authority, but outsiders played a critical role as well. Ladino schoolteachers determined to uplift the Indian race were one such group. During a period of democratic reform from 1944 to 1954, they tried to create space for their vision of a populist Guatemala by challenging ladino plantation owners. The resulting power struggles might seem to have led nowhere, particularly after the United States sponsored a right-wing takeover in 1954. But in hindsight, the populism of this period can be credited with nurturing the first indigenous schoolteachers in Ixil country. Meanwhile, Spanish priests were pursuing their own vision of uplifting the Indian race. By training young Ixil catechists to instill orthodox Catholicism, they undermined the authority of the elders in the town's traditional *cofradías* (saint societies). In each case, leadership struggles within the two ethnic groups encouraged changes in the power relations between the two groups. Thanks to cross-ethnic alliances, Ixils were making headway against the local system of domination before the arrival of the guerrillas in the late 1970s.

The Second Conquest of Ixil Country

But whose fault was it? It was the fault of the people because they refused to buy the land. . . . Now we are just in the middle of the finca's pasture. We are just about to die of hunger. We have no food, and we have no milpas. But things would be good now had the elders of those days bought the land. Then there would be land today. But they didn't buy it. Rather, they got angry over it. Aah, the elders have already committed many sins! . . . Well, due to all of this the Ladino has us in the palm of his hand today. Because of him we have no land. . . . Who can ignore what our plight is now, for the elders, our fathers, our grandmothers and grandfathers are responsible!

—Diego Chavez, "How the People of Ilom Lost Their Lands," 1975[1]

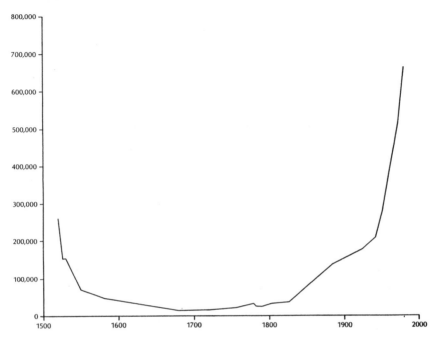

FIGURE 1 Population Change in the Cuchumatán Highlands, 1520-1980 (*courtesy of George Lovell*)

The Ixils have been on the periphery of Mesoamerican society for most of the last millennium. Three bloody expeditions by the Spanish and their Mexican allies were necessary to subdue them. Nebaj was stormed and burned in 1530, but the area did not attract Spanish settlers for lack of opportunities to enrich themselves. Like much of the Guatemalan highlands, the Ixil towns were off-limits to non-Indians unless they were representing the Crown or the Catholic clergy.[2] The *padre* became the most important representative of colonial authority. Unfortunately, the practice of concentrating the population into town centers to impose Christianity and tribute was, as elsewhere, followed by devastating epidemics of smallpox, typhus, and other diseases. The population reached its lowest point around 1700 (see figure 1). How low is unclear owing to the practice of avoiding taxation by fleeing into the mountains.

Toward the end of the colonial period, the Catholic clergy made regular complaints about Ixil intractability. The most visible issue was control over the all-important saint societies, an institution imported from Spain that Mayas captured for their own purposes. Catholic priests also realized their parishioners were frequenting caves to pray to their old gods, the lords of the hills. Following independence from Spain in 1821, a half century of republican strife continued to leave Ixils to themselves. Until the end of the 1800s, the only non-Ixil inhabitants of the three municipalities appear to have been a beleaguered priest and a few ladinos who were living like Indians[3]—that is, without becoming a distinct, extractive class like later settlers.

What opened up Ixil country were the political and economic changes associated with Guatemala's Liberal Revolution (1871). Export agriculture, above all coffee for the United States and Europe, was Guatemala's only development hope in the late nineteenth century. In Costa Rica and Brazil, coffee was grown mainly by smallholders, but in Guatemala it was dominated by large landowners whose politics choked off possibilities for stable development. Dignified by occasional elections and the ideology of progress, the Liberal party and its heirs set up one dictatorship after another from the 1870s to the 1940s. Meanwhile, through labor drafts and debt peonage, planters were coercing Indians into working for the coffee economy. Ladinos were encouraged to settle in Indian towns and title private estates, with the result that Mayas became subordinate ethnic groups in their own homeland.[4]

Forced labor systems tend to emerge when peasants have enough land that, given the choice, they refuse to work for large landowners. In Latin America, elites have often ensnared labor by monopolizing land, that is, by enclosing so much of it that peasants are forced to work for estates to survive. In the case of nineteenth-century Guatemala, David McCreery points out, the Liberals adopted a different approach. Instead of trying to wrestle land away from Indian towns known for stubborn resistance, the Liberals attacked the labor problem directly, by forcing Indians into debt servitude through forms of labor coercion dating from the Spanish colony.[5]

The most blatant of these was the forced-labor draft (*mandamiento*), an order from the department governor to a town's mayor to round up a certain number of laborers for a particular plantation. The institution was so at variance with the free-wage ideology espoused by Liberals that, in the course of relying on it for half a century, they outlawed it and told foreign visitors that it no longer existed.[6] Critical to expansion of the mandamientos, according to McCreery, was the rule that Indians could not be drafted if they were already bound to another kind of labor contract. As a result, Indians protected themselves from mandamientos by taking refuge in another kind of forced labor, debt peonage; that is, they built up personal debts with labor contractors and plantation owners. Once most of a town had opted for that tactic, planters desperate for labor—so desperate they were willing to bribe the department governor to authorize a mandamiento—sent their recruiters to more distant towns. The Cuchumatanes region was sufficiently remote that, prior to the Liberal era, it seems to have been touched only lightly by the system. By the 1890s, however, the demands of the new coffee economy were so voracious that mandamiento orders were arriving in places like Nebaj.[7]

How labor recruiters inserted themselves into a town of defiant *indios* is an intriguing question. The careful manners of contemporary Ixils toward outsiders are quite a contrast to the stony reception they gave would-be colonizers in the 1890s. One early settler was prevented from putting up a house for several years, because every time she gathered the materials they were burned.[8] When the traveler Robert Burkitt visited Nebaj at the turn of the century, he reported that ladinos "were evidently in some awe of the Indians."[9] A few years before, in 1898, labor recruiters had brought down a massacre on themselves and other ladinos in the neighboring municipio of San Juan Ixcoy.

The culmination of the San Juan episode—even bloodier massacres of Indians—demonstrated the new relations of force that weighted calculations on both sides. Armed with repeating rifles and a new telegraph system, the Liberals used ladino militias to overawe Indian towns and exert a new level of control over the countryside. Uprisings that had been common were, by the end of the nineteenth century, a rare occurrence.[10]

The newcomers to Nebaj were a heterogenous lot, including Spaniards, Italians, and Mexicans as well as Guatemalans.[11] The majority of the latter came from Huehuetenango Department to the west, particularly the ladino municipio of Malacatán. Many started and ended their lives on the same level as the Ixils did, as subsistence farmers. In the new surroundings, however, some were able to work their way up through opportunities that the Liberal regime offered ladinos in Indian towns, especially labor contracting, bartending, moneylending, and foreclosure.

Municipal secretaries played a revealing role: invariably ladinos and usually from another town, they were appointed from above. Because their responsibilities included authorizing labor contracts, it was easy to go into business for themselves.[12] In Nebaj the first labor contractor, Captain Isaías Palacios, came to town with such an appointment, which he obtained for services rendered the governor of Huehuetenango during an uprising. From authorizing labor drafts for plantation agents who arrived with mandamiento orders in their pockets, it was a small step for Palacios to exempt Ixils from the mandamiento by signing them up for his own labor contracts.

Events in Nebaj corroborate McCreery's point that the initial impact of the coffee economy often came, not in the form of expropriating land, but of recruiting labor. "Advances and wages injected unprecedented amounts of cash into local economies, which hastened the conversion of land into a commodity, drove up prices, marginalized the poor, and hastened social differentiation."[13] Among other things, coffee earnings "gave the Indians unprecedented wherewithal to drink."[14] True to long experience in exploiting native labor, the most effective way to snare Ixils for plantations was selling them liquor and getting them into debt. When Burkitt visited Nebaj a second time in 1913, he saw "an unceasing coming and going of labour contractors and plantation agents getting out gangs of Indians for the Pacific coast. . . . The place stinks of [rum]. The Indians are drunk from morning to night. . . . In the days I was in Nebaj you could hardly see an Indian on the street after nine o'clock in the morning who was not already dizzy. I used to think that Chichicastenango was the drunkennest town in the country, but now I think it is Nebaj."[15]

Ixils had long gotten drunk to honor the saints. But even ladinos admitted that it was their own compatriots who were "responsible for increasing the amount and strength of the liquor for the purpose of enriching themselves."[16] The words belong to Jackson Steward Lincoln, the North American anthropologist who came to Nebaj in 1939 and, before he died of pneumonia, left us the first ethnographic account of the town.

The practice of distilling alcohol is said to have been introduced by Malacatecos, the ladino peasants from Huehuetenango whose descendants still comprise an identifiable social group. Sugar cane for distilling was the first cash crop introduced by ladinos, not the coffee which later dominated,[17] and nearly all operated a liquor dispensary at one time or another. Gradually, local manufacture passed into the hands of enterprising Ixils, whose home-made kuxa is cheaper and more popular than the officially taxed aguardiente (literally, "burning water" or firewater). But despite alcohol's prominence in local moral discourse, as we shall see in later chapters, it was only an instrument for the destructive effects of monetizing a subsistence economy.

"Some of the Ixil found employers and some drank a lot," the prayer-maker Shas K'ow told Benjamin and Lore Colby. "Employers gave them money then, sometimes a lot of money, like 1,000 pesos. The Ixil would take the money and go to the saloon. . . . Yes, the money disappeared. . . . So they borrowed more from their employer. The employer would get them out of jail, and little by little they became indebted to him. Some had handed over their land to their employer as collateral, so he increased his holdings."[18]

By selling liquor and loaning the cash needed to go on binges, ladinos separated Ixils from much of their best arable land. If a simple advance was enough to get Ixils into a labor gang, acquiring their land required loaning money at a usurious rate of interest. Whether the loan was needed for a medical emergency, to sponsor a fiesta, or simply to drink, anything less than prompt repayment meant that the house or land put up for collateral could change hands. Moneylending became so accepted that, even today, interest of 10 percent a month does not evoke surprise or protest, even though it is illegal and unenforceable in court.

The other method for obtaining Ixil land was available only to ladinos who had connections in Guatemala City, along with enough money to bribe officials. By obtaining titles from the national registry in Quezaltenango, they could take advantage of Liberal legislation to override the Mayan system of use rights. Under the Spanish colony, land tenure had usually not been a burning issue because the indigenous population declined so precipitously. Land was assumed to belong to a town and its people, who worked as much as they needed.

Now under the Liberal regime, the municipio was given title to all land within its jurisdiction—except for what could be staked out by a surveyor, certified by a notary public, and recognized by the national registry.

Titling land may not seem the most obvious way to lose it, but such has been the experience of indigenous people, because what can be titled can be alienated. In theory, land already occupied by Indians could not be privatized, but in practice it often was. Owing to the expense of titling, most Ixils continued to hold their land under the authority of the town and its municipal title, not through the national land registry, which meant they could be invaded by an outsider with a private title and enough money to sway the courts in his favor. According to registry research by Elaine Elliott, the first of the Ixil municipios to title its surrounding lands, Cotzal in 1885, also lost the greatest percentage to plantation owners. The last of the Ixil municipios to title its community lands, Nebaj in 1903, lost the least (table 2.1).[19]

Because Indians lost so much land to the coffee economy along the southern piedmont of Mexico, Guatemala, and El Salvador, it should be emphasized that Ixils never lost most of their land. Nor, consistent with patterns elsewhere in Guatemala, did plantation owners ever try to monopolize it.[20] What Ixils lost was the lower-lying *tierra templada* (warm country) on the northern and eastern edges of their territory, down to altitudes of a thousand meters. This was of more interest to coffee planters than the high-lying *tierra fría* (cold country) surrounding the three Ixil towns at two thousand meters. Nor was land titling simply imposed by the Liberals after their victory in 1871. According to documents examined by Elaine Elliott and David McCreery, the Ixils of Nebaj were agitating for title to their community lands even before the Liberals took power,[21] to fend off fellow Mayas including Cotzaleños and Chajuleños.

By the 1890s Ixils also wanted municipal titles to protect their land from ladinos. Nebaj and Chajul suffered the most serious losses to the north, in warm, fertile valleys suitable for sugar cane and coffee. Two long-established Ixil settlements—Sotzil and Ilom—remained with little but the land on which their houses sat while several others—including Chel, Sacsihuán, and Ixtupil—also lost their most productive land. The most prominent claimant was Lisandro Gordillo Galán, a Mexican-

TABLE 2.1
Percentage of Ixil Municipios Claimed in National Land Register

	Year Municipal Title Granted	Area in Caballerías According to National Institute of Statistics[1]	Caballerías Deeded to Municipal Ejido According to Natl. Land Register[2]	Cabellerías Deeded to Individuals According to Natl. Land Register[2]	% of Total Area Deeded to Individuals
Nebaj	1903	1340	1237	87	6.49
Chajul	1900	3359	2424	157	4.67
Cotzal	1885	401	388	180	44.89
Ixil Triangle		5100	4049	424	8.31

1. One caballería = 112.12 acres or 45.374 hectares (see table on page 37).
2. Figures courtesy of Elaine Elliott, personal communication, May 2, 1990.

born figure who makes his first known appearance in 1895 as municipal secretary of Chajul. Eventually, his steady purchase of previous land grants included one in the name of Manuel Estrada Cabrera, the dictator (1898–1920) memorialized in Miguel Angel Asturías's novel *El Señor Presidente.* Unfortunately for Gordillo, his titles proved to be for less valuable land to the west, not the ground he was occupying, which had already been titled to Chajul. In 1928–29 two lower courts ruled that Gordillo had invaded land belonging to the Chajuleños, only to be reversed by the country's supreme court. Disregarding Chajul's preceding boundaries, the highest court legalized a fraudulent title—a decision from which there was no appeal.[22]

Several stages occurred in the formation of fincas in Ixil country. The first was a period of land speculation in the 1890s, which collapsed with a fall in coffee prices.[23] While a number of personal titles date to this period, few ladino owners tried to claim their property for another two decades, whereupon they met resistance. Hence Isaías Palacios was never able to take possession of the fifteen *caballerías*[24] he claimed in Acul, although eventually the Ixil villagers were persuaded to buy the title from his heirs. An old settler near Sotzil says that in the 1920s his father fended off regular attacks from surrounding Ixil communities. In 1924 the people of Ilom jailed a surveyor who had to be rescued by the militia of Nebaj and Cunén.[25] On another occasion, according to a descendant, Lisandro Gordillo and the gunmen accompanying him

Signing up to work on a plantation

killed three Ilom protesters. To avoid persecution, the planter fled to the capital to make a personal appeal to dictator Jorge Ubico.

By the 1920s, moneylending, foreclosure, and the ladino capture of town halls were producing other plantations or, in local parlance, *fincas*. They clustered in the lowest and warmest valleys of Ixil country, for growing sugar and coffee, but several near the town of Nebaj were cleared for cattle, while other cold-country lands in Cotzal became *fincas de mozos*. These were plantations parceled out to Ixil farmers in exchange for working as *mozos* (seasonal labor) on the sugar plantations of the Pacific Coast. Significantly, not all fincas in Ixil country were owned by ladinos.

Defense of municipal land was led by principales, some of them descended from the pre-Conquest Mayan nobility, who had worked their way to the top of the town's civil and religious hierarchies. According to the ladino elders interviewed by Lincoln in 1939–40, the principales who ruled Nebaj at the turn of the century were despotic extracters of tribute from lower-caste Ixils.[26] Colonists would, of course, cast aspersions on the indigenous system of authority they were supplanting. But even now that the great principales should be acquiring the mantle of nostalgia, Ixils recall them with mixed emotions. While descendants defend the good name of their progenitor, describing him as a tribune of the Indian race, others paint the same man as an oppressor and turncoat who extracted contributions from his people, then sold out to acquisitive ladinos.

Memories of betrayal are strongest in Cotzal, which lost almost half its land base to finca owners. Table 2.1 suggests the intensity of titling there: while the municipio includes only 404 caballerías, the town hall and private titleholders claimed a total of 568 caballerías.* Interpreted literally (which is probably a mistake), 164 caballerías, or 41 percent of the actual land area, was contested. Pride in the defense of municipal land is strongest in Chajul, where the town's leaders fought the Finca La Perla for half a century and fended off the powerful Brol family in the 1960s.

To defray the cost of defending town land—trips to the capital, legal fees, and the like—principales demanded contributions from their constituents. Suspicion that they had kept the money for themselves or been paid off by the adversary was never stronger than when, as frequently occurred, they lost the case. Education in the titling process also led principales to claim large extensions in their own name. The rationale was to preserve the land for community use. But eventually it ended up in the hands of their children and grandchildren, if it was not lost to a ladino as the owner progressed from the manufacture of bootleg alcohol to addiction.[27]

Two of the most powerful principales during Lincoln's time deprecated Ixil customs, dressed as ladinos, and treated their fellow Ixils at least as badly as ladino land-grabbers did. Three of the nine plantations in Nebaj were owned by principales who had learned to copy ladino methods, Lincoln reported, and several also became labor contractors. The great principal Gaspar Cedillo was said to seek out particularly strapped neighbors to offer loans, then foreclose, making himself the largest Ixil landowner in Nebaj.[28]

As for ladinos turning municipal land into fincas, they were assisted by the fact that Nebaj was, simultaneously, waging boundary dis-

---

* Land measures in Ixil country have the following equivalents (after Stadelman 1940:130, with 1 hectare=2.471 acres=22.77 cuerdas):

Cuerdas	Manzana	Caballería	English Equivalent	Metric Equivalent
1			.108 acres	.044 ha
16	1		1.736 acres	.703
1,033.3	64.58	1	112.12 acres	45.374 ha

putes with six neighboring Indian municipios, not to mention K'iche' Maya colonists from southern Quiché and Totonicapán. In each case, Mayan peasants from land-poor towns were encroaching on tracts that had yet to be occupied by the relatively land-rich Nebajeños. Given the importance of political influence in the capital, local ladinos were perceived as important allies in these conflicts until they were settled (more or less) in the mid-twentieth century.

Ladinos were also assisted by the Ixils' need for patróns to protect them from Liberal labor laws. When President Jorge Ubico (1931–44) abolished mandamientos and debt-peonage in 1934, his new vagrancy legislation required all but the wealthiest Indians to prove they were doing wage labor for 100 to 150 days a year. Meanwhile, ladino planters had obtained more land than they could put into cash crops, leaving a surplus that could be loaned to Ixil tenants in exchange for their labor. To ensure the necessary number of days in their workbooks—and avoid migration to distant, disease-ridden plantations on the Pacific Coast—many Ixils accepted a local finca owner as their patrón, sometimes the same one who had taken their land.

The relations between ladino patróns and Ixil clients were not just economic: they became strongly personal, in keeping with a society that prefers to express economic dependency in terms of reciprocity and kinship, even if the reciprocity is unequal and the kin relation has to be invented. Hence the importance of *compadrazgo*, the godparent relationships between ladinos and Ixils, with the Ixil client typically asking the patrón to serve as godfather to his child. Another practice was the presentation of Ixil women to ladino patróns,[29] whether demanded as collateral or offered in expectation of a favor. Some ladinos boasted of dozens of children from such relationships, and there were enough of them to visibly affect the Ixil gene pool. Nebaj became populated with half-brothers and half-sisters on either side of the ethnic divide, some raised as Ixils and others as ladinos.

With the help of Guatemalan law, distilled alcohol, and Ixil principales distrusted by their own people, the "ladino principales" took over the town hall. For half a century, from the 1920s to the 1970s, every mayor was a ladino, more often than not a finca owner (see table 7.1 in chapter 7) The majority of town councilmen were ladinos, with Ixils reduced to subordinate roles. All the salaried jobs in the town hall were

Table 2.2

The Growth of Ladino Population in Nebaj

Census Year	Ladinos	Indians	% Ladino	Total
1893	66	5,879	1.1	5,945
1921	421	10,436	4.0	10,857
1940	c.650	12,339	5.0	12,989
1950	1,101	12,152	8.3	13,253
1964	1,800	21,574	7.7	23,374
1973	2,167	25,092	7.9	27,259
1981[1]	2,231	15,903	12.3	18,134
1984	2,122	13,066	14.0	15,188

SOURCES: All figures are from the national census except for those listed for 1984, which were gathered by the local government health center. The figures for the 1893, 1921, and 1950 censuses are courtesy of Pierre van den Berghe. The figures for the 1940 census are calculated from Lincoln 1945:9. The figures for the 1964 census are calculated from Colby and van den Berghe 1969:193.

1. The leap in the ladino percentage from 1973 to 1981 and 1984 is because the violence made it impossible to count predominantly indigenous portions of the rural population.

occupied by ladinos, while Ixils were required to serve in unpaid positions as message-boys and burden-bearers.[30] Since mayors also functioned as justice of the peace, they used their authority to help labor contractors collect their debts; some used their authority over municipal land to put more of it under private title.

By 1950 Nebaj had a ladino population of 1,101 (see table 2.2). While comprising only 8.3 percent of the total municipal population of 13,253, two-thirds of them lived in the town center where they made up 21 percent of the population.[31] Their success in acquiring land is confirmed by table 2.3. Derived from the 1964 census, it shows that ladinos were only 9 percent of farm owners in Ixil country but controlled 27 percent of the farmland, with those who did not live in town scattered through coffee-growing areas.[32]

Closer examination of the figures (table 2.4) suggests a substantial class difference among ladinos. While a few owned properties averaging 665 manzanas (467 hectares, or 10.3 caballerías), most ladinos had much smaller holdings that averaged only 23 manzanas (16 hectares or about one-third of a caballería). If we adjust for anomalies in reporting, particularly a number of fincas in Nebaj and Chajul that were disguised in the smallholder category, what emerges is a population of ladino smallholders whose farms did not average much larger than Indian

Table 2.3
Land Holding by Ethnicity According to the 1964 Census

	Total Number of Farmers	Total Area in Farm[1]	Nonindigenous[2] Farms and Farmers					Indigenous Farms and Farmers				
			Number of Farmers	Area	% of Total Farmers	% of Total Area	Avg. Size Holding	Number of Farmers	Area	% of Total Farmers	% of Total Area	Avg. Size Holding
Nebaj	3,593	32,686	279	6,072	7.77	18.58	21.76	3,314	26,614	92.23	81.42	8.03
Chajul[3]	1,600	21,943	194	6,641	12.13	30.26	34.23	1,406	15,302	87.87	69.74	10.88
Cotzal	1,754	21,307	119	7,517	6.78	35.28	63.17	1,635	13,790	93.22	64.72	8.43
Total	6,947	75,936	592	20,230	8.52	26.64	34.17	6,355	55,706	91.48	73.36	8.77

SOURCE: Dirección General de Estadística 1968:232, 249.

1. Land measures are in manzanas (1 manzana = 16 cuerdas = 1.736 acres = .703 hectares: see table on page 37).

2. For the purpose of simplicity, I assume that all properties with personaria jurídica (an incorporated status) were owned by nonindigenous farmers.

3. From Chajul I excluded two anomalous properties totaling four manzanas which are listed in the source documents.

Table 2.4
Ladino-owned Properties in the Three Ixil Municipios

	Total No. Ladino Farmers	Total Area Ladino Farms[1]	Ladino Farmers with Deeds (Large Properties)					Ladino Farmers Without Deeds (Small Properties)				
			No. of Ladinos	Area with Deeds	% of Total Ladino Farmers	% of Total Ladino Area	Avg. Size Holding	No. of Ladinos	Area Without Deeds	% of Total Ladino Farmers	% of Total Ladino Area	Avg. Size Holding
Nebaj	279	6,072	2	125	.72	2.06	62.50	277	5,947	99.28	97.94	21.47
Chajul	194	6,641	5	271	2.58	4.08	54.20	189	6,370	97.42	95.92	33.70
Cotzal	119	7,517	3	6,253	2.52	83.18	2,084.33	116	1,264	97.48	16.82	10.90
Total	592	20,230	10	6,649	1.69	32.87	664.9	582	13,581	98.31	67.13	23.34

SOURCE: Dirección General de Estadística 1968:232,249.
1. Land measures are in manzanas (1 manzana = 16 cuerdas = 1.736 acres = .703 hectares; see table on page 37).

farms in the 8 to 11 manzana (5 to 8 hectare) range. This and other contrasts among ladinos proved significant in how Nebaj responded to the country's democratic opening from 1945 to 1954, and again in the 1970s and 1980s when Nebajeños survived the war between the army and the guerrillas.

Schoolteachers and Plantation Owners

We built the "Gerardo Gordillo Barrios" School to incorporate the Indian to the currents of culture. It began with boys because that was thought advisable, that girls didn't need to go to school, but today we have both male and female Ixil teachers, because that school educated the first bilingual promoters. We started schools even in remote communities like Sumal Chiquito, Sumal Grande, and Ixtupil. According to the ladino principales, this was communism. The indio doesn't like school, they said. After the indio has gone to school, he'll want to be as important as a ladino, they said. Civic fiestas which previously were especially for the aristocracy, the few families of ladino principales, were now fiestas for everyone, without social distinctions. We talked about cooperativism and organized the first agriculture cooperative here, Lacuvan Canal or "We're Going to Triumph" (another communist plot). A storehouse was organized for the people and, when corn rose to ten quetzals for a hundred pounds, it was on sale there for four quetzals.

—*Former ladino mayor recounting his*
accomplishments in the early 1950s

The Liberal era came to an end in 1944 when the dictator Ubico was overthrown by a popular uprising led by middle-class professionals. During the next ten years, elected governments introduced numerous reforms. Vagrancy laws were abolished; workers and peasants were allowed to organize unions; land was redistributed. The Guatemalan Left remembers the period as a springtime of democracy, but the threat of disorder and a return to military rule lurked beneath the surface. Only the intervention of army officers extracted General Ubico from the national palace in 1944, and only the reformists among them saved the revolution from lapsing into a new dictatorship. President Juan José

Arévalo (1946–50) was a university philosopher by profession, but his successor Jacobo Arbenz (1950–54) was one of the colonels who over-threw Ubico.[33]

The Arbenz government's land reform was just starting to change northern Quiché when it was destroyed by the U.S.-backed counter-revolution of 1954. There were arrests but apparently no bloodshed in Ixil country, and the agrarian movement there left behind few hopes and memories. But before the democratic period ended, it provided a temporary opening for dissident ladinos and Indian leaders to defeat local planters in elections. The resulting struggles suggest the fault lines in Nebaj society that, in subsequent decades, enabled Ixils to reassert themselves in the town hall.

When Nebajeños recall the 1944–54 revolution, they are most likely to invoke the name of their congressman Gerardo Gordillo Barrios. He was one of many out-of-wedlock offspring of the planter Lisandro Gordillo Galán but was "recognized," that is, acknowledged as an heir, perhaps because his mother was a ladino schoolteacher. Jackson Stew-ard Lincoln esteemed Gerardo's knowledge of Ixil customs: he was one of the first Nebajeños to study beyond secondary school. His political career began at San Carlos University, as president of the student asso-ciation under Ubico, whom he helped overthrow in 1944. According to local memory, it is Gerardo Gordillo Barrios who brings the revolution to Nebaj, arriving heroically in a touring car with a pistol on his hip and wearing a shirt from Jorge Ubico's closet.

The stories about the younger Gordillo suggest a populist from the lesser plantation bourgeoisie who, early in the reform period, arbitrated a series of compromises between the two most visible factions in Nebaj politics: the *viejos, señores, principales ladinos,* or *oligarquía* on the one hand, and the *jovenes, progresistas,* or *comunistas* on the other. Despite webs of marriage and descent, ladino society had differentiated consid-erably since the arrival of the first settlers, into upper-class *sociales* (soci-ety) and lower-class *obreros* (workers).[34] The conservative faction was led by plantation owners, anxious over the revolutionary rhetoric filling the air. To avoid offending the ruling party, they proclaimed their loyalty to the reform presidents Arévalo and Arbenz just as they had to the dicta-tor Ubico. But as land reform approached, they gravitated to new right-wing political parties. The opposing faction was led by progressive young schoolteachers, who felt sufficiently empowered by the national reform movement to challenge the planters to whom some were closely related.[35] Given the small scale of ladino society in Nebaj, the conflict pit nephews against uncles and in-laws against in-laws, at a time when, in the words of historian Jim Handy, "the national press and the local ladino elite sounded shrill alarms at the organization of Indians in rural areas . . . claiming to see impending Indian massacres at every turn."[36]

Two ladino reformers were elected mayor in 1947 and 1949, backed by some of the Ixil principales, only for both to be driven from office. Their refusal to jail Ixil debtors, citing the relevant prohibition in the national constitution, did not sit well with labor contractors accustomed to mayoral backing. The second of the two mayors, a young schoolteacher, was a particular thorn in the side. Fond of making speeches, he used the town's new public address system to criticize patróns for failing to pay the minimum wage. Another schoolmaster, meanwhile, was teaching pupils to celebrate May Day with speeches attacking imperialism and cartels. When the local conflict came to a head in 1951, the Arbenz land reform was still a year away but the national congress had just announced the expropriation of part of the Finca La Perla, the second largest plantation in Ixil country.[37] Planters accused the mayor of being a Communist who was plotting to seize other men's land and women. Fearing that agrarian reform would affect their own holdings, Ixil principales wavered and the mayor was forced to leave town.

Under Decree 900 of 1952, many Ixil peasants claimed local fincas. During my interviews thirty-five years later, the subject never came up spontaneously, and I had no idea of the extent of the expropriation decrees until my colleague Elaine Elliott did archival research. From the Finca La Perla in Chajul, fifty-two caballerías (2,343 hectares) were expropriated for surrounding Ixil villages. While the owner doubtless interpreted the decree as a vendetta, even more caballerías (86, or 3,875 hectares) were taken from the Finca San Francisco, whose owners included Arbenz's minister of agriculture Nicolás Brol. Municipal land in Cotzal and Chajul was expropriated for peasant smallholders, as were parts of several smaller fincas near La Perla, but apparently nothing was expropriated in Nebaj, perhaps because of the victory of the planters prior to Decree 900.[38] Judging from available information, there were no land invasions, no violence, and no land actually changed hands before the reform was aborted by the 1954 invasion of right-wing exiles and the army's mutiny against Arbenz.[39]

One of the schoolteachers who led the progressive faction in Nebaj insists that the main bone of contention with "the oligarchy" was, not land reform, but Indian education, a subject in which reformers took keen interest. On the principle that a little education is a dangerous thing, ladino patróns feared that *indios* would put on airs and turn into troublemakers. (Eventually plantation owners reconciled themselves to Indian education, to the point that one serving as mayor is said to have ordered the town police to round up reluctant pupils.) Here Gerardo Gordillo Barrios enters our story again, as the congressman who, in 1945, encouraged two ladino teachers to start a special school to teach Ixils Spanish. The *Escuela de Castellanización* was one of a number of government experiments to prepare Indian pupils for a standard primary school. The teachers were all ladinos, but pupils started out with those who knew some Ixil before passing to others who taught only in Spanish. The school survived the political turmoil of the early 1950s and was sufficiently novel a decade later for one of the founders to be invited to the capital to reproduce the experiment for other Mayan language groups.

Starting in 1967, the new program trained bilingual *promotores*, that is, Indians who had only minimal education but could prepare Indian children for primary school. Among those involved were North American Bible translators from the Summer Institute of Linguistics, an evangelical mission hoping to teach Mayas to read the New Testament in their own language. Moving Indians into the national educational system also appealed to the U.S. embassy. With subsidies from the U.S. Agency for International Development (USAID), the program expanded to include hundreds of promoters in the various Mayan languages, including forty-five in the three Ixil towns.

The language of bilingual education was, by current standards, paternalistic. It would uplift the Indian, raise his cultural level, advance him economically, and integrate him into the nation. The intent was clearly to increase the slender loyalty of Ixils and other Maya-speakers to the Guatemalan state. But the promoters were the first Ixils to become *profesionales*, that is, members of a salariat with an announced profession, in this case, of helping other members of their *raza* through schooling. They operated in their own language and were supposed to promote the interests of their ethnic group. As Benedict Anderson has pointed out, ethnic cadres whom states train to implement nation-building policies can also help their people defend themselves.[40] Bilingual promoters were a new kind of indigenous leadership in Nebaj, and in the disorder of the early 1980s they became a crucial one.

The Catholic Action Revolt Against Gerontocracy

These cofradías burn money. They just burn money.
—*Ixil catechist, Christian Democrat and merchant, 1989*

Another vehicle for new kinds of Ixil leadership was the Catholic Church, an institution of great influence in towns like Nebaj, although not always in the way it intends. When Catholic missionaries imposed their religion following the Spanish Conquest, Mayas interpreted it in terms of their own beliefs, a subtle revenge that produced the famous ritual systems of Guatemala and southern Mexico. Among the Catholic institutions imported from Spain that Mayas turned to their own ends were the *cofradías* (religious brotherhoods). Each cofradía was organized around the worship of a particular saint, for an annual cycle of rituals which became part of the civil-religious hierarchies governing a town. Starting in their youth, men climbed a ladder of community obligations, typically alternating back and forth between the saint societies and the town hall. Some had to be forced to undertake the duties, yet such *cargos* (the same word for a burden carried on the back) were rewarded with prestige. Men reaching the top of the hierarchy became *principales*, the elders ruling the community.[41]

Vestiges of the civil-religious hierarchy can be found in any Mayan community, and some saint societies continue to thrive, but the system has been undermined by national reorganization of local government, the introduction of political parties, and other forces.[42] Leading the assault in the western highlands was, ironically, the Catholic clergy. To a new generation of Spanish and North American missionaries who arrived in the 1950s, the fiestas honoring saints had become excuses for idolatry and debauchery. To discourage such behavior, priests organized chapters of Catholic Action, a pastoral organization intended to turn Mayas into orthodox parishioners.[43] In Ixil country, Catholic Action was introduced by Padre Gaspar Jordan, the solitary Spaniard who represented the Catholic Church in Ixil country and surrounding regions for several decades. Lincoln paints him as a merry friar itinerating through an almost medieval world of pomp, incense, and superstition, but Nebajeños still remember his clashes with the saint societies. On one occasion, the town elders sent a delegation to the department capital to accuse him of being an *evangelista*.[44]

The twelve saint societies in Nebaj are each served by ten men and their spouses, a new group of whom enters every year, for a busy calendar of jointly celebrated processions and fiestas. Little about the cofradías is orthodox: certainly not the names of the saints they parade through the streets. Six of the saints are organized into man-woman pairs (Rosary Man and Rosary Woman, Cross Man and Cross Woman, and Conception Man and Conception Woman) suggesting the androgynous nature of Mayan deities. Ixil traditionalists believe that propitiating the saints is essential to the town's welfare, but to deal with personal crises and bury the dead they go to their own Mayan priests, men whose calling can be traced to before the Spanish Conquest. Without any sense of contradiction, Ixil *baalbastixes* (literally, "fathers before God") pray both to the Catholic saints residing in the church and to the *aanheles* ("angels") who, visualized with the same European faces as the saints, live in the mountains surrounding Nebaj. At various wooden crosses located around the town center, and before piles of crosses heaped in the town cemetery, the priests also pray to the souls of departed ancestors who reside with the *aanheles*, or lords of the hills. Baalbastixes are entrusted with crucial prayers for the saint societies, for the maize harvest, and for new political officeholders. Some are also *aaq'ii* (or "day man"), the diviners who preserve the day count of the Mayan calendar from before the Spanish Conquest.[45]

When Benjamin and Lore Colby recorded the worldview of Ixil priest Shas K'ow, what emerged was an ethic of great forbearance toward humans and other living things. But, like any religious system, Ixil *costumbre* (custom) is not completely successful in resolving society's contradictions. Traditions stressing the power of ancestors, as have those of the Ixils and their neighbors the Akateko Mayas, provide obvious rationales for the authority of elders, that is, for gerontocracy. Where principales and other elders rule, the young depend on them to inherit land and acquire a spouse. When a gerontocratic society is more or less in equilibrium, much of the inequality that exists works itself out over the life-cycle. Younger men and women perform labor service for their elders and, as they themselves grow older, are compensated by the labor service they receive from their juniors.

Unfortunately, Ixil society has not been in any kind of equilibrium. Two developments after 1900 complicated relations between the generations, by reducing the amount of land that fathers could pass on to sons. One was alienation of land to finca owners. Cotzal lost up to 45 percent of its land base this way (see table 2.1), but Nebaj and Chajul lost much less (5–6 percent), even if certain aldeas like Sotzil and Ilom were practically swallowed up. The other, more pervasive phenomenon reducing inheritances was population growth, perhaps sixfold in the last century (see figure 1 on p. 37 and table 2.5). According to George Lovell, it took the population of the Cuchumatanes more than four centuries to regain the level that existed at the time of the Spanish Conquest. Once that point was reached, around 1950, it took only a generation for the population to double.[46]

The effect on the amount of land available for inheritance can be seen in table 2.6. In 1893 the inhabitants of Ixil country enjoyed 19.13 hectares per person, but by 1950 the figure had declined to 7.52 hectares, and by 1989 to 3.30 hectares. Also keep in mind that the number of hectares available for each Nebajeño (1.86) and Cotzaleño (1.01) in 1989 was much smaller than for each Chajuleño (7.85), and that the amount of arable land per capita was even smaller.[47] According to Nebajeños, the land their fathers actually owned and passed to them is indeed smaller than the above figures would indicate.

To illustrate this point, table 2.7 compares two very different groups: (1) the "town elite," a diverse collection of religious leaders, labor contractors, merchants, and professionals whom I sought out because of their prominence and who therefore are not necessarily a representative sample, and (2) an outlying cantón of the town, including many families (48.5 percent of the total) displaced from outlying villages by the war, for which my interviewers and I surveyed every household. The town

Table 2.5

Demographic Collapse and Recovery in the Ixil Triangle, 1529–1989

Period/ Year	Source	Nebaj	Chajul	Cotzal	Total
1529	estimate				20,000– 25,000
1670s/80s	estimate				2,000
1740	estimate	228	352	404	984
1850s	estimate				6,700
1893	natl. census	5,945	3,329	2,825	12,099
1921	natl. census	10,857	4,968	4,590	20,415
1950	natl. census	13,253	8,258	9,244	30,755
1964	natl. census	23,374	13,497	12,150	49,021
1973	natl. census	27,259	18,092	12,698	58,049
1981	natl. census	18,134	15,713	10,944	44,791
1981	natl. census projection	37,953	29,598	16,742	82,293
1983/84	govt. health centers	15,188	6,360 (urban only)	5,530 (urban only)	27,078
1986/87	govt. health centers	23,906	13,467	12,246	49,619
1989	U.N. estimate	46,383	18,103	17,940	82,426
1989	corrected U.N. estimate	32,709	19,423	17,940	70,072
1989	natl. census projection	45,438	38,672	17,669	101,779

SOURCES: Estimates for 1529 to the 1850s are from Colby and van den Berghe 1969:61–2. Census figures for 1893 and 1921 are courtesy of Pierre van den Berghe. Census figures for 1950 and 1964 are reproduced in Colby and van den Berghe 1969:193, while the figures for 1973 are from Dirección General de Estadística 1973. National census projections for 1981 and 1989 are from Instituto Nacional de Estadística 988:24. The 1989 United Nations estimate is courtesy of the Nebaj office of the Program for Refugees, Repatriates and Displaced Peoples (PRODERE) of the U.N. Development Program.

leaders report that their fathers owned an average of 11.6 hectares, that they inherited an average of 2.1 hectares, and that they now own slightly more than that, an average of 2.7 hectares. As for the poorer Cantón Xemamatze, its household heads report that their fathers owned an average of 4.2 hectares, that they inherited an average of 1.7 hectares, and that they now own even less, an average of 1 hectare.

Even if respondents are underreporting their actual holdings, as peasants often do, such figures suggest the minimal amounts of land Ixils are inheriting from their fathers. The sense of betrayal this can engender is suggested by the man from Ilom quoted in the epigraph on page 28. Even though his village was subject to blatant aggression by a

Table 2.6

The Decline in the Hectare Per Capita Ratio in the Three Ixil Municipios, 1893–1989[1]

	Area Km²	1893 Popu-lation	1893 Ha/Person	1893 Persons/km²	1950 Popu-lation	1950 Ha/Person	1950 Persons km²	1989 Est. Popu-lation	1989 Ha/Person	1989 Persons/km²
Nebaj	608	5,945	10.23	9.78	13,253	4.59	21.80	32,709	1.86	53.80
Chajul	1,524	3,329	45.78	2.18	8,258	18.45	5.42	19,423	7.85	12.74
Cotzal	182	2,825	6.44	15.52	9,244	1.97	50.79	17,940	1.01	98.57
Ixil Triangle	2,314	12,099	19.13	5.23	30,755	7.52	13.29	70,072	3.30	30.28
Department El Quiché	8,378	92,753	9.03	11.07	174,911	4.79	20.88	557,044	1.50	66.49

SOURCE: Derived from preceding tables.
1. This is total land, not arable land.

Table 2.7

Land Inheritance and Ownership in Contemporary Nebaj[1]

	Avg. Cuerdas Owned by Father[2]	No. of Cases	Avg. Cuerdas Inherited (if Father Dead)	No. of Cases	Avg. Cuerdas Owned Now	No. of Cases	% Who Claim to Have Enough Land	No. of Cases	% Who Claim Sufficiency in Maize	No. of Cases
Town Elite	265.90	155	47.96	80	61.23	167	49.7	157	45.1	153
Cantón Xemamatze	95.13	88	38.33	39	24.02	98	26.0	96	26.3	95
Total	203.22	244	44.80	119	44.44	265	40.6	253	37.7	248

1. Sample: Cantón Xemamatze included all or nearly all the households in the cantón. But "town leaders" are not a representative sample since I instructed my interviewers to seek out certain kinds of prominent Ixils including teachers and bilingual promoters, Catholic leaders and evangelical pastors, men who had served as heads of saint societies, labor contractors, vehicle owners and merchants. While some are rather poor, on average they are a more privileged group than Cantón Xemamatze, which includes many people displaced by the war.

2. One cuerda = .108 hectares = .044 acres and 22.77 cuerdas = 1 hectare (see table on page 37).

ladino planter and the Guatemalan legal system, he blames Ilom's elders—"our fathers, our grandmothers and grandfathers"—for not being sufficiently prescient to buy the land back. Or as an evangelical pastor commented on his own family's loss of its land: "Many don't want to work, they fall into vice, selling their land, houses and milpas, leaving their children with nothing." Such feelings of deprivation are the mood in which youth can be expected to question the verities of their elders and experiment with new forms of authority.

From a comparison of seven Mayan communities in southern Mexico and Guatemala, George Collier has derived an association between the scarcity of land, its inheritance from fathers to sons, and the strength of patriarchal authority. As land becomes scarce owing to population growth or other factors, Collier's comparison indicates, patriarchal authority in the family increases. It continues to grow until land becomes so scarce that the size of the inheritance dwindles to insignificance and so does its influence on sons, at which point patriarchal authority deflates.[48]

Just such an inflation and deflation of patriarchal authority seems to have occurred in Nebaj, which used to be known for the power of its elders. One indication are the stories of tyrannical principales extracting tribute well into the twentieth century, then the popularity of the Catholic Action movement which rejected their authority. What is certain is that the authority of fathers over sons, land inheritance, and religious loyalties were connected issues in Nebaj. "Fathers used to be respected, but now it is not the same," an elder told me. "'Our real father is not here, our father is in heaven,' rebellious sons say. There are some parents who preferred to sell their land, because their children no longer showed respect."

For Ixils, a common way of experiencing their dwindling resources was an agonizing reappraisal of the cost of their ritual duties, especially serving as the head of a saint society. Hence the evangelical pastor who recalls how his father had to sell his bull, then his cow, to pay for eight nights of marimba music to honor a saint. Men without animals had to borrow money from a ladino, who might end up taking their land. Or a second pastor whose *principal* grandfather and two uncles drank up the family property, leaving his father and himself without an inheritance.[49] Differences sharpened in the 1950s when Spanish priests recruited young Ixils into Catholic Action. Requirements for joining the new group included doctrinal instruction, getting married in church, and going to confession. Most important, catechists were prohibited from participating in the saint societies, which the priests condemned as pagan. To instill orthodoxy, the clergy were encouraging young catechists to defy elders whose authority was already being undermined by the land squeeze.

In Nebaj, only generational strife can explain the zeal with which catechists assaulted traditional symbols of religious authority.[50] When *costumbristas* (traditionalists) came into church drunk, catechists snuffed out the candles they were lighting and threw them out the door. They even burned the wooden crosses in the chapel at Juil, the center of the Ixil universe.[51] Catholic Action "behaved with the arrogance and confidence of youth," Pierre van den Berghe recalls of his 1966 fieldwork in Nebaj. "They were rough with the costumbristas. No doubt that Catholic Action versus costumbre was a generational thing, a resentment of young against old, of young breaking the rules and disrespecting elders."[52] Confrontations between rival processions sent one worshiper to the hospital as late as Good Friday 1973.[53]

The Emergence of Evangelicals

In Catholic Action there are still baalbastixes, there's hardly any change. There's still copal, marimbas, shooting off fireworks, the very priest uses incense and candles at mass. Evangelicals don't do this because we're baptized in the Holy Spirit.

> —Ex-Catholic Action president turned evangelical pastor

After the Catholic Church became a victim of army persecution, it became easy to overlook policies that Ixils might regard as coercive. No such inhibitions were felt by Horst Nachtigall, the German ethnologist who studied Nebaj in 1973. From disaffected traditionalists, Nachtigall heard that the priest was refusing to baptize their infants.[54] Because baptism is an essential marker of human identity in Mayan towns, this would have been a punitive measure. Years later, traditionalists and catechists agree that baptism was always available to traditionalists—

so long as they took doctrinal classes from catechists. The parish priest in the 1970s, Javier Gurriarán, was a young, energetic Basque belonging to the Sacred Heart, the Spanish order entrusted with Quiché Department. Despite the army's effort to discredit his name, he is remembered affectionately by most Nebajeños, including a number of his catechists who turned into evangelical pastors. As long as traditionalists took care not to show up drunk for mass, and submitted to the required classes to baptize their children, Padre Javier provided them with the ritual services they desired. During his time, Catholic Action became less exclusive and the saint societies performed their ceremonies in peace. In the countryside, Catholic Action is said to have held its services at sacred Mayan sites and asked villagers to bring their maize for blessing.

Catholic Action did not lose its sectarian edge in Nebaj in the 1970s due solely to Padre Javier. The catechists of the 1950s and 1960s were getting older, some of them lapsing into the rich, alcohol-driven rituals of their town.[55] Ironically, the growing tolerance of Catholic Action toward Ixil tradition became a stimulus for Ixil interest in Protestantism. Through Catholic Action, the clergy had provided an outlet for tensions between the generations. So long as Catholic Action maintained a sectarian attitude toward the traditional religious system, by excoriating the saint societies and their fiestas, it provided a platform for young Ixils predisposed to revolt against the authority of their elders. It also happened to preempt the potential appeal of evangelical Protestantism as a form of rebellion. But when Catholic Action became more tolerant and inclusive, evolving from the discipline of a sect toward a broader church body according to the well-known typology, it no longer provided the same satisfaction to Ixils intent on breaking with costumbre.[56]

Hence the numerous catechists who left to become Protestants, often before the violence. They complain that Catholic Action failed to maintain its standards, forcing them to worship beside traditionalists who smoke and drank, as if that made them feel polluted. "Padre Javier left the traditionalists in peace," complains a puritanical catechist who turned evangelical in the late 1970s. "And this was the problem. When we came to mass, the cofradías over there were drinking and smoking in church, getting drunk inside, making an uproar. This was why we thought that God was not going to come. . . . 'If there is disorder, depart from there."' Clearly, puritanical catechists and evangelicals were developing a rather different idea of the holy from the traditional one. The new religion in Nebaj emphasized self-control, as if to discipline the self to compete more effectively with ladinos.

The Revolutionary Party and the Christian Democrats

Nebaj provides an interesting reversal of the usual assumptions about opposition politics in the Guatemalan highlands of the 1960s and 1970s. Catholic Action catechists were, true to their own interests and the modernizing objectives of the Catholic clergy, predictable dissidents against local power structures. Traditionalists, on the other hand, seemed predictable defenders of the status quo. During the early 1950s, social researchers recorded the opposition of principales to agrarian reform in a number of Indian towns,[57] and during the early 1980s in Nebaj the number of principales killed by the guerrillas (I received reports of at least six) suggests a continuing lack of enthusiasm for social transformation. Yet both catechists and traditionalists resented ladino prerogatives, and in Nebaj it was traditionalists who achieved the symbolic victory of breaking the ladino monopoly on the mayor's office.

As Colby and van den Berghe studied ethnicity in 1966, the first Ixil-controlled political party in town, a branch of the Revolutionary party (PR), was running a slate headed by an Ixil. The candidate's father was Sebastián Guzmán—the town's leading principal, the first Ixil to buy a truck and also one of the first to become a labor contractor. Like only a few Ixils before him, Guzmán had learned how to compete with ladinos on their own terms. Unlike several of the most powerful principales before him, he also upheld Ixil traditions with pride. For Colby and van den Berghe, Guzmán was a soft-spoken, unassuming man who gave little indication of his authority as the power broker who summoned other principales to his house to deliberate on town affairs.

The announced purpose of the Revolutionary party was to restore the social reforms of 1944–54. Although it was soon co-opted by the Guatemalan army and discredited, some Ixils still appreciate its organizers for teaching them how to take their problems to the appropriate government ministry in the capital. Ixils also remember the PR for establishing ethnic equality in the town hall. What focused Ixil resentment was a vestige of the civil-religious hierarchy, the requirement for Indian men to provide unpaid service to the town hall, which ladino politicians turned into unpaid service to themselves. "The ladinos had the *indígenas* like slaves," an elder recalls. "While ladinos in the town hall all received salaries, sixty or more Ixils were obliged to work without pay." "For us indígenas it was . . . just giving away our day . . . [we were] just errand boys nothing more," an old PR leader explains. "When there was a fiesta, they sent us to bring back pine boughs, half for the fiesta and half for them. For free. So we thought a lot about why we were giving away our day for free and they were not. This was the politics of how the Revolutionary party won the elections."

Translating the numerical advantage of Ixils into an electoral victory was not easy. Notwithstanding universal franchise, most illiterates failed to vote unless induced with drink or coin provided by party activists. Of those Ixils who were literate or opposed to selling their vote, many were catechists at odds with the traditionalists led by Sebastián Guzmán. The bitterness of the struggle between the two Catholic factions is why, in 1966, Colby and van den Berghe found that the catechists had thrown their support to the ladino-dominated and army-allied Democratic Institutional party (PID). Strife between catechists and traditionalists is also why, despite the growth of a conscientious Ixil vote, the ladinos of the PID were able to win the 1966 election.[58]

Only in 1970 did the Revolutionary party win its first election in Nebaj—with a ladino for mayor who, along with his brothers, owned the largest finca in Ixil country. Enrique Brol had promised to end unpaid Ixil labor for the town hall. Once elected, however, he succumbed to the entreaties of fellow ladinos and failed to do so. The PR's undisputed head in Nebaj remained Sebastián Guzmán, and for the next election in 1972 he ran another of his sons, who became the first Ixil mayor in Nebaj since the 1920s. The new mayor was careful to parcel out municipal jobs to ladinos as well as Indians, but one of his first decisions was to liberate the unpaid Ixil youths serving the town hall without pay. They were replaced with a smaller number of paid offices that have since been apportioned by the winning party.

Absent from the two anthropological accounts of Nebaj in this period was the soon-to-be main opposition party in Guatemala, the Christian Democrats (DC). According to Nebajeños, the local branch of the DC dates to 1965 when it was organized by 120 men. The majority were Ixils from the Catholic Action movement, but there were also ladinos, some dating to the reform movement of the late 1940s and early 1950s. The new DC branch was not a contender in the 1966 election because it was still fighting to be legalized on the national level. When the catechists of the DC reacted against the traditionalists of the PR by throwing their support to the army-allied PID, they could not have known that, a decade later, the PID candidate would put members of both parties on a death list.

Reform Without Revolution?

Now they've woken up. They know they have rights.
                    —*Former ladino mayor of Nebaj, 1992*

When a people are colonized, the techniques used to control them are likely to take advantage of preexisting contradictions in their cultural practices. Traditions that were both cherished and oppressive become implicated in new kinds of oppression. In the case of the Ixils, a society dominated by old men and given to ritual drunkenness provided plentiful opportunities for the agents of a new export economy. Ladino colonists stepped into the same position of authority occupied by Mayan principales but used that power for new ends, such as obtaining laborers for plantations. Oppression is easiest to visualize in terms of an external class and ethnic agent, such as a ladino planter. But it was also an internal problem, of cultural practices that, in a rapidly monetizing economy, could lead to personal destruction. Traditional obligations to honor the saints could be used to put Ixils into debt and take away their land.

One way of looking at the resulting inadequacy of Ixil tradition is in terms of leadership. When existing leadership fails, as occurred for Ixils in the first half of the twentieth century, a demand for new kinds of authority results. The elders of the civil-religious hierarchy were, on the whole, too illiterate, monolingual, aged, and alcoholic to defend Ixil interests in an era of rapid commercialization. Of those principales who did learn how to deal with ladinos on equal terms, several of the most prominent also learned how to use ladino methods to exploit their own people. The result was what Eric Wolf has called "a crisis in the exercise of power," in which Ixil society began to generate new kinds of authority figures.[59] As is often the case, new kinds of authority were shaped by incorporative ideological forms of the colonizing society. Catechists, pastors, and promoters were intended by missionaries and government educators to convert and uplift their neighbors. In chapter 7, we shall see how these figures merged into the figure of the promoter, who has supplanted the principal as the most visible example of ethnic authority.

Through schools and reformed religion, Ixils were learning to hold their own with ladinos in new ways. Although politics in Nebaj was shaped by ethnicity, it did not divide into opposing ladino and Ixil blocs. Instead, transactions between members of the two ethnic groups illustrate James Scott's "moral economy" of reciprocal, if unequal, obligations between members of different social classes. Instead of colliding in open conflict, Ixils and ladinos constructed a shared moral universe in which they could agree, for example, on what constitutes proper behavior for patróns, clients, and public officials. Factions competing for the town hall typically drew on members of both ethnic groups, if only because Ixils comprised a large majority of the population and had profound disagreements over how to comport themselves in the new era. As for ladinos, differences of class led to noticeable differences in ideology. Ladinos led the populist coalitions of the 1944–54 period and again in the 1970s, even as their disproportionate power began to wane. Partly because of the many alliances between members of the two ethnic groups, in the 1970s the local political system was able to respond to Ixil demands for more equitable treatment.

The gradual gains registered by Ixils were part of a wider trend in the western highlands. Northern Quiché is on the periphery of the highland market system, meaning that its indigenous population still focuses on growing maize and, as a result of increasing land shortages, has become more and more dependent on seasonal migration to plantations.[60] Yet, when Carol Smith surveyed the regional market system in the 1970s, she found that "many fewer people from peripheral communities, including the Ixil area, were seeking plantation work."[61] She found a greater diversity of local employment, with artisans and merchants meeting more of the demands generated by local markets. More people in peripheral communities were working in government construction projects, and they were exporting more goods to the rest of the highlands. Ladino control over commercial possibilities was diminishing. Ixils were developing alternatives to plantation work and absorbing more of their labor at home.

Given the political violence that engulfed Ixil country after 1979, is there any evidence of insurgency being generated by the local relations between Ixils and ladinos? The answer is, rather little. However much Ixils suffered from colonization, violence against ladinos was a rare response on their part. In the 1920s Ixils confronted planters surveying their new properties around Ilom, but the only fatalities appear to have been Ixils. In 1935 a peaceful protest against labor abuses in the Nebaj plaza turned into an "Indian revolt" when a ladino comandante panicked, but the only deaths—seven of them—were, again, Ixils rather than ladinos.[62] In 1969, as we shall see, Ixil politicians in Cotzal conspired with guerrillas to rob and kill a plantation owner. But such widely spaced incidents hardly indicate a history of simmering revolt in Ixil country.

THREE

The Violence Comes to Ixil Country

*Captured guerilla holding an unloaded weapon at an
army rally in Nebaj, 1988*

We were the bees and the war was the honey.
                                    —*Mario Payeras, Days of the Jungle, 1979*

THEY came into Nebaj early on Sunday market day, January 21, 1979. First they took strategic points such as the telegraph office. The treasury agents surrendered without a shot, but a pair of national police held out for two hours before one surrendered and the other escaped. There was a single fatality, the plantation owner Enrique Brol. Perhaps because one of his brothers had been killed by guerrillas and another ransomed at great expense, the ex-mayor grappled with the woman taking him prisoner and died of the resulting gunshot. Ironically, Enrique was one of the finca owners known for numerous liaisons and offspring. Now he had died at the hands of a young woman about the same age as his concubines. Around each of the assaults gathered crowds of townspeople, who followed the prisoners to the marketplace for the rally that the guerrillas were announcing.

"So this is the Guerrilla Army of the Poor, finally they have appeared," townspeople said with anxiety and wonder. But there is disagreement about who these hundred or so guerrillas in fresh green uniforms really were. According to one account, they were mainly Indians, while according to another they were mainly university students from the capital.[1] A North American detained by the guerrillas for a few hours recalls that most seemed young, inexperienced, and nervous, but she thinks that they were not local, nor heavily ladino, nor simply campesinos. If each of the above perceptions is accurate, they point to a very special social group that has provided the first recruits for more than one guerrilla movement in recent years: urbanized, educated youth from indigenous backgrounds who return to the countryside to make the revolution.

A few of the guerrillas had stocking caps pulled over their faces, as if to avoid being identified as local men. Two others without masks were recognized as Ixil youths who had disappeared and been presumed dead. The more well known, a Christian Democratic activist, had not been seen since his uncle and father-in-law were kidnapped by a death squad. Three years later, he was making a triumphant return in the uniform of the Army of the Poor. "The old people know how the town used to be," he told the crowd in the marketplace. "We used to have land. The people used to have food when there were no labor contractors. You know how we have been losing all our land to powerful families, like that of Enrique Brol. You know how we live, that at times we have tortillas to eat, and that at times we don't have even tortillas. At times, we go for months eating tortilla with greens while others, not because of their work but because of their ability to rob, eat whatever they want, spend all kinds of money, and then when they get rich leave town for good."[2]

The audience is said to have applauded, but how Nebajeños really felt about the EGP's brief takeover is another subject for disagreement. Some claim there was a warm reception, due to anger over a series of crimes by security forces, but others say that many in the crowd were simply ingratiating themselves to a display of authority as Nebajeños customarily do. Doubtless, feelings were complex. After pointed warnings to labor contractors, the guerrillas helped themselves to supplies at various stores and released their prisoners. "We're going, but we're not really going," they said as they left town. "The army says that we are bandits in the hills, that we live there. But it's not true. We are among you. We know what you are going through."[3]

The army took the guerrillas at their word. Three years after the EGP occupation, on a December morning in 1981 that is not recorded in any human rights report, the Guatemalan army ordered all the men in town into the park in front of the Catholic church. Then it sealed the exits. One by one the Nebajeños were ordered into the community hall next to the church, a bright new place where they used to meet with Padre Javier. Instead of the parish priest sat the dread figure of an *encapuchado* (hooded one), a presumed guerrilla who, probably under torture, had agreed to identify his comrades. This judge of life and death never spoke a word from under the hood, only shook his head from side to side or nodded up and down as each man passed before him. Soon the community center was full of men, thrown on the floor and trussed up like pigs for slaughter, upon whom soldiers were methodically stomping. Some were eventually let go; dozens of others were never seen again.

Our understanding of what set off massive political violence in the western highlands is still shaped by the terrible images that reached the outside world. In 1978, for example, the army machine-gunned a crowd of unarmed Q'eqchi' Mayas who were demanding land titles in the plaza of Panzós, Alta Verapaz. Farther north was the "transversal strip," a belt of rain forest scheduled for colonization, cattle-raising, and oil exploration. Owing to the keen interest of army officers in acquiring land at the eastern end of the transversal, soon it became known as "the zone of the generals." When the Guerrilla Army of the Poor surfaced farther west in the strip, the organization was interpreted as a popular reaction to military land-grabbing.[4] Then there was the massacre at the Spanish embassy in January 1980. Peasants from northern Quiché—mainly Uspantán but also the Ixil towns—had come to the capital to protest the kidnapping of relatives. To draw attention to their plight, they occupied the Spanish embassy. Government security forces attacked and the protesters burned to death, along with most of the embassy staff and a former vice president of Guatemala.[5]

As atrocities made their fleeting appearance in the international media, most scholars and journalists rejected the Guatemalan army's rationalizations, including the claim that it was reacting to subversive attacks. Instead, they looked to the Catholic Church and the revolutionary movement for an accurate picture of events. Some of the people who died at the Spanish embassy were members of the Catholic Action movement, catechists who were becoming political militants. Catechists were also said to play a leading role in the Committee for Campesino Unity (CUC), a semiclandestine organization leading mass strikes on sugar and cotton plantations.[6] CUC was the radical wing of a broader peasant movement which included many cooperatives organized by the Catholic clergy. The idea of raising the consciousness of the poor, of encouraging peasants to organize themselves against oppressive social structures, was spreading in the Catholic Church and starting to be called liberation theology.[7]

As for Guatemala's national security state, it seemed bent on destroying any attempt by Mayan campesinos to improve their lives.

Government repression, concluded the eloquent 1982 Oxfam report *Witnesses to Political Violence in Guatemala,* was "less an attempt to wipe out a guerrilla insurgency than an effort to suppress a rural development movement."[8] One scholar hypothesized "an underlying rationale" for repression—the need to free up Mayan wage labor for the plantations.[9]

Government massacres made it seem self-evident that the violence originated in the intolerance and brutality of Guatemala's rulers. This is true in terms of what the Left calls "structural violence," the long history of domination that bred the failed reforms of 1944–54 and then the guerrilla movements. But if we focus on military violence in northern Quiché, there was none until after the Guerrilla Army of the Poor made its first raids in 1975. Indeed, there was little military presence of any kind before the EGP's arrival: the western highlands were ruled by a police state that had no reason to militarize the area. When local people describe what happened, their grim accounts of army violence usually refer to earlier actions by the guerrillas. This simple chronological point is obscured in the literature, however, as if our revulsion against the Guatemalan army is so great that we have been unwilling to acknowledge how local people talk about the violence.

What, then, set off the mayhem in northern Quiché Department? Fortunately, we have *Days of the Jungle,* a revealing account of the first years of the Guerrilla Army of the Poor. Writing under the nom-de-plume of Mario Payeras, the author was educated in Guatemalan and foreign universities, led the EGP's advance into the Ixcán rain forest under the nom-de-guerre "Comandante Benedicto," served in the EGP high command, and led a split from the organization in 1984. *Days of the Jungle* can be accused of triumphalism, as can the Guerrilla Army of the Poor, but it stands apart from the uninformative, ideological tracts usually produced by guerrilla organizations. Payeras is frank about the many reverses of the EGP's first years, and his poetry of warfare is revealing about the implications of starting a guerrilla movement. "For the great machine of war to move," he writes, "the motor of clandestine organization had to be set in motion."[10] In this chapter I will argue that the violence in Ixil country was not an outgrowth of local social struggles. Rather, it was the result of insurgents choosing a backward area where state authority was weak. The predictable overreactions of security forces would help the guerrillas start a movement.

The Army of the Poor Comes to the Ixcán Jungle

They said "we're going to change the law. We are the Guerrilla Army of the Poor. You don't have to worry about necessities anymore because we're going to take the fincas to give them to the people."

"We're going to start a war for the lands we don't have, the lands which the patrón robbed from us, and because they don't pay us well." We thought, "that's fine, maybe it's true." Everyone liked the lie they told us.
—Nebajeños describing how the EGP appealed to them around 1980

On January 19, 1972, a small band of guerrillas crossed from Mexico into the Ixcán rain forest of northern Quiché. They were survivors of an earlier insurgency in the eastern part of the country, which had been suppressed by the Guatemalan army with great loss of life. Like other survivors of that debacle, dispersed into an array of factions, the founders of the Guerrilla Army of the Poor were casting about for a new place to start a national liberation war. In the Ixcán they found some of the most remote, intimidating geography in the country. So dense is the tropical vegetation covering its broken terrain that, two decades later, after dozens of counterinsurgency sweeps, it still protected thousands of refugees at a short distance from army garrisons. The Ixcán was on an international frontier, crucial for logistics. And it bordered the population the guerrillas wanted to organize, the Mayan peasantry of the western highlands, thousands of whom were descending into the Ixcán to carve farms out of the forest.

Now that agrarian reform had become politically impossible, the Ixcán was to provide land for campesinos from the crowded highlands. The migration included spontaneous flows of land-hungry families from Ixil country, southern Quiché, Alta Verapaz, and Huehuetenango. There were also projects of the U.S. Agency for International Development and the Guatemalan government's National Institute for Agrarian Transformation. But the most impressive Ixcán settlements were sponsored by the Catholic Church, including the North American Maryknoll order in Huehuetenango and the Spanish priests of the Sacred Heart in Santa Cruz del Quiché. It was because the Catholic colonies were already so well organized that the EGP was attracted to them in its search for a popular base.[11]

While Ixcán settlers suffered great hardship during the first years, the land produced abundantly as soon as it was cleared. Maize could be harvested twice a year, not just once as in the highlands, as well as fruit, coffee, and cardamon, a spice in great demand in the Middle East. The mid-1970s price for cardamon was high and, unlike other Guatemalan exports, it was not monopolized by plantations. Instead, some of the profits went to small farmers. The better-organized settlements were booming, particularly the Catholic ones. With the help of mission subsidies, settlers built well-equipped cooperatives. They had their own schools, churches and health clinics, electric generators and two-way radios; a subsidized transport/marketing system stretching to the capital; and a collective land title being processed by the national authorities.[12]

Winning the colonists over was no small problem for the guerrillas, who were all outsiders and mainly ladinos. Guerrilla poet Mario Payeras describes a successful uphill struggle, but the receptions he describes are mixed, including lots of deep suspicion.[13] When Ixcán settlers do warm to the armed strangers, Payeras is usually dissatisfied with their level of understanding and commitment. While some colonists allow guerrillas to help them farm, and a few join the organization, only one of their local recruits in the first two years stays with the organization.[14] By 1974–75, Payeras reports, "a constant stream of peasants sought out our local cells, bringing with them their ancient burden of grievances." Yet when an armed column marches on the Finca La Perla, the hardships so discourage the new recruits that they all return home before the attack.

Whatever the relation between a dozen or so revolutionaries and the Ixcán settlers, it became the basis for a new stage in how Guatemalan revolutionaries thought about their task. The movements in the eastern part of the country had been inspired by the example of Fidel Castro in Cuba. According to the resulting *foco* theory, a few committed militants could become a catalyst for revolution, without the long, painstaking task of first organizing the local population.[15] Emboldened by this romantic doctrine, throughout Latin America city-bred intellectuals slipped away to Cuba, returned home to intern themselves in the mountains, and issued proclamations, only to be overwhelmed by U.S.-equipped government forces. The most famous exponent of *foquismo*, Che Guevara, met his end in Bolivia in 1967, the same period his Guatemalan admirers were also being tracked down with the help of Green Berets.

In Guatemala, Mayan peasants were generally slow to warm to armed strangers preaching against the government. The revolutionary movement had always been dominated by ladinos, who tended to deprecate the revolutionary potential of a population that was doubly handicapped, according to orthodox Marxist thinking, by being indigenous and peasant. Since most ladinos do not speak a Mayan language, they faced special difficulties in communicating with peasants whose Spanish was rudimentary. With few exceptions, Indians did not participate in the 1960s guerrilla movements, not least because of the punishment that was sure to follow. Santa Maria Tzejá was one of a number of Ixcán locales where the budding EGP found it was not welcome. After an earlier guerrilla column passed through the area and purchased a pig to eat, the army hung men from trees.[16]

With the effigy of Che Guevara on its banner, the EGP never abandoned its *foquista* assumptions, that is, the idea that professional revolutionaries from outside an area could set off a chain reaction leading to revolution.[17] But in the Ixcán, it did succeed in integrating part of the wider population into its movement, first in the form of clandestine cells and networks, later in the form of entire villages. The new approach required patience. The EGP took more than three years to attack its first target, in 1975, and waited nearly another four years before openly entering Ixil aldeas in the highlands to the south. It would be a "prolonged popular war," based on long-term preparations and special efforts to recruit Indians into a ladino-led organization. After "implantation" in the Ixcán and nearby highland municipios, there would be "armed propaganda," followed by guerrilla warfare, the creation of liberated zones, and mass insurrection. In debates with the rest of the revolutionary movement, the EGP argued that the Indian peasantry of the western highlands would provide mass support to defeat the Guatemalan army.[18]

The Cotzaleños Who Went to Greet the EGP

People appear the same, but who knows with whom they've been talking?
—Mayor of Cotzal, 1976–80

The first Ixils to respond favorably to the EGP's overtures were not impoverished seasonal plantation laborers, as its strategists seem to have expected. Instead, they were prominent men from San Juan Cotzal, relatively well-situated merchants and labor contractors, who wished to enlist the guerrillas in the bitter political feuds of their town. The people of Cotzal are, like Nebajeños and Chajuleños, quite conscious of themselves as a distinct group: the women do not wear the famous red skirt and their speech may be less closely related than the other two dialects of Ixil. According to local wisdom, Cotzaleños also stand apart in personality: they are the most *listo* (clever) and quarrelsome.

They also happen to have the smallest land per capita ratio, and lost the largest percentage of their municipio to ladinos (see tables 2.1 and 2.6 in the previous chapter). Above all, they lost control of the warm, fertile valley that descends to the Finca San Francisco, the largest coffee plantation in Ixil country.[19] San Francisco was put together by Pedro Brol (1877–1942), an Italian emigrant who, Lincoln believed, was exceptional among ladinos in having acquired his property fairly and honestly.[20] Fifty years later, Cotzaleños say their grandparents were forced to acquiesce "by fear and the law." That is, Brol purchased national-level titles beyond the ken of Cotzaleños who were simply farming municipal land inherited from their fathers. As far as Cotzaleños are concerned, they welcomed ladino families like the Brols as new neighbors; sold, bartered, or lent them land for their needs, as was the custom between Ixil neighbors; then watched the Brols bring in surveyors, draw boundaries, and expand inexorably over the landscape. What to ladinos was a legitimate transaction in the capital, the sale and transfer of properly certified titles, was to the Ixils a *robo* (robbery).

Many Cotzaleños felt betrayed, not just by a distant law in the capital, but by their own leaders. The same sense of betrayal can be found in the other Ixil towns, but it seems strongest in Cotzal and is applied

The Finca San Francisco

to an entire generation of *principales* who, as mayors in the 1920s and 1930s, certified that municipal land was unoccupied and could be sold to ladinos.[21] Of these men, a former small finca owner recalls: "They loved writing. There were many who learned how to make public documents, to buy and sell land, just like a notary even though, being Indian, they were not. They made out purchase and sale documents for everything, without the need to go to [Santa Cruz del] Quiché. They didn't know how to do this in Nebaj, but in Cotzal yes. A very knowledgeable type they were."

Such men are referred to as *guisach* (interpreters) and they serve as intermediaries with the ladino legal system. Of a current guisach, one Cotzaleño remarked, "He has a lot to do with the judges. He charges people a lot. He himself says people talk badly of him. He makes up legal documents, including false ones, but manages to fix them with some lawyer, and then they are legal. He always goes with people to Quiché." Guisachs are often the only recourse for a campesino in legal straits, and during the agrarian reform they could be agitators. But inevitably, their performance reflects the available opportunities for redress, which are few, and exploitation, which are many, and they tend to become an extension of the power structure.

In the years leading up to the violence, the leading guisach in Cotzal was Gaspar Pérez Pérez. As the son of a wealthy man, he was able to go to school in the capital, returned to become a labor contractor and, like a number of better-off Ixils in Cotzal, adopted many ladino ways. During the Arbenz land reform, Pérez was a member of the Cotzal agrarian committee, involving him in attempts to expropriate every plantation in the municipio. When the U.S.-backed invasion overthrew Arbenz, he was one of the local leaders taken to jail in the department capital. Two decades later, he was the only mayor who could claim to have recuperated municipal land from the Finca San Francisco, which he parcelled out to Ixil claimants. But true to the paradoxical role of a guisach, by this time his many enemies reviled him as an ally of the Brol family, not their opponent.

The Finca San Francisco became the most divisive issue in Cotzal. Under the 1952 land reform, a *Unión Campesino de Cotzal* and competing groups of *colonos* (resident workers on the finca) made several claims against it. Even after the expropriation decree was overturned four years later,[22] various Ixil politicians became accustomed to warning the Brols of threats to their property, as a way of obtaining financial support and the captive colono vote, and the town hall became dependent on the finca. After 1968, new administrators at San Francisco set off labor trouble: they prohibited *quinceneros* (literally, "fifteen-dayers" who worked for the finca half the month and tended their own crops the other half) from planting coffee on the finca parcels they cultivated for themselves.[23] In 1972 quinceneros refusing to sell their improvements back to the finca were hauled off to jail. Coinciding with the expulsion, a government commission came to investigate abuses and a union was organized, only to be broken when the finca expelled hundreds more workers.

Gaspar Pérez Pérez had, meanwhile, become a political boss. Like a cacique in rural Mexico, he had emerged from local agrarian struggles only to become an agent of wider power structures. Like Sebastián Guzmán in Nebaj, he combined ritual leadership in the town's religious hierarchy with labor contracting and political brokerage. Unlike Guzmán, Pérez was a stalwart of the military wing of Guatemalan politics, the Democratic Institutional party (PID) and a frequent ally, the National Liberation Movement (MLN). His opponents in the Revolutionary party (PR) charged that he never won an election honestly. The fraud emanated from the Finca San Francisco, they claimed, with the laborers voting under pressure from administrators and the dead voting twice.

Because the PR was in power on the national level, its local affiliates were able to win the Cotzal town hall in 1968 and 1970. Early in the PR administration, in June 1969, the town was rocked by the murder of a plantation owner, an unprecedented event in Ixil country. Jorge Brol had been driving the payroll to the Finca San Francisco when he and an assistant were stopped in the road and shot. Robbery was assumed to be the motive, with various signs pointing to members of the PR administration. One of them—a labor contractor named Domingo Sajíc—was later kidnapped from a coastal finca to which he was delivering laborers. He is said to have paid for his involvement in the Brol murder by being placed in the Finca San Francisco's coffee-drying furnace.[24] The source of this latter story is Mario Payeras, who reveals that Sajíc had been among the Cotzaleños who agreed to sell supplies to an earlier group of insurgents—probably the Rebel Armed Forces (FAR), who tried to open a new front to the east in 1968–69.[25] According to Payeras, the assassination of Jorge Brol grew out of this alliance.

It was three years later, in September 1972, that the future EGP made its first contact with Ixils—itinerant traders from Cotzal who came to the Ixcán for the occasion. Their precise motives are not clear from *Days of the Jungle*, but may well have included making money (the guerrillas already had a reputation for paying well);[26] avenging their dead compatriot Domingo Sajíc; and planning their comeback in the Cotzal town hall, which had just been wrested away by Gaspar Pérez in the latest election.[27] One of the EGP's first contacts was Xan Cam, a veteran of the Guatemalan army as well as a PR partisan. Rising quickly in the EGP organization, he was in Guatemala City for clandestine training when, always eager for action, he joined in a holdup to raise money and was killed during the getaway.[28]

Assassinating the "Tiger of the Ixcán"

The Indians comprehended their strength. . . . They confirmed that local power in Guatemala, the hundreds and thousands of little centers of

power dispersed throughout the territory, were not articulated among
themselves nor articulated nationally. There was no authority giving
them cohesion. They were made up of the mayor, the police chief, the land-
lord, the truck owners, previously the priest and the military commis-
sioner. A handful of men. In each zone, powerful but isolated. When the
Indians confronted them openly, a nightmare ended and a reality began. . .
. . Following the destruction of local power wherever it was found came
the confrontations with the [Guatemalan] army.

—EGP spokesman in Mexico, 1980

To create a revolutionary movement, the guerrillas felt they needed
a symbol of oppression against which to rally the hodgepodge of eth-
nicities and factions populating northern Quiché. Since the Ixcán consisted mainly of smallholders, one of the few plantation owners within
reach was Luis Arenas, lord and master of the second largest coffee
finca in northern Quiché. His Finca La Perla was located in a lush,
warm valley between the steamy jungles of the Ixcán and the high, cold
Ixil country. According to Mario Payeras and *Days of the Jungle*, he was
known as the "Tiger of the Ixcán" for his cruel treatment of workers.
Gunned down at the finca on a payday in June 1975, Arenas left this
world to the accompaniment of deep-throated cries from his assembled
workers, according to Payeras, who adds that the Ixil village of Ilom
put on two days of fiesta to celebrate his demise.[29]

The career of Luis Arenas illustrates the intimate relation between
plantations and political patronage. Having made the down payment
for La Perla in 1941,[30] he convinced reform president Juan José Arévalo to build a road into the region. The project fell apart, partly because
of his tyrannical behavior toward the government engineers. He was
accused of participating in a 1949 conspiracy against Arévalo and soon
organized the Party of Anticommunist Unification (PUA). In 1953, the
year before the United States masterminded the overthrow of the
Arbenz administration, Arenas told North American diplomats, "Of all
the exile figures . . . only he was fit to lead a revolt"—if they would give
him $200,000. When the embassy turned him down, he threatened to
fly to Washington to appeal to Vice President Richard Nixon, whom he
referred to as his friend.[31] Sometime after losing the Finca La Perla to
the bank in 1962, Arenas obtained an appointment as head of the state

development agency for the Peten (FYDEP), proceeds from which are said to have bought back La Perla four years before his death.

By assassinating *el Tigre*, the Army of the Poor wanted to broadcast its cause to the campesinos of northern Quiché, and the symbolism of that blow has resonated through the revolutionary interpretation of events ever since. Fifteen years later, unfortunately, the consequences look rather different than was intended, owing to a distinction familiar to anyone who has studied plantation conflicts. Two different kinds of worker were standing in line for their pay when the EGP shot Arenas.[32] *Voluntarios* are temporary workers recruited for the coffee harvest. They come from the same villages whose land was expropriated to create the finca. For Arenas, he was simply taking possession of the land on his deed, but it had been legalized fraudulently before he bought it and, being the man he was, he took possession forcefully. It is easy to believe the guerrilla report that, after the assassination, old Indians "took our hands and looked long into our eyes in gratitude."[33] In 1989 I discovered that inquiring after the fate of *Don Luis* could still bring a smile to Ixil elders whose land he and his predecessor seized. He starts to look like the towering figure of violence and desecration painted by Mario Payeras in *Days of the Jungle*. But contrary to Payeras, he was not called "the Tiger" by local campesinos, at least not until after the EGP started calling him that. The name was coined by a newspaper columnist in the capital: when killed, he was approaching seventy and so crippled by gout that he could barely walk.

The other category of worker at La Perla are *colonos*, a mixed population of ladinos, Ixils, and Q'anjob'al Mayas who, unlike *voluntarios*, are completely dependent on the finca for their living. None of the five eyewitnesses to the assassination I interviewed would admit that they or any other worker cheered the killing of their patrón.[34] Whatever the true feelings of La Perla's dependents, they were not gladdened by the subsequent bankruptcy of their only source of wages. In contrast to Ixils from surrounding villages, colonos are more likely to recall Don Luis with nostalgia, if only because during his time they did not live in the middle of a war zone and their purchasing power was higher. Consequently, instead of joining the revolution, the colonos became a mainstay of the army's counterinsurgency drive. In 1982 civil patrollers from La Perla accompanied soldiers to nearby villages and helped commit the worst massacres of the war in the area. When I visited seven years later, the army so confided in the La Perla civil patrol that it had withdrawn the last of its troops, in contrast to heavy garrisons to the north, south, and east.

Fonseca's Betrayal

To save his life, it is said that he told them who his companions were here in Cotzal, who was collaborating, who was working with him in the guerrilla movement. . . . Because of that list, the army came.
— The capture of Fonseca according to a Cotzaleño in 1987

Once the guerrillas had announced themselves by shooting Luis Arenas, even the rumor of their presence was enough to set off reactions by Guatemala's national security state. Were local political bosses so disposed, they could now accuse rivals of subversion, with confidence that the army would give their list of targets prompt attention. Although many innocents died in this way, more was involved than rumors. In February 1976 the army captured what Mario Payeras describes as the EGP's most precocious organizer in the highlands. The light skin of "Fonseca" suggests descent from a ladino finca owner although he was raised as an Ixil: his revolutionary career ended at the age of eighteen, during a drinking bout in Chajul.[35] On the fourth day of interrogation and torture, according to *Days of the Jungle*, Fonseca began to name the people he had organized. Soon they were being arrested and killed, with their relatives and neighbors falling under suspicion. "Hundreds of innocent villagers," including entire families with children, were taken to the army base at Santa Cruz del Quiché.[36] Their misfortune led to the first denunciation of army kidnappings of Ixils in the national press,[37] but without explaining the reason thanks to the usual conspiracy of silence between insurgents and counterinsurgents.

Fonseca's betrayal was quite a setback for the Guerrilla Army of the Poor. Yet according to the polarizing logic of insurgency, it opened up Cotzal to guerrilla actions like never before. Even though it was the EGP's reliance on an immature youth that had provoked reprisals against hundreds of Cotzaleños, many do not blame Fonseca or the EGP for the epidemic of kidnappings and assassinations. Instead, they blame the MLN/PID's local political boss, Gaspar Pérez Pérez, for giving the army the names of his political enemies. Shortly before or after Fonseca's capture, he invited an army detachment to take up quarters in one of his houses. It was one of his last political decisions. As the unit used the house to arrest, interrogate, and dispatch fellow Cotzaleños, Gaspar Pérez received the blame. "The people got angry because he brought the army," a sympathizer explains. "People did not know what a guerrilla was, but the army was coming to Chichel and grabbing people. It was not understood why."

The leadership of the Revolutionary and Christian Democratic parties suffered particularly. Over the next several years, in reaction to waves of kidnappings, Cotzaleños became the first Ixils to flesh out EGP columns and proselytize the other two municipios. A son of the PR's Domingo Sajíc—killed earlier in reprisal for the murder of a Brol—was tortured by the army before being released. He went on to become a guerrilla leader and, in 1989, was said to command one of the two EGP columns still operating in Ixil country. Two Christian Democratic candidates for mayor, each the victims of electoral fraud according to their supporters, also joined the guerrillas. Fifteen years later one was dead and the other was said to be an EGP leader. Pérez himself was killed at the end of the same year he welcomed the army to Cotzal, in December 1976, while talking to friends in a field. When you ask now about him and his family, the response is a monotonous litany of *lo mataron*—"they killed him." His son and an assistant were killed while driving their bus to the Finca San Francisco. His cousin José Pérez de la Cruz, another ex-MLN/PID mayor, was shot dead in 1980 after seeing his four sons killed one by one. By 1980, the guerrillas were ambushing the army inside town.

The Death Squads Come to Nebaj

There was very little I could do, really nothing. It was difficult to clarify who was who. Many things were said but not verified. There were personal reprisals, political reprisals, of every type, and really it was not known who was who. —Mayor of Nebaj, 1976–80

I watched the Indians in the area. People did not rush to join the guerrillas. They did not take the decision lightly. People gradually began to speak of the CUC, of the EGP, of the other guerrilla groups, but not much. I could feel it, clearly, the people came and went, but they still didn't know what to think. "We don't trust anyone" is all they would say. Until they realized that this movement was for them. Then, suddenly . . .

—"Padre Leonardo," ex-parish priest in Ixil country

The first kidnappings in Nebaj occurred in March 1976, shortly after Fonseca's betrayal fifteen kilometers away. Perhaps the abducted Nebajeños were connected to the guerrilla network in Cotzal, perhaps not. Even if they were not, the excuse for the kidnappings was provided by the EGP's appearance in the region. Local politicians who had disgraced themselves in office and were being defeated in elections could now denounce their opponents to the army. The military party's candidate for mayor in 1974 was Francisco López Villatoro, a ladino who had once helped lead Nebaj's reform movement. After the U.S.-backed counterrevolution in 1954, he and his brother Santiago went to jail briefly for their pro-Arbenz sympathies. Over the years the brothers became involved in labor contracting, moneylending, and adding to the land they owned. Santiago became military commissioner, which put him in charge of local military conscription and made him the army's eyes and ears. When conflicts arose over his other activities, Santiago took advantage of his immunity as military commissioner.

Allegations hang heavy about the 1974 voting which made Francisco mayor: that Ixils were trucked in from outlying villages "dominated by fear and paid twenty-five cents to vote, told that the Christian Democrats were communist and the Revolutionary party too." Nationally, this was the election that the army high command stole from the Christian Democrats and their presidential candidate, a reformist general named Efraín Ríos Montt. Francisco's term is widely remembered as corrupt and intimidating. As the next election approached, in 1976, the López Villatoro brothers chose their closest confederate as the MLN/PID's candidate for mayor. He was Catarino Urizar, the government health inspector, who had a reputation for using his post to extort money.

Like Gaspar Pérez in Cotzal, the Villatoro brothers and Urizar are widely blamed for bringing government kidnappers to town and fingering a list of opponents, ladinos as well as Ixils. In Nebaj, their misrule stirred up sufficient feeling to bring together the traditionalists of the Revolutionary party and the catechists of the Christian Democrats. Their candidate for the 1976 election was a young ladino, the stepchild of a finca owner, who had distinguished himself on a civic committee that built schools with the help of aldea committees, Padre Javier, and the U.S. Agency for International Development. On election day, the ladinos and Ixils of the PR/DC coalition discovered where the ruling party was manufacturing votes. As the López brothers and Urizar celebrated their victory, the challengers were en route to Guatemala City, where the electoral commission decided in their favor.

In office, the new mayor antagonized Santiago López Villatoro and other labor contractors by refusing to jail debtors, an illegal practice to which contractors had become accustomed. As military commissioner, unfortunately, Santiago continued to have close ties with the security forces—including the Mobile Military Police (PMA), the G-2 intelligence branch of the army and the *judiciales* (the detective branch of the National Police). All were taking an increasing interest in the Ixil area. More victims were kidnapped, with ladinos who had masterminded the PR/DC victory the first to suffer. Another target was an Ixil leader in the village of Xoncá who had won a lawsuit against Santiago López over a piece of land. It was as Santiago visited his property at Xoncá, in February 1978, that the EGP killed him and his bodyguard. Francisco López left town and died in the capital. Catarino Urizar was killed by the EGP not far from Xoncá in June 1979, as he inaugurated a health center. A North American living in Nebaj at the time remembers "quiet rejoicing" over his death. Yet both Catarino and Santiago left behind lists of political enemies for the security forces to target.

What can we surmise from the sequence of events? The EGP seems to have found it harder to recruit Nebajeños than Cotzaleños. The guerrillas entered highland villages for the first time in early 1974[38] and were killing army collaborators in Cotzal in another two years. But in Nebaj it took them four years to hit their first target, the military commissioner Santiago López. Only after young political activists went into hiding from the 1976–78 kidnappings can the first Nebajeños be detected in the EGP. With more Ixil-speakers, in 1979 the guerrillas were able to move onto the next stage in their strategy, "armed propaganda," as exemplified by the lightning occupation of Nebaj described at the start of this chapter.

At dozens of subsequent rallies in outlying aldeas, guerrilla columns arrived and called the people together. At one such meeting in Salquil Grande, the guerrillas included women as well as men, and K'iche's from the Finca San Francisco as well as Ixils. According to an evangelical pastor, they "talked about the poverty of the people, said there was no need for a mayor anymore, and declared that they would change the law so that everyone eats the same. Workers were not receiving the value of their work: they were paid Q3.50 for picking a quintal of coffee which the patrón was selling for Q500 and keeping the difference. 'A rich man doesn't work but goes around in a truck, in an airplane,' the guerrillas said. 'The poor work but they don't travel in a car, they have to walk. Forget all your debts and get ready to kill the patróns,' they said. Then they pulled down the jail where debtors were kept."[39]

The guerrillas had already tried to establish clandestine networks of sympathizers, with the occupations of 1979–80 signaling the move from underground cells to organizing entire aldeas. But arriving with several dozen combatants and calling a meeting is not, in itself, a sign of broad support. Many Ixils admit that they were attracted to the guerrilla message, but what observers stressed at the time was the importance of repression, as if government kidnappings had backfired and increased support for the Guerrilla Army of the Poor.[40]

According to the anonymous parish priest quoted previously, the guerrillas consisted largely of "Indian farmers from the area who a few years previously had fled from the Army's repression." He adds that it is only after August 1979 (seven months after the occupation of Nebaj) that the EGP "stops being a group of outsiders to area farmers. It is no longer small or large. It becomes a popular force and a nucleus of peasant organization because of the massacre and the military occupation endured by the people during the past three years." The end of 1979 was also the period when, according to the same observer, "small groups, but each day growing larger, unable to endure the poverty and repression, have begun surfacing in each village. Out of these groups have been born the first manifestations of campesino resistance to the Army. . . . The villages in the area begin their own protests giving the conflictive situation the first indications of a revolutionary process."[41]

Confronting the Army

In these years of struggle, the Indian people recognized their face and recovered their blood. They had lived in resignation. They did not make history. Instead, it was made at their cost. Then they made their decision. . . . The poor villagers of the mountains told their stories and became inflamed.
   —*"Julio" of the Guerrilla Army of the Poor, 1980 interview in Mexico*

For more than 400 years we Indians have been looking for roads of life for our people. We've tried commissions to the president, denunciations, lawyers, political parties, religion, uprisings. Every road we try, the rich and the government cut us off, it always remains the same. Just one door remains open, the road of war. Although we don't like it, there's no other way, that's where we're going to walk.
   —*"Pedro Ixil," from "Sebastián Guzmán: Principal de Principales"*

The success of EGP organizers was obvious in the protests that broke out in each of the Ixil towns between October 1979 and March 1980. In Cotzal, a large crowd of men, women, and children marched from the plaza to the army garrison, demanding that the soldiers return their kidnapped relatives and leave. The following month, after the army attempted a three-day civic action campaign, a crowd of Cotzaleños responded the same way—with loudspeakers, a demonstration in the plaza, and demands that the army leave.[42] But local opinion was divided. According to an evangelical who went on to become a civil patrol leader but is appalled by army killings, the marchers were instigated by the guerrillas. He says they were from the hill aldea of Chisis, carried flags and sharpened sticks, and put women and children in the front.

According to a more sympathetic report, from a parish priest, "women and children begged the soldiers to return their kidnapped relatives or at least their remains. The lieutenant answered that he was not a killer of the people and that Communists had instigated the demonstration. The people answered, `We don't know what a Communist is but we do know the damage the army has caused our community.'" A month later, according to the priest, the guerrillas killed a lieutenant in the plaza. Afterward soldiers shouted "Cotzaleños, guerrilleros, catechists, guerrillas, we will go to the mountains, we will eat guerrilla" and conducted a house-to-house search, dragging prisoners to the garrison where they were interrogated and beaten.[43]

The hardest of the Ixil towns for the EGP to organize seems to have been Chajul. Although Chajuleños stubbornly resisted the loss of the Finca La Perla, they do not face an acute shortage of maize-growing land in the municipio as a whole, nor are they very dependent on working for plantations except around La Perla. If the EGP's calculations had been correct, the killing of Luis Arenas in 1975 should have helped it organize the municipio. And if Catholic Action had been the locus of guerrilla organizing, as army and solidarity accounts agree, then Chajul should have been in the vanguard because it had the largest Catholic Action organization in Ixil country.[44] Yet Chajul was surprisingly quiet for another four years. When the guerrillas won over the Chajuleños, townspeople claim, it was by executing local cattle thieves—that is, by appealing to them as small proprietors rather than as semiproletarians.

Before the violence, some Chajuleños enlarged their stock of cows with the help of a Catholic cooperative and the U.S.-based Heifer Project. Their prosperity overpowered the scruples of certain of their poorer neighbors who are said to have organized a gang. Perhaps because a church cooperative was involved, the owners showed sufficient restraint to organize a committee and send a petition to the national government, but without result. The guerrillas were more than pleased to offer their services. How many cattle rustlers were administered revolutionary justice is unclear: while one estimate went as high as twenty or thirty executions, some of the thieves seem to have escaped to the coast, and I could confirm only two deaths. In October 1979 a mob attacked an accused thief as he was hauling firewood: while being dragged to the cemetery, he was beaten to death, as was another that same day.[45]

Actually, Chajuleños have their own tradition of lynching cattle thieves: during my fieldwork, the mayor told a crowd he could not let them extract a local rustler from the town jail because, if they did, higher authorities would hold him accountable. This raises the question that if Chajul cattle-owners can lynch thieves on their own, why would they ask guerrillas for help? Perhaps they are simply blaming presumed outsiders for homicides that, at least in the two documented cases, were carried out by townspeople.

The parish priest quoted above also associated the two killings with the army-guerrilla conflict, although for different reasons. Two days before the lynching, according to his report, the EGP occupied Chajul and held a meeting in the plaza. The next day, the guerrillas killed three soldiers on the road to Juil, brought their bloodstained weapons into town to show to the people, and advised the latter to organize, as the army was certain to retaliate against them.

On the third day, according to the priest: "An army patrol occupied Chajul and began a systematic search, beating and abusing the people. When the traditional shout of the Chajules began, men, women, youths, children and old people came out of their homes armed with stones, sticks and machetes and the whole town confronted the Army in the central plaza. Between the two groups were the bodies of the three soldiers killed by the guerrillas. An army helicopter began to fly over the group as they talked. The people demanded that the army leave and if they didn't do so, they were prepared to attack them. They said that they would kill more than the army could. One citizen demonstrated he had been beaten by the soldiers. The lieutenant in command asked for a stick and began to beat the responsible soldier leaving him almost dead. The people again demanded that the army leave and began to push the soldiers until they left the town. Indignant over the situation they had endured . . . , they decided to lynch Pedro Pacheco and Melchor Xinic, army collaborators and informers."[46]

Whatever the role of cattle-thieving, events in Chajul suggest how the EGP was setting up the population for reprisals. How intentional this was is a matter of interpretation. Consider a widely reported massacre in the Nebaj plaza. During a Sunday market day in March 1980, the Mobile Military Police suddenly ordered all the men to form long lines outside army headquarters to receive identification cards. On the second day, with rumors flying that men inside were being tortured, hundreds of women marched into town from several outlying aldeas, shouting slogans and demanding the return of their men. When the soldiers fired into the air to disperse the crowd, according to one account, a bullet clipped a power line that sparked, startling the troops who then machine-gunned the demonstrators, killing as many as fifteen.[47] In human rights reports, the incident is another unprovoked massacre.[48] Yet various people in town that day told me they had seen dead or retreating demonstrators who turned out to be men dressed as women. They claim the demonstrators were organized by the guerrillas and regard the massacre as an EGP provocation.

Civilians as Surrogates

The EGP tactic, which later became that of the army, was to create a climate in which neutrality was impossible. —*Joel Simon on the Ixcán*

The Guerrilla Army of the Poor hoped to transcend the errors of *foquismo* by incorporating the local population into its struggle. Yet in at least one critical respect, the EGP's advance in revolutionary theory and practice looked distressingly like the previous stage. That the army's reprisals would be indiscriminate was clear from its performance in eastern Guatemala in 1966–67. To get at no more than five hundred guerrilla combatants, of whom it killed forty to fifty, the army killed two to three thousand civilians.[49] Unfortunately, "prolonged popular war" aggravated the most serious problem with guerrilla *focos* from a humanitarian point of view: the army would blame nearby civilians for guerrilla attacks and treat them accordingly.

This is why Ixils often explain army killings as emotional reactions to guerrilla attacks: "Some groups of the army arrive as friends, yes, others angry because there was an ambush." Not all massacres can be explained in these terms. The waves of kidnappings in 1976–78 were carefully planned operations based on death lists. Nor does heat-of-the-moment explain the army's subsequent policy of burning down the settlement pattern. But Nebajeños do recall many examples when the army lashed out at them immediately after guerrillas killed soldiers. "What did you expect?" an army officer asks a widow whose husband and son have just been executed by soldiers. "They killed my boys. My boys had reason to be mad. Many of them died today, and you people killed them."[50] *Castigo* (punishment) is how Nebajeños describe this kind of retribution, which was based on the EGP's claim that it represented the people and the army's assumption that it did.

Evangelical missionaries were convinced that the guerrillas were counting on "provoked repression" to bring Indians into their movement.[51] James Morrissey, the Catholic priest-anthropologist studying the Maryknoll colonization projects in the Ixcán, calls such calculations "the cornerstone of their revolutionary methodology."[52] Calculated provocation certainly has been part of other insurrectionary projects, including the Reagan administration's Contra War in Sandinista Nicaragua,[53] but such reasoning is not explicit in the few EGP documents available to me. Payeras even writes of planning "a limited military operation, limited so that the enemy's reaction would not exceed either what the people were prepared to understand or what we were capable of withstanding and defending at the local level. The wind we set in motion should not be so strong as to strip the blossoms from the tree."[54]

What the EGP expected the local population to withstand was clearly a lot, unfortunately. James Morrissey illustrates the problem with an incident not reported in *Days of the Jungle*. Shortly before the assassination of Luis Arenas, the EGP organized cooperative members near the Xalbal River, then encouraged them to focus their resentment on a local ladino landowner and murder him. After the guerrillas vanished into the jungle, the army was able to identify the local men who were responsible, round up more than thirty, and take them to the military base at Santa Cruz del Quiché for the usual rituals of elimination.[55] According to the stories that reached Morrissey, the EGP had imposed itself on the small Indian settlement by force. But even if the Xalbal settlers were willing collaborators, Morrissey's point is worth quoting.

"An army needed recruits, so the guerrillas adopted a strategy for getting them by making people de facto participants in guerrilla activities. This would automatically place them in opposition to the military, which in turn would place them on the side of the guerrillas. [The guerrillas] tested this strategy at Xalbal by coercing the Maya to act as their surrogates for an assassination. They succeeded in making their operational surrogates, surrogates in suffering military reprisals as well, while they escaped unscathed. They did not succeed in getting the

Maya to think of themselves as their allies, much less their colleagues. Nevertheless, it was inevitable that as increasing numbers of Maya came to share the lot of the guerrillas, as targets for military reprisals, an increasing percentage of them would decide to join their ranks."

The Guatemalan army went on to adopt a compatible strategy of turning civilians into surrogates, Morrissey continues. "The massive retaliation which followed guerrilla activities was deliberately aimed, not at the guerrillas, but at civilian populations anywhere near where the guerrillas had operated. . . . The intent was clearly not only to make people reluctant to have anything to do with the guerrillas, but to make the consequences of the guerrillas' operations so repugnant that the guerrillas themselves would refrain from action rather than risk having people suffer such barbarism. The guerrillas . . . and the military . . . had each developed a strategy for warfare which was considerably safer and probably just as effective as engaging each other directly in armed conflict."[56]

Solidarity Explanations for the Violence

In 1975, the national army arrives in Nebaj, then troops sent by the Somoza dictatorship of Nicaragua, on the pretext of maintaining order. But the truth is that this region has access to the Northern Transversal Strip, an area rich in minerals.
—Opening line of the Declaración de Iximché, Committee for Campesino Unity, February 14, 1980

It was like an avalanche. Entire villages, whole communities, from one day to the next we realized that they had joined the organization. They would say, "This is the only answer to our problems."
—"Padre Leonardo," ex-parish priest in Ixil country

Now that we have looked at the chronology of how political violence emerged in Ixil country, let us review solidarity explanations for what set it off. Since there is wide agreement that Mayas flocked to the revolutionary movement only after indiscriminate army repression, the question becomes, what motivated the army to behave as it did? Three complementary explanations appeared in revolutionary publications, human rights reports and scholarly interpretations. First, army officers were seizing Indian land in the Northern Transversal Strip or "zone of the generals." Second, army officers and their finca-owning allies wished to free up Mayan labor for their estates. Third, the same elite was reacting against any form of indigenous organizing and consciousness-raising, again to protect their supply of cheap labor. In each case, the Guatemalan security forces fire the first shot, so to speak, and the guerrillas assume the role of a defensive reaction.

Jeffrey Paige provided a useful summary of the solidarity view. "The generals' . . . slaughter of entire Indian villages at Chajul, Cotzal, Nebaj . . . and Panzós in this region combines a grim economic as well as political logic. Eliminating the population will eliminate the guerrillas and also free the land for development. The parasitic relationship between the hacienda and the Indian village is being destroyed by military agribusinessmen whose viciousness apparently knows no limits. If they survive the generals' onslaught, the peasants' last connection to the land will be severed and they will be completely dependent on agro-export wage labor."[57]

Like a number of writers in the early 1980s (including myself), Paige took at face value EGP claims that army officers were systematically driving Indians off their land. It is true that high-ranking officers, including President Romeo Lucas García, carved out estates farther to the east in the Northern Transversal Strip, in the Department of Petén. In that same area, and probably others too, ruined smallholders were a source of recruits for the guerrillas, although ecological failure and market forces may have been more responsible for driving them off their land than rival claimants.[58] Finally, it is true that Indians often lose disputes over land titles, and the guerrillas tried to convince the Ixcán settlers that they were about to lose theirs.

Yet estate owners were not expanding in the staging areas of the EGP, that is, the Ixcán and Ixil country, before the violence. In the Ixcán, most conflict over land was between successive waves of smallholders sponsored by the government and competing factions of the Catholic Church.[59] In the highlands, most of the land still in Mayan hands is of little interest to plantation owners: it is too steep, eroded, high and cold for export agriculture. For Ixil country, the explanation breaks down completely. Aside from not being located in the Northern Transversal Strip, military officers were unlikely to lust after it. Except for the two large fincas already in ladino hands, land around the Ixil towns was worth sufficiently little that one of the government's first counterinsurgency moves was to investigate the possibility of redistributing it.[60] The extensive holdings of one absentee owner—the Herrera Ibargüen family—actually were handed out in the midst of the repression, which therefore was not motivated by the desire to create new estates.

But what about the argument that the army was trying to shake loose more Mayan labor for the plantations, what Carol Smith calls "economic reorganization" of a regional Mayan economy becoming too self-sufficient for the needs of agribusiness? In studies of the regional economic system, Smith found that highland communities became less dependent on seasonal migration to the plantations in the 1970s. Instead, thanks to innovations like chemical fertilizers and the organization of cooperatives, they were able to invest more of their labor in personal enterprises such as petty commerce, coffee, and other cash crops, as well as more productive maize farming—hence the army's interest in smashing Mayan self-improvement schemes. But if this were the motive for repression, the army would logically attack the most developed parts of the highlands, around Totonicapán, where Mayan entrepreneurs have had the greatest success in ending dependence on the plantations. Instead, as Smith notes, this was the part of the highlands least touched by repression.[61]

The third solidarity explanation for the violence is that the army wanted to destroy the new grassroots organizations through which Indians were addressing their problems. It is true that army officers often acquire land in the course of their careers, hence share the interest of finca owners in suppressing labor organizers. Ladino store owners were not favorably disposed toward new cooperatives undercutting their prices, nor did labor contractors appreciate catechists who preached against taking wage advances.

Illustrating such tensions is the case of La Estancia in southern Quiché. As an aldea of Santa Cruz del Quiché, the department capital, its inhabitants were more involved in agricultural innovation and commerce than were most Ixils, hence becoming less dependent on plantation labor. That put them on a collision course with local commercial interests. Because of its location, moreover, La Estancia was also much closer to church-state conflict than was Ixil country. Catholic Action was especially strong, as was the cooperative movement and the Christian Democratic party. As a result, the aldea became implicated in a lengthy conflict between the Spanish priests of the Quiché diocese and the ladino dons of Santa Cruz.

After the army stole the 1974 election, the Catholic Action chapter of La Estancia helped organize the Committee for Campesino Unity. Also participating in this pivotal event were students from Santa Cruz and an independent pastoral team of Jesuit priests. The latter groups understood their work in terms of "consciousness-raising" and were evidently establishing ties with the Guerrilla Army of the Poor (see chapter 6). By early 1980, army assassins were targeting La Estancia and some of its youth were going north to join the EGP. Larger massacres followed, and the aldea was soon abandoned.[62]

La Estancia's accessibility made it a well-known case of how repression against grassroots organizing created support for the guerrillas. But it was hardly a typical aldea. Many La Estancia activists may not have been aware of their associates' ties with the guerrillas, but suspicions were rife, hence references to "spies." Also suspecting EGP connections was the army, prompting the holocaust of alleged cadres in 1980. Once we bring the realities of clandestine organizing back into the picture, La Estancia does not illustrate how the army set off the violence by suppressing peaceful cooperative and educational programs. Instead, it shows how the sub rosa battle strategies of the Guatemalan Left and Right reached out to penetrate and destroy an Indian community.

Significantly, repression did not focus on areas where indigenous organizations were strong but the guerrillas had little presence, such as around Totonicapán and Quezaltenango.[63] Instead, it concentrated on where the guerrillas were trying to organize. The four areas of greatest government violence—northern Quiché and northern Huehuetenango, southern Quiché and Chimaltenango[64]—follow the EGP's swathe as it moved south to cut the Pan-American Highway.

True, the army targeted Catholic catechists, Christian Democratic activists, and cooperative leaders. It is also true that repression was often guided by local elites. But this was not just a knee-jerk reaction to self-improvement projects and reformist politics, as the solidarity explanation would have it, for two reasons. First, the local bosses giving death lists to the army were reacting to the arrival of actual guerrillas. Second, the radical wing of the Catholic Church joined the insurgents in the late 1970s and played an important role in widening their base.[65] Jesuit priests working in popular education and organization were involved, as was part of the Catholic Action movement and perhaps a few members of the Sacred Heart order. Their most well-known achievement was the Committee for Campesino Unity, but Catholic radicals also became involved in the "mass work" of the EGP and its incorporation of CUC activists.[66]

The locus for the alliance was not in Ixil country but to the south around Santa Cruz del Quiché. The key constituency was apparently not seasonal plantation workers or farmers fighting for their land, but Mayan students, catechists, and promoters who tended to be from better-off families. At least a few Ixils were involved in radical Catholic networks, but they seem to have been students whose careers were taking them away from Ixil country.[67]

Doubtless there is a history of organizing in Ixil country that has yet to be told, but it is not the same history as that of the mass of Ixil townspeople and villagers, as their reactions to the violence will suggest. Because a clandestine movement was trying to take advantage of Catholic popular organizations, the people being orchestrated would have had little idea that some of their catechists and promoters were part of a revolutionary network. What several authors have referred to as "Christian base communities" around Nebaj apparently were not called that by catechists themselves, who do not recognize the term.[68] Significantly, CUC did not establish a presence in Ixil country, even though its campaign to raise plantation wages should have appealed to the tens of thousands of Ixils who descended to the coast every year. Even the government kidnappings of real or imagined EGP cadre in 1976–78 did not visibly stir large numbers of Ixils.[69] Only after EGP military units appeared, ambushed soldiers, and provoked wider reprisals against the population did thousands of Ixils join the revolutionary movement, to protect themselves from the army.

Stripping the Blossoms from the Tree

The guerrillas said that they were stronger than the army. They said they were going to bring weapons for the people. Cuba and Nicaragua would

help us. In Vietnam the people had triumphed, and in El Salvador they
were about to. — *Refugee leader at La Pista, November 1982*

Why, then, did it become popular to argue that the violence was triggered by the army's wish to grab Indian land, enlarge the reserve army
of labor, and smash reformist efforts by Indians to improve their situation? Obviously, even if these do not explain what set off the violence,
they represent an attempt to get at the structural context of land
monopolization, labor exploitation, and repression needed for any
analysis of political violence in Guatemala. Moreover, in areas like the
south coast where plantation owners were quick to use violence to control their laborers, death squads may not have been a response to guerrilla organizing as they were in northern Quiché. Just because solidarity explanations break down in one key area does not mean they are
without validity elsewhere.

Still, solidarity explanations have played an apologetic function for
the revolutionary movement, by mystifying what happened in at least
two ways. First, they have minimized the gap between revolutionary
politics on the national level and the politics of the western highlands,
that is, between the ladino-dominated Left and Mayan Indians. Second, solidarity explanations have minimized the responsibility of the
guerrilla movement for triggering the escalation of military violence in
the late 1970s.

There is a clear lineage of revolutionary politics in Guatemala, but
Mayan Indians usually have played only lesser roles in it.[70] It is not that
they lack a tradition of armed rebellion: Mayas rose up against Liberal
reforms on various occasions in the early 1800s. But they did not
respond in the same way to land expropriations following the Liberal
Revolution (1871), if only because the balance of forces had turned
against them. Notwithstanding the hopes and fears of outsiders,[71] the
traditional Indian *tumulto* (riot) has been in abeyance for more than a
century.[72] The revolutions of 1920 and 1944 were ladino affairs, and
Mayan peasants failed to rise in defense of the Arbenz land reform in
the critical month of June 1954.[73] Generally speaking, as Carol Smith
points out, Mayan resistance has not taken the supralocal, coordinated
form in which the Left understands revolutionary politics.[74] When

Mayan intellectuals became politicized in the 1970s, many did so along indigenista rather than Marxist lines.[75] They defined the oppression of their people primarily in ethnic rather than class terms, questioned ladino control of the Left, and were reluctant to collaborate with revolutionary groups.

Mayan disinterest in insurrectionary politics is what has made consciousness-raising such an important part of the solidarity explanation for the violence in the western highlands. The very existence of such a model suggests distance between peasants and whoever thinks their consciousness needs to be raised. As interpreted by revolutionary sympathizers, *concientización* connects the reformism typical of Indian campesinos with the Left's far more ambitious hopes for revolutionary transformation. Consciousness-raising offers to recruit cautious local communities with ameliorative objectives into a scheme for global transformation. Last but not least, it connects the pastoral efforts of church organizations with the insurrectionary plans of guerrilla organizations—a connection that probably was tenuous in many areas but that both the army and the guerrillas wished to make, with lethal consequences for Catholic parishioners.

If we take the consciousness-raising thesis at face value, Catholic catechists in Ixil country would have supported the guerrilla movement at a fairly early date, say, after the first kidnappings in 1976. But there is little sign that they did. Instead, the army seems to have attacked catechists for more extraneous reasons, such as their participation in local Christian Democratic politics (as transmitted to army headquarters via local MLN/PID politicians), the national role of the Catholic Church in challenging army abuses, and perhaps the political ties of a few Ixil students returning home to organize their communities. In any case, surviving catechists, Christian Democrat founders, and cooperative leaders vehemently deny that their dead associates had any special relation with the guerrillas.

What solidarity explanations also represent is the claim to innocence so common in debates of this kind—an attempt to shift the burden of responsibility for triggering military violence off the shoulders of the guerrillas and onto the army. First comes an army strategy of seizing land, forcing Indians into greater dependence on the plantations, and smashing reformist self-help schemes. Only then do victimized peasants rise up in rebellion, and the Army of the Poor makes its appearance. What the solidarity explanation systematically elides is the provocative role of the guerrillas. Regardless of the structural factors at work encouraging political violence, the chronology of events show that army repression began in reaction to guerrilla actions. The point may seem so obvious that it does not need to be stated, but the revolutionary movement has systematically avoided acknowledging it, to obscure its own responsibility for triggering the violence.[76] Giving proper emphasis to this fact will also make it easier to understand why support for the guerrilla movement evaporated so quickly.

FOUR

The Civil Patrols, Ríos Montt, and the Defeat of the EGP

Presumed guerilla shot by civil patrol, 1989

W e have taken more than eleven municipal seats. . . . More than 250 villages are ours.　　　　　—*EGP spokesman in Mexico, 1980*

We're in between.　　—*Nebaj civil patroller to author, November 1982*

IT was getting dark when I came into Cotzal for the first time, a few nights before Christmas 1982. Not a single house was inhabited along the hour's drive from Nebaj, and most were in ruins. An evangelical pastor pointed out where villages had stood. In a ramshackle office, a government cooperative organizer told me that, of the twenty-nine aldeas on his list, only three still existed. A lieutenant walked in and, with his eyes darting everywhere but toward me, railed against North Americans who printed lies about the army. At the imposing old town hall, up on a covered porch above jail cells, a long row of civil patrollers sat under a few dim light bulbs, staring grimly into the darkness and gripping bolt-action rifles with their butts on the floor. Inside, in a room with a high ceiling, the mayor interrupted a meeting to receive me. What the town needed most, he said, were more guns. He described how civil patrollers had died in this and that confrontation, then counted the armament at hand: twenty-four M-1s, twenty shotguns, and three .22 rifles. "With a hundred arms we'll finish them off," he vowed.

Up the street, in a room lit by candlelight, I found the man I was looking for, the evangelical pastor credited with organizing the Cotzal civil patrol. Nicolás Toma never smiled during a long conversation, and it was obvious that he had been deeply wounded by his experiences. He was a handsome man with deep-set, steady eyes, like many Cotzaleños, and spoke such educated Spanish that I assumed he was a seminary graduate. It turned out that he had only finished primary school and supported himself by farming. But what most surprised me were his reasons for helping to organize the civil patrol. He never justified supporting the army in religious or ideological terms. Instead, he spoke about survival, telling me how the army had killed his brother and brother-in-law, and how "thousands" of other Cotzaleños had died. If he had not helped the soldiers, Pastor Nicolás told me, they would have killed him too. "The guerrillas only provoke the army and then they go," he said bitterly. "We are the ones who suffer the consequences."[1]

Looking back on this period, the people of the three Ixil towns refer to it euphemistically as *la bulla*. "The uproar," literally, was the peak of violence in the time of dislocation extending to the present which they refer to more generally as *la situación*. Since the same army that smashed through Ixil country in the early 1980s continues to rule the country, many bystanders assume that Guatemalans live in an unbroken state of terror—cowering in their homes at night and wondering if they will live to see the morning. But many Ixils under army control say that kind of fear is past. Asked what changed the situation, they invoke the name of Efraín Ríos Montt, the born-again general who seized power in 1982.

No matter that Ríos Montt's impact on the army's behavior was questionable. Or that the changes he achieved could impress Guatemalans only because of the stark terrorism of the preceding regime. Or that his projection of personal rectitude only made them feel safer because of a new, more effective form of coercion revolving around the civil patrols. However limited Ríos Montt's reforms, their meaning is clear to people around the three towns. "Lies, lies!" an Ixil promoter shouted when I insisted that his beloved general had covered up massacres. "If it wasn't for Ríos Montt, we all would have disappeared! Before there were killers waiting on the corner, you couldn't even go out because they would kill you. But Ríos Montt took away all that!" Another of my friends, a Catholic, associated the general with the "*Ley de Amistad*" (Law of Friendship), actually the "*Ley de Amnistía*" (Amnesty Law) that Ríos offered refugees.

The general was deposed by fellow officers after only seventeen months in office. But when he made a comeback in 1990, by running for president, he was the most popular candidate in Ixil country. At campaign headquarters in Nebaj, I was surprised to find that the first three activists to show up were, despite the general's well-known feelings about alcohol, amiably drunk. It was Sunday afternoon and they were

Catholics of the old school. Never mind that their candidate was a Protestant general, or that he was accused of persecuting the Catholic Church, or that the Guatemalan army had destroyed every rural settlement in their municipio. No, they found something to admire in Ríos Montt that still eludes his critics. Even after he was barred from the election on constitutional grounds, supporters came close to winning all three town halls in Ixil country.

This chapter explores the shift in loyalties that occurred around the three Ixil towns in 1982. The subject of "support" or "loyalty" is a slippery one given all the elements of coercion and concealment in a guerrilla conflict. Hence, some readers will draw conclusions that differ from mine. Still, I will venture that Ixil support for the EGP was not primarily a function of preexisting grievances, of consciousness-raising or ideological mobilization, although these played a role. Instead, I will argue that Ixil support for the EGP was primarily the result of "dual violence," that is, the coercion produced by an armed confrontation that forces civilians to align themselves with one side or the other to save their lives.

Actually, many observers have suspected that Mayan support for the guerrillas was, first and foremost, a reaction to the chaotic violence of the security forces in the late 1970s and early 1980s. My innovation (if any) is twofold. First, I stress the role of the guerrillas in provoking repression, in order to dispel the aura of an indigenous revolutionary movement. Second, I stress how Ixils were under pressure from both sides, not just the army. These points should also help explain why Ixil support for the EGP proved to be relatively fleeting. Unlike campesinos pressed to the wall by land monopolists—such as the peasants of Morelos who followed Emiliano Zapata in the Mexican Revolution—many Ixils soon decided that it was the adventurism of the insurgents that had placed them in such jeopardy. The offense might have been forgiven if the guerrillas had led them to victory, or at least been able to defend them. Unfortunately, the EGP never gained the upper hand militarily, making it vulnerable to a new counterinsurgency strategy. As the army imposed a new form of social control in the civil patrols, then offered amnesty to guerrilla collaborators, a growing number of Ixils cast their lot with a superior force that offered to return them to a semblance of their prewar existence.

Benedicto's Visit

> *I'm fighting because I saw old man Catarino's body strung from a tree alongside the road, castrated. Thank God he was dead. I'm fighting because Mec's brothers and mother were forced to disappear like many of my relatives have disappeared due to the soldiers. And I'm fighting because I have no other choice. If I stayed at home, the soldiers would come and kill me anyway. At least this way I have a chance not to die in vain.*
> *—EGP fighter, c. 1980; from the unpublished memoir of a*
> *North American who lived in Nebaj during this period*

Guatemalans attribute a unique level of violence and insecurity to the administration of General Romeo Lucas García (1978–82). Death squads have terrorized dissidents before and since, villagers have been massacred, elections have been stolen along with the national treasury, but no other regime has earned quite the same reputation for mayhem and misrule. No one felt safe from government killers, not even the wealthiest families in the capital. The Lucas García regime was of the kind that alienates the widest range of society, including the upper class, and is most vulnerable to overthrow by a revolutionary movement.[2]

As a reputed bastion of the Guerrilla Army of the Poor, the Ixil municipios suffered more heavily than most parts of the country. At first, the security forces targeted individuals rather than the entire population: they attacked presumed members of the EGP's underground network, men (and less often, women) who had been betrayed by an EGP organizer like Fonseca in Cotzal, or who had been denounced by personal enemies, or whose name had been ejaculated in the torture sessions before a captive dies. Following the EGP's first public meeting in January 1979, uniformed units occupied Nebaj and began committing random homicides. Their drunken abuses were punctuated by visits from better-disciplined units who emphasized smiles and friendship in U.S.-style civic action campaigns.[3]

Combining force and persuasion, utmost brutality with candy for children, is not new in warfare for hearts and minds, but it is not just a calculated strategy. Army killing could also be an emotional reaction to guerrilla attacks, of the kind to be expected when irregular fighters melt into a civilian population. In more technical terms, Timothy Wick-ham-Crowley describes insurgent strategy as one of conflating combatants, noncombatants, and logistics,[4] which practically guarantees that governments will use terror to crack the three apart. In Ixil country, village massacres began in 1980, following EGP ambushes that killed soldiers. The army presumed that nearby civilians knew about the impending attack and failed to warn it; Nebajeños argue that, since the guerrillas warned members of their network to leave the area before an ambush, the bystanders whom the army killed were the innocents. One of the worst such incidents occurred at Xecax just outside Nebaj, around February 1981, when guerrillas blew up a military truck and soldiers burned some forty-five people to death in their houses.

By early 1982 the army was massacring villagers without the provocation of an ambush, simply because an informer accused them of helping the guerrillas. By this time the EGP did enjoy widespread support, if only in reaction to the army's behavior, and the only safe assumption for soldiers was that they were surrounded by enemies. "They had a guerrilla-phobia of all the Ixils," a ladino observes. "All the Ixils of Nebaj, Cotzal, and Chajul they considered guerrillas. They were afraid of their own shadow."

It was said that the army did not control anything beyond its own barracks. According to Nebajeños, the troops became so trigger-happy that, at any sign they were approaching, the only safe response was to clear out as fast as possible. The result of indiscriminate reprisals was to create the appearance of total support for the EGP, among ladinos as well as Ixils. So great was the revulsion against the army that, even now, Nebajeños debate only whether sympathy for the guerrillas was widespread or universal.

Numerous ladinos sought haven elsewhere. None dared run for office in the 1980 municipal election, nor did any right-wing party, leaving the field to the Ixils of the Christian Democratic and Revolutionary Parties. The winner was the first Ixil elected by the Christian Democrats, but one of his duties became retrieving the bodies of his party's leaders. The town's treasurer—one of the last surviving ladino reformers who had saved the 1976 election from being stolen—was gunned down by government killers in front of the town hall. The vice mayor went out to the countryside on a visit and returned only three years later, after being captured by the army. Another member of the town council was with the guerrillas for the better part of a year, while a third was killed by the guerrillas. After an attempt to firebomb the municipal building, two other Ixil office-holders fled to the mountains where one became a well-known EGP leader. Many of the auxiliary mayors—the mayor's appointed representatives in the villages—stopped reporting to him because the guerrillas had appropriated their staffs of office.

In the streets of Nebaj there were EGP slogans painted on walls and nocturnal exchanges of gunfire. Above the road hung a banner celebrating the second anniversary of the Sandinista Revolution that the army did not bother to remove. In July 1981, Nebajeños told visiting journalists that between eight hundred and a thousand Indians had been killed in the three towns.[5] Many of the deaths came out of personal quarrels, when small-town enemies denounced each other as subversives or army informers. One woman is said to have charged vengeance-seekers money to take denunciations of their enemies to the army—until the army realized what she was doing and took her away too. Even the town fools who made their living by begging were shot, for wandering around after curfew and startling sentries. There were so many dead that the town ran out of planks to make coffins. Out in the aldeas, the dead were wrapped in whatever was available and buried together in mass graves.

By December 1981, the guerrillas were so confident of their support that they assassinated Sebastián Guzmán, the head of the traditional religious hierarchy, in the middle of a saint procession. Early the next morning, they launched the heaviest attack of the war on the soldiers quartered around the Catholic church. The sound of machine-gun fire and grenades reverberated through the streets. After the fighting tapered off, two helicopters touched down. One was carrying Army Chief of Staff Benedicto Lucas García. Invariably referred to by his first name, to distinguish him from his older brother the president, Benedicto had the townspeople rounded up for an important message. It was more or less the same speech he delivered in a number of plazas during this period, but the people of Nebaj remember it well.

He wished them a merry Christmas and said that, if they did not refrain from further acts of subversion, he would burn their town to ashes. "Why are you supporting the subversives?" he demanded. "Who are they?" No one answered. "If this town doesn't clean up its act (*componerse*) in a month," he continued, "I'm going to put myself at the head of five thousand men, start at Chimaltenango, and finish off (*acabar con*) the entire population if I have to!" Nebajeños are a polite people and will applaud almost any speech, but they did not applaud this one. When Benedicto's helicopter lifted off, the guerrillas opened fire on it from a few hundred yards away.[6] As it turned out, Benedicto did send thousands of troops and they did burn all the outlying villages. But Benedicto had a better idea than burning Nebaj itself to the ground. Instead, he started the civil patrols.

The Civil Patrol in Cotzal

> To the army's surprise, there were few direct military confrontations, because the guerrilla units in [southern Quiché and the Ixil region] were in fact CUC bases and Indian supporters who had only very recently taken up arms. So the civilian, largely Indian population became the main target. —Luisa Frank and Philip Wheaton, *Indian Guatemala: Path to Liberation*, 1984

The civil patrols are usually associated with the name of Efraín Ríos Montt, who in 1982 expanded the system throughout the western highlands. But they originated in the last months of the Lucas García administration, under the command of the president's brother, Benedicto.[7] Organizing civilians to fight insurgents is not a new idea, but the scale of the Guatemalan effort was unusual. Eventually the army claimed to have more than a million men in the patrols, which would mean virtually every male in the western highlands between puberty and old age.[8] The coercion involved was also unusually naked. Investigators became accustomed to wide discrepancies between the army's claims about the system and what civil patrollers had to say. While officers always described the patrols as voluntary, patrollers just as reliably said they were forced to serve on pain of death.

Some of the first *patrullas de autodefensa civil* were organized in Ixil country between December 1981 and January 1982. Army planners were recommending them many months earlier, in terms suggesting the idea was a familiar point of debate. One reason for delay was the fear that, as soon as patrollers were outfitted with rifles, they would join the guerrillas.[9] Perhaps this is why one of the earliest patrols was at the Finca La Perla, where the permanent workers, fed up with the hardships created by the EGP's assassination of their patrón, seem to have been an island of loyalty or at least control. Another early patrol was in Nebaj where the army could draw on a substantial ladino population. But there was an obvious way to prevent patrollers from giving their rifles to the guerrillas: it was to avoid arming the patrols until enough blood had been spilled—patrollers killing guerrillas and vice versa—to confirm that they were on the army's side.

In Cotzal, the army had alienated the civilian population even more thoroughly than in Nebaj. Tit-for-tat kidnappings and assassinations started earlier, and soldiers were regularly ambushed in the center of town. What happened after the EGP's July 28, 1980, attack is particularly engraved in the memory of Cotzaleños. Soldiers occupied the neighborhood from which the guerrillas had fired, dragged all the men they could find to the barracks, and butchered them in the field behind. Sixty-four men died. A second group of about sixty men was herded together and nearly suffered the same fate. "You're all guerrillas," a colonel screamed, striking anyone who dared speak and shoving a youth up against a wall to shoot him point-blank. This second group, after listening to a discussion of how they too would be killed, was reprieved by another officer who arrived and said, "We are going to pardon you this time, but if it happens again you're all dead." Taking him at his word, many Cotzaleños left their homes, some going to the coast and others to mountain aldeas, leaving the town semiabandoned.

The next time the EGP attacked the Cotzal army post, on the tenth anniversary of its arrival in the Ixcán, the army responded differently, even though the January 19, 1982, raid killed several officers. A new commander arrived and identified himself as Captain Alfredo. To the town hall he summoned the remaining religious leaders, one of whom has provided the following account of his words:

"Now I want to ask you a question. Why have you let yourselves be deceived? You are not little kids. You are grown men. You are leaders. Why have you gotten involved with the guerrillas? Why did you take the bad advice of the guerrillas, that today we don't have money but tomorrow we are going to be rich, that we're going to have the wealth of the plantation owners?"

None of the religious leaders dared answer him. They all kept their mouths shut.

"Son of a bitch, don't be stupid, don't be idiots!" Captain Alfredo shouted. "Whether or not you're going to answer me, I came here to find out how much you care about your town and family, because they're going to die, they're going to be finished off on account of your stupidity.

"Because look, these officers who died four days ago, and all the soldiers who have died, what do they have to do with you? Son of a bitch, put your hand on your heart, what does the Bible say? The Bible says love thy neighbor as thyself. You're leaders of the church, how could you think to kill your neighbors? Damn it, answer me! I'm a man, I'm a person like you, I don't have horns, I don't have a tail that you have to be afraid of me. What I want to know is what you think."

First one, then another evangelical pastor spoke up, and Captain Alfredo began to calm down. "Now we're going to talk like men," he said. . . . .

"Is it death you want, or do you want to remain alive?"

Everyone said, "Look captain, please, why not let us stay alive? We don't want to die."

"Well now," Captain Alfredo laughed, "if you don't want to die, correct your people. Correct your members. How many evangelicals here will correct their members? How many Catholics here will correct their members? How many *costumbristas* here will correct their members? What you have to do is call out to God. Pray! Ask God for mercy and peace!" But Captain Alfredo warned that he wasn't promising anything. "I'm not going to tell you that you're in the clear, no way. Only if you have faith in God. That's all. Just remember two things. Maybe death, maybe life."

A few days later there was a loyalty ceremony in the plaza. "Do you agree to pledge allegiance to the flag, to stamp out the guerrillas here in Cotzal?" Captain Alfredo demanded. "Do you promise to follow Guatemala?"

"Why not?" the people answered. "Why not?"

"Are you sure?"

"Yes!" the people said. "Yes!"

"Well good. I certainly hope so, because this is where the guerrillas started. And this is where peace is going to start too. . . . But it's easy to pledge allegiance to the flag. . . . Anyone can do it. Even the king of the guerrillas because the tongue can do anything. I'm going to see if you're really sorry, by what you do!

"Everyone who did not present themselves today, those who really are guerrillas, bring them to me here. Tied up. But don't bring me innocent people. Don't bring me honorable people. And don't bring me people with whom you have some problem, over a piece of land, over a cow, over a woman, over money, none of that. But if he really is a guerrilla, if you have seen him with a weapon, if you have seen him with the guerrillas, if he did not present himself today, bring him to me here. This is the work that you are going to do. If you bring them to me, it will be a sign that Cotzal is supporting Guatemala and also supporting its army.

"Do you promise to bring me the guerrillas?"

"Yes!" said the people.

"And do you want to pledge allegiance to Guatemala?"

"Yes!" said the people. "We want to pledge allegiance to the flag! Down with the guerrillas! Guerrillas sons of bitches! We don't want anything to do with you! We want peace, we want our Guatemala!"[10]

This was the start of the civil patrol in Cotzal. Captain Alfredo had summoned Catholics as well as Protestants, but what he wanted from them was evangelical in tone: a confession of personal responsibility for subversion ("put your hand on your heart") followed by conversion to the army's side ("correct your members"). EGP assassinations of the town's right-wing leaders, and the army's own atrocities, had virtually destroyed the army's ability to communicate with the population. This forced Captain Alfredo to push down through a shattered political structure to a more basic form of social organization, the congregation. It is becoming fashionable to extol congregations for promoting self-help and cohesion at the local level, but in Cotzal what they had were leaders who could be intimidated into collaborating.

This still-extant social denominator in the Ixil towns did not necessarily bear Protestant colors, as we shall see in Chajul. But in Cotzal it was represented above all by the Full Gospel Church of God, the largest evangelical group in the municipio. The pastor happened to be a half-brother of Gaspar Pérez Pérez, the MLN/PID power broker who invited the army to Cotzal and was killed by the EGP. But the two brothers had become estranged over inheritances, and the pastor was not a political activist. Before leaving town, he appointed the church's deacon to replace him. Nicolás Toma had run for mayor in 1980, for the PID party, but lost to the Christian Democrats. Following the EGP's January 1982 attack on the barracks, he and a few members of his church took the desperate step of helping the army track the retreating insurgents. He placated Captain Alfredo and persuaded other members of his congregation that they could survive by helping the army.

Watching approvingly from a distance, evangelical missionaries from the Summer Institute of Linguistics and Ríos Montt's Church of the Word regarded Nicolás Toma as the spiritual leader of the civil patrols. His congregation provided the first head of the civil patrol, an ex-army sergeant who also became the town's representative to the Ríos Montt administration in the capital. When the army needed a new mayor for Cotzal, it went to Pastor Nicolás who recommended another prominent man in his congregation, an ally of Gaspar Pérez Pérez who had survived various assassination attempts himself. Soon Pastor Nicolás also became head of the Church of the Word's relief operation in Cotzal, vice mayor in the town hall and even chief of the civil patrol. He was functioning in all these capacities when, on March 12, 1983, he was ambushed and killed while riding to an outlying congregation.

The Civil Patrol in Chajul

They called together the people and told them there would be a class. When the people were all together, they made them form a line, took off their clothes and made them go to a bridge. They hung them from the bridge and killed them by machete. And from there they threw them in the river.

They rounded up a lot of men, women and children in the village hall, took the men out and shot them with everyone looking on. The women and

children were let go, only to find that the soldiers were setting fire to their
houses while they were burying the dead. Of all these people killed, only
three or four were guilty.

—The massacres at Chel and Ilom, aldeas of Chajul,
early April 1982, from accounts seven years later

In Chajul, the army also reached down to the religious leadership to organize the civil patrols. But here the mainstay did not consist of evangelicals, if only because the single congregation was just a few years old and still small. Instead, the army's collaborators were Catholic Action leaders who, in fear for their lives and seized by the Holy Spirit, joined a movement calling itself *La Renovación*. The "renovation" was charismatic renewal, a new wing of the Catholic Church. Like Catholic Action, charismatics reject the saint-worship of the cofradías, but they also pursue the same spiritual gifts as pentecostals—speaking in tongues, healing by faith and prophecy—hence the accusation of being crypto-Protestants. After being reprimanded by unsympathetic priests, many have indeed left for evangelical churches.

In the capital, the upper-class Catholics who turned charismatic in the late 1970s included Efraín Ríos Montt, and among the evangelical groups they joined was the Church of the Word, of which the general became a member. Out in the countryside, meanwhile, charismatic renewal was a peasant movement stimulated by the fear and dislocation of the violence. In northern Quiché encouraged by the Maryknoll priest in nearby Barrillas, Huehuetenango, it first emerged in some of the same Ixcán settlements being visited by the Guerrilla Army of the Poor. In June 1980 the army murdered the parish priest of Chajul, and Catholic Action leaders fled to the town's colonies in the Ixcán. Here they took refuge with other Catholic catechists who had already turned charismatic. When they filtered back to town, they came bearing a message of escape from political confrontation.

"Instead of becoming furious [over army killings]," a charismatic leader explains, "the people saw that they were being punished by God. Instead of getting angry for suffering so much, they asked God for pardon." The movement swept the town. Charismatics claim that they staked out a neutral position between the army and the guerrillas, so that they were left in peace. According to an evangelical missionary, the charismatics practically ran the civil patrols but were also strongly opposed to the army.[11] According to others, charismatics used spiritual renewal to define themselves against the guerrillas. The army certainly saw it that way: while littering the streets of Chajul with bodies, it allowed charismatics to go door to door with their message of repentance. Because a few charismatic leaders had the courage to approach the killers at the army base, they quickly achieved influence as go-betweens, and a source of salvation in the most immediate, physical sense. When the local army commander summoned the male population to organize the civil patrol, the man chosen to lead it was the most prominent charismatic leader, a former catechist named Domingo Rivera Asicona. The army was so impressed that soon it appointed him to be mayor as well.

As to what happened next, some Chajuleños say "the devil snared him. . . . he lost his mind." Others say he succumbed to the same temptation as a number of other civil patrol chiefs, to extort money and eliminate personal enemies. Of the many accusations against Chajul's charismatic prophet—including relatively minor mayoral abuses such as extorting illegal fines and jailing people without cause—the most serious is that he was responsible for the series of prisoners whom soldiers hung from the balcony of the town hall in 1982. When Chajuleños went out in the morning, there they were hanging by the neck.[12] Having taken to drink in violation of his religion, Domingo Rivera was the object of so many complaints that, in December 1982, Ríos Montt's government replaced him with an evangelical pastor.

"Everyone pays in this life," moralizes a Chajuleño recounting the end of Domingo Rivera. Still head of the civil patrol after being replaced as mayor, he is said to have stayed behind drinking when the civil patrol went out with the army and fell into a devastating ambush. Accused of having tipped off the guerrillas, he was taken to the army base at Santa Cruz del Quiché. There is a more sympathetic version, that after being dismissed as mayor, he went back to his religion and led the town's defense of its lands at Juil against an army plan to redistribute them. This becomes the reason he was taken away and, like so many others, died in the army's hands.

The Civil Patrol in Nebaj

"Come on Lasho, help the Major out, collaborate with him. Tell him what you know. I told him that I used to collaborate with the guerrillas 'cause they threatened me and he didn't do anything to me. Come on, they'll give us guns and we can go out at night and kill those communist assholes. We can wear masks so no one will know who we are, the soldiers will protect us. Look it, Lasho, don't you want to keep on living here, don't you like us?"

"Lasho, I was at the town meeting. The President promised to build a new paved road into town. As soon as we get rid of these rebel bastards, we'll get rich, our land will be worth a lot of money. Think about it, you're not stupid, you're smart Lasho. Help us finish 'em off, it'll be fun, just like a war movie."

—*Nebaj ladino in early 1982; from the unpublished memoir of a North American who lived in Nebaj during this period*

From Chajul and Cotzal, we might suppose that the Guatemalan army had a keen appreciation for the counterinsurgency value of hallelujah religion. But in Nebaj the army organized the civil patrol through a part of the population, local ladinos, who had almost disappeared from the other two towns. Immediately after the visit of Army Chief of Staff Benedicto Lucas on December 14, 1981,[13] an officer called together certain men, said they had been selected for being "honorable," and charged them with protecting the security of the town. "This is voluntary, the door over there is open for anyone who wants to leave," the officer harangued a member of the town's ambulance squad seeking an exemption. "But I tell you one thing. Here there aren't any pinkos. There is just white and red. Either you are with us or you are with them. But if you are with them, you'll die."

Soon the army forced the first patrollers, most of whom were ladinos, to start kidnapping guerrilla suspects, all of whom seem to have been Ixils. If a suspect was not at home, a member of his family would serve as scapegoat. To show a squad what the job entailed, a soldier plunged a knife into the first victim—a fourteen-year-old boy whose father was not at home. "You know who the subversives are," an officer told the patrollers, "so it's you who will go get them. We want two or three every night. Now we're all going to get our hands dirty." To overcome the patrollers' reluctance to kill the first victims, an officer ordered them to pick executioners by lot. Subsequently, a victim would be tied to a tree and everyone in the patrol ordered to stab him with machetes. Before long, some patrollers were volunteering to kill.

The original civil patrol in Nebaj consisted of various squads of twenty-five men each, one of which operated each night over a four- or five-day rotation. It went into action a few days after the army culled the male population of alleged subversives at the Catholic community center (described at the start of chapter 3), with a special interest in suspects who had evaded that roundup. Only when the town had been "cleaned up" in this manner, with more survivors fleeing to the mountains in panic, was the army ready to expand the civil patrol. Hence the first of many meetings in the plaza to which the army summons all the men, demands to know if they will collaborate, and teaches them to shout back in unison, like troops in uniform. Only at this point did the civil patrol become a predominantly Ixil institution, operating in daylight and incorporating the entire male population into the army's command structure.

One sign that the guerrillas were vulnerable to the army's new strategy was the discovery of storage pits on the outskirts of town. There were hundreds of them, Nebajeños claim, filled with clay jars of rice, grinding stones, soap, gas stoves, coffee and machines to grind it, personal documents of militants—everything needed for life in the mountains. Reputedly some of the storage pits were betrayed by men tortured in the community center, others by civil patrollers. Once the army promised the contents of the storage pits to the civil patrollers who found them, the race was on, to dig each one up before someone else did.

The General Who Was Born Again

I am trusting in God, my Lord and King . . . because only he gives and takes away authority. . . . Eight years ago I was cheated, four years ago they cheated us, they just cheated us again a few days ago. . . . [but] I hope that our Lord God will extend his cloak of pity and grace over Guatemala. . . . No more cadavers will appear along the highways; those who go

*against the law will be shot, but no more murders, we're going to respect
the rights of man. . . . The peace of Guatemala does not depend on
weapons, it depends on you sir, on you ma'am, on you little boy, on you
little girl. Yes, the peace of Guatemala is in your heart, once peace is in
your heart, there will be peace in your house and peace in society.*

—General Efraín Ríos Montt, head of the new
military junta, March 23, 1982

The born-again general is not easy to give his due. Consider the thousands of unarmed men, women, and children killed by the army while
he sermonized about morality, and he is a monster. Guatemalans
unnerved by his displays of religious fervor compared him to the Aya-
tollah Khomeini and lampooned him as *Díos* (God) Montt. Consider the
hopes invested in him by many Guatemalans, including poverty-strick-
en Catholic peasants, and he becomes a hero of mythic proportions.

Guatemala's first Protestant chief-of-state was from a family of
small-town patróns in Huehuetenango, not unlike the ladinos who
came to Nebaj where he has relatives. After the father lost his store, his
eldest surviving son enlisted in the army and quickly became an officer. Marrying into an important military family, the Sosa Avilas,
brought him valuable connections, including appointment as director
of the Polytechnic Institute, the country's military academy. His career
peaked in 1973 as army chief of staff. Since he obtained the job from
military president Carlos Arana Osorio, "the butcher of Zacapa" who
centralized the death squads under army control, critics have assumed
that Ríos shares responsibility for the thousands of political kidnappings during this period. But his time as chief of staff was brief. According to a biography published by brethren, his rectitude offended the
rest of the regime and he was bundled off to the Inter-American School
of Defense in Washington, D.C.

It is at this point, fuming in exile, that Ríos took on the role of the military reformer. He accepted an invitation to run for president as the
candidate of the Christian Democrats. It is of course possible that the
break with Arana was staged to co-opt the most popular opposition
party. But even in that case, his campaign was so convincing that it disrupted the intended outcome. Early returns on election night in 1974
showed that he was winning by a wide margin, forcing the high com-

mand to commit a blatant fraud to give the presidency to its candidate General Kjell Laugerud. Instead of becoming president, Ríos was sent into exile a second time, this time as ambassador to Spain. It was now that, bitter and disillusioned according to his church biography, Ríos turned evangelical. Actually, his entire life reflects a "protestant" hunger for discipline and self-improvement which has always been a current within Latin Catholicism. He was among the devout but spiritually restless Catholics who, in the late 1970s, experimented with charismatic renewal. Soon he joined a new Church of the Word being organized for members of the elite by California hippies turned evangelical missionaries.[14]

No one in the first months of 1982 foresaw the impact that this washed-up, retired general was about to have. His sudden resurrection as a political figure followed the script of the "reform coup," a familiar form of political theater wherever dictatorships founder. After years of congratulating the regime on its progress toward democracy, U.S. diplomats begin issuing glum predictions, and the boys in the back room go to work. Suddenly, idealistic junior ranks in the local military establishment overthrow the regime. Between making speeches about rooting out corruption and instituting democracy, they marshall the security forces for a showdown with the Left.

In Guatemala, the high command had just stolen another election when, on March 23, 1982, it was deposed by young officers. To head the new junta, the young officers chose their former superintendent at the military academy. They were only dimly aware that he had recently converted to a born-again church, but this became all too clear when, on the night of the coup, Ríos told the nation that it was God who had put him in power. His manic gestures and figures of speech were easy to ridicule, but harping on the restoration of law and order reassured Guatemalans terrorized by the security forces. He promised to end the abuses, so that law-abiding citizens would have nothing to fear. This is the usual rhetoric of a reform coup, but Ríos added evangelical hopes that had even wider appeal. In the midst of chaotic violence in which most people felt helpless, Ríos said they could make a difference. They could bring peace to Guatemala by changing their hearts.

The general quickly confirmed his law-and-order reputation by shutting down the elite police forces that were terrorizing the middle and upper classes. He announced a general amnesty, for both Left and Right, and forced all civil servants to pledge that they would not steal, rob, or abuse. Because the two other army officers on the junta were blocking his initiatives, on June 9 he ejected them from the government and declared himself president. He sidelined the civilian political parties that had supported the coup, promising elections only after thirty months of authoritarian rule that soon included restrictions on civil liberties, press censorship, and special state-of-siege tribunals. The general's attempt to rationalize army rule did not please civilian politicians, but they had such a reputation for corruption that the image of a righteous military dictator—an old tradition in Guatemala—seems to have gratified more people than it antagonized. His administration even tried to implement badly needed changes in taxation and foreign-exchange, to the fury of the upper classes, and broached the forbidden subject of land reform to their equal dismay.[15]

During the same months Ríos announced his reforms, the various guerrilla organizations—including the EGP, the Organization of the People in Arms (ORPA), the Rebel Armed Forces (FAR), and the Guatemalan Labor party (PGT)—were combining their forces in a new Guatemalan National Revolutionary Union (URNG). Predictably, the URNG rejected the amnesty, not least because the army's field command did not change during this period, let alone its strategy. The army had embarked on a scorched-earth policy during the last months of the old regime, and during the first four months of Ríos Montt its violence continued to escalate. Villages collaborating with the guerrillas were systematically destroyed, with survivors run across the border into Mexico or—as Ríos exerted his authority—corralled into relocation camps. To give some idea of the devastation, the Catholic Church estimated that, in 1981–82, 1.5 million people were displaced, which would be a fifth of the country's population.[16] Rural violence did decline after July 1982, but probably due more to the retreat and regrouping of the URNG than to any order from Ríos Montt, who in later months was unable to prevent security forces from resuming urban kidnappings.

When human rights organizations look at the seventeen months Ríos Montt occupied the presidential palace, to August 1983, what they see are the continuities with the previous regime and its antiguerrilla offensive.[17] But to survivors, including most people living under army control in the three Ixil towns, what counts is a crucial difference: how Ríos Montt replaced chaotic terror with a more predictable set of rewards and punishments, that is, what passes for law and order under the country's normal level of repression. Under the amnesties that he repeatedly offered over the airwaves, URNG collaborators who could no longer withstand the army's hammering were promised personal safety on two conditions, that they (1) present themselves to the army, and (2) collaborate with it from that point onward. The amnesty, along with the letup in chaotic repression, is why many Nebajeños credit him with ending the bloodbath in their town. "Under Lucas the people were just killed," an aldea leader told me. "Under Ríos Montt they were taken to Nebaj." Another Ixil observes: "He's the one who brought peace to Guatemala, no? Rios Montt was the same with everyone, rich and poor." Recalls a third: "The army had been killing people as if they were chickens, in rows. Then all of a sudden it was 'good morning,' 'good afternoon.' Before they just used to shoot."

If popular memory is checked against human rights chronologies, it turns out that Ríos Montt's advent in the national palace did not ameliorate army violence in the Ixil area at first, and this despite his almost immediate visit in April 1982. Instead, an army unit based at the Finca La Perla, accompanied by the La Perla civil patrol, committed an unprecedented string of massacres at Ilom, Estrella Polar, Covadonga, Chel, Juá, and Amajchel in the first days of April.[18] The killings, which totaled several hundred or more, were not hasty reactions to attacks on soldiers. Instead, they were prompted by mere accusations of involvement with the guerrillas. Later in April, in Acul, the army executed forty-six men, many of whom were fingered as collaborators by a hooded prisoner.[19] Another massacre occurred close to Nebaj on May 1, when soldiers slit the throats of twenty-nine men, women, and children at Tu Chobuc, beyond Tzalbal, after finding a guerrilla storage pit nearby.[20]

When Summer Institute missionaries visited in early July, they found their converts living in fear of the most menacing commander in the town's experience, a newly arrived lieutenant-colonel who flew into a rage whenever anyone tried to talk to him.[21] It was following appeals to higher authority by various townspeople—and a report to Ríos Montt by the Summer Institute missionaries—that he was relieved and the army changed the way it exercised authority in Nebaj. The new commander was not one of the young officers who had overthrown the Lucas García regime, but Major Tito Arias[22] epitomized their reform image. Nebajeños say "the situation calmed down" under the personable and sensitive Tito. His sense of humanity was relative to the situation, of course: to make an example of men shirking the civil patrol, he instituted the practice of dumping them into the town fountain. But unlike previous commanders, Tito assumed that he was winning over the people. Kidnappings came to an end. And as we shall see below, he was rewarded with a sudden influx of two thousand refugees from the EGP-controlled area of Salquil Grande.

This was the crucial (and not necessarily typical) command switch that turned Nebaj into a showcase for Ríos Montt's *fusiles y frijoles* (rifles and beans) program. The slogan was launched after the president's advisers realized they had a refugee crisis on their hands and would have to counter a barrage of adverse human rights reports. As the Summer Institute missionaries advised, there would be an effort to shelter and feed the refugees created by the army's offensive (the beans) at the same time that the army organized them to fight the guerrillas (the rifles). In July the elders of Ríos Montt's church announced the formation of International Love Lift, to supervise what the president said would be a billion dollar contribution from North American evangelicals. The aid channeled by Love Lift through its Foundation for Aid to the Indian People (FUNDAPI) never amounted to more than a few hundred thousand dollars, but most of what arrived went to Ixil country where Summer Institute missionaries saw that it was distributed effectively.

A human rights activist happened to be in town in early 1983 when Major Tito gave his farewell speech. He said he knew that many of the people listening to him were still crying for members of their family. But the army had lost some of its own as well, Tito said, so that for every dead soldier there was a family crying too. The visitor was amazed to see part of the crowd in tears. More than a few Nebajeños thought they would be dead if the army had not relented under Tito, and they could not be sure that his successor would not return to kidnappings and massacres. As it turned out, fortunately, subsequent commanders followed his precedent. But the army was only rationalizing its use of force, making it more predictable to make it more effective. In outlying areas, offensives continued to force EGP-administered people into concentrated resettlements that soon were being called model villages.

Not so much had changed as army apologists would have us believe, because the continuing offer of amnesty was accompanied by regular punishment of those who failed to accept it. While the size and frequency of army massacres diminished, these did not end. According to a man from Parramos Grande, soldiers cut down maize fields and burned houses in June, July, and August 1982, then again in May 1983, at which time they killed a man and six women who were unable to escape. During the next offensive, in September 1984, soldiers from the new garrison at Salquil Grande killed another twenty people from Parramos Grande—shooting some as they fled, killing others with knives, and strangling children with cords. Judging from the experience of peasants in the montaña, there was still plenty to fear from the Guatemalan army.

From Civil Patrol to Civil War

> *Since 1980, two things have changed: the army no longer trusts any Indians, and the Indians have become conscientizados. In this latter process, they cross over a much more important threshold: into a political awareness which includes Indian unity and the knowledge that the army is trying to destroy their Indian way of life. From this awareness, there can be no turning back even when they are forced to commit atrocities against their own people and even when living under totally controlled conditions.*
> —Luisa Frank and Philip Wheaton,
> *Indian Guatemala: Path to Liberation,* 1984

At dawn on June 15, 1982, an armed force surrounded the village of Chacalté, pounced on the just-stirring households and killed every per-

*Soldiers checking an Ixil man's identification
at the Nebaj airstrip, 1987*

son in reach. It had all the marks of an army massacre. Certainly no other case of Guatemalan guerrillas killing a hundred men, women, and children and wounding thirty-five more has been established, contrary to the army's propaganda claims, which are usually too vague and at odds with local testimony to be taken seriously. Yet the army communique blaming the EGP is unusually detailed: it paints Chacalté as a model of cooperation with the new civil patrol. The aldea had been "the first to organize themselves in self-defense patrols" and inflicted thirteen casualties on the guerrillas, including the death of a "Comandante Alvaro." Then the Chacalté patrol had helped the army find a guerrilla camp and kill seven more—all prior to the June massacre.[23] Significantly, Chacaltecans and Chajuleños also blame the guerrillas. The village had repented of collaborating with the EGP, according to these accounts, then beaten several guerrillas to death before the EGP decided to make a lesson of them.

This was not the first massacre that Chajuleños blame on the guerrillas. A month before, on May 18, men who appeared to be soldiers hurried into the village of Batzul, announced that the guerrillas were destroying a nearby bridge, and ordered the civil patrol to turn out with its guns. Some say that, as soon as the patrollers fell into line, they were machine-gunned; others say they were led into an ambush. Fourteen men died according to Amnesty International.[24] Chajuleños insist that it was guerrillas disguised as soldiers, not soldiers, who were responsible. That same day or the next, in the village of Chichel, seven more civil patrollers were killed, also reportedly by guerrillas disguised as soldiers.[25]

Should we believe Chajuleños when they blame the EGP? It would be nothing new for soldiers to go on the rampage disguised as guerrillas. The army used the tactic in eastern Guatemala in the 1960s, as it evidently did in nearby Sacapulas in 1980, when men wearing army-issue boots and driving death squad-style vehicles showed up in the village of Parraxtut, claimed to be the EGP, and kidnapped fifteen men.[26] What if Chajuleños are confused or afraid to tell the truth? But in Ixil country, people usually assign responsibility for large-scale killing with little sign of doubt, and in most cases they blame the army.[27]

Only immediately after the organization of the civil patrols do guerrilla massacres appear in local testimony, not before or since. Until that point, Ixils describe EGP killing of noncombatants as selective—a military commissioner here, a pair of accused Ixil informers there—which is the same way they describe EGP killing ever since. Another interesting datum is that, while the Army of the Poor denied responsibility for Chacalté, it did take credit for a massacre nine days before. On June 6, 1982, guerrillas extracted thirteen Cotzaleño civil patrol leaders and their wives from a bus, shot them one by one in the head, and ordered the driver to run his vehicle over the bodies, an action the EGP's *Informador Guerrillero* described as the execution of "thirteen leaders of paramilitary bands."[28]

Local testimony suggests that creation of the civil patrols turned a war between Ixils and the army into a civil war between Ixils. As an officer told the first patrollers in Nebaj, "now we're all going to get our hands dirty." Indeed they did. Under army orders to cooperate or die, patrollers began to participate in the arrest, interrogation, and execution of guerrilla suspects. Some were also forced to participate in the bloodiest episodes of the war. Perhaps the single largest massacre in Ixil country occurred on February 13, 1982, when the army ordered Cotzaleños under its control to punish the aldea of Chisis. Located in the mountains above Cotzal, the aldea had become a refuge for people fleeing from army reprisals; the day before, guerrillas had reportedly come through and burned a national flag. When the civil patrol at the aldea of Santa Avelina refused to comply, the army sent out patrollers from the town center who killed more than two hundred men, women, and children. Some time later, the skulls in the river were said to look like the smooth stones in the river at Sacapulas. One heart-stricken patroller said that he made the sign of the cross before killing each person.

Events such as this make it easy to see why the guerrillas might go on a rampage, to avenge their nearest and dearest. Judging from stories about Ixil EGP leaders being demoted or executed for abusing their authority,[29] it is possible that some of the killing was done by local militants who were violating orders. In any case it was not hard for the guerrillas to retaliate, particularly because the army was sending out patrollers without weapons, not even the bolt-action Mauser and M-1 rifles they later carried. In December 1982 the mayor of Cotzal told me that, since January, seventy-six of the nine hundred men in his civil patrol had been killed.

Much of the slaughter was in Xeputul, on a ridge occupied by smallholders above the Finca San Francisco. The municipio had long contested this warm and fertile area with the Brol family, with homesteaders holding out against finca surveyors and appealing to the town hall for help. Finally, in the early 1970s, shortly before he was killed by the EGP, Cotzal's strongman Gaspar Pérez Pérez was able to stabilize the boundaries and allocate land to smallholders. This was not the end of the conflict, however: in a small, crowded, and finca-dominated municipio, Xeputul represented the last open land, prized for its ability to grow coffee and two maize crops a year. Land claims are never more problematic than in clearing virgin forest and settlers were soon at each other's throats. Conflict between evangelical factions may even have been responsible for the murder of a Methodist pastor and two companions.[30] After 1979, Xeputul also suffered from serving as a corridor for guerrillas attacking San Francisco. As guerrillas entered local social relations, neighbors who felt they had been wronged in the distribution of land were presented with new ways to settle scores.

When I visited Xeputul in 1989, the only relic of the old settlement was a large, decaying temple of the Full Gospel Church of God, surrounded by the thatched huts of survivors who had just returned. Across the river was an EGP refugee zone, the scene of ambushes when the army tried to penetrate it. Coincident with my arrival, someone had just accused Xeputul's auxiliary mayor and military commissioner of supplying the guerrillas with salt. Now they would have to report to the army for questioning. So dangerous was Xeputul's reputation that, even though numerous Cotzaleños owned land there, few were returning to work it. The town hall was so eager to resettle the area, to keep it out of the hands of rival K'iche' Maya colonists from Uspantán and Cunén, that it was offering land to Nebajeños. As to whether previous owners might object, I was assured that they were either with the guerrillas, therefore of no account, or dead.

A civil patrol leader showed me the handwritten register the army required him to keep. The entry for March 4, 1982, reports that the Xeputul patrol dismantled a guerrilla encampment consisting of two women, four children, and seventy-nine household items including food, salt, female clothing, sleeping mats, and bedspreads. These were just a few of the forty-two people, mainly women and children, whom the Xeputul patrol captured over the next year. But patrollers paid dearly for turning over the families of guerrillas to the army. On May 10, 1982, according to a survivor, twenty-five patrollers armed with seven shotguns and .22 rifles ran into a guerrilla column that killed twelve of them, wounded another four, and captured another six who were never found. Some days later, the army arrested ten more Xeputul patrollers, on suspicion of helping the guerrillas: they were never seen again either. The following month, in June, another five civil patrollers were picked up by the guerrillas and disappeared. Of the forty-nine original members of the Xeputul civil patrol, according to this account, thirty-three were dead or missing.

How Much Support Did the EGP Have?

During the months of May and June, the guerrilla forces of our Ho Chi Minh Front completed a successful series of military operations, which were executed despite the gigantic counterinsurgency operation which the genocidal army of the rich, headed by the fanatical Ríos Montt,

*launched against our forces and especially against the civilian population,
in a desperate attempt to halt what is now impossible to stop: the growing
process of popular revolutionary war which day by day advances in our
country.* —*Guerrilla Army of the Poor, June 1982*

The increasing visibility of the EGP encouraged the idea that Ixil country was a guerrilla bastion. It claimed to have broad support and the army agreed, as did church observers, journalists, and diplomats.[31] Yet such is the power of rumor, of presumed knowledge and imputed conspiracy, that entire towns had a reputation for guerrilla sympathies before most of their inhabitants had any contact with the EGP, let alone displayed any position on the matter. As soon as army kidnappings began in Cotzal in 1976, that town was becoming known as *guerrillero*, and the same was true of Nebaj as soon as the EGP began holding village rallies in 1979. So assumed the army, whose reactions did so much to turn Ixil villagers into guerrillas, just as the EGP did so much to bring on the war simply by showing its face and declaring itself at one with *el pueblo*.

In this whirlwind of assumptions creating realities, any claim about how Ixils felt is probably too broad. People feel every which way in the midst of terror; only the ideologically committed are likely to define themselves with much precision. Certainly many Ixils had grievances against labor contractors and plantation owners, and most if not all understood their disadvantageous position in the social order. So when an "army of the poor" showed up with weapons in hand to preach equality with the wealthy, it had appeal. The arrival of death squads, oriented by local politicians associated with the Finca San Francisco in Cotzal and labor contracting in Nebaj, sharpened the point. So did the way that government kidnappers targeted reformist politicians, catechists, and cooperative leaders seeking alternatives to dependence on plantation labor.

In the Ixcán rain forest colonies to the north, where the EGP had a longer history of organizing, observers detected sympathy for the guerrillas in the late 1970s before the onset of massive repression. Leaders of these new settlements had high expectations that were being frustrated by exploitative middlemen and institutional roadblocks.

They were mainly catechists and, thanks to Catholic educational efforts, were becoming more aware of how they were exploited. Like Eric Wolf's "middle peasant," they had the tactical mobility to become dissidents; like Samuel Popkin's "rational peasant," they thought they were gaining something from supporting the guerrillas; and as postulated by Joel Migdal, the EGP apparently was able to institutionalize mutually beneficial exchanges with them.[32]

As a long-settled traditional population in the highlands, Ixils seem to have received the guerrillas with greater caution than the multiethnic Ixcán settlers. But we can infer at least two stages of Ixil participation in the revolutionary movement. At first the EGP attracted frustrated political activists, survivors of government kidnappings, traders seeking profits, and youth looking for adventure, none of these categories being mutually exclusive. As the EGP extended its clandestine networks, government reprisals became more indiscriminate and the number of recruits increased, with the two antagonists effectively working together to create the movement. A second stage began in 1979 in Nebaj (and possibly earlier in Cotzal), as the guerrillas became a military presence. The security forces responded with even more indiscriminate attacks, prompting wider swathes of inhabitants to identify with the guerrillas.

An old ladino populist observes that the guerrillas "had a good organization"; that is, they could give the impression of wider support than they actually had, especially in exotic indigenous communities that outsiders assume to be more solidaristic than is actually the case.[33] The EGP's practice of holding village rallies gave the impression that it was relying on ideological persuasion. The rallies were also presented as evidence that villagers were becoming enthusiastic supporters. Many Ixils admit that they liked what the guerrillas offered—a world in which they would have electric light and new access roads to their aldeas, where they would recover fincas and enjoy the same luxuries as wealthy ladinos. But warming to a speech is not the same as joining an insurrection, and the EGP's organizing techniques were coercive, albeit in more subtle ways than the army's. Around Salquil, according to an evangelical pastor who led a mass defection to the army in 1982, militants would put up red flags at night. After soldiers came to take them down, other flags would appear, with the warning that if anyone tried to remove them it would mean opposing the guerrillas. When the army demanded to know who was putting up the flags, the people did not know or were afraid to say. As a result, complains the pastor, the army thought they were all involved with the guerrillas.[34]

Once the EGP had organized an aldea, the inevitable reaction of the army forced villagers to choose sides. Neutrality was no more acceptable to the guerrillas than to the army because the EGP could not tolerate the security risks implied by serious dissent against its plans. "The guerrillas said that those who didn't speak, who didn't get along with them, who didn't have anything to say, were `ears' (informers)," a man from Xoloché told me. The EGP usually did not report what happened next, although one of its communiques describes the execution of eleven army collaborators and four thieves on a single day in December 1981.[35] During my own interviewing, Ixils often mentioned family members or neighbors who had been executed by the EGP on security grounds.

Timothy Wickham-Crowley attributes guerrilla killing of noncombatants to two factors. One is the vulnerability of a clandestine revolutionary movement to "information leakage." That is the reason provided by Mario Payeras for the execution of two wayward EGP comrades in *Days of the Jungle*. The other reason is a guerrilla movement's claim to represent "the people" and constitute legitimate authority. When dissenters threaten that claim, guerrillas tend to respond the same way as the governments they challenge, with what Wickham-Crowley evenhandedly calls terror.[36] The contest between government and guerrilla coercion tipped initially in favor of the latter because, as Wickham-Crowley concludes from his comparative study, it is more selective and effective. Guerrillas tend to be closer to the people than counterinsurgents are, making it easier for them to distinguish friend from foe. By the heavy-handed standards of the Guatemalan army, in contrast, anyone who handed a guerrilla a tortilla was guilty of collaborating with subversion. The army was so indiscriminate that I heard of cases where even close family members of EGP targets fled to the guerrillas for protection, because they were much more selective in defining their enemy. In the competition between army and guerrilla coercion, the clumsier responses of the army pushed many civilians into the insurgency.

The EGP is customarily given credit for transcending the *foco* conception of guerrilla warfare "by embarking on a lengthy process of organizing civilians."[37] It certainly did organize civilians, but how much of the reason they joined was the situational coercion described above? How much did the collision of two armies create a misleading impression of support? Carol Smith has noted the lack of information about the relations between the guerrilla leadership and its social base.[38] The publications of the EGP shed little light on the subject. The only hint that the entire population does not support the EGP are occasional references to the execution of reactionaries and paramilitary leaders (civil patrol heads), with the disastrous year of 1982 summed up as "reinforcement of the social base of the revolution."[39] Retreats become a consolidation of forces, and defeats become advances in popular consciousness. The lack of information is so striking that it suggests EGP militants were ultimately defeated by the deep-seated neutralism so evident in Ixil campesinos today.

Abandoning the EGP

The start of it all was in 1978 when the guerrillas began to organize the people clandestinely. They said that the rich, the millionaires, the Spaniards had us enslaved and we didn't want that. They also said that the fincas paid us poorly. The people said, that's right. The guerrillas promised to help them economically when they won, that they would be given cash, house and car, and that they would finish off the Spaniards, that is, the rich. . . . Really all the people allowed themselves to be organized, but it was a fraud. Because the guerrillas promised them everything, and out of ignorance the people permitted themselves to be organized. When the guerrilla [combatants] showed up, they looked like military personnel. And they began to attack the army. But when they were not strong enough, they fled to the montaña, they left, and the army arrived to take vengeance against civilians, people who were unable to flee because they were old, young or female.

It was in 1980 when the guerrillas captured a military garrison in Cotzal. It is said that all the soldiers died. . . . Out of anger, the president sent helicopters to bombard all the roads and houses. The army arrived to kill people in Cotzal, then came up to Pexla and Bipulay. There in Bipu-

lay they found people who out of fear had fled from the road in Pulay. They killed about 45 people there in Bipulay. Three days later I helped recover the bodies. Just women and children living in little huts. . . . Fifteen days later the army came out of Cotzal again and killed about fifteen people in the aldea of Pulay, old people and children, either by machete or burning them in their houses. That's how it was. . . .

In Pulay there were educated people, civilized, who realized that the guerrillas were lying, that the army was killing but that the guerrillas were to blame. The guerrillas said they would protect the people but did not fulfill their promise, the moment would arrive and they would run away, so the people protested. [The guerrillas] replied, that's war. The people of Pulay got angry, turned their back [on the guerrillas], and went to town to tell the army. The army did not realize: it thought that all the people were guerrillas.

—1992 account of why part of Pulay surrendered
to the army ten years before

There is no denying that ideological mobilization occurred in northern Quiché. The guerrillas recruited many hundreds of Ixil militants and combatants, many of whom continue to hold out in the mountains to this day. What I am questioning is their relation to the rest of the population, that is, the solidarity assumption that the guerrilla movement represented "the people." The limits of solidarity thinking are illustrated by refugee patterns in 1981–82. While many Ixils cast their lot with the EGP, a surprising number of others stayed next to army garrisons or relocated there despite the evident dangers.[40] The pattern becomes even more evident with Ríos Montt's amnesty. According to an adviser, the army assisted forty-two thousand people in the Ixil Triangle between 1982 and 1984.[41] This would be almost half the population according to national census projections, the remainder being in the mountains with the guerrillas, in exile elsewhere in the republic, or dead.

Around the Finca La Perla, even the army's serial massacres in early April 1982 did not drive many of the survivors to join the guerrillas. From Ilom, most simply left their burned-out aldea for the nearby Finca Santa Delfina and, several weeks later, allowed themselves to be organized into a civil patrol. Remember that Ilom was the aldea that, according to *Days of the Jungle*, celebrated Luis Arenas's assassination with a marimba seven years before. The Chajuleños of Ilom were mainly seasonal plantation workers whose fathers and grandfathers owned the surrounding land before it was expropriated for plantations. If any Ixils were to be receptive to the EGP, it should have been them. Yet there was little sign of support at this critical moment. It is of course possible that, when the army executed eighty-five to ninety men in Ilom, it eliminated the guerrilla network with deadly accuracy. If this is the case, however, such a slaughter does not say much for the EGP's level of organization or preparedness. Across the Xalbal River at Covadonga, Q'anjob'al colonos arrested three guerrilla cadre warning them to flee to the montaña. Instead of following the cadres' advice, the colonos turned them over to the army. This was shortly before the army and the La Perla civil patrol returned, called the men of Covadonga together, and killed everyone who could not escape.

Now consider the area just east of Nebaj—around Río Azul, Xoncá, and Pulay. These were aldeas where ladinos had appropriated land, death squads had been active, and the EGP had executed military commissioner Santiago López and his ally Catarino Urizar. These were also the villages from which hundreds of women marched to confront the army in Nebaj on March 3, 1980. Over the next year, the army committed at least two major massacres in this area, at Bipulay (forty-five or more dead) and Cocop (sixty-eight), as well as enough others that more investigation will be required to distinguish them.[42] Early in 1982, the army ordered the people who were left to evacuate into town or be killed and many did so, spurning guerrilla pleas to flee to higher elevations instead. Testimony from nearby Pexla Grande suggests that its people were barely acquainted with the EGP before army massacres forced them to choose between fleeing to the montaña or the town. That EGP organizing and the army reaction split these villages down the middle is suggested by the sizable contribution they made to the early civil patrol. Soon after the patrols were organized in early 1982, two men from Pulay and Río Azul led five hundred to six hundred people—roughly a quarter of the population—into the town center and became two of the first commanders of the Nebaj patrol.[43]

The clearest sign of discontent with the EGP was a mass defection from the well-organized area of Salquil. Here the guerrillas were clearly in control. Few people responded to the army's demands to come into Nebaj in early 1982. As the army stepped up its attacks, the population obediently melted back into the hills according to the EGP's defense plans. Then in August 1982, a lay pastor of the Full Gospel Church of God, the same group playing such a prominent role in Cotzal, led a mass surrender to the army. A commentary from the EGP describes Pastor Miguel (not his real name) as a *compañero*, a helpful man with a brother who was a combatant, but also better off than most because of his occupation as a tailor and butcher. The organization began to have problems with Miguel when his worship services became so prolonged that they interfered with revolutionary tasks, that is, the work assignments being given Salquileños now that they were under siege from the army.[44]

According to Miguel, the guerrillas killed four members of his church for filling in stake-pits that the EGP had dug as a defense measure. The evangelicals did not want to be blamed when soldiers fell into them. Two months later, in May, it was the army who murdered members of Miguel's denomination, twenty-nine of them, after finding an EGP storage pit nearby. As a result, he and his brethren felt increasingly "in between" the two forces. The guerrillas had said they would win the war by the March 1982 election. But these were lies, Miguel said when I interviewed him at year's end; instead, more people were being killed. Over the radio, meanwhile, he was hearing Ríos Montt use evangelical language to promise amnesty. "Spies" from town may also have provided assurances from the Summer Institute missionaries. Under Ríos Montt's protection, they had just returned to Nebaj and, during these same weeks, were wondering how to convince Salquil evangelicals that the amnesty was genuine.

On the night of August 3, to avoid detection, Pastor Miguel led 237 men, women, and children—most of them evangelicals—out of Salquil by a roundabout route. The desertion caught the EGP by surprise. The guerrillas were even more upset when men from the first group returned, accompanied by soldiers, and rounded up another 1,740 Salquileños, including many Catholics. Judging from the EGP's denunciation of "infiltrators" for persuading refugees to surrender, many of these people gave themselves up more or less voluntarily.[45] As the army escorted them to Nebaj, it put on a show of fraternity, with soldiers carrying children on their shoulders, for the thousands of Salquileños who remained in hiding. The debate over whether to surrender continued to spread, encouraged by taped radio appeals from Pastor Miguel offering safety, food, and medicine.[46]

In my conversations with the pastor and other Salquil refugees, ideological rationales for turning against the guerrillas—such as loving thy neighbor and obeying the government because it is put over you by God—were accompanied by vivid descriptions of the hardships they had suffered. They had come down because they were, in the words of one, "without clothes, without medicine and there had been many deaths among us. We no longer had food, and we no longer had shelter." They could no longer go to the coast for their accustomed source of cash because the guerrillas had taken their identification papers. After several years of political warfare, the overriding concern of these people was physical security. When I interviewed them at the army's new refugee settlement at the Nebaj airstrip, dubbed Camp New Life, they professed satisfaction with a ceremonial display of firepower by the army.[47] What they wanted most was to be on the stronger side.

Obviously, the defeat of a revolutionary movement does not provide the best conditions for assessing popular feeling about it, but then a revolutionary victory may not either. Because so much coercion and concealment is involved in this kind of warfare, how can we be sure that statements of neutrality or alignment with the army are anything but tactical, James Scott's "public transcript" as opposed to a "hidden transcript" of support for the guerrillas? There is indeed no way to be certain on this point, but Nebajeños had more scope to express themselves at the end of the decade than at the start, and what they say contradicts the claims of the EGP as well as the army.

At the most public level, that is, face to face with the army, Ixils mimic its rhetoric, as when civil patrollers volunteer that "we're protecting our communities from the subversives." Almost as public, that is, offered to just about anyone except perhaps an army officer, are protective statements of neutrality such as "we're between two fires." Not coincidentally, the same kind of claim happens to be popular in Peru, where insurgents as well as the security forces are known for brutality. This is the safest possible presentation of self, the least compromising in many situations where one's interlocutor is not clearly marked politically.[48] Needless to say, sharper feelings operate below the surface, voiced only in what James Scott calls the "hidden transcript." While some Ixils speak mainly against one side or the other, what is most common are expressions of having been abused by both sides. The most hidden sentiments are identification with the EGP on one or another level, such as sympathy for relatives who are still with the guerrillas, pride in the ability of Ixil fighters to defy the army, and attraction to the EGP's vision of a just society.

However, putting such sympathies into practice by collaborating with the EGP runs against a great deal of clear and expressed feeling in the three Ixil towns. To presume that large numbers of Ixils want to see the guerrillas make a comeback is to presume that they are willing to go through another period like they did in the early 1980s, which I find very hard to believe. This is why I have chosen to take at face value what Ixils say they want, which is peace. To deconstruct their stated wishes in terms of "resistance" or a "hidden transcript," or to argue that peace can be achieved only with justice as does the guerrilla movement, can be used to impose an agenda for continued war.

Why the Army of the Poor Lost Support

> We cried a little; we suffered a lot. . . . We spent two years in the montaña. Every time the army arrived, people died. Women, little ones, the old people. If we stay here, we said, we're going to die. If we go to town, we'll die too. In any case, we're going to die. We're not alive, we're not dead, just with God we came in. —Elder from Aldea Xoloché, 1989

The EGP has never acknowledged that it was defeated in 1982. But two years later dissidents left the organization and, calling themselves October Revolution after the popular national uprising of 1944, began to ventilate what had happened. One of the dissidents was Mario Payeras, who described the destruction of the EGP's urban network in a second and grimmer book than his first, therefore less welcome and less known. According to Payeras, the EGP had been caught off-guard by the intensity of the repression. It did not have the organizational capacity and weapons for the thousands of recruits flocking to it for protection and leadership.[49] In the words of solidarity writer Philip Wheaton, the EGP "knew that not enough attention had been paid to security; that often unarmed communities had not been taught how to defend themselves; they realized they had not taken adequate steps to integrate the new Indian cadres into the ranks of the armed guerrilla units. Yet the responsibility for the mass killings was not theirs."[50]

If this is the explanation, it should refer mainly to the EGP's failures where it opened so many new fronts in the early 1980s, only to see them fail.[51] It should apply less to Ixil country, where the EGP supposedly had sunk deep roots. Gradually, more revealing intramural criticism has surfaced, of how the EGP imposed military priorities on grassroots activists which exposed them to deadly reprisals, if not destroying popular organizations altogether.[52] One example is the Committee for Campesino Unity (CUC), which originated in Catholic consciousness-raising efforts and agitated for higher plantation wages. Thanks to government kidnappers and guerrilla organizers, CUC's agenda came to include organizing the masses for insurrection, to the point that, by 1980, it was virtually a wing of the Guerrilla Army of the Poor, whereupon it was almost destroyed.

A critique of militarism is clearly called for, not just of the "army of the rich" but of the "army of the poor." That the EGP was counting on the popular reaction to army repression is suggested by how *Informador Guerrillero* spoke of the recruiting role of army massacres, somewhat wishfully, in late 1982. "These are experiences felt in one's own flesh, scenes seen and heard from the refuges and trenches. Hope and the desire to struggle are not lost, to the contrary, they are reborn like the grains of corn which give life to our families, our people, our Revolution."[53] Army massacres certainly did increase support for the guerrillas, but this was not the only response of Ixils. Another was to blame the guerrillas for putting victims in harm's way. "It was for the guerrillas that they died," says a man of his aldea Bijolóm, near Salquil, "because when there were clashes with the army, many died."[54] Such reactions help explain why, even before Ríos Montt, some survivors were aligning themselves with the same army that had committed massacres.

Another equation that needs to be viewed skeptically is the common one between Catholic popular organizations—in Ixil country, Catholic

Action—and the guerrilla organization. Although this kind of radicalization was planned by the guerrillas, presumed by the army, and incarnated in the trajectories of some lay Catholic leaders, it describes only part of the local Catholic leadership. Surviving catechists insist that Catholic Action was never *subversivo*, and it is certain that numerous catechists refused to join the revolution, as dramatized by the transformation of much of the Catholic Action leadership in Chajul into the charismatic movement, soon to become the basis for organizing the civil patrol there.

The civil patrol is usually approached as a form of coercion imposed by the army on an unwilling population. This is quite true, as we have seen from the horrifying way the patrols were established in the Ixil towns, but the civil patrol is more than that. Because Ixils do not see *la situación* as brought about exclusively by the army, instead blaming the guerrillas as well, they do not see the civil patrol as an obligation imposed only by the army. Joining the patrol became a way to protect self, family, and community from the guerrilla contacts that triggered army massacres. Hence the worry we shall see as the civil patrols began to disintegrate in the late 1980s.

FIVE

From Montaña to Model Village

Civil patroller at Xolcuay

The civil patrol is very necessary, but it's a big waste of time.
—Nebaj town councilman, 1989

NORTHERN Quiché Department is one of the few places where the guerrillas hung on after their defeat in 1982. Here the Guerrilla Army of the Poor regrouped as it withdrew from areas to the west and south where its organization had disintegrated. Except for a few pockets to the east in Verapaz and the Petén, only in Ixil country and the Ixcán to the north did displaced populations remain beyond government control. One reason is geography. In contrast to Huehuetenango Department to the west where tens of thousands of refugees were able to flee to Mexico, jungles, swamps and rivers north of Ixil country make the journey to the border almost impossible for families.[1] What a trapped population could do, on the other hand, was provide the EGP with maize and adolescents to be turned into fighters.

The unusual level of resistance in Ixil country led to an unusual level of militarization. The destruction of the rural settlement pattern was far more complete than in neighboring municipios, where the army left some homesteads and neighborhoods standing while burning others accused of subversion. For the revolutionary movement, the displaced villagers became, together with a similar population in the Ixcán, the "communities of population in resistance" (CPRs). But in Nebaj, most returned refugees say simply that they were in the *montaña*, that is, the more forested parts of the surrounding mountains. Despite the connotation of wandering far from home, life in the montaña for the majority of Ixils meant staying close to their fields, throwing up a rude shelter at a less accessible point, getting by without trade goods, and cooperating to a greater or lesser degree with EGP-appointed authorities. Rather than a refuge or place apart, the montaña was a state of existence without the comfort of the old adobe-and-tile house, subject to persecution by the army, cut off from town and the larger world.

Because part of the population was continuing to support the EGP, the Guatemalan army set up a special system to control the area. While civil patrols were organized across the highlands, only in a few areas—and in none so intensively as Ixil country and the Ixcán—did the army remake the settlement pattern. Hence the controversial "model villages," described as a bold new development model by the army and as concentration camps by critics. Conceived under Ríos Montt, these concentrated resettlements were actually built under the defense minister who overthrew him, General Oscar Mejía Víctores (1983–85). Hoping to make the program palatable to foreign donors, the army produced another euphemism for the model villages which became infamous, that they were "development poles."[2]

In 1990, as part of the Central American peace process, the Catholic Church and the human rights movement took up the cause of the remaining people in the montaña. Representatives of the communities of population in resistance protested army bombardments, denied that they were part of the EGP's Ho Chi Minh Front, and demanded the right to return home without joining the army's civil patrols. My information came from a different source: refugees who had been captured by the army or surrendered to it and were now living under its control. They confirmed the bombardments, but their stories were of disillusion with the revolutionary movement and accommodation to army rule. This chapter will describe how, in the late 1980s and early 1990s, Nebajeños talked about both sides and behaved toward them. It will also show how they turned the army's most important instrument, the civil patrol, into a way to protect themselves from soldiers as well as guerrillas. How they talk about their experience from montaña to model village suggests that they are not repressed revolutionaries (although they have been repressed) or willing army collaborators (although they are collaborators). Instead, most Ixils are best understood as determined neutralists.

The Pursuit of Neutralism

Civil Patroller: How much time are you losing, patrolling and Putting Your Life in Danger, instead of working and struggling so that your family does not die of hunger? The army threatens and coerces you because it

does not want to do its dirty work in the service of the rich. Don't obey
what you're ordered to do. Look for a way to deceive them. No one can
stop the struggle of the people.

—*Guatemalan National Revolutionary Union*
(flier distributed in Nebaj 1988–89)

When gunfire erupted on the outskirts of Nebaj, we would hear the pop-pop-pop of the civil patrol's bolt-action rifles, interspersed with short measured bursts of automatic fire from guerrillas conserving their ammunition. More often than not, the shooting was coming from up the valley in Xevitz. This was a new resettlement along the road that climbs out of Nebaj for the department capital. Guerrillas often stopped traffic there, leading to shoot-outs if soldiers or civil patrollers happened by. But the guerrillas took a special interest in creating uproars at Xevitz, perhaps because it was a safe, convenient place to taunt the army and remind Nebajeños that the soldiers were afraid to face them.

Who the army did send was the civil patrol, but no one ever seemed to get hurt in the resulting encounters. After many a crossfire, not even the glass had been blown out of the new school. Did everyone just shoot in the air? Not true, insisted a civil patroller: while the guerrillas might shoot in the air, the patrollers were aiming as best they could "but without result, for lack of a training course." Another curiosity was that the guerrillas never approached the nearby refugee camp at Xemamatze, even though it was full of people who had just been brought in from the mountains and were only lightly guarded, if that. It would have been easy for an EGP unit to rescue captured refugees, yet nothing of the sort occurred. They were not being kept there by brute force.

La situación in Nebaj by the late 1980s was quite a contrast to the body-strewn scene at the start of the decade. Now it was an almost ritualized affair. Around the three Ixil towns, the dead were relatively few and consisted mainly of combatants. Unlike in 1982, the guerrillas usually avoided shooting civil patrollers: the EGP was said to have standing orders forbidding it, on grounds that the patrollers were just poor people being forced to carry the army's guns. Patrollers were more likely to express fear of the army than of the supposed adversary, their sense of security illustrated by the bunched-up, unmilitary way they slumped across the countryside. Even a Nebaj civil patrol leader whom the guerrillas could blame for the death of comrades circulated without protection or apparent fear. "They tell people to keep on working, that their quarrel is only with the army, that's why there's no problem," he assured me blandly. "They don't have anything against me. Why should I worry?"

This was a war in which the two sides rarely challenged each other seriously, being content to justify their presence through occasional displays of shadow-boxing. Both the army and the EGP were playing a waiting game in which the civil patrols performed a half-hearted surrogate role. When the guerrillas staged an action, the army's usual response was to send out a column of civil patrollers whom the guerrillas would not engage unless trapped. Despite the army's unimpressive military performance, it clearly had the upper hand. Take the EGP's 1985 (or 1986) occupation of Xix, a K'iche'-speaking village in Chajul, as recounted by an itinerant merchant from there.

"[The guerrillas] took us by surprise at five in the morning and began to shout, that the patrol not run away and instead surrender its weapons. Those of us who had rifles left on the run, with the rifles, because otherwise the guerrillas take them. And the army demands to know why [we lost them], if there wasn't even one death. . . . [The guerrillas] held a meeting [in Spanish], asking why we returned to town to live in sheds when the government had failed to rebuild our houses. . .

"Then one of the women answered them: 'Why do you come to deceive us again? We've seen what you've done. It's because of you that we don't have shelter, that they burned all the houses. . . . Why do you come to bother us, so the army comes to do us harm? It's because of you that they do what they do. Please get out of here, because the soldiers are already on the way.' The guerrillas asked for the patrollers' weapons, that they give them up, but no one spoke."

Eventually, the fleeing civil patrollers found each other at the edge of the settlement and began to fire their guns, prompting the guerrillas to withdraw. No one had been injured, nor had any patroller from Xix become a casualty several years later, in a testimony to guerrilla forbearance. Such episodes might sound like comic opera, but they frightened villagers by threatening to upset their delicate relationship with the army.

In 1989 the guerrillas took the inhabitants of Parramos Chiquito by surprise, shouting "this village has been taken!" and "don't be frightened!" As some of the guerrillas held a meeting with the people, others entered houses to help themselves to food and the community medicine chest. Ordinarily the EGP pays for what it takes, but in this case the guerrillas were angry because the civil patrollers had managed to hide eight of their rifles. Refusing to give up the rifles was why the guerrillas took five prisoners, threatened to kill them, and only released them after administering a thrashing. Worse for Parramos Chiquito, the guerrillas had been able to capture the aldea's other two rifles.

When the patrollers reported to the army, the response was: "What happened, boy! You have to be ready, you were sleeping! We don't give you rifles so that you give them to the guerrillas!" "They always get mad," a villager observed of his experiences with the army. "But what can we do with ten rifles if there are so many [guerrillas]?" Drunk in town afterward, several of the patrollers moaned over and over that they had lost two M-1s, as if they couldn't believe the enormity of their offense.

Whether in the name of revolution or defending the nation, both sides were keeping up their pressure on civilians. But this was only the quieter and less costly side of the war. Farther away there was another, which we glimpsed only when an A37 attack jet streaked overhead or a line of refugees escorted by soldiers straggled across the plaza. The warplane was heading north on a bombing run, to a place called Amajchel, and the refugees were from there too. This was the other side of the army's counterinsurgency strategy. Even as it was allowing Ixils under its control to return to their land around the three towns, it was systematically persecuting those beyond its control by cutting them off from trade, burning their houses, chopping down their crops and, whenever possible, snatching them away to a refugee camp.

The Army of the Poor

Actions of the URNG from January to July 20, 1989:
975 political-military operations in 11 departments including the capital
1,392 casualties inflicted on the army, among them 12 officers

60 garrisons attacked
74 weapons recovered
1 PC-7 Pilatus airplane shot down
1 A37-B airplane blown up and another damaged
1 helicopter shot down
27 helicopters damaged
6 commando trucks destroyed
26 trucks seriously damaged
6 machine gun nests destroyed
1 military launch sunk and 2 damaged
The URNG Advances!
　　　　　—Flier left after guerrillas burned a government truck,
　　　　　　　　　　　　　　　　September 1, 1989

As we settled into Nebaj, it proved to be laced with ex-guerrillas who had accepted the army's amnesty. Given the army's reputation for foul play, I was surprised they were still alive. But it served the army's interest, to show other EGP veterans that they could give themselves up. All had surrendered or been captured after leaving active duty, not while part of a combat unit, and they did not give the impression of being vanquished. To the contrary, they seemed to hold themselves more erect than anyone else in town. "Who's the better soldier?" I asked one. "Ah, the guerrilla combatant," he answered, "because while they die by ones and twos, soldiers die by ten or fifteen. The soldiers move only by day, not the combatants, they're ready [with an ambush] whenever the soldiers come out. Only a few guerrillas die."

　　Still, the stories of ex-combatants conformed to the narrative of disillusion expressed by other refugees within the army's pale. One ex-combatant was pregnant with the child of a guerrilla commander when she surrendered. For three years her job, she explained while bouncing her baby on her lap, was ambushing the army. Ana (not her real name) belonged to the cohort of guerrillas produced by the violence of the early 1980s. To avoid being killed by *envidia* (envy)—denunciation by a personal enemy to the army—she and her family escaped to the Army of the Poor.

Typical of this period, death came to Ana's family from all sides.

Back in Nebaj, an uncle was taken away by the army; three months later his body was thrown into the street. A brother who joined the EGP was killed fighting the army. Another brother, fed up with the guerrillas, died mysteriously as he was leaving for Nebaj. Her father, a maize buyer for the EGP, was killed when children accidentally discharged a combatant's weapon. As for her own children, the first two died in infancy, which she attributed to the neglect of their father the EGP officer. In October 1987, during an army offensive, Ana and her mother joined a hundred refugees who escaped from the EGP-controlled zone of Sumal. When the army discovered who she was, they dressed her up in a military uniform and photographed her for a propaganda poster. When I met her a year and a half later, she was being left in peace.

The EGP was now one of four revolutionary organizations in the Guatemalan National Revolutionary Union (URNG), the name on the fliers left behind on roads. But local units were still part of the Ho Chi Minh Front, one of the two *frentes* surviving from the seven that the EGP set up at its height. The other remaining front was named after Ernesto "Che" Guevara: it operated in the Ixcán lowlands to the north. Each of these two battalion-level formations was divided into two columns or companies, for a total of four: the one most active around Nebaj was the July 19, named after the anniversary of the Sandinista Revolution in Nicaragua. The Ho Chi Minh Front's other company bore the name of Fernando Hoyos Rodríguez, an ex-Jesuit priest who died fighting for the EGP in 1982. It tended to the east, around San Juan Cotzal and the Finca San Francisco.

Each company was supposed to have a hundred fighters, although actual strength in 1988–89 seems to have been less. There were also smaller formations that operated apart. These included the platoons, of which the Ho Chi Minh Front was supposed to have six with twenty persons each. They covered less distance than the companies and specialized in harassing army garrisons. Attached to the civil-political structure (to be described below) were the *fuerzas irregulares locales* (FIL), as many as fifteen to thirty reservists in each community who lived with their families, carried burdens for the guerrillas, and performed defensive tasks such as digging stakepits, but usually did not have firearms.

The majority of people carrying weapons were Ixils, with most of the rest K'iche's and Kaqchikels, the two largest Mayan language groups in the country. Ex-combatants usually described command in terms of multiethnic committees including, for example, an Ixil, a Kaqchikel, a K'iche', and a ladino. Command was exclusively Guatemalan except for two Cubans who, in the mid-1980s, performed an important function as "secretaries." *Comandantes* exercised authority at the level of the *dirección de frente*, while *mandos de columna* (also sometimes referred to as lieutenants) presided over the companies. *Mandos* (roughly, sergeants) and *jefes de escuadra* (corporals) commanded small units, whose fighters were addressed as *combatientes*.

No one was paid, ex-combatants insisted, and they were given nothing but shoes and a uniform. The majority of recruits were from the Ixil population in the montaña, including many who had lost parents in government kidnappings and massacres. No one claimed to have been conscripted, although several who were barely adolescents when they joined said they had been deceived by false promises. While a few combatants had carried arms for seven or eight years, turnover was high. Fighters were allowed to return to their families after putting in a request, although two ex-combatants harbored fears that *commandantes* might, subsequently, order one's quiet elimination. Women fighters were part of every EGP action I was told about, to the point that two male ex-combatants claimed that half or more of their units had been women, one reason being that they stood the hardship better. Also common were fighters who looked fifteen or less, a cohort to be found in the Guatemalan army as well, and probably every other armed force in Central America.

The feelings of Nebajeños about the Army of the Poor were complicated. The town was filled with the ghosts of persons who were missing but not necessarily dead, people who might be near but had not been seen, spoken to, or touched for the better part of a decade. The next cadaver the army dragged into town could be one of them. A term of humor and respect for the guerrillas was *boxnay*, the Ixil word for a root that is eaten in time of hunger and has the connotation of something hidden. Another was *canche* ("blondie"), ordinarily a term for gringos and fair-haired Guatemalans, which became an ironic reference to army claims that the guerrillas were led by foreigners. Knowing that a majority of combatants were Ixils, Nebajeños rarely expressed fear of the guerrillas, certainly less than they did of the army. But identification with the rebels was mixed with anger, over a war that seemed like it would never end. "This town used to be prettier before," an Ixil elder told me, waving at the surroundings. "But the guerrillas came to bother (*fregar*) us. Before there were aldeas. Now they are refugees. Now we have to patrol without pay, without rations, without anything."

The Guatemalan Army

Combatant: The organization has offered you triumph. Where are you?
What it really has given you are wounds, hunger, cold, fear. It has taken
you away from your family. Come and help us celebrate our fiestas.
　　　　　　—*Your brothers (sign on the path to Acul, June 1989)*

If the attitude of Ixils toward the Guatemalan army could be summed up in a few words, it would be "keep the beast calm." When Mayas learned to mimic the army's discourse in the early 1980s, visitors concluded that they were being confused or brainwashed. Evangelical churches were particularly suspect, as if they had the ability to obliterate consciousness of oppression. But on further acquaintance, such interpretations become impossible to sustain. Ixils had learned how to use the language of counterinsurgency, but it was not hard to elicit frank descriptions of how the army imposed itself in the early 1980s, and few or none could be said to share the army's point of view. Even ex-army sergeants, civil patrol leaders, and military commissioners recounted their experiences from the in-between position of the beleaguered civilian.

The army's discourse had a certain impact, but only when it spoke convincingly to Ixil experiences, that is, reinforced a conclusion they were already drawing themselves. One shared interpretation was that the guerrillas had "deceived" Ixils with their offer of an imminent new social order. *El error* of placing credence in the guerrillas explains the resulting *castigo* (punishment) administered by the army. Another contact between army propaganda and Ixil experience was the contrast between the "old" and "new" army. Needless to say, both were led by the same officers, the main difference being that the new army was more discriminate in its use of force. Yet this was a crucial difference for Ixils around the three towns, because it meant they could align themselves with the army with *más confianza* (greater confidence).

The security forces were never a monolith to Nebajeños, who learned to evaluate officers on whether they could be approached for personal appeals. Some are remembered as *muy humano* (humane), others as *matones* (killers), with a certain amount of disagreement stemming from the vagaries of individual experience. The different personas presented by officers and units also reflected the division of labor in a national security state. The S-5 or G-5 officer represents the socially conscious side of the army, the civic action (or psychological warfare) branch. These are the officers with college degrees, in charge of befriending villages and impressing journalists. S-5 troops in Nebaj always included women who specialized in reassuring newly arrived refugees, among them a Chajuleña who translated political talks.

Other officers were in charge of units dedicated to kidnapping, most notoriously the intelligence section (G-2 or S-2), which is feared and loathed in Nebaj even though, during my visits there, it was not being blamed for specific murders. The G-2 system is run from the highest levels and has Gestapo-style powers of surveillance over the army command structure. Its executioners are reputed to be captured guerrillas who joined to save their lives. However, many of the G-2's *especialistas*—"specialists" or civilian employees who work on a contract basis to be deniable—are probably just ex-soldiers with an aptitude for murder, the situation being further confused by their availability for freelance assassination. In Nebaj, one ex-soldier with G-2 ties offered to kill a personal enemy for a hundred dollars. While such men are immune from the courts, they are popularly believed to never leave the system alive. Even if this is not true, one reason for keeping them on a contract basis is to make them easy to eliminate should they become trapped and show signs of informing on higher-ups.

The army battalion headquartered in Nebaj was named the Kaibil Balaam Task Force, after a Mayan war god. The Guatemalan army was said to be the most effective counterinsurgency force in Central America, but around Nebaj in the late 1980s the troops did little but sit in hill forts. Officers exhorted the civil patrol to keep up its guard and go on long fruitless marches, but they rarely sent their own men after the latest guerrilla apparition. From the point of view of minimizing bloodshed, it was a commendable policy. When units did go on patrol, it was usually at the end of a tour, to get back to a main base, and they were likely to put civil patrollers in the lead as human buffers. The army suffered most of its casualties out on the new roads that had been built to control the area and were now the best place for guerrillas to stage ambushes. Army casualties were lower than the fantastic totals claimed by the EGP, but higher than the very occasional deaths reported to the Guatemalan press. From October 1988 to September 1989, at least seven soldiers were killed near the towns of Nebaj and Chajul without being reported in the press.[3]

Sophisticated military technology was not much in evidence. Troops usually took the field in trucks, then on foot, with a few Bell "Huey" helicopters ferrying commanders, transporting supplies, evacuating casualties, and sometimes providing fire support. The main weapon consisted of Israeli-made Galil assault rifles, known for their deadly spray at short range, but not for accuracy or range; in 1989 they were replaced by M-16s from the United States. Occasionally the army discharged a few rounds from its 105-mm howitzers into the surrounding mountains, or sent an A37 assault jet overhead on a sortie, but such displays of firepower were of little use against guerrillas.

The only target sitting in one place long enough to be aimed at were the montaña settlements beyond the army's control, civilians presumed (often accurately) to be supporting the guerrillas. In one illustrative month, according to the Guatemalan Church in Exile, the army dropped 103 artillery and mortar rounds on the Xeputul zone of refuge, wounding two young men and killing a mother and her child. In an offensive in March 1990, the Church in Exile reported from its local sources, a small fleet of helicopters and airplanes bombed, strafed, and rocketed civilian settlements day after day, forcing thousands to flee to surrounding heights and ravines.[4] Clearly, the main function of the army's firepower was to intimidate refugees beyond its control into giving themselves up.

The Civil Patrol

Civil Patroller: The constitution of the republic of Guatemala says, under Article 34, "The right of free association is recognized. No one is obliged

to associate with or form part of self-defense groups or associations. . . . ''
According to the law, no one is obliged to participate in the civil patrols.
But the army does not respect this and other rights of the people. Instead,
with threats and kidnappings, it obliges participation in the civil patrols
and commits many injustices.

Civil Patroller: Struggle for your rights to be respected! Join with your
neighbors and demand your rights! A people who organizes is a people
who triumphs. —*Guerrilla flier, 1988*

Entire human rights reports have been dedicated to the civil patrols.[5] In southern Quiché Department, a major struggle erupted in 1988 when thousands of men refused to continue patrolling. Guerrilla columns had disappeared from this part of the highlands, and patrol duty was especially onerous for the many campesinos taking up itinerant commerce. Supported by international human rights organizations, the Runujel Junam Council of Ethnic Communities (CERJ) took its stand on the 1985 constitution, which guaranteed the right not to patrol. Simultaneously, a widow's organization called CONAVIGUA (National Coordination of Guatemalan Widows) began to press for the excavation of clandestine cemeteries and protest abuses by civil patrol chiefs. The army's reaction was predictable: it encouraged the more loyal patrollers to threaten dissidents and, if they refused to conform, kill them. In a tragic reprise of how the army and the guerrillas set Mayas at each other's throats, the human rights campaign to enforce constitutional rights and uncover past crimes sharpened village conflicts.

The picture in Ixil country was different. In 1988–89 there was no visible human rights organizing, no open defiance, and little open discussion of the constitution. Nearly everyone resented being forced to patrol, some Ixils were becoming adept at dodging it, yet many described it as an unfortunate necessity. Why? Because four columns of the Army of the Poor continued to operate in northern Quiché, in contrast to the south where there were none. Were they to stop patrolling, village leaders explained, guerrillas would be free to contact the population again, and the army would return to kidnapping suspected infiltrators. Out of fear, many Ixils reluctantly supported the patrols as a form of protection from both sides, and they were rewarded with a certain precarious security. Despite the high level of EGP activity, there were no death squad murders or abductions in the three Ixil towns until December 1989 when, perhaps reacting to the disintegration of the civil patrol in Nebaj proper, hooded men wearing army boots executed a man said to have been speaking about his constitutional rights. Two months later, in February, a man and his son were extracted from their house at night and murdered by the same kind of group.

The fear motivating the patrol was most evident in Cotzal, as if *la situación* had not relaxed and little had changed since 1982. Even in town, men still did unpaid roadwork for the army and needed permission to go to the coast. To prevent villagers from selling goods to the guerrillas, they still had to buy a three-centavo authorization from the patrol to take their purchases home from market. The civil patrol chief in Cotzal was referred to as the *comandante*, in Nebaj a term reserved for army officers, and there were many complaints against him and his predecessors. Those who could not or would not patrol were accused of being subversive, sent to the army garrison, or thrown into jail. "*Puro Nicaragua*" and "*puro Cuba*" was the comment of one man whose family had been decimated by the EGP, by which he meant that the army regime in Cotzal was tantamount to communist totalitarianism.

My sources blamed the special rigor of the Cotzal patrol not just on the army but on the social relations between Cotzaleños. "Certainly the patrol is necessary," an ex-patrol commander said, in the midst of detailing the abuses of other men who had held the job. "If not, the guerrillas come into town and people start talking against each other. There's a lot of *envidia* here in Cotzal. If one has work, the others who don't have work envy him. If one is a butcher or a merchant, others are very envious. So that if guerrillas show up, the envious are capable of telling them, he's an informer for the army. Or of telling the army that he spoke with a guerrilla. This is why so many people died here." "There is *envidia* if we don't do our service," another Cotzaleño agreed. "The people say . . . that he gives food to the guerrillas. If we don't see him at the meeting, who knows what work he has? Who knows with whom he talks? He's like a ball in the street that no one picks up. If something happens, no one helps him. He who doesn't do his patrol, neither the patrol nor the army are going to worry about him, he'll be taken from his house and no one will care."

An unwanted civil patrol had, paradoxically, become an institution of solidarity.[6] Even in the town of Nebaj, where the patrol was disintegrating in 1988–89, many Ixil men still expected their peers to put up a show of cooperation. "We have problems here!" a patrol chief shouted in the midst of a shoving match with a resister (or shirker, depending on your point of view). "Nobody here is paid, I'm not paid, we have to stick together! He won't patrol, instead he drinks. If he doesn't want to help, he should take himself to some other place that's better." For the patrol chief, the issue was helping the community survive a confrontation between larger forces, a buffering function illustrated by the patrol's occasional challenges to abusive soldiers.[7]

In the late 1980s the civil patrols continued to be mandatory in all the aldeas, as well as in the towns of Cotzal and Chajul. Only in the town of Nebaj were they falling apart. Town-dwellers were not as afraid of contacts with guerrillas as villagers were. They were also emboldened by the example of Nebaj's many ladinos, as well as of Ixil schoolteachers and evangelical pastors, who had all taken advantage of the country's new constitution in 1985 to stop patrolling. Although Nebajeños did not speak out on the constitution, they were becoming aware of the discrepancy with the army's demands. "If we read the constitution, they kill us," an Ixil student said drawing a line across his throat.

The first conscientious objectors in Nebaj were the Jehovah's Witnesses, a small group organized by two ladino mentors who arrived around 1987. Throughout the world, the Witnesses are known for refusing to submit to military conscription or even salute the flag, in the conviction that nationalist ideologies violate the commandment against setting up false gods. An awed squad leader told me how half a dozen men from his cantón refused to patrol "because of what it says in their book." Full of trepidation, he went along when they were summoned to the base, where the colonel threatened to take them in a helicopter and drop them into the Ixcán to join their guerrilla friends. "Very well," my source quoted the Witness spokesman, "if that was the will of the Lord, it was fine with him, he was ready."

The more typical Nebajeño approach is illustrated by the organization of a Red Cross chapter, into which considerable civic energy was sunk in 1988–89. To foreigners being solicited for contributions, the new organization seemed a wasteful duplication of the rescue service already provided by the volunteer fire company. It was only after innumerable meetings, ceremonies, and fund-raising events that the new Red Cross workers—mainly Ixil youths—refused to continue patrolling. "They can't touch the Red Cross because it has international ties," one of the ladino organizers explained.

Until 1987, the Nebaj civil patrol had been organized by "companies," each drawn from all over town. That year I watched soldiers round up all the men in each neighborhood, for meetings to reorganize the patrol on a cantón by cantón basis. Henceforth, the men of each neighborhood would serve in their own cantonal patrol—thirteen in all—and elect their own officers—except for the three top commanders who would still be named by the army. Unfortunately for the army, the cantonal leaders whom it intended to whip their neighbors into line instead became co-conspirators. "There are times we pick up the rifle [from army headquarters where weapons are handed out] and just go to sleep in our houses," a cantonal chief confided. "At five in the morning we go around knocking on doors, get together again and return the rifles. That's it. Before this couldn't be done, because the men came from different cantóns and some might talk. But in the same cantón, they're not going to talk and, if they do, worse for them."

One Ixil friend, forced to become a squad chief because he could read and write, was rarely successful in persuading his men to report for their biweekly patrol. If it wasn't a bad foot, then it was a trip to Santa Cruz del Quiché or a pilgrimage to the Christ of Chajul. "Some say they've been operated on, others haven't gotten out of bed, others have to attend a wedding, everyone looks for a way out," the hapless Domingo reported after yet another failed roundup. Even on duty, patrollers were less likely to tote rifles than sprawl on the grass crocheting handbags for tourists. They never tired of pointing out the contrast between bored teen-age soldiers sitting inside army forts, while civilians who were older and had families to support were snatched from their work and sent on long, exhausting marches through the countryside without pay or provisions. There were bitter jokes about how the army liked hanging around town so it could be protected by the people.

When I left Nebaj in 1989, the town's cantonal patrol chiefs were voicing complaints with increasing boldness. Instead of appealing to the constitution, they pointed out obvious inequities in the struggle against subversion. Why didn't ladinos patrol? Or the Ixil teachers who received such enviable government salaries? Army officers responded with thinly veiled kidnapping threats. Don't come to us if unknown men start showing up at night and snatching you out of your houses, they warned. "If something happens to my soldiers," an officer threatened a cantonal chief reporting that his men no longer wanted to patrol, "they're going to hang." By the following year, some cantóns no longer patrolled, from others only five or six men could be mustered, and the head of the patrol since the early 1980s turned in his resignation.

Life in the Zones of Refuge

Our struggle is one of resistance against capture, persecution, bombardment, strafing, and the imposition of militarization by the army. We are in resistance here, creating a new way of living in liberty and equality, until in all our communities and the whole country true democracy is constructed.

—Coordinating Commission, Communities of Population in Resistance of the Sierra, 1991

Eighteen kilometers north of the town of Nebaj rise the rocky outcrops of Mount Sumal, six thousand feet above surrounding valleys. It is a huge, pitiless massif, on the flanks of which travelers can spend days struggling in and out of ravines thousands of feet deep. This is the height that Jackson Steward Lincoln climbed in 1939, hoping to glimpse a legendary city of the Mayas in the lowlands to the north, only to catch his death of pneumonia. In 1985 it was the EGP-controlled area that two North Americans were trying to reach when they were killed by civil patrollers from a neighboring municipio. For the Guerrilla Army of the Poor, its zone of refuge on Sumal was code-named "Namibia" or "Vietnam." Until the army offensive that ended it, more than five thousand people lived among the crevices and shoulders of Sumal, looking down on the world every morning and wrapped in clouds every afternoon. Even the briefest walk from one place to the next demonstrates what an effective refuge it was, a place whose inhabitants could not have been run down until they decided to give themselves up.

Sumal was one of three refugee zones defended by the EGP along the northern rim of Ixil country. Another was the mysterious Xeputul, located downriver from the Finca San Francisco and code-named "Camagüey" or "Tanzania." No refugees from there ever arrived in Nebaj, nor could anyone tell me about it except for a young ex-combatant who said that few people lived there, a claim belied by the efficiency with which the guerrillas repelled army and civil patrol incursions. The third zone of refuge was Amajchel, north of Chajul in warm, lower country the guerrillas code-named "Saygon."

In the early 1980s fifty thousand people may have taken shelter in the montaña of northern Quiché.[8] Judging from available information, less than half that number remained a decade later. From Sumal and Amajchel alone, the army offensives between October 1987 and the end of 1989 extracted at least five thousand people.[9] In mid-1992 an official of the communities of population in resistance said that there were about seventeen thousand internal refugees left in the sierra with another six thousand in the Ixcán.

The CPRs of the Sierra, on the northeastern edge of Ixil country, included Chajuleños, Cotzaleños, and K'iche's, along with a smattering of Q'eqchi's, Q'anjob'als, Kaqchikels, and ladinos. But according to refugees passing through the army's hands, a large majority were Ixils speaking the Nebaj dialect. Indeed, 72 percent of 766 refugees registered by the government between May and November 1988 were Nebajeños.[10] According to the CPR representative quoted above, twelve thousand of the seventeen thousand people in the montaña settlements were Ixils. These included some two thousand families of Nebajeños, two hundred families from Chajul, and only fifty families from Cotzal, plus a thousand families of K'iche's, three hundred families of ladinos, and a hundred families of Kaqchikels.

Why such a preponderance of Nebajeños? The Cotzaleños had been the first to join the guerrillas, a former EGP district director told me, but were also among the first to quit the montaña. As for the Chajules, fewer had joined the guerrillas in the first place, and most of them had also returned home within a year or two. That left the Nebajeños. Some had fled from the town center, others were from every corner of the municipio. But the majority seemed to be from the pre-violence population of Sumal and Amajchel. When trapped by the army counteroffensive in 1981–82, most stayed with the guerrillas for protection and continued to cultivate their land even after the army destroyed their houses.

Conceivably Sumal and Amajchel had been organized longer and more effectively by the EGP than the rest of Ixil country. What is certain is that they were harder for army troops to reach than Salquil, much of whose population surrendered in 1982–84. Geography gave them more time to escape army patrols, made it harder for dissidents to escape, and helped the guerrillas make army patrols so hazardous that the two areas remained what the army called a "red zone."

The three refuge zones in Ixil country were, like the EGP's fighting units there, administered by the Ho Chi Minh Front. Ex-militants describe EGP civil political authority in terms of multiethnic committees which, at the level of the front, consisted of a platoon-sized unit of eight directors and their staff. From this level of organization descended a hierarchy of three regions (the same as the three refuge zones), districts (five or six per region), and localities (three or four per district), each presided over by a committee whose three to four members supervised education and political formation, support for the guerrillas, and other community assignments. The lowest-level committees, at the level of neighborhoods, were originally known as *comités clandestinos locales* (CCLs). Disputes were adjudicated by an influential "area committee" whose position in the hierarchy was unclear, but to which we will return in chapter 9.

In practice, resistance to EGP authority created a spectrum of involvement ranging from considerable to minimal.[11] One conflict surfacing in refugee testimony involved the traditional pattern of authority, that is, domination of the young by their elders, with which the EGP felt obliged to break.[12] Hence the not-infrequent *ajusticiamientos* (executions) of principales in the early 1980s, on the accusation that they were passing information to the army.[13] Nor was the conflict confined to well-off traditionalists like Sebastián Guzmán. "Some of the kids of neighbors had ideas put in their heads by the guerrillas, who wanted them to come work for the revolution," stated a principal who became a catechist and spent several years in the montaña after the army kidnapped his son, a well-known cooperative leader. "I warned a neighbor whose children had been recruited: 'Now it's the kids who are in charge.' Now they think they're the big ones, forgetting how their parents suffered. It's a question of who has the right to command, parents or their children. We were always afraid that we would die because of a son or daughter."

According to refugees from Sumal who spent seven or eight years under EGP authority, their support for the revolution withered as the hardship dragged on. "They began to announce that we would work together," recalls a man from Sumal Chiquito who surrendered together with sixty-five other people in May 1988. " 'Because if you help us, we will have to help you.' One or two years passed in which the people were in agreement. But then the people began to refuse, because they no longer had a file for sharpening their hoes, machetes, and axes. This is why they protested. What do we get out of the collective if there is no longer a file for sharpening? There were no longer clothes, hats, sandals. But the subversives advised not to worry, because each year the movement advances, because we're shooting soldiers by the group, and little by little these soldiers will be finished off, and we will come to triumph in Guatemala."

The most common complaint against the guerrillas was the lack of trade goods that the people used to obtain in town. "At first the people were content," states another man from Sumal Chiquito, "but then they became discontent (*inconformes*), over promises that were not fulfilled. [The guerrillas] said that clothes would come that didn't come. They said that salt would arrive that did not arrive. They had salt but the population, no. . . . The civilian population no longer wanted to continue struggling, the combatants, yes." "The population began to make many demonstrations [of discontent]," says an ex-district director from Sumal. " 'This has to be confronted politically,' " his superiors said. "But the people are no longer satisfied with politics, they want to see practice," the ex-director told me, having resigned his post two years before surrendering to the army.

By 1989, most of the new refugees being brought to Nebaj were from Amajchel. The warm, fertile land here is located on the last escarpment before the drop to the Ixcán, and before the violence it was attracting

Ixil colonists, particularly land-poor evangelicals. "We were working peacefully," a prewar settler recalls. "We did not know what was going to happen. But there were some organizers who established the new law. It was 1981 when the war began. Old men, women, children, widows arrived. When the organizers showed up, they told us that people were going to come and that we should prepare food. So we did. Some four hundred arrived the first time, from Xix and Xolcuay in 1981. Then thousands arrived, from Sacsihuán, Ixtupil, Trapiches, in 1985."

"We were somewhat sad, because we did not know this new law," says another prewar Amajchel settler. "The road was closed, we could no longer leave, because we used to come here [to Nebaj] for [buying] things. Almost half the people were not in agreement, the other half yes. The [EGP-appointed] committees said: 'Sowing has to be done, a collective organized, we're going to call everyone together. . . .' But it was not work as we do it, as individuals, but together, in communal work. Even if one did not want this, he was obliged to. If not, there was punishment. . . . tied up for the night with a rope. That is why people were afraid and followed the order that the committee gave."

The majority of refugees I talked to in Nebaj did not describe growing food for the guerrillas in such a negative light. But the EGP's system of work groups, as well as mandatory sentry duty, shows that both sides obliged civilians to provide labor and military service, not just the army. Certainly, there was room for negotiation in EGP territory: according to another Amajchel refugee, his group of fifteen people eventually refused to continue collective work and the guerrillas agreed to buy food from them, a practice that seems to have become increasingly common as time went on. Other refugees also spoke of successfully confronting the guerrillas with collective demands, including being allowed to surrender to the army.

But according to refugees in Nebaj, before the guerrillas began to accede to such demands, they killed Ixils for conspiring to give themselves up. The height of such killing apparently followed the losses to Ríos Montt's amnesty, but before impatience with the war became more or less universal. From 1983 to 1985, according to a village cooperative leader who spent years in the montaña, the guerrillas and the army killed civilians "nearly equally." Anyone who surrendered would, of course, become a source of information for soldiers attacking the holdouts. How many civilians were killed by the EGP is impossible to say, but the ease with which Nebajeños produce names and dates suggests that they number in the hundreds.[14]

The Continuing Army Offensive

Civil Patroller:
Don't cut the corn
Don't persecute your relatives
And you won't fall into our traps.
Don't put your life in danger!
Long live the URNG
(read and pass this to your neighbors or trustworthy friends)
—*Guerrilla flier, 1988*

In late 1987 and early 1988, the army laid waste the EGP-administered settlements of Sumal. Following bombardments to shake up the population, thousands of soldiers and civil patrollers ascended to burn the shelters, destroy the crops, and capture whomever they could. The offensive was the army's greatest success since organizing the civil patrols. Thousands of campesinos were captured, other thousands gave themselves up. By the time my family and I arrived in late 1988, Sumal was no more. Removed to Nebaj, the captured refugees were organized into civil patrols and—sometimes within months—sent home again, this time to build new army-controlled settlements. Meanwhile, roughly half the population of Sumal retreated with the guerrillas to Amajchel, joining the thousands of refugees already there. The army was quick to follow and by 1989 there was a battalion dug into various hill-forts in the middle of the EGP's zone of refuge, reinforced periodically by civil patrollers marched up from the Ixil towns.

When asked about their policy, army officers painted a benign game, of waiting for refugees to come down out of the surrounding bush of their own accord. Thanks to the Guatemalan Church in Exile, a different picture emerges, from the reports of montaña communities themselves. Troops from hill-forts take advantage of darkness or rainstorms to steal up on dwellings only kilometers away, protected mainly by lookouts and broken terrain. Something causes the troops to start shooting, the majority of the people get away, some are captured, a few are killed. Before the troops withdraw, they destroy any huts, belongings, and crops in reach.

Such tactics were corroborated by the people brought to Nebaj. "Nothing is left anymore because the soldiers and patrollers burned everything" was one man's description that summed up everyone else's. "The soldiers and patrollers arrived every little while and no longer permitted us to cultivate. They dropped bombs, burned the forest, destroyed the yucca, the sugar cane, the maize, they chopped it down with machetes." It was the familiar combination of force and persuasion, with the army alternating its scorched-earth tactics with offers of amnesty from small airplanes, including messages of reassurance from relatives who had already been captured.[15]

In Nebaj, refugees explained the distinction between being *agarrado* (grabbed) by the army or civil patrol and *entregando* (surrendering). Sometimes the distinction was rather fine. Surrendering invariably followed a process of disillusionment punctuated by the shells and raids of government troops. In army accounts, of course, refugees invariably "escape" while in revolutionary accounts they are always "captured." In Nebaj those who had been "grabbed" or captured by force were often, by the time they talked to me several months later, reinterpreting their experience in terms of surrender (e.g., we were thinking of surrendering when they grabbed us). Surrenders in the midst of an attack might be expedited by patrollers rushing up and shouting amnesty in Ixil. Or refugees might simply wait, for sufficiently calm patrollers or soldiers to appear, and finally stop running way. "If the civilians, the patrol comes, we won't flee," some decided. But there were always others determined to escape, who fled deeper into the mountains.

Some of the families coming into army hands remained in Amajchel, clustered half a kilometer below the army base in a new resettlement. The purpose was to show the thousands of people in the surrounding hills that the army had not killed its new charges. To further demonstrate the army's good intentions, the families were showered with food supplies, tin roofing, and tools brought in by helicopter, including an occasional U.S. Army Chinook or Blackhawk sent by the U.S. Southern Command in Panama. As a result, the refugees ate better than the soldiers. The Guatemalan army is notorious for failing to feed its troops, especially at remote posts to which supply lines break down. "Look at us and who do you think is the Army of the Poor?" a hollow-eyed major told one visitor, who watched a soldier sell his underpants to a refugee for two pieces of bread.

The Special Commission for Aid to Refugees

Nebaj no longer exists, the church no longer exists, the people all dead or gone—this is what the guerrillas tell the people in the montaña. That if they go to Nebaj, they are sure to die. —Returned refugee, 1989

The efficiency of the army's offensive against Sumal was not matched by any preparations to care for the refugees it created. During late 1987 and early 1988, hundreds of refugees at a time were kept in the Nebaj army compound or nearby buildings, many of them seriously ill from exposure to the elements and bad sanitation, with the crowded condi-tions encouraging epidemics. Civilian relief workers were over-whelmed.[16] To handle another class of refugees—those returning from Mexico, mainly to Huehuetenango and the Ixcán—the government had recently set up the Special Commission for Aid to Refugees (CEAR). The people being forced out of the mountains in Ixil country were in more desperate straits than the returnees from Mexico. Yet CEAR's main funder, the United Nations High Commissioner for Refugees (UNHCR), refused to allocate money for them. By charter, UNHCR's mission was confined to refugees who had crossed an inter-national frontier, to avoid the even larger problem of people displaced within their own countries.

This left the new CEAR program in Nebaj hobbling along on alloca-tions from other government agencies. During its first months in Nebaj, twenty-six children died in its care, mainly from pneumonia. By the time we arrived in October 1988, the epidemics had been contained and the refugees moved to a compound on the edge of town. Over the next year Camp Xemamatze housed a fluctuating population of one hun-dred to two hundred refugees who had been brought there by the army and would be released after three months. Security was light. Sometimes a few soldiers were lounging around. On other occasions, there was only an unarmed civil patroller—one of the internees—sitting in the sentry hut and crocheting a bag. One such patroller explained the rules of internment as: (1) asking for permission to leave, and (2) not coming back drunk. Toward the end of their three months, men were allowed to work as day laborers, and I interviewed at least seven over lunch in town.

Keeping an eye on the Xemamatze refugees were Ixil "interpreters" or "guides" working for the army's civic action/psywar branch. All four at the camp in late 1988 were disgusted ex-guerrillas who had not been paid their miserable Q90 monthly salaries in so long that they were about to quit. One who remained a few months longer, said to be an ex-EGP lieutenant, left the army's employ after telling internees that they would go to hell unless they turned evangelical. According to a CEAR worker, who was disgusted at the interpreters for encouraging internees to demand pay for doing chores, the interpreters were informers and brainwashers. What the Guatemalan army called "political reeducation" had an Orwellian ring to it, but at Xemamatze the process did not seem very rigorous, with more time invested in soccer matches than political talks.

None of the Xemamatze internees whom I interviewed, mainly away from the camp in town, had serious complaints about how they were being treated.[17] They were measuring the camp against their years of being persecuted by the army in the montaña, against EGP warnings that rape and death awaited captives in Nebaj as it had in the early 1980s, and against the shock of being captured. One sign of how well the soft regime served the army were the internees who returned to Amajchel to persuade their relatives and neighbors to surrender. At the end of 1988, ten CEAR refugees were said to be away on such *comisiones*, taken there by helicopter, then left alone to take their chances with the guerrillas. One man I interviewed had been captured in February 1989: by the time I talked to him three months later, he had already been back to Amajchel twice, had brought out two groups totaling 109 people, and was arranging for the surrender of a third group of 42 people. Sixty refugees in all had gone out on such missions, a CEAR worker estimated, and some 10 percent had not returned, with a few rumored to have been killed by the guerrillas.

The Xemamatze refugees were most anxious about their families still in the montaña, many having become separated from spouses, children, or parents. They were also anxious about how they would make a living after leaving the camp. All their possessions had been lost in the army's offensives. While the United Nations was providing returnees from Mexico with start-up aid, internal refugees were getting almost nothing. The most common destination after leaving the camp was therefore the coast, to earn money to buy clothes and cooking implements before joining the rest of their aldea for the extremely tough move back to the land. Three relatively easy months at Xemamatze were a lure to return to the grind of peasant existence on the army's terms.

Another unknown for the refugees, especially those who had fought for the EGP, was whether the army would continue to respect their lives once the amnesty no longer served an immediate purpose. I interviewed eight ex-combatants in 1989, but most had returned only within the last year or two. Having been interrogated in army compounds and photographed for army files, anyone the army distrusted could be kidnapped at a future date. Nebajeños already told the story of a bilingual teacher named Miguel Brito who had worked for the guerrillas, accepted amnesty, and been warned by friends to make a new life for himself somewhere else. Just before Christmas 1987, he was called to army headquarters to receive a gift of maize and instead was forced to become a guide for an army patrol. The patrol fell into an ambush, a sergeant and a lieutenant were killed, and Miguel Brito never returned.

No civilian authorities in Guatemala, least of all the Special Commission for Aid to Refugees, dared challenge the army. Hopes in amnesty were predicated on a law-abiding officer corps, elements of which were, during our time in Nebaj, staging coup attempts in the capital and committing a variety of human rights violations around the country. No reports of missing Xemamatze internees came to light during our stay, although I did hear of a young man who was beaten up for resisting induction into the civil patrol.

The following year, in September 1990, army officers took away a young K'iche' woman whose family had become civil patrol resisters.

The woman's home village, Parraxtut in nearby Sacapulas, was about to become known for mobbing a government human rights commission. María Tiu Tojín's last words to fellow refugees on their way to the CEAR camp at Xemamatze were "I think they're going to kill me." She and her infant were never seen again. Soon the director of the CEAR camp, a former army cadet on good terms with many officers, was seeking political asylum in Canada because of his role in reporting the case.[18]

The Resettlement Villages

> *While the State Department calls them "half-way houses" and "rural settlements," they have been called "concentration camps" by everyone from rural religious workers to Nobel laureate Adolfo Pérez Esquivel. And they are models of nothing except confinement and misery. Where barbed wire and overt army presence are no longer necessary, fear and mistrust of one's neighbors provide sufficient control over villagers' movements.*
> *—Jean-Marie Simon, Guatemala: Eternal Spring,*
> *Eternal Tyranny, 1987*

The model villages of Ixil country were not detention and reeducation centers, contrary to some reports. Nor were they concentration camps, at least as this term was redefined by the Nazis in the Second World War.[19] Nor did they involve mixing refugees with members of other language groups or sending them to strange new territories. Technically, they are best described as nucleated resettlements to bring campesinos as close as possible to their fields while keeping the guerrillas at a distance. Life in them usually seemed grim, but I was surprised to find refugees in town petitioning the army to build new ones.

Besides the twelve model villages set up by the army as of 1985,[20] sixty more resettlements popped up during the next five years, after groups of refugees asked the army for permission to return to their land and agreed to organize their own civil patrol. Many of these people had been with the guerrillas only months before, and some of the resettlements were so well organized that they seemed to have carried over lessons learned in the montaña. In the army-controlled aldea of

The model village of Pulay, 1987

Amajchel, former montaña-dwellers continued to extract cane from a communal sugar plantation and work in fields assigned by the group, as they had under EGP administration.

The concentrated settlements were a success for the army because they served the needs of the population, not just because they regimented it. Human rights groups focused on the repressive function of the resettlements, which the inhabitants indeed resented. But the only reason soldiers had destroyed their former scattered homesteads was to get at the EGP, whom Ixils also resented. Only the pressure of living "between two fires" can explain their willingness, even eagerness, to live in the resettlements. Ecologically, they wanted to live as close as possible to their fields and firewood, to minimize the daily trek up mountainsides. To cover their subsistence deficit, moreover, the majority of Ixils still needed to go to the plantations every year, which the army could permit but the EGP could not.[21] Finally, there was what the army had taught Ixils to call the problem of "security," the wish to minimize future contacts with the guerrillas and the inevitable reprisals.

The original model villages of 1983–85 were, on the drawing board, imposing quadrangular layouts of wood-plank houses serviced by an electrical grid, potable water taps, schools, health clinics, markets, even police substations and telegraph offices. Together they were to become "development poles," thriving centers of production and commerce assisted by public and private agencies working together under a bureaucratic creation called the *Coordinadora*.[22] For better or worse, the energy to build the model villages—much of it provided by the Nebaj civil patrol, which was forced to trudge out day after day, week after week, to provide unpaid labor—ran out after the first twelve were in place. While achieving the physical layout, or at least the rough outline thereof, none of the settlements progressed much further toward the full, fantastic vision. As for genuine development assistance—that is, providing small-scale loans to help people produce and earn more—there was little. Economically, the model villages were dead except insofar as inhabitants were able to revive prewar agriculture and crafts.

The second generation of resettlements were less quadrangular but continued to satisfy the army's security criteria. Except for occasional donations, returning villagers were left to shift for themselves until 1988, when the Christian Democratic administration of President Vinicio Cerezo (1986–1991) launched a new drive, dubbed the *Multisectorial*, to coordinate the efforts of dozens of private and public agencies. While the Multisectorial succeeded in concentrating resources on eight or so villages—again, the grid of standardized housing, school, and so forth—dozens of others remained on waiting lists for even basic assistance, particularly tin roofing, to the point that many families spent several rainy seasons under plastic sheeting in a bronchitis-inducing climate. Like the army, the Multisectorial emphasized physical infrastructure, especially the expensive public buildings beloved by contractors and politicians for the lucrative kickbacks they provided. Of actual help to build up production and income, there was still rather little. While various public and private agencies had plausible schemes for experimenting with new crops, buying handlooms, and financing new cooperatives, usually they lacked an operational budget to do much.

Refugees faced their most vulnerable period during the months when they returned home to rebuild, before harvesting the first maize crop. In the best of cases, agencies provided building material and technical help while the returning villagers provided the labor, ideally compensated by the standard local wage (approximately U.S. $1.15 per day) or equivalent in foodstuffs. In the worst of cases, villagers returned to their little patch of scorched earth with nothing but a few M-1 rifles from the army, threats ringing in their ears from the nearest lieutenant, and a bit of maize and plastic sheeting from the parish priest. Amid the coming and going of dozens of institutions dedicated to rebuilding Ixil country, the most consistent source of emergency aid for returning refugees was the one based in Rome that had been there for four centuries.

The physical effort required to rebuild was tremendous. Consider the skimpy maize diets on which Ixil villagers based their energy expenditures—the other staple of the traditional Mesoamerican diet, black beans, being all too often out of reach—and their sobbing exertion was a miracle of human metabolism. The trails to off-road villages were lined with innumerable wads of spat-out sugar cane being devoured by ants. On the trail up to one barren, cloud-wrapped ridge, I met a skinny ten-year-old boy who was carrying his own weight in two roofing beams, a fact I verified by lifting first his load and then him.

However poor these people had been before the war, they had always been able to return from the plantations to solid adobe-and-tile houses stocked with spare clothes, blankets, and tools, surrounded by domestic animals, and proximate to maize fields. Now they had lost everything down to their cooking utensils. At Sumal Grande, high in the mist of what had been, a year and a half before, an EGP stronghold, I found a new settlement where roofing was so scarce that the people only thatched the hut serving as a Catholic chapel when clergy were expected. When the visit was over, they removed the thatch to cover their houses.

Villagers rebuilding their homes faced heavy, contradictory demands on their labor from the civil patrol, from official development projects and private ones, at the same time that they needed to put in their crops and go to the plantations to earn cash. Every time a contractor's truck passed through, an aldea could lose a few more inhabitants to the coast. To prevent entire villages from leaving for the plantations, the army ordered the civil patrols to maintain a minimum strength, so that more men could not go until others came back. Construction projects came to a halt when the army ordered civil patrols out on sweeps.

Even after the hardships of getting in the first harvest, resettled villagers did not necessarily eat as well as they had under the EGP. "With the guerrillas there was always something to eat," a village official in Sumal Grande claimed, apparently because the population lived farther apart, making it possible to cultivate a larger area. Living close to their fields had also helped farmers protect their crops from wild pigs, an impossibility after they were concentrated at a single location. But once in town, refugees denied that they had been better off in the montaña. They cited the impossibility of going to the plantations to earn money, the lack of medicine, clothes, and salt, and of course the army's raids.

The condition for being allowed to return was, in the words of a lieutenant, "that no coyotes get in there with you." That is, villagers had to maintain a civil patrol, live close together, and make sure that the guerrillas could not quietly pressure or persuade a family to collaborate with them. "We know that some of you have the idea of helping the subversion," a lieutenant told patrollers resettling at Trapiches in 1989. "But we're going to know, because nothing is hidden, and we'll take drastic measures."

The great temptation was to trade with the guerrillas, a proposition made when the latter stopped Ixils on trails. "Bring me sugar or a pair of pants and I'll pay you well," they said. There were stories about how so-and-so had profited from business dealings with the EGP, to the point of capitalizing a permanent stall in the marketplace. I heard of a furious debate in one village over whether to go for the money or tell the army. Trading with the EGP was extremely dangerous: in 1988–89 there were at least two nocturnal encounters in which guerrilla buyers and their trading partners were trapped with mortal consequences. In the Chajul case, one of the surreptitious merchants taken away by the army was an ex-member of the town council who was considered well-off. His motives for helping the guerrillas did not appear to be ideological: a son was in the army and he had just run for town council on the ticket of the right-wing National Liberation Movement. Two other men killed near Ixil towns were, quite possibly, fathers from the montaña trying to meet the needs of their children for salt and clothes.

In the fields surrounding the resettlements, still dotted with adobe ruins from the previous settlement pattern, nocturnal activity was considered evidence of trading with the EGP. Another zone of ambiguity and danger was the trail from Chajul to the Finca La Perla, reopened in 1987–88 but still subject to guerrilla overtures and army paranoia.

"If you don't leave your load [with them], the guerrillas accuse you of being an army guide, " a K'iche' merchant from Xix complained. "If you do leave the load, [the army] will say you're helping the guerrillas. At first, the army just investigates. But among campesinos there is much envy. It's very possible that, when one falls into the hands of the guerrillas, others have something against him, they can accuse him of being a guerrilla."

The same kind of dilemmas were created by cattle rustling. In one case, a Nebaj civil patrol leader was caught butchering a stolen cow, but conventionally such losses were attributed to the guerrillas. Unfortunately, because guerrillas usually pay for what they take, any bereft owner could be suspected of having invented a theft to cover up a sale.

Prolonged Popular War

Have you forgotten about us? Never forget about us because we're still committed to the struggle. The war is never going to end because we are even shooting down airplanes. We are not making war against the civil defenders but with the military. If you realize that we are passing near the village, don't start a shoot-out with us. Even if you realize that we are beside the trail, we don't want problems with you. Pass on by, don't bother us, because if you bother us, we'll finish you off. There are thousands of us, we're not just one or two hundred. Don't insult or mistreat us. Don't trust the soldiers. We have to finish them off to end the war.

—Guerrillas to Ixil travelers, 1989

Please let us pass because you're burning us, because we don't have communications with you anymore. Because then the military causes us lots of problems when word leaks out that we were together with you. We're not thinking about you. You're the ones who are attacking us on the trail. Please let us pass. Better that you change your route because we don't want to meet you.　　　　　　*—Ixil travelers to guerrillas, 1989*

Refugee family that has just returned to
Batzchocolá under army control, 1989

By 1988–89 Nebajeños most often saw the guerrillas along roads, as they stopped trucks to buy food, clothing, and canvas tarps. The stepped-up requisitioning reflected the erosion of the EGP's agricultural base, the people in the montaña who had supplied it with maize. I was never in the right place at the right time, but the guerrillas were usually described as polite and nonthreatening, insisting on what they wanted but almost always paying for it, sometimes generously. In fact, the wads of cash displayed at roadblocks were proverbial, as if the guerrillas were advertising their prowess as trading partners. But only discipline and a supply of cash stood between them and a common fate for unsuccessful rebels, that of turning into bandits.

Living in Nebaj forced me to conclusions I would have preferred to avoid. One was that the Guatemalan army had a remarkable ability to turn survivors of its massacres, indeed guerrilla supporters, into the mainstay of its counterinsurgency operation. This was illustrated in the late 1980s when the army allowed inhabitants of the first concentrated villages—huge antiecological agglomerations of as many as seven hundred families—to disperse across the landscape into much smaller settlements where farmers could live closer to their fields. Obviously, villages as small as twenty-five households[23] could never muster enough civil patrollers to keep out the guerrillas by force. So why did the army allow it?

A civic action officer had an explanation. The army previously had to concentrate rural households because, scattered as they were, guerrillas could intimidate and co-opt them one at a time. Now smaller villages would suffice, Captain Gómez said, because the people had learned the high cost of subversion. So long as households clustered together, they would be able to watch out for each other's security;[24] that is, guerrillas could not visit houses without being detected. Now the army was relying on social control; it could trust Ixils to turn in neighbors who were endangering their alliance with the army.

The army's version of events in Ixil country is, for the most part, not very credible. Local testimony usually contradicts its claims that dead civilians were actually armed guerrillas, that it was the EGP who burned all those aldeas, that the inhabitants spent seven years in the montaña because they were kidnapped, and that the civil patrols are purely voluntary. Yet the army's claims do make contact with popular experience in two important ways. First, when Ixils echo the army's theme that guerrillas "deceived" them, they are also describing their own reaction to the years of hardship that followed the EGP's promises. Let us recall that the Army of the Poor offered Ixils "a new law" that would end discrimination and exploitation. The guerrillas also said that villagers would be able to defend themselves against the army and, organized into the EGP, win the war in short order. Instead, the army's punishments became more devastating, to the point of discrediting the "new law" and obliging Ixils to return to the "old law," which had superior force behind it.

This brings us to the second way in which the army's claims have communicated with Ixil experience. Once the army began to prevail, it geared its strategy to the needs of peasants by resettling them in the vicinity of their land and allowing them to go to the plantations to earn cash. It made itself the champion of returning to a more or less normal existence, in contrast to the guerrillas, who could now be blamed for disrupting the ever-precarious efforts of peasants to earn a living. While Ixils around the three towns have not adopted the army's point of view, they do accept its definition of what is possible in these two basic respects because it is corroborated by their own experience of the realities of power.

SIX

The Holy Ghost in Northern Quiché

Catholic priest officiating at a procession for a saint

"Look," I told them, "I don't want to give information to anyone. Not to the army or to you either. Because, I'm telling you, I'm not against anyone. I'm not against you and I'm not against the soldiers. I'm not your friend nor am I the friend of the army. The only friend I have is Jesus Christ."

"And if the soldiers find you, what are you going to tell them?" they asked me.

"I won't tell them anything either," I said. "I don't want you to go off and kill someone because of my word. And I don't want you to die because of my word. None of that. I'm not on the side of anyone except Christ."

—Pentecostal pastor to guerrillas, 1981

IN just two years, from the murder and expulsion of Catholic clergy to the presidency of Efraín Ríos Montt, born-again religion became the dominant form of religious expression in Ixil country. In Cotzal and Nebaj, pentecostal congregations became the most visible, active religious bodies while in Chajul a form of Catholicism influenced by pentecostalism, the charismatic renewal, occupied the same position. One pastor helped organize the Cotzal civil patrol; another led a mass defection of refugees from guerrilla control in Salquil Grande. Missionaries from the Summer Institute of Linguistics and Ríos Montt's congregation, the Church of the Word, worked closely with the army during this crucial period in 1982–83, their aid to refugees becoming an important part of the pacification program.

The intervention of evangelical missionaries led to an outcry, and not just from exiled Catholic clergy, because it seemed to make them complicit in mass murder. Fortunately, the army did not subsequently butcher the refugees attracted by the missionaries, strengthening the latter's argument that they were helping Ríos Montt ameliorate the situation and save lives. Meanwhile criticism of the evangelical role in the Ixil Triangle became part of a wider alarm over evangelical growth in

Latin America. Catholic bishops denounced an "invasion of the sects" that they attributed to a political conspiracy coordinated by the U.S. government. When Ríos Montt used evangelical rhetoric to defend his scorched-earth policy, it heightened fears of a "religious war" that were soon augmented by the activism of the U.S. religious right in the region.[1] Not only were most evangelical missions in Guatemala clearly progovernment, despite the military's record of brutality; some, like the North American elders of the Church of the Word, saw themselves as frontline fighters against communism.

Fortunately, unlike North Americans shaped by the cold war, Ixil evangelicals never talk like counterinsurgency strategists. Instead, they use an older, more reputable evangelical language, of neutrality, which proved more appropriate to their situation. In chapter 4, looking at the formation of the civil patrols, we saw how some Ixils responded to the army's threats with a language of spiritual rebirth which distanced them from the revolutionary movement. That the army encouraged this response is demonstrated by Captain Alfredo's "put your hand on your heart" speech, in which he simultaneously threatened Cotzaleños with death. But while the language of rebirth made evangelicals and charismatics the army's de facto allies, it was also a language of diffidence and ambiguity, expressing the wish of most Ixils to escape the confrontation between the army of the poor and the army of the rich. As a result, when evangelicals are asked about their new religion and the violence, they respond with a language of neutralism, distancing themselves from the conflict rather than positioning themselves as partisans.

The new spiritual language of Ixil country is, together with its charismatic variant in the Catholic Church, pentecostal. Pentecostalism revolves around baptism in the Holy Spirit, as manifested by faith healing, speaking in tongues, prophecy, and other manifestations of the miraculous. It is the most popular wing of Protestantism in Latin America, attracting as many as three-quarters of all evangelicals. To understand the appeal for survivors of political violence, recall the original Pentecost, in the Book of Acts (2:1–4), when Christ's disciples are huddled together awaiting persecution. Suddenly tongues of fire descend and they are filled with the Holy Spirit, empowering them to go out and preach in languages they have never known. Among people traumatized by violence, a Catholic priest pointed out to me, clustering together to chant and clap rhythmically hour after hour is an obvious way to rise above feelings of isolation and fear. It was hard for me to sit long in the services: I was bored by the repetitiveness of the ritual language. There seemed about as much theology as in calisthenics. Gradually, it dawned on me that perhaps this was the point of pentecostal worship in Ixil country, to say very little.

The Suppression of the Catholic Church

I was quite blind, because I always had faith in development, in doing good work. . . . I was very blind to the end, and I struggled up to the end, trying to push cooperatives and everything else. But the people kept insisting, trying to make me see. Once they said, "Padre you . . . just don't understand." So I was forced to open my eyes. It was a change. I remember that we [the clergy] were always speaking about peace, about peaceful ways. —*"Padre Leonardo," ex-parish priest in Ixil country*

The tablets to their memory can be found at the altars where they used to say mass. The one for Padre José María Gran is in the huge old church in Chajul. He was returning from warm country, on June 4, 1980, when soldiers cordoned off the trail to shoot him and his sacristan. The tablet for Padre Faustino Villanueva is in southern Quiché. Formerly the parish priest of Cotzal, on his final visit there he had to be smuggled to safety. Army hit-men caught up with him on July 10 in Joyabaj, shooting him in his office. It was at this point that Bishop Juan Gerardi ordered his priests to close their churches and leave the department, in a desperate attempt to draw the world's attention. The tablet for the third Sacred Heart priest killed in Quiché, Padre Juan Alonso, is just over the ridge from Ixil country in the church at Cunén. It was early the following year that Padre Juan returned to the towns he had served for so many years. He believed that, because of his disinterest in politics, the security forces would leave him alone. It was just after he presented himself as the new priest in Nebaj, in February 1981, that he was kidnapped and murdered.[2]

When I visited Nebaj for the first time in November 1982, a machine gun poked out of the bell tower of the Catholic Church. Parish buildings had been converted into barracks. Army officers attributed the absence of Catholic clergy to their complicity in subversion, by hiding guns and recruiting peasants. As it happens, none of the three Sacred Heart priests whom the army murdered in Quiché was known for political activism. More to the point, the Sacred Heart was publicizing the army's human rights violations in Quiché. A few months before the murder of José María Gran, he had witnessed the marketplace massacre in Nebaj. After the diocese contradicted the army's version of events, Gran was confronted by a captain who accused him of being the source.

Unfortunately, the army's allegations against the Catholic Church did not lack plausibility. Guerrilla priests are part of Latin American folklore. In southern Quiché and Chimaltenango, other clerics—in particular, a group of itinerant Jesuits—joined the revolutionary movement in the 1970s as clandestine organizers. At odds with local bishops, to whom they did not report, various Jesuits from Spain helped organize the Committee for Campesino Unity (CUC) and also encouraged Mayan activists to join the Guerrilla Army of the Poor.[3] Two of the Spanish Jesuits joined the EGP, as did two other priests working in southern Quiché after the army began killing their colleagues.[4]

During this period, the mainly Catholic movement known as liberation theology was reaching its apogee in Latin America. Long years of pastoral work seemed to be creating a groundswell for political change. Theologians extolled the church's "option for the poor" as the vanguard of reform and, if necessary, revolution. In Central America, Catholic pastoral networks became a bridge into revolutionary organizations. The martyrs created by the inevitable reprisals—in Guatemala alone nine priests during 1980–81, plus hundreds of lay leaders—seemed to strengthen the "popular church." Yet in the most affected areas, it was becoming unsafe for parishioners to identify themselves as Catholics. While some survivors of repression were joining revolutionary groups, many more were seeking haven elsewhere. Many joined evangelical churches, a rival movement just starting to attract notice.

The western Guatemalan highlands was one of the main arenas for these developments. Prior to the war, the Catholic Church had built up the most extensive network of popular organization in the highlands, with a legitimacy no other institution could match, including the state.

When the Guerrilla Army of the Poor set up its own network, it began to expand rapidly only after making common cause with Catholic radicals who, according to one version, took over the lower and middle levels of the EGP around 1978. Not long in picking up the trail were government security agents whose methods—kidnapping and interrogation under torture—produced long lists of targets. As Catholic clergy became the main source of human rights reporting, selective kidnapping of their local leaders turned into general persecution.

The Jesuits who helped organize CUC and entered the EGP's fighting forces in 1980 were not the only ones to join the revolutionary movement. After being forced out of Quiché, several Sacred Heart priests started the Guatemalan Church in Exile, a revolutionary support group that served refugees and publicized army atrocities. The bishop of Quiché disavowed the Church in Exile, not wishing to join the revolutionary movement, and the majority of Sacred Heart priests accepted assignments in other countries. But the Church in Exile carried on an outspoken campaign from Mexico and Sandinista Nicaragua, and a decade later it was still speaking out.

When a parish priest sees his local leaders snatched away to be tortured to death, what might be most unbearable is the thought that their sacrifice was unnecessary and avoidable, that it served no higher purpose. Perhaps for this reason, the clergy of the Church in Exile resurrected their pastoral work in the 1970s as a preparation for the Armageddon at the end of the decade. According to this interpretation of the struggle, the Catholic Church raises the consciousness of Indian peasants, organizes them into cooperatives and base communities. Refusing to tolerate the efforts of Indians to better their lot, the army unleashes a terrible wave of persecution. Local activists have no choice but to join the guerrillas. Ensues "the Hour of our People," a Christian drama of martyrdom, revolution, and redemption.[5]

Vindicated by army massacres, the Church in Exile had quite an impact on how journalists and scholars interpreted northern Quiché. Its accounts also spoke powerfully to the solidarity groups in foreign countries who sought a moral explanation for the violence. As to be expected of a survivor narrative, the Catholic exiles placed their pastoral program at center stage, as if this had been the main target of the holocaust. When I was able to interview extensively in Nebaj after

1987, I found deep nostalgia for the prewar Catholic Church. But Ixils do not give it a prominent place in their accounts of the violence. Priests and catechists are seen less as protagonists than as early victims of a contest between two groups of armed contenders from outside the area. Nebajeños corroborate the repression that the clergy divulged to the outside world, but they explain it differently—as a reaction, not to peaceful Catholic social projects, but to the arrival of guerrillas.

One of the central figures in the Church in Exile was the former parish priest of Nebaj, Javier Gurriarán. Another was his cousin Luis, also a member of the Sacred Heart, whose career illustrates the tension between Catholic social activism and revolutionary politics. Luis worked in the department capital of Santa Cruz del Quiché. Via small airplanes, he organized colonization projects in the Ixcán. His energetic promotion of cooperatives cut into the profits of ladino merchants, whose complaints led to his expulsion from the country on two occasions in the 1960s. Willingness to confront power structures did not mean that Luis believed in working with revolutionary groups, however. When three U.S. Maryknoll missionaries became involved with guerrillas during the same period, it was Luis who decided that they were endangering the church, informed the archbishop, and triggered their expulsion.[6]

As for Javier, many Nebajeños used to believe (incorrectly) that their former parish priest was in the mountains with the guerrillas.[7] Before the events of 1979–80 he does not seem to have been any more radical than his cousin, nor do Nebajeños recall him as a prophet of revolution. He is still remembered fondly, even by evangelicals who believe they have improved upon his interpretation of the Bible, as well as by a few who echo the army's claim that he "brought the subversion."[8] What he is most remembered for are development projects. They included organizing the town's largest cooperative, introducing a new breed of honeybees from Italy, financing cement-block houses with low-interest loans from the Catholic charity CARITAS, donating an ambulance to the town's volunteer firemen, and helping villagers build new schools, chapels, and potable water systems. These would not seem the actions of a man preparing campesinos for a war that, as it turned out, destroyed most of what he built.

Many Nebaj catechists and cooperative leaders were associated with the Christian Democrats, but Javier is not remembered as a partisan in local elections. Nor did his sermons against injustice, including admonitions against going to the coast, lead to confrontations with local power brokers. The clandestinity of a revolutionary movement makes it hard to pinpoint when someone joins. But judging from the testimony of Nebajeños, including former catechists who turned evangelical, Padre Javier was not a member of the EGP's political wing because he did not try to recruit them. By 1979, however, he saw the guerrillas as an inevitable response to army brutality. With the closing of the diocese the following year, he became a revolutionary.

The Sacred Heart withdrawal from Quiché was to be temporary. If unable to return to their churches, the priests planned to resume their pastoral work "from the catacombs."[9] But where was the church in the catacombs? Certainly it existed in the mountains with the guerrillas, but most of the dozens of refugees I interviewed in Nebaj said there had been little organized religion there. A church in the catacombs no doubt also existed in the towns among the Catholic catechists who survived, remained loyal to their church, and eventually resurrected it. But here, too, the usual commentary is that catechists were too afraid to meet together. In small settlements under rigorous military control, it was practically impossible.

Despite hopes of solidarity triumphing over persecution, the Catholic Church fragmented when it was deprived of the central figure of the priest. Lay leaders were forced to choose contradictory survival strategies and divided into factions. In chapter 4 we saw how the army's persecution of Catholic Action leaders in Chajul inspired many to suddenly turn charismatic. The "renovation," as this Catholic form of pentecostalism is known, first appeared locally in the besieged colonies of the Ixcán. A priest who knew the movement there in the late 1970s denies that it had any pro-army markings; to the contrary, he suspects that the first charismatic leaders sympathized with the guerrillas, like many other Ixcán catechists at the time. When charismatic renewal reached Chajul in late 1980, however, catechists were taking the brunt of army repression, and the many identifying themselves as charismatics were trying to distance themselves from the prewar Catholic Church and its Catholic Action movement. Baptized by the

Holy Spirit and claiming to be neutral, the charismatics of Chajul broke with what was left of Catholic Action and spread the renewal elsewhere. One Chajuleño prophet is said to have "preached for forty days without an itinerary, in Sacapulas, Chiul, Chajul, throughout the aldeas, La Perla, Ilom, wherever the spirit led him."

In Nebaj few Catholics were coming to church when, toward the end of 1980, the renovation arrived. As already had occurred in Chajul, the president of Catholic Action—an Ixil under tremendous pressure from the army now that the priest was gone—became the leader of the charismatic renewal in Nebaj. Vicente Gómez had inherited the face of a bearded ladino from one of his grandfathers, a Spanish finca owner who sowed his seed widely, but not his lands or money, because for a living Vicente repaired shoes. In the last months of his life, in obedience to the Bible's command to show humility, Vicente the cobbler went barefoot. As he went from house to house, spreading the charismatic message of repentance and reconciliation, there was more resistance than in Chajul. His group was forced to stop meeting in the church, and it is said that both catechists and traditionalists denounced him to the army. The guerrillas, meanwhile, are said to have threatened him for preaching the gospel of the gringos and the rich. At the end of Holy Week 1981, the rest of the Catholic Action leadership in Nebaj expelled him, and in June he was killed with a machete while walking home from a village service.

The Evangelical Refuge

This comes from the chapels which Padre Javier organized in every can-tón and aldea. There they began to read the Bible for themselves and real-ize what the Gospel was. . . . The situation got worse and people knew they were going to die, so they wanted to get ready. At that time everyone thought they were going to die, so they were thinking about God. The majority of evangelicals didn't have problems, but the Catholics yes. . . . Also many people began to preach in Ixil, [unlike] before [when preaching was] almost always in Spanish. This was another factor which con-tributed: they heard the Word in their own language. When the aldeas began to surrender, the only aid committee was the one advised by FUN-

DAPI, which was supported by Ríos Montt. They sent sugar, beans and clothes.
—*Former evangelical leader explaining the success of Protestantism, 1989*

In closing the Quiché diocese, the Sacred Heart priests did not anticipate how quickly evangelicals would fill the vacuum. Protestants had not seemed very significant in prewar Nebaj, numerically or otherwise. No one guessed at the role they would play, because no one guessed at the impending devastation. "The gospel," as evangelicals put it, came to Nebaj during the coffee boom of the 1920s with the Reverend Thomas Pullin, a pentecostal missionary and founder of the country's Church of God (Cleveland, Tennessee) mission. Pullin lived in Nebaj with his family and itinerated from it on horseback for much of the 1920s and 1930s. He enjoyed a moment of success, but not with Ixils. Infatuated with him were upper-class ladinos who attended services until a few lower-class brethren spoke in tongues and "an *indio* preacher from Momostenango started making scandals."[10]

A Primitive Methodist mission was only slightly more successful, again among ladinos. According to mission accounts, it was only in the mid-1950s that the first Ixil converted. He was a man from Salquil who bought Spanish-language Scripture from a missionary, to treat a case of *susto* ("fright," or oppression by evil spirits) that Ixil healers were unable to cure.[11] Until the late 1970s, just before the violence, there were only two small churches in the town center of Nebaj,[12] and not many more out in the aldeas. The only sign of what was to come was the small but growing number of catechists who were declaring themselves evangelicals.

The main conflict in religious life until this point was within the Catholic fold, between the tradition-minded, localistic saint societies on the one hand, and the clergy and their Catholic Action catechists on the other. The young Ixils who joined Catholic Action in the 1950s and 1960s had particularly strong feelings about drunkenness. Getting drunk in fiestas is an act of worship according to the traditional Mayan scheme, yet addiction to alcohol has been the ruin of many a household. As long as Catholic Action drew sharp lines between itself and the inebriated practitioners of costumbre, it was a refuge from the effects of alcoholism. But as Catholic Action became more inclusive, more accepting of backsliders and traditionalists, the catechists who most hungered for a new sense of purity and discipline began to look elsewhere.[13]

Another source of leadership for the coming evangelical boom was the Primitive Methodist Church. Frequently evangelical growth in Latin America is attributed to largesse by foreign missionaries. In the case of Nebaj, the many good works of two North American couples, one from the Primitive Methodist Mission and the other from the Summer Institute of Linguistics, earned more gratitude than converts. The missionaries did attract various young men who later became pastors, but their most important contribution was a careful dose of ecclesiastical subversion. What they subverted was ladino control of the town's Primitive Methodist congregation, a common situation that missionaries often blame for the stagnation of their work. Nurtured by the missionaries, Ixil converts collided with ladino elders and, in the late 1970s, began to organize their own churches.[14] When the army forced Padre Javier and the evangelical missionaries to leave in 1980, an incipient Ixil leadership was on hand to welcome the flood of converts.

The correlation between the evangelical boom and the war is inescapable. A decade before the violence hit Nebaj, in 1969, two Primitive Methodist missionaries counted 139 baptized converts "in the entire Ixil zone."[15] Ten years later, a linguist estimated that the Protestant community had doubled. Yet he also described it as "minute and concentrated in a few scattered communities" including Nebaj, Vicalamá, Ilom, and Amajchel. "It has the virtual status of a pariah group, and believers, especially in remote aldeas (e.g., Ilom) report being ostracized by their neighbors."[16] At the start of the violence, the Primitive Methodists could attract sixty to eighty people to their services in town. Meetings of the Church of God, the Central American Mission, and the Assemblies of God were even smaller. By 1981, in contrast, an army strategist estimated that the area was 20 percent evangelical.[17] A year later under Ríos Montt, according to the Church in Exile, as much as 95 percent of the town of Nebaj was claiming to be evangelical.[18] Even after the violence tapered off, a large minority of Ixils continued to say the same—23 percent of family heads in Chajul, 30 percent in Cotzal, and 37 percent in Nebaj.[19]

The most obvious reason evangelical churches prospered amid the violence was the army's animus against Catholic clergy. In frequent announcements from the Nebaj plaza, army officers pointed to the departure of the priests as proof that they were subversives, jacking up the pressure on local Catholic leaders. "Many left the church for fear, because Padre Javier was accused of being communist. If you were Catholic, the army said you were communist," a Catholic in Nebaj explains. The army vendetta was especially devastating because of the irreplaceable role of the *padre* in the Catholic system. "Without a single priest here, there was a total breakup in the program, with groups going here and there in their own direction," a later parish priest told me.

The army did not attack evangelical authority in the same way. While some leaders died or fled for their lives, the majority were able to continue functioning. "We never suspended services," a Cotzal pastor claimed. "At times there was just me, the deacon and one person listening. The three of us. Soldiers would pass by in the street, the dead [would be carried by], but we never suspended services." Fortunately for evangelicals, the army did not occupy their temples as it did the more substantial and central Catholic installations. Turning Catholic churches into barracks and torture centers proved to be quite a stimulus to the evangelical alternative. "Lots of Catholics came to the church over there in Cantón Vitzal," a successful pastor of the period recalled, "because the army was occupying the parish buildings and the people did not want to show up there."

Under Ríos Montt, an influx of evangelical relief suggested that the wave of conversion was being encouraged by handouts. Loyal Catholics mutter that evangelicals changed their religion for this reason, and pastors acknowledge that there is some truth to the charge. Explained one: "It's the experience of all that, when a church pulls in people with handouts, later they go on to other churches." The role of inducements and political pressures in religious identification is illustrated by Las Violetas, the refugee camp on the edge of Nebaj that has become a new neighborhood. "Everyone here is evangelical," the camp representative claimed in 1982: he happened to be a pastor himself. Yet seven years later, Las Violetas showed a relatively low percentage of evangelicals, at 22 percent.[20]

The Las Violetas population changed during the interval, as many of the first refugees returned home, but the politics of survival also changed. The displaced people coming into Nebaj in the early 1980s were far more likely to describe themselves as evangelical than those arriving in the mid- and late 1980s. Perhaps because the army had become more predictable and the Catholic Church was now the most consistent supplier of emergency relief, the montaña refugees captured by the army in its later offensives were one of the least evangelical parts of the Ixil population.

Returning to Las Violetas, the resettlement became a focus for Catholic aid following the arrival of a new resident priest at the end of 1984. Although the parish provided assistance without regard to religion, it seems to have contributed to the resettlement's relatively high (78 percent) level of Catholic identification. The neighboring cantón of Xemamatze provides an interesting contrast. It received large numbers of displaced people in the early 1980s; they did not receive any special attention from the Catholic priest; and only 57 percent of the household heads identified themselves as Catholic in 1989.[21]

But evangelical groups did not prosper simply because of the army's persecution of the Catholic Church. They grew rapidly from the start of the violence, before their apparent immunity from army repression. In fact, young evangelicals being schooled in the department capital seem to have felt the same attraction to the guerrilla movement as Catholic students, and the Primitive Methodists suffered heavily.[22] Only after Ríos Montt came to power in March 1982 did a clear identification between the army and the evangelical message emerge. Even then, as the born-again general preached amnesty and reconciliation over the radio, his troops were burning down evangelical churches along with everything else in the countryside.

Well before Pax Montt, however, the language of spiritual rebirth was helping evangelical leaders step aside from the unequal contest between the Catholic Church and the army, in a language of neutrality soon adopted by catechists turning charismatic. A recurring story is that of the evangelical who, helpless and with a gun to his head, overawes his guerrilla captors by asserting a higher allegiance to Jesus Christ. Catholics tell similar stories about the agonizing decision to surrender to the army. Convinced they will die if they stay in the mountains and die if they turn themselves in, they commend themselves to God (see the epigraph on page124. In each case, Ixils transcend an impossible situation by declaring their neutrality and sanctifying it with an appeal to divine will. "I am not bitter against the army," an evangelical told Mark Coffin in 1981, just after the army had murdered his father. "It doesn't help to be bitter. God sees all and knows what is going on."[23] Catechists and traditionalists could also adopt the language of neutrality, but evangelicals seemed to use it with the most skill. In contrast to Catholic Action's language of commitment to the community, conversionist religion offered a convenient rhetoric of escape.

The Chaos of Congregationalism

People say the campaign went very badly. The evangelist didn't show up, a band that was going to come didn't either, even the coordinator didn't arrive. The pastors had disagreements: they say it went badly because they weren't united. It's also said that one of the pastors, of the Jehovah Our Justice Church, went on a drinking binge for ten days and had to be replaced.

—Nebaj pastor commenting on an interdenominational crusade, 1988

Until the late 1970s, there were only two Protestant churches in the town of Nebaj, the Primitive Methodists and the Full Gospel Church of God. By 1989 there were twenty-one. For the entire municipio and its forty odd aldeas, the number of congregations was around ninety (see table 6.1). Evangelical churches grew so rapidly during the violence that, seen from afar, they looked like the proverbial "invasion of the sects." The rhetoric of North American missions seemed to confirm the accusation: they claim to have "planted" so many new churches last year and announce that they will "plant" even more next year. But looked at from the ground up, most new churches are not started by outsiders. Instead, they originate in other local churches, when leaders fall into scandals, fight over money, or refuse to share authority. Losers take part of the old congregation with them, set up their own and, in hope of pastoral legitimacy, gravitate to a new denomination, often going to the capital to find one.

Table 6.1
Evangelical Churches in Nebaj, 1989

Name of Denomination	Date Appears	Origin	U.S Affiliation?	Theology	Baptized Members	No. Congs. & Subcongs.
1. National Methodist Church	c. 1982	Split from U.S mission	No	Holiness	c. 100	2
2. Methodist Church, Ixil Center	1983	Split from National Methodist to rejoin mission	Primitive Methodist Mission	Holiness	270+	10
3. Central American Church	1980–81	Split from Methodist Church	Central American Mission	Dispensational-fundamentalist	c. 30	2
4. Church of God, New Jerusalem	c. 1981	Split from Methodist and Central American Churches	No	Pentecostal	20–25	3
5. Monte Basán Church	1981	Split from Methodist and Central American Churches		Pentecostal	505	10
6. Nazarene Church	mid-1980s	Split from National Methodist	Church of Nazarene	Holiness	38	2
7. Full Gospel Church of God	1920s		Church of God (Cleveland, Tennessee)	Pentecostal	c. 900	7 +
8. Full Gospel Church of God #2	1986	Ixil-speaking split from main congregation	Church of God (Cleveland, Tennessee)	Pentecostal	10	1
9. Pentecostal Voice of God Church	1988	Split from Church of God	No	Pentecostal	15	1
10. Assemblies of God	1977	Nationwide A/G Campaign	Assemblies of God	Pentecostal	210	5
11. Evangelical Association of the Prince of Peace	1979	Founded by Catholic Action catechists	No	Pentecostal	c. 268	5

f God when members felt obliged to adopt the New Testa-
ctice of washing each other's feet. By way of compensation,
Peace soon acquired a new congregation in the same aldea,
g of thirteen families who felt obliged to leave the Bethany
n the nearby village of Tzalbal, Prince of Peace also picked up
wo Methodist factions. The two groups had become hard to
ish after the two pastors, despite ill feeling between their
ors, became fast friends and tried to merge their followers.
d by this ecumenical gesture, the majority of both Methodist
asked a Prince of Peace pastor to minister to them. When one of
laced pastors tried to claim the humble chapel in Tzalbal, his
flock mobbed him.

all evangelical attempts at social organization were this chaotic.
gest and best organized church in Nebaj managed to turn up-
ming members into the leaders of its own expansion. The Full
Church of God belonged to one of the country's two largest
inations, national in leadership but with a strong connection to
urch of God (Cleveland, Tennessee) in the United States. During
olence of the early 1980s, the Church of God provided a warm
ative to the cramped regime over at the Methodist Church, not
ecause it was pentecostal but because it was not dominated by
os. "There's no discrimination there," an Ixil evangelical told me.
e end of the decade, the congregation in town numbered several
red members, with another several hundred in Salquil Grande,
t least five other village congregations.

cording to the typology of David Scotchmer, a Presbyterian
ropologist working with Mam Protestants in San Juan Ostuncal-
he Church of God has a "hierarchical" style of organization: it is
nstitutionalized body with carefully defined norms and levels of
onsibility. While central authorities appoint the local head pas-
significant decisions are reserved for consensus decision making
he local level. The more stable churches tend to be of this type,
tchmer observes. But the majority of evangelical churches in
aj are what he calls "authoritarian." That is, they revolve around
charismatic authority of an individual who left another church,
ether in disgrace, in pursuit of his call from the Lord, or both. Such
urches are subject only to the headstrong individuals who start

Church	Founded	Origin	Foreign connection	Type	Members	
12. Voice of the Divine Teacher Church	c. 1983	Split from Prince of Peace	No	Pentecostal	195	5
13. Resurrection Church	1987	Split from Voice of Divine Teacher	Tex Sawyers Ministries (Richland, Virginia)	Pentecostal	48	4
14. Pentecostal Prince of Peace Church	1986	Brought to town by returnees from the south coast	No	Pentecostal	94	3
15. Wellspring of Eternal Life Church	c. 1985	Split from Prince of Peace	No	Pentecostal	292	7
16. Jehovah Our Justice Church	1986	Split from Monte Basán	No	Pentecostal	48	1
17. Living God Church	1981	Split from Prince of Peace	No	Pentecostal	290 (but seems rather smaller)	5
18. Bethany Church	1982	Split from Catholic charismatic renewal	No	Pentecostal	300	5
19. Jesus Saves and Heals Church	1986	Branch of main church in Chajul came out of Catholic charismatic renewal	Gospel Outreach (Church of the Word)	Pentecostal	c. 35	1
20. Emmanuel Mission	1988	Initiative of Guatemalan businessman and founder of mission	No	Holiness	20 (out of attendance of 200)	5
21. "Church of God, Sabatica" or "God of Israel, Sabatica"	1980 or earlier	Said to have spread from Huehuetenango Department	Apparently not	n.d.	small	3
22. Jehovah's Witnesses	1987 or earlier	Started by ladino missionaries	Watchtower Society	Nonorthodox in evangelical terms	25–30 attending	1

SOURCE: Author's interviews in Nebaj, 1988–89.

The twenty-one congregations in Nebaj ranged from successful, expanding bodies with hundreds of members to others with a few families. Nearly all were affiliated with a *misión* headquartered in the capital or a provincial town. Contrary to the English connotation, most missions were denominations controlled by Guatemalans, not foreigners. Although several of the more prominent churches were affiliated with U.S. denominations, a large majority were not. Since most Nebaj congregations were splinters from earlier ones, usually it was the local leader who invited the mission to Nebaj, not the mission that started the local church.

A disproportionate number of splinters came from the Primitive Methodist Church, the main evangelical network in Ixil country prior to the violence. The many stories of departure from Methodism revolve around two themes. One is the wish of Ixils to worship in their own language, an aspiration encouraged by North American missionaries in hope of broadening their appeal. The other is the attraction of Ixils to the emotional practices of pentecostalism, the most popular current of Protestantism in Latin America. The Primitive Methodists were not alone among older denominations in drawing the line at pentecostalism and losing members to it.[24]

Surpassing the Methodist Church in sectarian fecundity was, ironically, Catholic Action. Of the twenty-one congregations in the town of Nebaj in 1989, nine were currently led or had been organized by former catechists (see tables 6.1 and 6.2).[25] The spiritual odyssey of six catechists from Pulay illustrates how such leaders organized dozens of new congregations. In 1978 the group was studying a new Bible from Padre Javier when they concluded that Catholic Action was flouting Mark 16:15; that is, the Catholic practice of baptizing infants was no substitute for the evangelical practice of waiting for the age of consent. Not long after the start of their evangelical apostolate, they cured a paralyzed woman. When the army burned the houses of Pulay and ordered the inhabitants into town, the six obeyed and helped bring part of the population with them.

In 1989 three of the six ex-catechists were pastoring their own congregations while a fourth, an ex-Catholic Action president and the most effective, had withdrawn from leadership. Diego Martínez was the town's most successful preacher in the early 1980s. "By applauding,

shaking, and shouting he took aw aldeas," a rival pastor remembers. Martínez built up one of the largest c the Prince of Peace Church in the capit literate and precise and had a bright North Americans instinctively trust. W Church arrived in 1982 to set up a relief coordinator. On another occasion, Nortl gered his life when he answered their qu and the local commander traced the infor

Unfortunately, Martínez succumbed t ting his congregation into as many as six t other churches, leaving behind a remnant deep convictions but was illiterate. Martín Pulay Six, led a similar career. After split Prince of Peace Church, he brought anoth morally and was forced to resign as pastor, t still another mission, appropriately named tl tion. When I visited in 1991, he had lapsed ag disintegrated, and all that was left was a va temple having been carted off to an aldea wl another ecclesiastical adventure.

As the preceding episodes suggest, congre sion tend to the tenuous. One reason for havin rity of *personería jurídica* (legal recognition), whi for congregations to obtain on their own. Other religious instruction and philanthropic donatic often than not go unrequited. In 1988–89 only f tions sent professional evangelists with any regul much with the biggest expense of church life, chapel. The most subsidized was the Jesus Saves Chajul, which received money from the Church of equipped band, a handsome temple to play it in, project. Arguments over how the money was spei half the congregation breaking away to form a new

The ties between town and aldea congregations Acul, for example, the Prince of Peace congregatic

Church o ment pra Prince of consistin Church. most of distingu supervis Disturb groups the disp former Not The la and-co Gospe denom the Ch the vi altern just b ladin By th hund and A anth co, an i resp tor, at Sc Ne the wl ch

them, have only weak ties to denominations, and tend to be unstable.[26]

Only four of the churches in Nebaj are not pentecostal, and even two of these have adopted the pentecostal practice of praying out loud. Consequently, a visitor may find it hard to distinguish between pentecostal and nonpentecostal services. There are the same invocations of the Bible, the same hymns set to bouncy Mexican *ranchera* music, and the same shouted prayers for divine healing. Where nonpentecostal leaders draw the line is at speaking in tongues and prophecy. Unlike the intelligible speech of praying out loud, speaking in tongues consists of rapid-fire strings of seemingly nonsensical syllables that manifest baptism by the Holy Spirit. Tongues can also lead to prophecy, that is, verbal guidance from the Holy Spirit, when another worshiper translates the expressions into directives for the rest of the congregation. This kind of extra-Biblical revelation opens the door to heresy but, to date, prophecy in Nebaj consists mainly of familiar bits of wisdom to raise members' spirits.

As an ideology, evangelical Protestantism in Nebaj does not seem markedly otherworldly. Rather it is "presentist," that is, focused on day-to-day needs. The main sentiments expressed are giving thanks to God for whatever humble blessings have been bestowed, and asking for more. Only unusually prepared preachers are likely to dwell on the need for repentance, let alone points of doctrine and, more often than not, these are guest evangelists from outside of town.

Because evangelicals appeal to the Bible as their source of legitimacy, Protestantism is supposed to be a great spur to literacy. In Nebaj it is true that evangelicals customarily arrive at services with Bible in hand, but many are unable to read it because they are illiterate.[27] This includes a surprising number of their spiritual shepherds. "It's no problem, because even Jesus Christ did not study," one illiterate pastor says he was told by the Prince of Peace mission in the capital. According to the pastor of a relatively literate congregation, everyone says they want to read the Bible but no more than 20 percent know how, and many do not care enough to learn.

All Nebaj pastors say they want to study the Bible, but not all consider doing so a prerequisite to starting their own congregation. Take the young vendor of handwoven clothing who led two families out of

Table 6.2
Evangelical Pastors in Nebaj, 1989

Current Denomination	Ethnic Idenity	Age	Years as Evang.	Years as Pastor	Occupation	Education	Church Origin
National Methodist	Ixil	47	32	5	dentist/milpa	4th grade plus some Bible Inst.	
National Methodist	Ladino	47	c. 25	7	dentist/cobbler	12th grade plus Bible Institute (ordained)	
Methodist, Ixil Center	Ixil	37	14	6	tailor/pickup truck owner	6th grade plus some Bible Inst.	
Methodist, Ixil Center	Ixil	80	31	31	carpenter/milpa	self-taught plus Bible seminars	pre-Catholic Action catechist
Central American	Ixil	60+	19	9	milpa	2nd grade	Catholic Action/ Methodist
Church of God, New Jerusalem	Ixil	59	11	7	milpa	little	Catholic Action (ex-president)/ Methodist
Monte Basán	Ixil	33	10	8	woodcutter/milpa	self-taught plus some Bible Inst.	Catholic Action/ Central Amer./ Methodist
Full Gospel Church of God	K'iche'	48	33	30	vehicle owner	Bible Institute (ordained)	
Full Gospel Church of God	Ixil	38	11	10	tailor/butcher/ carpenter	8th grade plus Bible seminars	Catholic Action
Full Gospel Church of God, #2	Ixil	33	10	3	weaving seller	self-taught	Church of God
Pentecostal Voice	Ixil	36	16	1	cobbler/radio repair	self-taught	Church of God

Church	Ethnicity	Age			Occupation	Education	Previous affiliation
Assemblies of God	Ixil	30s	14	7	full-time pastor supported by congregation	self-taught plus 3 years Bible Institute	Methodists
Prince of Peace (inactive)	Ixil	42	11	10	carpenter/milpa	4th grade	Catholic Action (ex-president)
Prince of Peace	Ixil	37	15	1	woodcutter/milpa	self-taught	
Voice of the Divine Teacher	Ixil	30	11	4	small shopowner/milpa	2nd grade plus Bible seminars	Catholic Action/Prince of Peace
Resurrection	Ixil	45	11	7	woodcutter/milpa	3rd grade	Catholic Action/Prince of Peace
Pentecostal Prince of Peace	Ixil	29	8	0	carpenter/milpa/promoter	self-taught	Church of God
Wellspring of Eternal Life	Ladino	37	13	2	civil servant	12th grade	Prince of Peace/Monte Basán
Jehovah Our Justice	Ixil	36	13	4	carpenter/milpa	self-taught	Catholic Action (ex-president)
Living God	Ixil	43	6	5	woodcutter	self-taught plus Bible corrspdnc.	Catholic Action/Charismatic
Bethany	Ixil	34	9	7	tailor/clothing seller	6th grade plus Bible seminars	Catholic Action/Charismatic
Jesus Saves and Heals	Ixil	20s	n.d.	2	canecutter on coast	little	Charismatic

SOURCE: Author's interviews in Nebaj, 1988–89.

the Church of God so they could worship exclusively in Ixil. Never having attended school, he just asked the Lord to learn to read. He had no time for pastoral studies, being too busy eking out a living in the marketplace. "The greater part of the leaders have the idea that study is not important, that it's enough to read the Bible by itself," complained one of the few trained pastors in town. All but one of his peers work to support themselves, generally with a trade or commercial calling in addition to maize farming (see table 6.2). The four churches that pay partial salaries from the national level are all nonpentecostal, tend to have better-prepared pastors, but have not been the most successful in drawing members.

Evangelical missionaries were eager to harvest the new adherents of the early 1980s, but the resulting growth was the kind of which they were most afraid. Violence and need sent droves of people into evangelical churches, but as much to save their lives as change them. Carrying around Bibles had become fashionable, but few knew how to read them. The congregational social form had become popular, but above all as a form of self-assertion by men who started more congregations than they could hold together. Many new members moved from church to church until they finally stopped attending.

The Rebirth of the Catholic Church

> *Don't be sad, because this is my fate. If as Saint Paul says, they kill me for preaching the word of God, I'm not afraid of death, because the Renewal will not die, the Renewal will continue. When my hour comes I'm going to rest with God.*
>
> —Last words of Vicente Gómez, the first charismatic leader in Nebaj, *according to a follower nine years later*

When Catholic clergy began returning to Ixil country for short visits in 1983, the most immediate problem they faced was not the evangelical churches popping up everywhere. It was the unplanned reformation that had occurred among Ixils who still called themselves Catholics. In Chajul a majority of the most committed parishioners belonged to what they called "the renovation." They appealed to the Holy Spirit in pen-

Heading home after a fiesta.

tecostal-style meetings, addressed each other with the evangelical salutation of "brother" or "sister," and were being courted by evangelical missionaries. Over in Nebaj, where the leader of the charismatic renewal had been murdered in June 1981, his successor lasted only ten months before organizing an evangelical church which, along with others, collected most of the town's first charismatics. All over Latin America, charismatic Catholics were defecting to evangelical churches after their new sense of empowerment collided with unsympathetic priests.

In Chajul the charismatics were now led by an ex-catechist and brother-in-law of Domingo Rivera, the prophet turned civil patrol commander and mayor whose downfall was recorded in chapter 4. The ex-catechist was now home again from the capital, where he had served as a Mayan delegate to the Ríos Montt regime, become acquainted with the Church of the Word, and been hired by the Summer Institute of Linguistics to work as a translator. He finally broke with the Catholic Church during Holy Week 1984, the holiest period in the ritual calendar (and from an evangelical point of view, the most idolatrous), when a priest told him to clear out and he took almost half the charismatic movement with him. With up to a thousand people, the ex-catechist organized Chajul's first large evangelical group, the Jesus Saves and

Heals Church, joined it to the Church of the Word, and became administrator of the Summer Institute's relief program.

Since the army was too hostile for the Sacred Heart priests to return, the Quiché diocese was turned over to a Guatemalan bishop who recruited a new pastoral team. Men from Italy, Germany, Mexico, Peru, the United States, and Guatemala were among the volunteers. So were Maryknoll nuns and the Sisters of Charity, the latter founded in France but staffed in Nebaj by Guatemalans and Salvadorans. The first to take up residence in Ixil country was Padre Guillermo, at the end of 1984. Three years later he moved to southern Quiché and was replaced by Padre Miguel, one of three new priests taking charge of the Ixil parishes. Both Guillermo and Miguel were energetic Guatemalans in their thirties. Both were willing to work where the army had killed their predecessors, where they would be subject to categorical suspicions, and where they would have to thread their way through compromising situations. Both saw the effects of the war, not Protestantism, as the main threat to their parishioners. But to the problem of how to bring together traditionalists, catechists, and charismatics they responded somewhat differently.

Padre Guillermo was an upholder of orthodoxy who distinguished carefully between the three groups in his charge. That put him closest to the catechists, while at a greater distance from traditionalists and charismatics. Because Catholic Action had been reduced to small, intimidated groups and the population had not seen a priest for years, at first Guillermo dispensed baptism and other sacraments without conditions. But he laid down the law with remaining charismatics, and by 1987 he was insisting on prewar sacramental requirements. Henceforth, parents seeking baptism for their children would have to know various prayers, the Ten Commandments, the seven sacraments, the five commandments of the church, and the various requirements for a good confession and good communion.

While Guillermo was a ladino, his successor Miguel was a K'iche' Maya from Chichicastenango, a town that is one of the country's most popular tourist attractions and suffered some of the worst massacres in the early 1980s. Miguel also believed in maintaining ecclesiastical standards. But he was quick to point out the defensive function played by Mayan tradition and was deeply pained by its loss. What Miguel cared about most was bringing the three factionalized groups together, particularly reassuring traditionalists that they were welcome. He invited the town's baalbastixes to mass for the town fiesta and pressured Catholic Action into joining the saint societies for their processions every Friday of Lent. He also tried to bring together catechists and charismatics. For the night before Christ's resurrection on Easter morning, he introduced a candle-lit procession from the cemetery to the church that became a moving evocation of the town's dead.

The Catholic clergy of Ixil country were impressive men and women, but I did not expect them to be very successful in reviving their church. This was one of the surprises of fieldwork. When I reconnoitered the Ixil area in 1987, Catholics appeared weak and divided. Catholic Action seemed a shadow of its former self. Padre Guillermo suspected that up to 70 percent of his parish's catechists were gone—dead, fled, converted to the charismatic movement or to Protestantism. Out in the aldeas there seemed to be nothing, he said in a pessimistic moment: those who were left could not even recall simple prayers. During the town fiesta in August, two hundred people accompanied Guillermo on a procession past the army garrison, their only image a magnificent gold chalice representing Christ. These were the remaining catechists of Catholic Action, and they were quite sober. Meanwhile, another hundred Catholics paraded from one cofradía to the next, in a state of inebriation and bearing the statues of their saints. That evening, the three largest evangelical churches in Nebaj drew two and a half times as many people. Over in Chajul, the only substantial Catholic group were the charismatics, some of whom continued to join evangelical churches. In the intimidating atmosphere of Cotzal, the Catholic Church appeared to have practically disappeared as an institution.

Two years later, Catholics were visibly coalescing around their new priests and sisters. In Cotzal, where I had seen only a few dozen people gather in 1987, a thousand or more packed the huge old church to greet Bishop Julio Cabrera. According to Padre Guillermo, the absence of a priest had forced the catechists of Cotzal to hold their people together and they had done so. If he was correct, there had been a "church in the catacombs" after all. In Nebaj, Catholic Action counted 560 members in town and a total of 1,200 for the municipio.[28] But the most spirited, best organized Catholic group consisted of the charismatics, more than 300 by 1991, who met in a separate chapel with the priest's blessing and maintained a busy round of prayer meetings in each other's homes.

Catholics were feeling less inhibited by the army, but they continued to feel watched and tested. Priests and sisters were often on edge, straining to interpret the subtle cues of a town that had been militarized for more than a decade. They distrusted the relatively open atmosphere in Nebaj, fearing that the forces of repression were simply waiting for heads to pop up again before chopping them off. One priest in Ixil country habitually referred to his hopes and plans with the disclaimer, "if the apocalypse doesn't come again." Discrimination against Catholics was not overt, but Nebajeños often said that, if *la situación* took another turn for the worse, it would be safer to be an evangelical. Any priest could tell of parishioners or evangelicals taking a complaint against him to the army. Even though the army usually did not intervene, the most petty dispute could carry a warning.

A Religion of Survival

> *I was one of those people who said we must always speak the truth, that it is better to be killed than to kill. But there came a moment when too many had been killed; there were too many martyrs. . . . We had to go under water and submit to unthinkable terrible cruelty and repression, and submit without saying a word. It was important that each of us survive for the survival of the race. That didn't mean we condoned what was going on; it meant taking a longer view, saying there is hope, but not for now.*
> —Catholic sister in Guatemala, on learning from Mayas how to survive; quoted in Berryman, "Churches in Conflict," 1991

Why did the Catholic Church lose so much ground in Ixil country? Persecution is an important part of the answer, but it does not explain why some catechists were turning evangelical before the violence. While the evangelical boom in Ixil country coincided with repression, this is not the case in many other parts of Guatemala. As Timothy Evans points out, evangelicals have grown to roughly a third of the population even where there was relatively little violence.[29] In certain Mayan towns, evangelicals were a fifth or more of the population before the war.[30] Such comparisons suggest that, while political violence can be a catalyst for evangelical growth, it is not the only such catalyst, and that the underlying cause lies elsewhere.

If we look at the origin of evangelical church leaders in Nebaj, the institution most responsible for raising them up is the Roman Catholic Church. The man most responsible for introducing the Bible to aldeas is probably Padre Javier. This is not the first time that the Catholic structure of authority has become a cradle for Protestant reformation. Many a friend of the Catholic Church in Latin America has noticed that, no matter how egalitarian and dedicated a priest or bishop is, there are always too many people waiting around for the chance to talk to him. Too much of church life revolves around one man who is usually foreign and always in short supply. A strong priest gives the impression of a strong church. Where a strong clerical figure is absent, the church seems weak.[31] Not only did the removal of such figures have catastrophic implications for the Catholic Church in Quiché: this was a disaster waiting to happen.

Meanwhile, the persecution of the Catholic Church led to a characteristic Exodus narrative about the violence, its most dramatic rendering by the Guatemalan Church in Exile. To sum up the picture in a few bold strokes, Catholic missionaries mobilize the people for reform. In retaliation, the army unleashes a terrible persecution. As the Catholic Church is driven underground, its activists join the guerrillas. Fundamentalist Protestants flood in to pacify the area, hence the apparent drop in support for the revolution. But while much of the population is held in concentration camps, thousands of others hold out in the montaña where, organized into free communities, they continue the historical struggle for indigenous rights.[32]

Significantly, this version of events omits the EGP's role in infiltrating Catholic structures and attracting persecution. The Church in Exile has also assumed that armed revolution was based on a broad popular consensus. Most observers believed the same in the early 1980s, but as events undermined such an interpretation the Church in Exile clung to it. Its definition of "the people" in terms of revolutionary militancy minimized the growing number of Ixils who were opting out of the struggle by casting their lot with the army. As a result, the Church in Exile lost touch with much of the Ixil population in significant ways.

Because the Catholic Church suffered alongside the people of Ixil country and has been the best source of information about events there, it has been hard for observers not to adopt an implicitly Catholic frame of reference. Besides wanting to show solidarity with the victims of human rights violations, many of us have found the sociological frame of reference adopted by liberation theology compatible with our own. Certainly it is easier for secular intellectuals to identify with liberation theology than with fundamentalism. But the theology of liberation may fit the religious experience of Ixils less than a theology of survival.

Alongside the narrative of consciousness-raising and radicalization propagated by the Church of Exile, we need another. As the guerrillas surfaced and the army reacted to their presence, the people of northern Quiché experienced waves of military violence like they had never known. The shock produced, not just political mobilization and resistance, as liberation theology emphasizes. There was also religious experience of a kind that liberation theology regards as escapist. It involved surrender of the self to divine power, declaration of separation from the two armed contenders and, in practice, submission to the army. Some who led the wave were evangelical. Others were leaders of Catholic Action who turned charismatic. As a result, religious reform in Ixil country did not culminate in the language of political struggle. Instead, it was superseded by a more oblique language of personal salvation. The paradoxical result of consciousness-raising and revolutionary mobilization was a wave of conversion to born-again religion.

Pentecostalism has long been interpreted as the religion of marginal, dispossessed people whose flights of spiritual fancy compensate for their oppression.[33] But in Ixil country, what may have looked like escapism in the early 1980s must now be explained differently, if only because charismatics and pentecostals include much of the community leadership. Their worship groups have become a widely accepted religious alternative, with members involved in the same kind of activities as catechists before the war. These include pursuing school educations, starting new businesses, managing aid projects, organizing cooperatives, and running for office. Evidently the otherworldly language of pentecostalism has not prevented engagement with the problems of this world, a conclusion other researchers are drawing throughout Latin America.[34]

In a perceptive account of Norwegian pentecostals, Stanley Johannesen argues that pentecostalism is not necessarily "an expression of social and economic dispossession, or a compensatory fantasy of social power," but can also reflect "cultural fluidity, an absence of clear cultural boundary, a weakened, or absent, or threatened, cultural hegemony." Johannesen's Norwegians, including his own father, immigrated to New York City early in the twentieth century. Despite the many disadvantages they faced, they did not feel inferior to native-born Americans. To the contrary, they looked down on the people who discriminated against them, in a way roughly analogous to Ixil feelings about ladinos. Instead of a "resentful retreat," according to Johannesen, their pentecostal worship was "a practice extending and cultivating ambiguity by the embracing of a rite of membership based on a language of no-place and no-one."[35]

Responding to a breakdown of cultural boundaries by cultivating ambiguity is a tantalizing description of pentecostalism in Guatemala. In a survey of religious change around Quezaltenango, the largest urban center in the western highlands, Timothy Evans found that pentecostalism was associated with Mayas moving into new forms of integration with the national and world economy.[36] This process was well under way before political violence encouraged pentecostalism in peripheral areas like Ixil country. Evans found that the majority of pentecostals were made up of "former Indians" trying to pass as ladinos, certainly an ambiguously bounded part of the population, while more securely established ladinos tended to remain Catholic.[37] The ambiguous material referents of baptism in the Holy Spirit have proven equally useful to Ixils who survived the violence. Indeed, it could be said that pentecostal discourse less distinguishes adherents from the rest of Ixil society than exemplifies the prevailing attitude of apartness from the warring contenders. Evangelical discourse does not fulminate against plantation owners, or preach against going to the coast. While evangelicals acknowledge the inequities of Guatemalan society, and with considerable feeling, confronting the power structure is not the point of the new religion.

SEVEN

The Ixil Recovery of Nebaj

Rion Montt's campaign for president in Cotzal, 1989

Don Julio was a dignified old gent and a moralist. Under the dictator Ubico, he was fond of saying, government schools had required students to take a course in Morals and Civic Urbanity. They had learned to get up early in the morning, scrub to their elbows, and respect their parents. It was the failure to teach civility to the youth of Guatemala that explained the country's sad state according to Don Julio. A son of the first ladino plantation owner in Nebaj, he felt threatened by both sides in the violence, sold his property, and went to live in another part of the republic. On a return visit, he was shaken to learn that a cousin had sold the family's burial vault, including the bones of his father, to buy an airplane ticket to the United States.   *—Nebaj, 1989*

THE Nebaj I read about in human rights reports was a town of captives, the army's headquarters for a pitiless counterinsurgency war in the surrounding mountains. Now that the aldeas had been destroyed, the army was bringing survivors of its offensives into town sick, malnourished, and in rags. Once they had been processed, indoctrinated, and inducted into the army's system of civil patrols, they were sent out to "model villages," little better than concentration camps, which they could not leave without the army's permission. The time demands of the civil patrols had strangled commerce and seasonal migration to the coast, to the point that the economy was almost dead. Representatives of the Catholic Church were forced to tread with extreme care, while evangelical sects flourished by preaching obedience to the government.[1]

The human rights reports of the mid-1980s were not false, but they failed to account for the bustling scenes of reconstruction I witnessed. In the last chapter we saw that, while evangelical churches grew dramatically in the early 1980s, the Catholic Church experienced a dramatic revival at the end of the decade with the arrival of new parish priests. Thousands of refugees were in fact being extracted from guerrilla-controlled zones north of town, at a high cost in suffering and death, but the majority were soon returning to farm their own land. They did so under army auspices, organized into new civil patrols, but after petitioning to do so, and often only months after being captured. They were eager to go home, even if it meant being ordered around by soldiers. Although they had practically nothing but each other, they were proud of having survived.

Over in the plaza, opposite the Catholic church, the town hall was being run by Ixils. The Christian Democratic (DC) party had survived the violence to become the dominant electoral force. Throughout Quiché Department in the 1985 and 1988 elections, the ladinos and army-affiliated parties who had dominated local government were replaced by Mayan-controlled DC branches. Ironically, the army contributed to this outcome through the countless meetings to which it had summoned townspeople. Ladinos having fled or lying low, the assemblies consisted mainly of Ixils, who dealt directly with officers from a national institution without the usual ladino intermediaries. Because the power structure was in disarray, the army had to deal with Indians more directly than before. Despite its persecution of Indian professionals, the army's concept of control and development required promoting more of them.[2] In the midst of the most ferocious assault on Ixil society since the Spanish Conquest, more Ixils were becoming schoolteachers, while others were becoming administrators of new government programs and aid agencies.

Other Ixils were taking over the town market a block from the plaza. Until the violence, the permanent stalls were occupied mainly by K'iche' Mayas from Totonicapán and by ladinos. Now all but a few of the outlets were operated by Ixils. The market was much larger than before, Ixils having opened dozens of new permanent stalls, and dense crowds flocked there every Sunday. More Ixils were acquiring buses and trucks, to the point of owning half the local fleet, and they were also buying real estate around the plaza which had been lost to ladinos early in the century. Even labor contracting had changed significantly. Now all the contractors were Ixils, the ladinos having been intimidated by the guerrillas, and contractors were unable to retaliate against debtors.

These developments are surprising only if we view army repression as targeted against any attempt by Indians to improve their situation, and only if we view the guerrilla movement as a response to local exploiters whose exactions had become unbearable. These are claims made by the revolutionary movement, but as we saw in chapter 3 there is little evidence for them. If instead Ixils were making incremental gains in the 1970s, as I argued in chapter 2, with the violence triggered by the blows and counterblows of outsiders, then mass violence could easily accelerate preexisting trends, to the point of Ixils dislodging ladinos from positions of power. Nor would Ixil gains be surprising in view of what anthropologists have reported from other Mayan towns.

On the basis of a massive survey of the regional market system, Carol Smith believes that, in the 1970s, Maya Indians were turning their backs on the plantation economy. They were doing so by investing their labor in their own towns, farms, and enterprises.[3] Duncan Earle has called it the "reconquest" of the highlands, a peaceful, incremental process unlike the original from Spain, and well under way before it was interrupted by the violence.[4] Better-off ladino families were withdrawing to the capital for careers in business and the professions, with poorer ladinos who tried to step into their shoes being frustrated by more knowledgeable and effective Mayan strategies. Mayas were developing new commercial capacities, lessening their dependence on plantations, acquiring educations, and winning local elections. The question is whether, despite all the setbacks of the violence, they could continue those trends.

The Decline of Ladino Power

There's no security. After fifty years, I'm not young enough to start again. The cycle is ending.
     —*Finca owner explaining why he was selling his land, 1988*

When Colby and van den Berghe studied ethnicity in Nebaj in 1966, ladino power was pervasive. But they saw that it was being undermined as Ixils learned to compete with ladinos on the latter's terms. Government schools, the Catholic Church, and evangelical groups were contributing to a new indigenous persona, the *preparado* ("prepared one"), who was literate, sober, and commercially acute. Two decades later, after a period of terrible repression, ladinos say that Ixils are asserting themselves like never before. A remaining finca owner reported that his formerly submissive colonos were not willing to work for him half the month as before: they had other priorities now, which he attributed to their years in the montaña with the EGP. "Now the people are waking up, they don't have the fear of before—it's fairly general," commented a ladino leading a new political party composed mainly of Ixils.

Ladino power in Nebaj peaked before the violence. The electoral strength of the Ixil majority was organized first by Sebastián Guzmán and the Revolutionary party, then by the catechists and Christian Democrats. The children of the more established ladino families were already moving to larger centers for careers in the national system, to be replaced by the most commercially minded Mayas.[5] The ladino retreat was part of a wider phenomenon in the western highlands, and when the violence came it had contradictory effects. In Chinique, in southern Quiché, ladino patróns displaced by Catholic cooperatives were able to use the destruction of those cooperatives, and the army's establishment of the civil patrol, to reassert their authority.

In Ixil country, on the other hand, the ladino retreat was hastened by the war. In the early 1980s, the smaller finca owners found themselves trapped into delicate negotiations with the guerrillas, then wiped out by an army which, while respecting their persons, burned their installations and stole their animals. A member of one well-known ladino clan, many of whom used to live scattered through predominantly Ixil aldeas before the war, estimated that only a quarter as many did so now. Some men in the family had been killed by the guerrillas, others by the army, forcing still others to spend years in the montaña. Other survivors moved into town, returned to the family seat in Huehuetenango, or left for other parts of the country.

Ladinos with smaller properties were less likely to leave. Even if their property could be sold, the proceeds would not establish them in a more cosmopolitan town. The withdrawal was most noticeable among better-off families. The Brols who owned the Finca San Francisco left entirely, with the surviving brothers who had run the finca since the 1940s joining their scion in the capital. Left behind were numerous children born out of wedlock: those who had been "recognized" (as off-spring but not as heirs) were ladinos whose father provided the where-withal to buy a store, vehicle, or small finca, while those not recognized were raised as Ixils and poorer. The third-generation Brol administering the Finca San Francisco came and went every month in a helicopter. Of the formal heirs of the ladino principales—Brols, Tellos, Palacios, Samayoas, and Migoyas—only two individuals still resided in Nebaj, and even they only part of the time.

Mutual charity was the usual tone Ixils and ladinos adopted in discussing ethnic relations with me, but a few older ladinos were willing to express a sense of disenfranchisement. "At the beginning there was a colony of Spaniards here, labor contractors, from that they lived," a former reform mayor from the 1944–54 era told me. "They came here poor, with patches on their pants. Five or six years later they were rich and displacing the Ixils from their properties. Now, the opposite is happening. The Ixils are displacing the ladinos. The mayor is *indígena*, the priest is *indígena*, the majority of the teachers are *indígenas*, the whole town hall is *indígena*, they're all *indígenas*. Why? Because the majority of voters are *indígena*. Now they just want *indios*"—reserving a term of racial condescension for last.

"Owners of lands and businesses don't get involved in politics because you finish with a bullet in the head," another ex-mayor stated curtly. "Politics ends in jail, in exile, or the tomb. It means death." Now that the most important ladino families were gone, in the view of this elderly patrician, they had been replaced by opportunistic Ixil promoters. "The situation has changed completely," he complained melodramatically. "Of ladino power, now there is nothing. It has all been dissolved. We went to the coast, to the capital, to the United States seeking better horizons. One whole family went to San Francisco, California. Now there is nothing. We don't have voice or vote in the town. Now it's the bilingual promoters who organize everything, have their meetings, and organize fiestas. What used to belong to the ladino sector, to us, now belongs to them. Now we hardly get together anymore. We don't meet, we don't have fiestas, there's nothing. Now we are the dominated and it's the *indígenas* who dominate."

The ladino presence in Chajul and Cotzal had always been weaker, and it plummeted with the violence. But this was not the case in Nebaj, where rural ladinos moving in from aldeas and new civil servants arriving from the capital may actually have increased the ladino proportion of the urban population.[6] Some ladinos continued to have great influence through working as teachers, serving on committees, or knowing influential figures in the capital. But they had lost their near-monopoly on mediation with national power. Now the army-appointed military commissioners were Ixils, all but one of the men on the town council from 1988 to 1990 was Ixil, and so were a growing number of schoolteachers, not to mention the leaders of the civil patrol, catechists, charismatic leaders, and most evangelical pastors.

Most government agencies in Nebaj were run by ladinos (nineteen of twenty-three in late 1988, with two others run by K'iche' Mayas from out of town and the two remaining by Ixils), but these were mainly appointees from outside the area, temporary players who did not own local property. Ladino leadership was less pronounced among private relief and development agencies: of the thirteen I counted in late 1988, only seven were run by ladinos, with five by Ixils and one by Europeans. The town's secretary and treasurer were both ladinos, but unlike their predecessors at the start of the century, they did not have a monopoly on literacy and clearly served at the behest of the Ixil mayor. Other ladinos remained active in town affairs, but their niche was the ad hoc civic committee. During elections, some helped lead political parties whose members and candidates consisted mainly of Ixils. The figure of ladino power represented by the saloon owner and moneylender, labor contractor and finca owner, was being replaced by a figure of ladino influence such as a schoolteacher. Planters were being replaced by civil servants.

Labor Contractors

Why would I lie to you?   —*Popular expression in Guatemala*

One of the more obvious signs of the shifting ethnicity of power in Nebaj is labor recruiting. The changing ethnic composition of the contractors themselves is revealing: from the turn of the century to the 1970s, the business was dominated by ladinos. When Colby and van den Berghe did fieldwork in Nebaj in 1966, they reported just one Ixil family engaged in labor contracting, that of Sebastián Guzmán.[7] Just seven years later, when Nachtigall did his research, eight of the nineteen contractors were Ixils.[8] Three of the largest contractors in the 1970s—a ladino, an Ixil, and a K'iche' Maya—met untimely ends during the subsequent decade of violence, prompting an exodus of others from the business. As a result, ladino labor contractors have been replaced entirely by Mayas, all but one of them Ixil.

When asked why they stopped contracting, ladinos cite wartime financial losses and the danger. "Because if an *indito* complains against you, the guerrillas may kill you," one said. Another simply pointed a finger at his head like a pistol. In a situation that places a premium on negotiating skills, speaking Ixil and being able to appeal to ethnic solidarity offers a bit more security. But the shift in power relations goes deeper than the relative advantages of Ixil ethnicity, to the relations of contractors with their laborers. The indicator here is the *anticipo* (cash advance), the short-term, interest-free loan that the recruiter gives a laborer against future earnings. Because labor contracting is an obvious way to extract surplus value, it tends to be analyzed only as a form of exploitation. But as is the case with virtually any such relationship, the laborer does not lose all maneuvering room. The size of the cash advance, whether and how it is repaid, make it a crucial negotiating point. Once the laborer has the cash in hand, will he show up for the trip to the plantation? If he does not, will the contractor go to the town hall to enforce the debt? Changes in how labor contractors handle advances suggest changes in the relative strength of patrón and peon, labor demand and supply, and the social context in which such transactions are negotiated.

For Indians selling their labor, the temptation is to take the advance and run, becoming what contractors call a *faltista*, from the verb "to be missing." Actually, this has long been the most typical form of labor resistance in Guatemala according to David McCreery,[9] who reports that enforcing debt agreements with laborers who borrowed too much, spent it on alcohol, and failed to work was a problem in the mid-nineteenth century.[10] Even if a peon's debts piled up, it was not hard to escape by running away to another labor-scarce finca.[11] In Ixil country, the system of debt, obligation, and evasion was pervasive before the war. Padre Javier estimated that 40 percent of Ixils were in debt to labor agents.[12] The more daring faltistas collected advances from several contractors before disappearing, and the punitive steps taken by contractors fed the grievances tapped by the EGP.

Enforcement of labor obligations reached down to the level of aldeas, where no-shows could be held in small jails. All but a few of the contractors, Mayan as well as ladino, paid the national police and the mayor to jail laborers who failed to report for work. The debt to be repaid was calculated to include interest, travel expenses, the bribes needed to activate the authorities, and a mysterious fine for "smirching the paper." No one in authority seemed to care that, except for certain kinds of fraud, indebtedness was no longer a punishable offense under Guatemalan law. When the reform mayor from 1976 to 1980 refused to jail debtors like his predecessors, it encouraged the more abusive contractors to set up private jails in their own houses.

During this time there was also a rise in anticipo-jumping, with Ixils making the rounds from one contractor to the next before disappearing with the advances they had collected. According to one source, it was motivated by growing poverty among Ixils.[13] But the most immediate cause may have been the relaxation of enforcement from the town hall, and the wave of *faltismo* peaked in 1980–81 with the arrival of the EGP. Contractors lost thousands of quetzals to no-shows, forcing them to cancel agreements with fincas. As far as contractors were concerned, unscrupulous Ixils were simply milking the system for all it was worth before heading for the hills. But perhaps some of the faltistas no longer dared come to town. In any case, many contractors went out of business and advances plummeted to zero at a time when thousands of Ixils were anxious to get out of the area at any cost. Some plantations turned away Ixils looking for work on grounds that the entire ethnic group was subversive.

As late as 1985, Nebajeños were so desperate for wages that they would go to the coast for little or no advance. This meant that Ixils with very little capital could try their luck at contracting, which dozens did. By 1988–89, there were so many recruiters—I counted eighteen in Nebaj, the majority of them new—that they were now bidding up advances to fill their crews. Workers were able to avoid plantations with the worst reputations. Contractors also alleged another wave of laborers collecting advances and failing to show up for work. But unlike before the war, most contractors chose not to complain to the authorities, even though the mayor could still lecture offenders, and the justice of the peace (since 1988 a separate official) could penalize blatant fraud.

Why were contractors not appealing to the town hall? "It doesn't suit me," explained an evangelical who lived in a squalor of discarded paperwork, oil drums, and dirty laundry. "Some show up and pay me back, others don't. I make more money confiding in what's above," he said, looking heavenward and waving good-bye with his hand. "I don't like to look for problems. I never go to the courthouse ever," agreed a contractor whose older brother used to jail debtors in his house, was chased out of town by the guerrillas, and in 1989 was murdered by bandits in the capital. "Sometimes I lose a thousand. But if you lose one month, you gain the other month. I don't like to screw people. There are months that gain, there are months that lose."

The easy-come, easy-go persona adopted by most Ixil contractors, at least in their interviews with a foreign anthropologist, suggests that appealing to ladino enforcement mechanisms had become an unacceptable rupture of Ixil solidarity. "Yes, there's a law," said another, who claimed to have lost Q4,500 in advances when a crew of 175 left the finca to which he had sent them for another. "But they're not going to pay and with 175 [deadbeats] I would have to be in the town hall every day. If we wage war on people, then there's a lawsuit, the whole world knows that one is with the judge and they begin to criticize." With fewer enforcement mechanisms than before the war, and afraid to use what remained at their disposal, the new generation of Ixil contractors leaned toward persuasion. "Look kid, we're from the same place, we're indígenas, and we have to help each other out," another contractor told faltistas.[14]

Contractors were quick to attribute the rise of no-shows to the rise in cash advances, which they in turn blamed on competition among themselves. "Three or four years ago business was very good, the people flocked to sign up with me," another contractor reported. "Now I do fewer because of all the envy among people. With so many contractors, the people go from one to the other." One young contractor, burdened with a long list of no-shows who owed him Q1,700, tried to organize an association with his competitors to put a ceiling on advances. But only a few contractors showed up for meetings, with the most successful preferring to trust in their sagacity and cash reserves.

Plantations used to provide the larger, more reliable contractors with funds for advances. This ended with the violence, leaving contractors with a commission of Q.15–.25 (U.S. $.045–.075) in 1989 for each day of work by each member of their crew. If a contractor is paid Q.25 per work day, then a crew of forty that works twenty-four days on a typical one-month contract will earn him Q240 (U.S. $80)—probably less than the amount he put at risk in advances to sign them up.[15] That is only about twice as much as each member of the crew earns, and for greater financial risks. Plantations reimburse contractors for the cost of hiring buses and trucks to take their workers to the coast, but only after the crew has settled down to the job. This is how fincas protect themselves against another costly form of worker resistance, the *saltistas* ("jumpers") or *fugos* (fugitives), who accept transportation to a finca and then "jump" to another, making it impossible for the contractor to recoup expenses. Jumpers are usually reacting to abysmal conditions— bad food, harsh foremen, or a lower wage than promised—but recruiting by a rival contractor can also be a factor. Since Ixils often bargain for higher advances in kin and village groups, they tend to both sign up and defect in groups, which makes "jumping" costly indeed for their recruiters.

Since contractors lack the coercive power and plantation advances of before, it is in their interest to avoid plantations with the worst conditions. They claim to keep an eye on how fincas treat workers, citing bitter experience with particular plantations and how they would like to find better ones. In the late 1980s Nebaj contractors were singing the praises of Cobán, the coffee district around the capital of Alta Verapaz Department. "There we set conditions for the patróns, like if they're going to provide meat on Sundays. . . . And they pay up to six quetzals a day, for three-quetzal tasks that are small." Significantly, Alta Verapaz gained an evil reputation in the late 1970s as the site of the Panzós massacre and repeated expropriations of Q'eqchi' Maya smallholders. Now Verapaz finca owners were going all the way to Ixil country to find their labor and paying well for it by Guatemalan standards. According to Ixils, the Q'eqchi's were no longer willing to work for patróns because

Secondary students parading in Nebaj, 1989

their land was warmer than Ixil country and could grow two crops of maize a year, not to mention cardamon, coffee, and oranges.

Promoters and Teachers

There were not many Ixil professionals at the start of the violence, and they suffered heavily. Apart from a few university students, several of whom died or joined the guerrillas, the main body of Ixils with specialized training were the bilingual promoters, twenty-five or so in Nebaj plus another twenty in Chajul and Cotzal.[16] They are said to have sent delegates to the Committee for Campesino Unity (CUC), which was working with the EGP, and three Nebaj promoters disappeared in army hands inside the Casa Communal in early 1982. Three other Nebaj promoters were also probably killed by the army, while another three are said to have been killed by guerrillas,[17] for more than a third of the Nebaj bilingual promoters. Of the fifty or so regular schoolteachers in Nebaj, seven died or disappeared under circumstances that pointed to the guerrillas as well as the army. Four victims were ladinos and three were Ixils, but the latter seem to have included all the first Ixil teachers.

The circumstances of some of the deaths remain obscure, but the general reason so many Ixil promoters and teachers died is not mysterious: it was their vulnerable social position. They were a highly visible new kind of leader, mainly catechists[18] who expressed the energies of the Catholic Action movement and its effort to reform community life, who were young and therefore breaking with Ixil gerontocracy. In contrast to most of their elders, they were literate, had educational experiences outside Ixil country, and were working for the Ministry of Education, which put them in contact with new levels of power and dissent. Active on behalf of their people and tempted to break with customary Ixil reticence over abuses, they came under suspicion from the army, which pressured them to prove their loyalty by denouncing subversion. If promoters and teachers complied, that put them in jeopardy with the guerrillas. Despite all the deaths, however, the Ixil promoters came out of the massacres with more influence than before. Three mayors in a row after 1982 were bilingual promoters, products of the *castellanización* or Spanish-teaching program started by Arévalo-era reformers forty years before.

Ironically, the original castellanización program was taught exclusively by ladinos, the first Ixil teacher having quickly returned to farming. Ixils only began to lead classrooms after 1967, through a bilingual program started by Guatemalan indigenists and supported by North Americans from the Summer Institute of Linguistics and the U.S. Agency for International Development. This was not the first time that gringo enthusiasm was needed to overcome biases in Hispanicist educational bureaucracies against working in indigenous languages. The new bilingual promoters were recruited from castellanización alumni, but few had advanced beyond sixth grade, let alone earned the high school degree needed for a teaching job, so they were not hired as full-fledged teachers. Instead, they were entrusted with a two-year preschool course that started in the mother tongue of Ixil children and built up their competence in Spanish.

The Ixil professionals who resulted from this pedagogical bridge-building were eager to learn ladino ways, but not at the cost of rejecting their indigenous identity.[19] Terms like *indígena* and its opposite *ladino* tend to be regarded as racial, and Guatemalans describe the two as *razas* (races). But in practice, the categories refer more to cultural conditioning than biological inheritance. Whatever distinguishes the two, it is not their shared gene pool. In Nebaj, the philandering of ladino plantation owners has produced Ixils who could pass as whites in the United States. Ladinos tend to be somewhat lighter in complexion than Ixils, and more than a few are white by North American standards, but others are quite Mayan in their physiognomy. In Guatemala, paradoxically, members of one *raza* can switch and become members of the other *raza*.

Anthropologists differentiate "ladinoization" into several processes.[20] First, individuals may try to "pass" as a ladino and abandon their indigenous identity altogether, generally by moving away from where they were born. A second process is far more widespread: it is for individuals and entire communities to adopt ladino practices, such as wearing shoes or speaking Spanish on buses, without abandoning their indigenous identity. The third process can only be measured in hindsight: it is the gradual erosion of indigenous identity as Mayan communities adopt more and more ladino ways. Bilingual promoters are a useful index in this regard, owing to their advanced "acculturation" to a ladino-dominated stratum of society. Their ability to learn ladino ways, function effectively in Spanish-dominated spheres, and raise Ixil families suggests that Ixils will expand their Mayan identity rather than lose it, just like other indigenous professionals who have become more vocal in expressing their identity as Mayas.

The first Ixil primary teachers not having survived the violence, the eighteen working in 1989 had been hired only a few years before, by the military administrations of Ríos Montt and Oscar Mejía Víctores, who took the unusual step of giving Ixil-speakers preference for local openings. Even though it might seem best to hire applicants who can communicate with children in their mother tongue, the national teacher's union and educational establishment have defended Spanish as the language of instruction. To admit that bilingualism was an important qualification would disqualify most ladino candidates. Under the Christian Democrats (1986–90), political patronage returned as the main criterion in hiring teachers. Otherwise, Ministry of Education officials were said to demand Q3,000—the better part of a year's pay—for an appointment.

Still, the proportion of Ixil teachers was likely to increase, if only because ladino appointees from other departments usually failed to stay in such a provincial location, especially if they were assigned to a village. Local ladinos and Ixils were more likely to settle into their jobs, hoping merely for reassignment to the town center. Of the ninety-one primary teachers working in Nebaj in 1989, only eighteen were from outside the Department of Quiché. Seventeen others were from southern Quiché, with the rest (62 percent of the total) from Nebaj. Of the fifty-six Nebajeños, thirty-eight were ladinos (42 percent of the total) and eighteen were Ixils (20 percent).[21]

Besides strengthening the Ixil position in teaching, the violence also boosted school enrollment. Thanks partly to the concentration of population, the March 1988 enrollment in Nebaj (3,320) was more than two and a half times the 1979 enrollment (1,273), not including another 1,108 pupils in the preprimary bilingual system.[22] The government was also putting up dozens of new schools to replace all the ones destroyed by the army. Unfortunately, enthusiasm for construction was not matched by an operating budget, which was essentially zero except for teacher salaries. Student absenteeism remained high, as much as two-thirds when parents took their children to the plantations. The majority of Ixil children, including most out in the aldeas, were still not getting past the first years of primary school. Still, a substantial demand for the next level of schooling had built up. By 1991, 325 students were enrolled in *Básico* (grades 7–9) in day and night sessions in Nebaj, perhaps 85 percent of them Ixils. Somewhat fewer than a hundred students were in *Diversificado* (grades 10–12) outside Nebaj for training as teachers, nurses, accountants, or agronomists.

Ixils who became teachers were, by definition, joining another social class than that of their campesino kin and neighbors. One indication is that even Ixils assigned to aldea schools went to considerable expense to return to Nebaj every afternoon unless geographically impossible. Underlying tensions were brought out by the 1989 teachers' strike and the reaction to it. Bilingual promoters joined the work stoppage even though they felt discriminated against by their teacher supervisors, even though their own wages were not at issue, and even though the national teacher's union had recently demanded abolition of the bilingual program. To continue drawing pay, the teachers and promoters showed up at school every day but refused to hold classes. The tactic infuriated Ixil parents who felt that teachers were already overpaid for physically undemanding work, not to mention resentment of teachers who came to school late and left early, missed days altogether, or showed up drunk, yet were tolerated by their colleagues.

Hence the confrontations in a number of aldeas and in Chajul, where parents asked the mayor to put the teachers in jail until they agreed to go back to work. The most serious incident occurred in Cotzal, where the mayor and the civil patrol chief summoned a crowd of several hundred parents who, armed with sticks and stones, assaulted two dozen ladino and Ixil teachers. The pedagogues were rescued only by soldiers beating back the crowd with rifle butts. A lieutenant shouted that the teachers were only obeying orders from their union, hence could not be blamed for not working. "Thank God the army arrived to save us," an Ixil promoter told me. In other words, the strike was so unpopular that the teachers needed the army to protect them from the civil patrol. The next day the teachers left Cotzal, which was not the only case in which strikers were run out of western highland towns.

A teaching job was enviable only from the point of view of a land-starved peasant. Salaries were plummeting in buying power in the late 1980s, to the equivalent of U.S. $100 per month—half what teachers made before the war—out of which they were expected to cover classroom as well as personal expenses. Before the violence, teachers with the good luck to be posted to their home town probably already had a house to live in, a bit of land to farm, and a family network helping to cut costs here and there, enabling them to save part of their salaries. Over a decade or two, savings could turn such teachers into small proprietors who raised cattle and hired laborers to tend their crops. This was doubtfully possible by 1990, yet teaching was one of the few ways to escape a life of menial labor, motivating great sacrifices to meet the costs. Many more Ixil youths were working for teacher degrees than would ever get jobs in the school system. On the national level, the forty thousand teachers employed by the Ministry of Education were outnumbered by another sixty thousand waiting for an appointment. But a teacher's degree opened up other possibilities and, in the eyes of up-and-coming Ixils, was the first step to a desk job with a salary. The demand was so great that, in 1991, a new teaching academy opened and quickly enrolled fifty-eight students, forty of whom were Ixils.

Promoters Take Over the Town Hall

The structure of power in Nebaj is completely disarticulated. We ladinos are demoralized, replaced by opportunistic bilingual promoters. What rules here is a politics of opportunism, of each man grabbing what he can. Economically powerful men still meddle in politics but under the table, without taking an active part. Because they fear retaliation from the other side once it gets in power. —Elderly ladino patrón, 1988

One ironic result of the army's victory was the disappearance of the army-allied political parties from before the war, and the triumph of the persecuted Christian Democrats. The decline of the National Liberation Movement (MLN), the Institutional Democratic party (PID), and the Revolutionary party (PR) was a national phenomenon: the MLN and PID had prevailed only through force and fraud, and in the process of co-opting the PR they discredited it. Even the Christian Democrats survived the violence only by becoming more conservative. But never having been allowed to win a national ballot, they became a magnet for democratic hopes when Guatemala returned to civilian rule. Hence their landslide victory in the 1985 election, nationally and in Nebaj where they took 65 percent of the vote.[23]

The category of men running the town also changed. Just as the ladino principales were sidelined, so were their Ixil counterparts. Nebaj used to be known for the power of the elders who had served as cofradía heads in the civil-religious hierarchy. Sebastián Guzmán was the last "principal of principales" who summoned all the others to meetings in his house. He was also the labor contractor and large landowner assassinated by the EGP in 1981. In a familiar pattern for a dependent hinterland, he was what Eric Wolf has called a "cultural broker." That is, he controlled a wide patronage network among his people, represented them to ladino authorities, and was resented for manipulating public affairs to his own advantage.[24]

Since Guzmán's death, no one has replaced him as the "principal of principales." Older men of principal rank still serve on the town council, but they are quick to voice feelings of marginalization. "We hardly understand this *muchacho*," one such councilman said of a bilingual promoter who had become mayor. "He's very abusive. He's taking money. He doesn't consult us, we feel like ornaments. I hardly go to the town hall anymore, I'm thinking of resigning." The rapidly changing scene in Nebaj had undermined the ability of leading families to reproduce themselves. The sons of Gaspar Cedillo, the town's most feared principal when Lincoln visited in 1939–40, were forced to sell his property and never attained his rank. Descendants of another famous principal, Miguel Brito de la Paz, were more successful in maintaining leadership, but mainly through new avenues such as bilingual education and truck ownership. Where principales were still obviously influential was out in larger aldeas like Acul and Salquil Grande. Here they were defined less as former cofradía heads than as former auxiliary mayors. They deliberated together on matters facing the aldea, such as development projects and whom to pick as the next auxiliary mayor.

In town the principales were being displaced by younger men, especially the bilingual promoters who provided three mayors in a row from 1982 (table 7.1). The first was appointed by Ríos Montt and left office with his reputation intact, but not the two successors elected by the Christian Democrats. The promoter elected mayor in 1985 was known for organizing village projects, and he was also a founder of one of the larger evangelical churches, Monte Basán. Some say it was the rum at official functions that did him in, while ladinos point to his politics of ethnic resentment against themselves. In any case, he quickly disgraced himself with flamboyant purchases beyond his means including a car, a television, and two houses. As justice of the peace, he sent personal enemies to jail in the department capital for costly judicial purgatories. All but his closest allies describe him as consistently petulant, overbearing, and drunk, to the point of threatening people with the pistol he carried.

The DC mayors elected in 1985 and 1988 enjoyed a sudden rise in municipal resources—the endlessly discussed "8 percent" of the national budget that the 1985 constitution awarded local governments for public works. In 1988, according to the town treasurer, the new revenue-sharing plan returned Q400,000 to Nebaj—quite a sum compared to the Q61,000 in local taxes he managed to collect. Opposition activists could detail one scandal after another in the town hall as well as the national government's main agencies on the scene, the Committee for National Reconstruction and the Ministry of Development. During my

Table 7.1
Mayors of Nebaj Since 1946

Ethnic Identity	Date in Office	Political Party	Occupation
Ladino	1946–47	FPL	finca owner
Ladino	1948–49	FPL	small finca owner
Ladino	1950–51	FPL	schoolteacher
Ladino	1952–53	PUA	finca owner
Ladino	1954	MLN[2]	finca owner
Ladino	1954–55	Named by military junta	n.d.
Ladino	1956–57	MLN	agriculturalist and shop owner
Ladino	1958–59	MLN	finca owner
Ladino	1960–61	RND	labor contractor
Ladino	1962–63	n.d.	butcher
Ladino	1964–65	Named by military junta	n.d.
Ladino	1966–67	PID	store owner
Ladino	1968–69	DC	small finca owner/ labor contractor
Ladino	1970–71	PR	finca owner
Ixil	1972–73	PR	agriculturalist
Ladino	1974–75	MLN/PID	store owner
Ladino	1976–79	PR/DC/CAN	driver
Ixil	1980–82	DC	agriculturalist
Ixil	1982–85	Named by Ríos Montt	biling. promoter
Ixil	1986–88	DC	biling. promoter
Ixil	1988–90	DC	biling. promoter
Ladino	1991–	DC	health inspector

SOURCE: Author's interviews in Nebaj, 1988–89.

1. CAN = Central Aranista/Auténtico Nacional; DC = Democracia Cristiana; FPL = Frente Popular Libertador; MLN = Movimento de Liberación Nacional; PID = Partido Institucional Democrático; PR = Partido Revolucionario; PUA = Partido de Unificación Anticomunista; RND = Redención Nacional Democrática (of General Ydígoras Fuentes).

2. For the period prior to 1966, my Nebaj sources seem to use the MLN label to refer to the National Democratic Movement (MDN) of Colonel Carlos Castillo Armas which the MLN replaced.

stay in 1988–89, food supplies for widows were being subtracted from the municipal storeroom by the senior civil servant in town. He stored his appropriations at the property of a K'iche' couple, owners of one of the two largest stores in Nebaj, who had been subject to more than one official crackdown without going out of business.

"Many factors degenerate into corruption," another functionary told me. "Employees are badly paid, so when they're caught they always argue that they are paying themselves back for work-related expenses, perhaps truthfully. Since most people are hired on account of *influencias*, the ministries fill up with people who owe their jobs to political patrons and who are not likely to move against abuses. When leadership changes, they are easily purged, making them even more cautious. Complaints sent to a higher level don't get a response and, in the worst case, you could suffer reprisals as a result. Wouldn't it be good if gringos came here to administer the aid?"

I was always mystified by the behavior of the Christian Democrats. Why proclaim ambitious new programs to attract voters, then steal most of the money so that the programs fail and the voters reject your party in the next election? The announcement of grand new projects for the model villages was reinforcing typical Guatemalan attitudes toward electoral politics, as a way of "making false promises in order to use the state for one's personal gains."[25] This might not seem much different from how North Americans view politicians, but the presumption of corruption was more sweeping. "To be a politician is to be a bandit," observed a ladino businessman. "The great lack in our country is that we don't have entrepreneurs. Instead of getting ahead by producing, they get ahead by being a politician, which is easier. Anyone can be a politician, because all it means is taking money from others." Constantly trading rumors of malfeasance, Nebajeños viewed municipal affairs as a succession of personal appropriations of public funds, to the point of converting every public work into a monument to suspected fraud.[26]

Officeholders in Nebaj quickly admit to feeling helpless over structural constraints. According to Richard Fagen and William Tuohy, in a centralized and hierarchical system like Guatemala's, each level of government below is "weaker, more dependent, and more impoverished than the level above."[27] Resources are channeled unreliably from the top, with the result that municipal authority is undercut by lack of an independent financial base. John Watanabe calls it "the politics of marginality" in his account of Santiago Chimaltenango, a Mam community in Huehuetenango. "Few, if any, ideological differences separate Chimalteco politicians," he points out, "the principal dynamic being the incumbents' defense of their record and the oppositions' usually justified accusations of bureaucratic sloth." Unfortunately, the national government is unresponsive to local needs no matter which party wins the local election. As a result, the leaders of even ruling political parties do not wield the same authority as the old principales, and the electoral process fails to provide community leadership. Meanwhile, unfulfilled offers of help from the national government discredit local politicians in the eyes of their constituents. The town's mayor becomes a hapless figure for whom, as Watanabe notes, alcohol is a major occupational hazard.[28]

Patronage and Protest Under Army Rule

It being 10 A.M. on the 22nd of March, 1988, a great number of the population having gathered before the town hall with the object of asking Mayor____ to resign for the following reasons:
1. Abuse of authority.
2. Threats to opposition activists. . . .
7. Obliges persons working on municipal drains to canvas for the official candidate. . . .
10. The only drain project is in front of his own house and those of persons belonging to the DC party. . . .
16. During the administration of Mejía Víctores, the aldea of Tzalbal received the donation of a television which the mayor removed without any justification, the return of which the aldea now demands.
17. The people have information that the mayor has relations with the subversion . . . INFORMATION WHICH WAS PUT AT THE DISPOSAL OF THE MILITARY DETACHMENT:
• on February 12, 1988 Sr.____ denounced that the mayor tried to bribe him with a thousand quetzals and offered to put a bullet in his face if he did not cooperate.
• on February 12, 1988 Sr.____ reported that the mayor followed him in a pickup truck trying to run him over.

—The indictment against Nebaj's DC mayor

If the army stages coups in the capital, why couldn't they stage one of their own? Thus reasoned the Nebajeños who, one morning in 1988, gathered in the plaza and called a meeting that quickly focused on the town's Christian Democratic mayor. The first men in the plaza were, according to one witness, carrying the rifles of the civil patrol. "WE ALL HAVE RIGHTS AS NEBAJENSES," said one banner. "THE PEOPLE UNITED AND CONSCIENTIOUS WILL NEVER BE DEFEATED," said another. As a mainly Ixil crowd of more than a thousand gathered, speaker after speaker hurled accusations at the mayor, who called on the army and civil patrol to help him, then escaped in a car with the crowd chasing after him on foot. Conspicuously absent was the army, except for a civic affairs officer chatting with protesters. Finally the crowd rushed the town hall and forced the municipal secretary to write out a declaration deposing the mayor. It was what Nebajeños proudly called their "municipal coup."

Running mayors out of office is a popular activity in K'iche' Maya towns to the south. During this same period, the DC-appointed department governor's main function was going from town to town rescuing his party's mayors from their constituents. On the second day of the Nebaj coup, as the crowd in the plaza worked out its plan of government, the governor showed up accompanied by the mayor and twenty national police. He bawled out the crowd of Ixils as ignoramuses who did not know the law. If they had a complaint against the mayor, he thundered, they should take it to the courts. Meeting no resistance, he threw two of the ringleaders into jail (only briefly) and restored the mayor to his office.

Nebajeños attribute the coup to the civil patrol heads and the disaffected vice mayor, one of the founders of the local DC two decades before. He was a son-in-law of Sebastián Guzmán but had broken with him before his death. Now he was the most successful Ixil in the marketplace, to the point of owning a bus and a truck. Smarting under the mayor's abuses, he was just one of the prominent DC members who now broke with the party, alleging that it had fallen into the hands of opportunists. Together with some of the Ixil promoters and teachers, until this point identified mainly with the DC, he joined with civil patrol leaders to organize an independent campaign for the 1988 election. Backed by many of the Ixils with small businesses in the market, they named their civic committee after the *cotón*, the red-braided jacket worn by Ixil men on ceremonial occasions. For a slogan they chose "Todos Nebajenses" (colloquially, "we're all Nebajeños") for their willingness to join with sympathetic ladinos, two of whom—including a former reform mayor from the Arbenz era—headed the electoral slate.

Despite the unpopularity of the incumbent mayor, his party won the 1988 voting. One reason was that opponents split their votes three ways, between Cotón (913 votes), the Union of the National Center (504), and the Solidarity Action Movement (347), whose combined tally would have bested the DC's (1,737) by 27 votes.[29] But the DC had demonstrated an impressive ability to withstand popular resentment. Arriving in town a few months later, I heard rumors of vote-buying, but no one would admit to seeing money change hands. Instead, the DC warned Ixils that, if it lost the election, they would lose their relief supplies. "Perhaps not so much with liquor and money but in a more effective way," explained a former mayor. " 'If we lose the election,' they say, 'dry fish won't come anymore, food supplies won't come anymore, all the help that arrives won't come anymore.' " "Unite yourself with power" (*únete al poder*) the DC painted on walls. In just two days, the DC congressman wrecked Cotón's chances by touring villages and asking, if it didn't have the president and didn't have the congressman, what could it obtain for the people?

Intimidation of this sort was most apparent among war widows, the most desperate clientele in Ixil country. There were 1,550 of them in Nebaj according to an official census in 1989,[30] the majority in straits, with the result that they were strung along on irregular handouts, summoned to appear in full ceremonial regalia for visiting dignitaries, and considered a captive vote for the Christian Democrats. Nothing could repress their seething resentment, and the men running the town hall considered them a continual headache. Still, I was surprised when a widow leader said that the mayor had threatened her before the 1988 election. "If you wag your tongue, they're going to kidnap you," she quoted him.

How promises of patronage and threats of violence came wrapped together was illustrated by the visit of the DC presidential candidate in 1990. The Christian Democratic party is with God and helps the campesinos, Alfonso Cabrera repeated time after time. In case anyone failed to get the point, he handed envelopes from the Minister of Culture standing next to him to each of the town's cofradía heads. Each envelope contained a thousand quetzals (about U.S. $300), for the avowed purpose of protecting the town's cultural traditions. Again and again, Cabrera invoked the memory of the violence, when women had to shut themselves inside their houses at night and didn't know if they would see their husbands again, to remind his audience that they did not want to return to those days. We don't want any more fear, he kept repeating: now the government respects the campesinos.[31] The message that came across, at the time if not in the telling, was that Nebajeños should support the DC unless they wanted the kidnapping to start again.

Cabrera's visit coincided with the DC government's defeat of the teacher's strike, a pyrrhic victory because it alienated a key stratum of the party's patronage structure. His speech was obviously intended for traditionalists and illiterates, those Ixils most inclined to vote for whomever was in power. It was a different constituency from the founding members of the DC in Nebaj: catechists, cooperative members, and small entrepreneurs. From the vanguard of reform in Nebaj, the DC had become an official party relying on handouts and the threat of losing them. So disappointed were Nebajeños with the DC's Ixil mayors that, by the time of the 1990 election, the six candidates for this office were all ladinos save one. Even though most of the other candidates for the town council remained indigenous, many Ixils wanted a ladino mayor in the hope that he would avoid the drunkenness, thievery, and scandal of the previous two.

With the Christian Democrats in the hands of *corruptos*, many Nebajeños were also ready to turn to *el general*—Efraín Ríos Montt. Two years before the voting, in late 1988, pocket calendars bearing the image of the former dictator began to circulate through the Ixil towns, his face serene and trustworthy. "He didn't collect his salary as president, just as a cabinet minister," stated one of his more devoted followers, an evangelical leader and schoolteacher (who, while on strike, grimly vowed that he and his union would gladly fight even if it meant civil war). "Guatemalan sociologists say that he could help the poor. He was a campesino as a child. He knows what it's like to haul wood."

The Guatemalan establishment still considered the Ríos campaign a bad joke when an Ixil campesino took the initiative to journey to the capital, find his way to the general's house, and come home to organize a local chapter of the first Riosmontista party. The Republican Front of Guatemala (FRG) was known colloquially as La Mano for its symbol, a hand presenting a three-fingered salute like a boy scout's, dating to the time when Ríos obliged all civil servants to swear that they would "not lie, abuse, or steal." In Nebaj the Mano attracted Catholics, while evangelicals gravitated to the other Riosmontista group that soon arrived, the Reform Party of Guatemala (PREG), known colloquially as La Llave after its symbol, an old-fashioned door key. Many of the people joining the two parties came out of the Cotón civic committee.

Even after Ríos was forced out of the race on constitutional grounds, his supporters won the town hall in Cotzal, where their predominantly evangelical slate was headed by a Catholic elder. The Riosmontistas also came close to winning the two other Ixil towns. In Chajul they placed a close second to the Christian Democrats, who also squeaked by in Nebaj with only 28 percent of the vote, the Riosmontistas having split over 50 percent between separate Mano and Llave slates. Ríos Montt was so popular that he resurrected the fortunes of Nebaj's Ixil congressman, an evangelical who was elected by the DC in 1985, became an object of derision for not accomplishing much, and now won reelection by jumping to Ríos Montt. Wrapped in nostalgia, a former dictator with a horrendous international reputation had become the image of good government in Ixil country. Rhapsodizing over Ríos Montt's virtues as a righteous military man was an acceptable way for Ixils to position themselves in regard to the slaughter of the early 1980s, the Guatemalan army, and their struggle to reestablish personal guarantees.

EIGHT

Ecological Crisis in Ixil Country

Xeputul, 1989

Across a gorge from the Finca La Perla is the Ixil aldea of Sotzil, its hous-
es piled atop each other on a steep hillside, producing an aesthetic effect as
mist rises from the river. "Who got here first?" I ask the elder serving as
auxiliary mayor. "The people of Sotzil were here first," he replies. "But
they did not have a deed, it was not certified, it was not on the map of
Guatemala. So the patrón in Guatemala looked at the map and sent sur-
veyors." "First Lisandro [Gordillo] took some, then Luis [Arenas] more,"
adds the president of the development committee, drawing on the dirt
floor with a stick that slices away at Sotzil until only a narrow ribbon
remains. The entire community has 225 hectares for a thousand people.
"There are more and more people and there's no room for them," the pres-
ident tells me. When I ask to which agencies he has given development
proposals, his answer is a lost, wishful look.   —*My visit to Sotzil, 1989*

ONE of the most misleading aspects of Nebaj was the prosperity and
bustle in town. On Sundays the market was mobbed with thousands of
people. It had exploded in size from before the war, as had the number
of permanent stalls open through the week, even though most Ixils said
they were poorer than before. I often wondered how sellers could multiply if the purchasing power of buyers had plummeted. One reason
consisted of new sources of capital. These included the government
agricultural bank BANDESA, whose loans could be diverted to set up
market stalls; merchants in regional centers who advanced goods to
junior Ixil partners; and the mysterious opportunities of war. There
were civil patrollers who had appropriated cattle from destroyed villages, and montaña refugees said to have brought back nest eggs from
their transactions with the guerrillas.

   Commerce was also thriving because of a larger market of buyers,
both geographically and socially. Geographically, army engineers had
built an impressive new road twenty-four kilometers out to Salquil
Grande, bringing a string of aldeas totaling twelve thousand people

within an hour of town in pickup and freight trucks. Socially, the counterinsurgency state was bringing hundreds of new salaries to the Nebaj market. Soldiers were the single largest group of new buyers, although there were also schoolteachers, program coordinators, and the staff of an expanded health center. In 1989 I counted twenty-three institutions from the national government operating in Nebaj, not to mention another thirteen private voluntary organizations. But the most important reason for the growing marketplace was probably the increasing dependence of Ixils on the money economy. In a continuation of population and resource trends from before the war, Ixils were being forced to buy more of their food.

Clearly, this was a situation with both winners and losers. Sources of social mobility in Ixil country centered on the towns, particularly Nebaj. Paths for upward movement included recruiting plantation labor, operating trucks for hire, and obtaining government jobs. Some of the larger contractors and merchants were clearly prospering, along with builders employed by the government, the local directors of aid institutions, and older teachers who had managed to invest savings in agriculture. There also seemed to be a mild trickle-down effect among the urban population, with shortages of agricultural labor boosting wages to U.S. $1 or more per day, about as much as Ixils could hope to earn on a coffee plantation.[1] In the outlying neighborhood of Xemamatze, I was surprised to find that, of fifty-five household heads who worked outside the municipio in the previous year, only 18 percent said they were migrating to work more than before the violence. More household heads (24 percent) said they were doing less seasonal migration than before the war (with 58 percent saying they were doing the same as before).

Unfortunately, I was not able to survey an aldea, let alone quantify the amount of labor migration out of Nebaj.[2] But Ixils living outside the town center almost always say that seasonal migration has increased from before the war, which they attribute to smaller maize harvests and the loss of domestic animals. For some farmers, smaller harvests result from no longer being able to afford chemical fertilizer. For others, living in concentrated villages has made it impossible or less productive to cultivate fields they once did. As villagers ran out of maize, they found it necessary to sign up with labor contractors. Except for the tough, dangerous job of cutting sugar cane, which could pay up to U.S.

$5–6 a day but which only the most determined men undertook, plantation labor was not very remunerative. Since most adult workers could hope to bring back only $30–40 for a month's work, another key reason for going to the coast was the daily food ration.

Agricultural labor was, together with coffee, Ixil country's most important export.[3] Before the war, Padre Javier and cooperative organizers tried to discourage Nebajeños from going to the coast. Creating new income sources locally was the alternative they preached, with the help of grassroots development agencies like the Heifer Project and the Peace Corps. Judging from wider trends in the western highlands reported by Carol Smith, the various cooperatives may indeed have helped Ixils invest more of their labor in their own enterprises, at least until the war swept the co-ops away. Now that the violence is abating, Ixils face the same constraints that drove so many to the plantations before the war.

How we characterize those constraints is a politically loaded question. The economy of Guatemala is dominated by plantations, and it has the highest Gini Index for land concentration in Latin America.[4] While Third World countries average 67 on the Gini Index, Guatemala's score increased from 82.42 in 1964 to 85.05 in 1979. That same year, 88 percent of Guatemala's farms were too small to provide for the needs of a family and, taken all together, occupied only 16 percent of the country's farmland.[5] The most obvious reason for the disparities in land tenure is that agribusiness has monopolized the most productive land. Guatemala's southern coastal plain is occupied almost entirely by cattle ranches and sugar and cotton plantations.[6] Much of the south coast was not occupied by anyone until recently because it was so swampy and malarial, but plantations did appropriate Indian land in crucial eco-zones such as the coffee-growing piedmont that rises to the highlands.

In Ixil country the inroads of large landowners are also evident. Yet even as they appropriated much of the best land, the peasant economy continued to prosper.[7] Peasant households produced surpluses of maize and tended pigs, sheep and cattle, for whose export the area was known. Ixils enjoyed a surplus of land compared to their neighbors to the south, hence the migration of K'iche' Mayas into sparsely occupied pockets. The ample land available for milpa and grazing was due to the population collapse following the Conquest (see table 2.5 in chapter 2). Only around 1950 did the population return to its pre-Conquest levels, according to George Lovell,[8] but since then it has more than doubled. Hence, the most immediate pressure on the person/land ratio is population growth and the subdivision of inheritances among an ever-increasing number of heirs.

Perhaps because Guatemala's political system is so oppressive, demography does not figure prominently in most accounts of the country's tribulations. But geographers and anthropologists have repeatedly identified it as a basic factor in impoverishment and ecological degradation.[9] The ample lands occupied by a few families in the nineteenth century are now a patchwork of tiny, fragmented holdings. In Nebaj, the role of population growth in pushing farmers below the level of subsistence is suggested by the declining size of family holdings from 1964 to 1979, a period in which losses to fincas were no longer a major factor. According to the national agricultural census (see table 8.1), there was a 60 percent increase (1,856 to 3,043) in the number of family holdings below five manzanas (3.5 hectares), with holdings under one manzana (.7 hectares) more than doubling, while holdings above five manzanas declined a precipitous 37 percent (1,737 to 1,099). Of the 4,142 holdings counted in 1979, the census classified the 972 less than one manzana in size as *microfincas*, the next 2,674 as *subfamiliares*, with only the 496 above ten manzanas (7 hectares) as *familiares* in size. In other words, only 11.97 percent of the holdings met the standard size considered sufficient to support a family.[10]

Burgeoning families and dwindling inheritances are so central to the growing land poverty of Ixils that, at the start of my fieldwork, I wondered if the death and destruction of the war could alleviate the pressure by lowering the person/land ratio. Consequently, this chapter explores the impact of the violence on population and land tenure. I will argue that, despite huge apparent losses, the violence has not made much difference in the amount of land available per person. The war has indeed had an impact on land tenure, but not through expelling peasants from their plots. Instead, the violence encouraged many finca owners to put their land on the market, making it possible for campesinos to recover part of their previous land base. The Guatemalan state has even pursued a modest program of breaking up fincas for back taxes. Yet parceling out such land to Ixil maize farmers has not addressed their long-term prob-

Table 8.1
Fragmentation of Land Holding in Nebaj, 1964 to 1979

Size of Holding in Manzanas[1]	No. in 1964	No. in 1979
<1.00	397	972
1.00–1.99	522	940
2.00–4.99	937	1,131
5.00–9.99	816	603
10.00–31.99	787	418
32.00–63.99	99	45
64.58–645.79	35	33
(1–9.99 Caballerías)		
Total	3,593	4,142

SOURCE: Dirección General de Estadística 1968:177–79; Dirección General de Estadística 1982:255–56.

1. One manzana = 16 cuerdas = 1.736 acres = .703 hectares (see table on page 37). The figures do not include 118 properties that were less than 1 cuerda, that is, less than .0625 manzana or .0439 hectare.

lems; instead, it has reinforced the dominant pattern of ever-smaller, below-subsistence holdings known as *minifundismo*.

Consequently, this chapter argues that the most serious threat Ixils face is the explosive growth of their own population. Wherever population growth is taxing resources, it raises basic questions about the cause and the most intelligent response. In response to the frantic calls of population-control organizations, many social scientists have pointed out that impoverished peasants have large families because these help them survive. Yet, as Alain de Janvry notes, while "more poverty implies the private need for more children . . . it is also true that more children imply the social cost of more poverty." In short, having large families is a survival strategy that worsens the overall situation.[11] In the case of Ixil attitudes toward family size, I will question the assumption that the large size of their families is the result of economic rationality, suggesting instead that an attitude of passivity, coupled with a lack of effective methods, produces larger families than many Ixils deem economic for their situation.

The Impact of the Violence on Population

Three to four thousand people from Nebaj were believed to be dead.
—*1985 field investigation, Washington Office on Latin America*

Table 8.2

Shortfall Between 1973 and 1981 National Censuses for Ixil Area

	1973 National Census	1981 National Census	Shortfall (%)
Nebaj	27,259	18,134	33.48
Chajul	18,092	15,713	13.15
Cotzal	12,698	10,944	13.81
Ixil Triangle	58,049	44,791	22.84

SOURCES: Dirección General de Estadística 1973, 1981.

Since the height of the violence, Ixil country has become known for its orphans and widows. When I visited in late 1982, a civil servant said there were 2,111 orphans in the three town centers and outlying camps controlled by the army. In Guatemala, orphans include children who have lost just one parent. But if some 25,000 people were under army control in Ixil country in late 1982,[12] and if roughly half were under the age of eighteen,[13] then 1 in every 6 children had lost a mother, a father, or both. In 1989 a government census counted 2,642 widows and 4,186 orphans among the people controlled by the government in the three municipios.[14]

As the Ixil area opened up following the worst of the violence, mayors of the three towns reported that up to half their people were missing.[15] The population showed a startling drop from the 1973 to the 1981 census, of 23 percent for the Ixil Triangle and 33 percent for Nebaj alone (see table 8.2), even though the 1973 count had fallen far short of the actual number of people. There were even larger discrepancies between the population projected by the national government and the number of people counted by local health centers (see table 8.3). For 1986–87, 48 percent of a projected Ixil Triangle population of 96,000 appeared to be missing. Could 46,000 people have died? Such figures are so disturbing that we must first ask how plausible they are, by examining the projections and head-counts on which they are based.

Counting people in a place like northern Quiché is never easy. The usual difficulties of quantifying a dispersed, mobile, and pre-literate populace were compounded by the war. With both the 1973 and 1981 censuses having derailed, the National Institute of Statistics (INE) went back to the relatively well-executed census of 1964 as a basis for pro-

Table 8.3

Population Count Shortfalls in Ixil Triangle

	Counted by National Census	1981 Projected by Natl. Statistic Institute	Shortfall (%)	Counted by Govt. Health Center	1986–87 Projected by Natl. Statistic Institute	Shortfall (%)	Corrected U.N. estimate[2]	1989 Projected by Natl. Statistic Institute	Shortfall (%)	INE's assumed annual pop. growth (%)
Nebaj	18,134	37,953	52	23,906	43,171	45	32,709	45,438	28	2.3–2.6
Chajul	15,713	29,598	47	13,467	35,667	62	19,423	38,672	50	3.9–4.3
Cotzal	10,944	16,742	35	12,246	17,135	29	17,940	17,669	none	1.1–1.6
Ixil Triangle	44,791	84,293	47	49,619	95,973	48	70,072	101,779	31	2.9–3.0

SOURCES: Dirección General de Estadística 1979:42-34. Dirección General de Estadística 1988:24. The 1986–87 figures are courtesy of the public health teams in the government health centers of Nebaj, Chajul, and Cotzal. The 1989 United Nations estimate is courtesy of the Nebaj office of the Program for Refugees, Repatriates and Displaced Peoples (PRODERE) of the U.N. Development Program.

1. The government health center counts are from 1986 to 1987, while the National Statistic Institute's projection is for 1987.

2. The figures obtained from the local U.N. office in Nebaj included an obviously inflated figure for the urban population of Nebaj (21,650), which I reduced to 9,296, in accordance with the health center's figure for 1989. I also made adjustments for aldeas that the compilers classified under the wrong municipio. However, I did not adjust head counts for various aldeas that looked too high but could be explained by seasonal labor migration.

jection. Once INE's projections for Ixil country are broken down into the three municipios, we find surprising differences in the missing population for each town. While the shortfall for Chajul remained at 50 percent at the end of the 1980s, Cotzal's declined steadily to the point of disappearing, with Nebaj holding a middle ground between the two. Such contrasts are surprising in view of the broadly similar experience of the three towns.

Looking closer at the projections, INE proves to have made very different assumptions about what the three towns' annual growth rates would be. While it assumes a population growth of between 2.3 and 2.6 percent a year for Nebaj, it assumes much higher growth rates of between 3.9 and 4.3 percent a year for Chajul, while for Cotzal it assumes rather low rates of between 1.1 and 1.6 percent. Interestingly, the distribution of assumed population growth parallels the distribution of supposed missing population, with Chajul's the highest, Nebaj in the middle, and Cotzal's the lowest. The surprising discrepancies between the percentage of missing population in each town could therefore be a function of INE's assumptions about how fast each was growing before the war.

Since I know of no basis for assuming such different population dynamics between the three towns, let us simply consider that our high (Chajul) and low (Cotzal) shortfall cases are based on questionable INE growth projections and concentrate on the middle case, Nebaj, for which I happen to have the most data. INE's projections could easily underestimate the high natural morbidity rates for Ixil country, particularly infant and child mortality, which would inflate the expected population. Yet for Nebaj, we have a 1980 health center count (35,810) that was just 3.6 percent below INE's projection for that year (37,156, see table 8.4). So at least for the case of Nebaj, let us assume that INE's projections are not greatly inflated. As for the Ixil Triangle as a whole, let us further assume that INE's over-and under-projection for Chajul and Cotzal cancel each other out, leaving a valid estimate of what the entire area's population would be if subject only to natural morbidity, not to the war. Hence, as shown in table 8.3, let us accept INE's projection of a 1989 population of 101,779 in the three Ixil municipios if the war had not intervened.

Now, what about counting the number of people who survived the war? We might think that counterinsurgency would include careful

Table 8.4

Population Count Discrepancies in Nebaj

Date	Source	Count	National Census Projection	Shortfall (%)
1973	National Census	27,259	31,576[1]	13.67
1980	Health Centers	35,810	37,156	3.62
1981	National Census	18,134	37,953	52.22
1984	Health Centers	15,188	40,394	62.40
1987	Health Centers	23,021 + 885 adjustment for non-reporting aldeas (177 households x 5) = 23,906[2]	43,171	44.62
1989	Health Centers[3]	21,512 + 4,390 adjustment for non-reporting aldeas (878 households x 5) = 25,902	45,438	42.99
1989	United Nations (PRODERE/UNDP)	46,383	45,438	none
1989	United Nations (PRODERE/UNDP) corrected[4]	32,709	45,438	28.01

1. I obtained a projected population for 1973 by taking the multiplier of 1.024 for the projected population increase from 1974 to 1975 (Dirección General de Estadística 1979:42–43) and projecting it backward for one year.

2. The multiplier of five for the presumed family size of households comes from the estimates of local observers, including public health inspectors (who estimate five to six) and Helen Elliott of the Summer Institute of Linguistics (who estimates five). I chose the lower figure because, when I surveyed Cantón Xemamatze in Nebaj, the average size of 97 households was 5.2. According to a questionnaire administered to 1,254 heads of displaced households by the Ministry of Development, their reported household size was 4.46.

3. This appears to have been a careful head count in the aldeas covered. For aldeas not included, I assembled various estimates of the numbers of households in each, selected the largest estimate unless I had other data contradicting it, and multiplied by 5 to obtain a population estimate.

4. The figures obtained from the local U.N. office in Nebaj included an obviously inflated figure for the urban population of Nebaj (21,650), which I reduced to 9,296, in accordance with the health center's figure for 1989. I also made adjustments for aldeas that the compilers classified under the wrong municipio. However, I did not adjust head counts for various aldeas that looked too high but could be explained by seasonal labor migration.

enumeration of households and men, who after being burned out of their homes would be eager to qualify for occasional relief supplies. But no authority has really been able to keep tabs on population movement. One source of flux is the shift to new aldeas as refugees return home, accompanied by confusion as to exactly who is where since refugees wish to hang onto their shelter in the old location and, if possible, avoid serving in the civil patrol in the new one. Another source of flux is seasonal labor migration. According to a staffer at the government health center in Nebaj, his vaccination drives could miss as much as 30 percent of the population, especially families away on the coast. If we add 30 percent to the Nebaj health center's adjusted 1989 count of 25,902, we get a total of 33,672, which is close to the United Nations 1989 estimate (32,709)[16] once its outlandish estimate for the town center is brought into line with the health center's.

The resulting shortfall from INE's projected 1989 population of 45,438 in Nebaj ranges from 26 to 28 percent. That corroborates the usual estimate of Ixil mayors in the 1980s, that a quarter to a third of their population was missing. So does the 31 percent shortfall between INE's projected 1989 population for the three Ixil municipios (101,779) and the United Nations' 1989 estimate of the number of people under government control there (70,072). For lack of better data, let us therefore accept that 70,000 of a projected population of 100,000 could be accounted for under government control.

What, then, happened to the other 30,000 people? As I interviewed refugees, it became clear that many of the missing were not dead. In 1992 the communities of population in resistance reported having 17,000 people on the northern edge of Ixil country, 12,000 of whom were Ixils.[17] Then there were the refugees of the early 1980s who went elsewhere, in an internal diaspora to the south coast and the capital. Many of these people eventually returned to Ixil country, but others did not. Unlike seasonal wage laborers, they no longer maintained a residence in Ixil country where they could be counted.

In contrast to refugees from Huehuetenango Department, very few people from Ixil country reached Mexico, a few hundred being the estimate of investigators familiar with the refugee population. There were also a few small colonies of Ixils in the Ixcán rain forest and to the east in Alta Verapaz Department, but again numbering in the hundreds.

The size of the Ixil diaspora is subject to conjecture, but the modest estimates of local observers suggest that it does not exceed 5,000. If there are another 12,000 Ixils in the montaña, that would boost the extant population to the level of 87,000 by 1989. Remaining unaccounted for are 15 percent of Ixil country's projected population of 101,779, 15,000 people who presumably died in massacres or starved in the montaña.

This estimate is based on many assumptions, which will have to be modified as more information becomes available. But if 15,000 people did perish in the Ixil Triangle, what difference would that make in the growth of the Ixil population? To answer the question, let us take the presumed current population of 87,000[18] and multiply it by the growth rate government demographers assumed for Ixil country from 1986 to 1990, of 3 percent per year.[19] If so, the population recoups its numbers to the 101,779 level in just six years, by 1995. If we continue multiplying by the same 3 percent annual growth rate, the 1989 population of Ixil country doubles to 174,000 in twenty-four years.

The Impact of the Violence on Land Tenure

Magdalena was an Ixil matron, one of the many past forty years of age who never appeared in public without a headband wrapped through her hair. In her bright red skirt and intricate huipil, she looked the very embodiment of Ixil culture. Together with her husband Nicolás, she lived in a shop where the two made hats; sometimes I would stop and ask for directions, and we would talk. They seemed a thoughtful, considerate couple. Magdalena was in bed one night when a grenade sailed in and blew her head off. The assassination occurred in 1991, not 1981, and various Ixils expressed grim satisfaction. Unbeknownst to me, Magdalena had earned a malodorous reputation as a guisach (interpreter) with lawyers in the department capital. A number of campesinos, mainly refugees from the montaña, had gone to her for help in recuperating their land from rival claimants; Magdalena had taken them to Santa Cruz del Quiché, and come away with the land for herself. —Nebaj, 1991

The violence has had a definite impact on land tenure in Ixil country, but not as we might suppose, by expelling large numbers of smallholders from their land. Civil war often concentrates ownership, as winners expropriate losers. In other parts of Guatemala, military officers are said to have taken advantage of the violence to build up fincas. In the Ixcán, there were cases of the army taking the land of refugees still in Mexico to award it to new colonists of its own choosing. In Ixil country, because so many refugees fled their aldeas for sanctuary with the guerrillas, we might expect a high level of expropriation. In Cotzal, the army did take the land of a father and son in the guerrilla movement to build two resettlements. But when refugees returned from the montaña, the army and town authorities generally respected their rights. The land disputes that came to my attention were, like the majority of such disputes before the war, between Ixil neighbors and relatives. For example, siblings or half-siblings would take possession of an abandoned house or field, claim to have lost a previous municipal deed, swear out a new one in their own name, and refuse to leave when the previous owner returned from the montaña. Actual rights to the property were often obscure, perhaps because a father had left heirs by different women.

In principle, if not always in practice, smallholder rights in Ixil country were unshaken, and returning refugees were usually treated sympathetically. There were several reasons for this. First, the majority of Ixils had suffered the same experience. Second, most of Ixil country is worth little to anyone but another peasant farmer. Last but not least, if anything could reawaken Ixil support for the guerrillas, it would be to violate their complex tapestry of ownership. The peril of tampering with local ideology of land ownership is illustrated by the Ixil reaction to one of the army's attempts at social engineering. Once it was setting up model villages, the army decided to give the inhabitants their own personal titles to nearby fields. The previous owners had never registered with the national government, and during the recent offensives they had mysteriously vanished. The conflict came to a head over the model village at Juil: finally even army officers were impressed by the silent masses of Chajules gathering to oppose the plan.

Town officials and CEAR functionaries all claimed to do their utmost to reunite refugees with their property. They were more or less helpless, however, if the rival claimant went to the expense of taking his case to the department capital. Where rights between rival kin were impossible to adjudicate because the owner was missing or in the montaña, the usual solution was to divide the already small parcel. Instead of consolidation, therefore, small holdings continued to splinter through inheritance and litigation.

Where violence has shaken up land tenure is in the finca sector, where numerous ladino owners have put their property on the market (see tables 8.5, 8.6, and 8.7). The two most important patronal families in Ixil country have not tried to sell out, but they have retrenched in other ways. In 1983 the Arenas family entrusted day-to-day administration of their bankrupt Finca La Perla to a worker's committee. Then the Arenases announced the sale of 40 percent of the finca to their five hundred *colonos* (permanent workers) as part of reorganizing it into a solidarity association, a technique for harmonizing worker-owner relations that Guatemalan businessmen have imported from Costa Rica.[20] Unfortunately, the enterprise was so indebted to banks that, as of 1990, the workers had yet to receive earnings, let alone pay for their shares. Like many solidarity associations, moreover, La Perla's was run by company foremen, many of whom came from a single, extended ladino family. Local skeptics questioned whether the association was really operative; I met at least two La Perla colonos who denied any knowledge of it. Nor did the association include the five hundred seasonal coffee pickers from surrounding Ixil villages who still regarded the finca's land as their own.

The Brols, owner of the other large coffee plantation in Ixil country, chose to withdraw from half a dozen outlying fincas that extended northeast into the Zona Reina of Uspantán. According to the finca's administrator, fifty-six hundred of the family's sixty-eight hundred hectares—all but the heavily planted coffee groves—were being transferred to five hundred of the finca's dependents in eleven-hectare parcels, as part of their worker's compensation. Blaming the labor conflicts of the 1970s on bank-appointed administrators, the Brols were returning to a more paternalistic style of management. Besides parceling out their peripheral property, they provided coffee seedlings to nearby smallholders; replaced outside administrators with men from the finca; built retirement housing for older workers; and, as if to consecrate the new era of labor relations, financed a handsome new temple for the Full Gospel Church of God.

Table 8.5

Fincas and Transfers in Nebaj, 1980–1991[1]

Finca Name	Location	Size in Cabs.[2]	Main Land Use	Ethnic Shift in Ownership from 1980 to 1991
1. Chemalá	La Pista/Cambalám	1.5–2	Cattle	Ladino to Ixils through church development project, for aldea of La Pista
2. N.d.	Bisan/La Pista	n.d.	Maize	Ladino to Ixils and ladinos through private purchase
3. Potreros Calderón	Above Xevitz	1	Cattle	Ladino-owned property, no change
4. San Antonio	Acul	3	Dairy	Ladino-owned property, no change
5. Las Vigas	Xeo	4	Coffee	Ladino to Ixils through church development project, for aldea of Xeo
6. Sichel	Sichel	3.5–4	Coffee	Ladino to ladino, within family
7. N.d.	Above Xoloché	1	Maize	Ixil-owned property, no change but for sale
8. N.d.	Bisan	7	Cattle	Ladino to army for military base
9. N.d.	Xoncá	3	Cattle	Ladino-owned property, no change but for sale
10. N.d.	Xoncá	2.4	Cattle/Maize	Ladino to ladino through private purchase
11. N.d.	Suchun	1	Coffee	Ladino to Ixil to pay off loan
12. N.d.	Sumal Chiquito	3.5	Coffee	Ladino-owned property, no change but for sale
13. El Cafetalito	Sumal Chiquito	1	Coffee	Ladino to ladino, private purchase within family
14. N.d.	Sumal Chiquito	1	Coffee	Ladino-owned property, no change
15. N.d.	Sumal Chiquito	1	Coffee	Still apparently ladino-owned
16. El Zapote	Sumal Chiquito	1	Coffee	Still apparently ladino-owned
17. N.d.	Sumal Chiquito	n.d.	Coffee	Ladino to ladino, private purchase
18. N.d.	Sumal Chiquito	.7	Coffee	Ixil to ladino, private purchase

19. N.d.	Sumal Chiquito	1.5	Coffee	Ixil to ladino, private purchase
20. N.d.	Batzchocolá	5–6	Coffee	Ladino to ladino, private purchase
21. Buenavista	Batzchocolá	6	Coffee	Ladino to ladino, private purchase within family
22. La Victoria	Sumal Chiquito/	3–4	Coffee	Ladino to U.N. Development Program, for aldea of Sumal Chiquito
23. La Soledad	Xeucalvitz	2.5	Coffee	Ladino-owned property, no change
24. Las Delicias	Xeucalvitz	.5	Coffee	Still apparently ladino-owned
25. El Imperio	Xeucalvitz	2	Coffee	Still apprently ladino-owned
26. La Quebrada	Xeucalvitz	4	Coffee	Still apparently ladino-owned
27. Las Pilas	Nw. corner of Nebaj	4	Maize	Ladino-held title disputed by villagers who are supported by Nebaj town hall
28. Las Americas	Nw. corner of Nebaj	4	Cattle	Ladino-owned property, no change
29. Las Amelias	Nw. corner of Nebaj	9	Cattle	Ladino-owned property, no change
30. Las Violetas	Outskirts of town	1	Cattle	Ladino to Catholic Church, for building resettlement neighborhood

1. This list is based on information I was able to collect in interviews, not on a survey of land tenure. It includes all the larger properties and all or most referred to publicly as "fincas," but not all properties in the 1–cabellería range, including a number held by Ixils as well as ladinos. Because the list is of larger properties, it does not include a number of sales by Ixil smallholders to ladinos around Sumal Chiquito.

2. One caballería = 112.2 acres or 45.374 hectares (see table on page 37).

Table 8.6

Fincas and Transfers in Chajul, 1980–1991

Finca Name	Location	Size in Cabs[1]	Main Land Use	Ethnic Shift in Ownership, 1980–91
31. La Perla, Santa Delfina and annexes	Ilom/Sotzil	80	Coffee/Cattle	Reorganized as solidarismo association
32 Estrella Polar	East bank, R. Xalbal	7	Coffee	Ladino to ladino, private sale
33. Covadonga and annexes	East bank, R. Xalbal	14	Coffee	Ladino-owned property, no change
34. Agro Aldea	Near town of Chajul	2	Vegetables	Ladino to Agros Foundation, for evangelical model village

1. One cabellería = 112.12 acres or 45.374 hectares (see table on page 37).

Table 8.7

Fincas and Transfers in Cotzal, 1980–1991

Flinca Name	Location	Size in Cabs.[1]	Main Land Use	Ethnic Shift in Ownership
35. San Francisco and annexes	Eastern end of municipio	111	Coffee	Peripheral 87 cabs. transferred to finca's colonos as part of worker's compensation
36. Finca Pacayal and annexes	Santa Avelina & Bichibalá	29	Maize/finca de mozos	Transferred to aldeas of Bichibalá and Santa Avelina by INTA
37. N.d.	San Felipe Chenlá	22	Maize/finca de mozos	Transferred to aldea of San Felipe Chenlá by INTA
38. Chinamaquín	Villa Hortencia I	29	Maize/finca de mozos	In process of transfer to aldea of Villa Hortencia I by INTA
39. Chipol	Villa Hortencia II	15	Maize/finca de mozos	In process of transfer to aldea of Villa Hortencia II by INTA
40. Esmeralda	Between Cotzal and Chajul	Small	Maize/Cattle	Ladino to 58 Ixils, private purchase
41. Monterrey	Santa Avelina	1.5	Coffee	Ladino to ladino, private purchase
42. Coalá	Road to Nebaj	Small	Cattle	Ladino to Ixil, private purchase
43. Los Angeles	Road to Nebaj	.8	Cattle to Vegetables	Ladino to Agros Foundation, for evangelical model village

1. One caballería = 112.12 acres or 45.374 hestares (see table on page 37).

Noblesse oblige is not what the world has come to expect of Guatemalan plantation owners. Nor do Guatemala watchers expect much of the National Institute for Agrarian Transformation (INTA), the government agency charged with implementing land reform. Often dismissed as a bureaucratic farce, INTA became active in Ixil country in the late 1970s, as the army tried to uproot EGP cells, and it received fresh impetus from the administration of Ríos Montt (1982–83), whose evangelical advisers wanted to distribute any unoccupied land to the shell-shocked survivors of the army's pacification program. Given INTA's reputation, I was surprised to learn that, at least in Ixil country, it had succeeded in partitioning a number of fincas for their colonos.

All the fincas belonged to the Herrera Ibargüens, one of the largest landowning families in the country. The Herrera properties were not lucrative coffee plantations, even though several were located in the valley below Cotzal on the road to the Finca San Francisco. Instead, they provided seasonal labor for the Herreras' vast plantations on the south coast. In return for cutting sugar cane every year, Cotzaleños living on the fincas received subsistence plots to grow maize for their own consumption. It is unclear exactly what triggered the Herrera family's abandonment of its Ixil holdings. But the decision was apparently made in the late 1970s, after the Army of the Poor kidnapped a Herrera serving as cabinet minister and obtained a large ransom for his release. Since the worst of the violence, approximately 350 families in three model villages—San Felipe Chenlá, Bichibalá, and Santa Avelina— have received individual titles to former Herrera land in exchange for legal fees of U.S. $10–20 each. The members of two other villages, Villa Hortencia I and Villa Hortencia II, were in the process of receiving title to Herrera land, for a total of 4,300 hectares.[21]

Comparing the three Ixil municipios, the finca sector has been most drastically affected in Cotzal, to the point of being dismantled except for the Brol property at San Francisco. This is due in large measure to INTA, which also supposedly influenced the Brols' decision to sell their outlying fincas, although the underlying shock of the violence is evident from the decision of several small ladino finqueros to sell (table 8.7). The war's impact is less obvious in Chajul (table 8.6), where my data are very limited, and in Nebaj (table 8.5), where a countervailing tendency appears. Around Sumal Chiquito, where the lower altitudes are suitable for growing coffee, the destruction of the EGP's refugee zone in the late 1980s encouraged a quiet land rush. New investors were buying up both small fincas and Ixil smallholdings. Local schoolteachers, other public employees, two ex-mayors, and an ex-civil patrol chief were among the new owners, who included Ixils as well as ladinos. Other buyers were coffee growers from Huehuete-nango, looking for a bargain away from their own overpriced land market.

Paradoxically, Ixils owed the good fortune of a shrinking finca sector to the misfortune that their land was not worth very much. Only the lower valleys had ever been very attractive to outsiders; now they were worth less because of the war, but perhaps only as long as the presence of the EGP discouraged investors. Meanwhile, transfers from finca owners to campesinos were usually financed by outside agencies on easy terms, not by Ixils making their way in the private market. As of the early 1990s, INTA was not starting new projects in Ixil country and development agencies usually turned down appeals to finance land acquisitions. As a result, Ixil aldeas and cooperatives were failing to make hoped-for transactions, with four of the five purchases being financed by church groups.[22]

The Effects of Finca Partition

Before our fathers had three hundred, four hundred, five hundred cuerdas. Now those who have the most have a hundred, and those who have less, two, three, or five cuerdas, with eight family members. We're splitting our land into tiny pieces. . . . As síndico it gives me pain to split land holdings instead of making them larger. I wish they were made out of rubber so we could stretch them. —The member of the Nebaj town council who mediates land disputes, 1989

In a region crowded with peasant smallholdings, the recuperation of fincas provides a rare opportunity for modernizing agriculture. But much depends on how the land is allocated. Respecting the wishes of Ixil maize-farmers who are already below the level of subsistence means reproducing the same pattern of the minifundium. In the case of the Herrera estates, the colonos regarded the land they farmed as their own well before the arrival of INTA. The first men to join the finca had been assigned as much as ten or fifteen hectares each, but late arrivals received as little as two, with the resulting inequities passed to subsequent generations. Under the old regime, colonos in need of cash even sold their rights to each other, for as little as Q1 or Q.50 per cuerda. They became sufficiently proprietorial that, when INTA apportioned the finca, it agreed to head off a row by respecting the existing boundaries, even though these were wildly unequal.

The viability of the result depended on the generation. On my 1989 visits to the former Herrera estates of San Felipe Chenlá, Santa Avelina, and Bichibalá, I talked mainly with older men who, as colonos of the finca, had received relatively large installments of land for nominal legal fees. They were no longer obliged to go to the coast and expressed pleasure over their new land titles. On my return in 1990, interviews with cultivators about land use and family size revealed a grimmer picture. These were younger men in their twenties and thirties, who had been forced to divide their father's land with brothers, and their inheritances were quite inadequate.

In Bichibalá I met a tailor who was growing black beans for market and obtained a thousand-quetzal harvest from a cash investment of a few hundred. But he claimed to be the only man in Bichibalá engaged in this kind of venture. Even in Santa Avelina, whose lower elevations provide more land for growing coffee, entrepreneurship was hardly flourishing. Under the finca, colonos were prohibited from planting coffee, a management policy to prevent them from building up a long-term investment that might compete with the finca's objectives. In nearby San Felipe Chenlá, an old colono told me, the finca foreman had threatened to send him to the national penitentiary for trying to plant coffee. Later the foreman was killed by the guerrillas and the colono was able to plant coffee during the height of the violence. Now he had a valuable income freeing him to pursue his calling as an evangelical pastor.

Only a minority of those in Santa Avelina have planted coffee, however: the rest are said to be too poor, with holdings too small to spare any land for planting a cash crop. The idea of taking out a loan from the government development bank BANDESA is vigorously rejected, even though there is a branch in Nebaj that offers relatively low interest rates and, just as important, has not shown any interest in seizing the land of defaulters. "People here do as their parents taught them," said the man who claimed to be Bichibalá's sole agricultural entrepreneur. "They're not the kind to borrow from the bank." "People here just want to work by themselves without loans," the auxiliary mayor of Santa Avelina told me, "but they want their *ayuda* ("help" or handout) because they are poor." He didn't want a loan either, and he was not criticizing his neighbors: former colonos expected someone to help them make ends meet regardless of the size of their families. "Those best off have up to fifty cuerdas, but these are just *ruinos* (roughly, "ruins"). They just want their *ayuda*. They don't want to borrow," the auxiliary mayor repeated.

The people of Santa Avelina and Bichibalá remember when much of the surrounding land was still wooded; now little is, requiring two to four hours round trip to carry home firewood. Few can afford fertilizer, and everyone described the land as *cansado* (tired). In December 1990 heavy rains caused the first major landslides along the steep-sided valley of the Río Cotzal that runs below Santa Avelina. The largest of the slides plunged hundreds of yards from deforested hilltops to the river below, while others perforated hillsides in serrated rows. Entire maize fields were washed away. "The owners are crying because all their land is wasted," the auxiliary mayor told me. "The landslide carried away the milpa and the poor guy went to the finca because what is he going to eat?"

The first finca partition in Nebaj followed the same lines as the INTA projects in Cotzal, that of reinforcing minifundismo. Here the decision makers were North American philanthropists who bought the 2-caballería Finca Chemalá for the nearby resettlement of La Pista. To be equitable, they decided against turning the property over to a nascent cooperative at La Pista because it did not include the poorer families. Instead, they divided the finca into 220 parcels of four cuerdas (less than one-fifth hectare), one for each household.

When the Finca Chemalá was purchased from one of Nebaj's larger landowners, it was still heavily wooded, with land cleared only along narrow valley floors for cow pasture. As a condition for retitling the finca to La Pista, the government insisted that the steeper hillsides be set aside in a vaguely defined forest reserve. During the lengthy process of surveying, the local administrators (a committee of evangelical pastors) began selling off firewood rights to pay for expenses, prompting bitter protests from La Pista. Additional quantities of firewood were extracted by civil patrollers under orders from the army, which typically did not offer any payment. Once in possession, the La Pista owners cleared the remaining trees off their plots so quickly that they are said to have depressed the local price of firewood. Finally, confident that no one would really mind, the La Pista committee in charge of the property divided up the forest reserve into another several hundred parcels, this time of two cuerdas (one-tenth hectare) each, whose new owners began to extract the wood there, too.

The Deterioration of the Maize-based Subsistence Economy

The people say they're getting ahead. The government provides houses, schools, bridges, and roads. In this sense the people have abundance. But the road is forty meters across, when we take into account the stones and damage, and it's kilometers long. So much is lost for cultivation. There are families who already have four, six, eight members and who have lost their farmland. At La Pista there are eight evangelical churches instead of one big church. That's eight building sites lost for cultivation. Before there used to be sixteen aldeas. Now there are thirty-three, and each one wants its own soccer field. On the one hand we think we're getting ahead, but on the other hand we're losing land.   —Nebaj's síndico, 1989

The resource pressures in Santa Avelina, Bichibalá, and the Finca Chemalá were evident wherever I went in Ixil country. Following ecologists Paul and Anne Ehrlich, human impact on the environment can be viewed as a function of the number of people, their average consumption of resources, and the environmental cost of the technology they use. Or as the Ehrlichs put it, Impact = Population x Affluence x Technology.[23] In the case of Ixil country, technology over the last century has changed little, except for the spread of motorized transport and very recently chainsaws for felling trees. Levels of consumption

Carrying firewood home to Rio Azul

have also not changed much. What remains as the variable increasing most rapidly is population.

Located as Ixils are on the periphery of the highland marketing system, they continue to rely heavily on cultivating maize even by Mayan standards. They have not diversified into new commercial crops like their southern neighbors the K'iche's. Many do not even intercrop the other staple of the Mesoamerican diet, black beans, because of somewhat unfavorable conditions. Historically, the extraordinary commitment to maize reflects the abundance of land Ixils used to enjoy. Ample land permitted new families to move into fresh, unexploited areas and obtain the yields they needed to maintain self-sufficiency in maize. But those days are past. By 1966, when Colby and van den Berghe did fieldwork in Nebaj, the area was already importing maize.[24]

As land per capita decreases, it is being worked more intensively, with fallow periods being shortened to nothing. Wide swathes of *chipe* (fern) surround many of the resettlements, indicating soil no longer worth cultivating. Invariably Ixils say their land is "tired" or that "the land no longer gives," and they have become accustomed to rather low yields. By common reckoning, maximum production is two quintales (two hundred pounds) per cuerda with fertilizer and, without it, one quintal or less, with some farmers persisting even when production drops to one-fifth quintal (twenty pounds) per cuerda.[25] At the freshly cleared and parcelled Finca Chemalá, none of six cultivators reported more than a quintal per cuerda, even on the flat bottom land.

Deforestation of steep slopes is another sign of ecological deterioration in Ixil country. The growth of a subsistence farming population is not the exclusive cause: when the army retook the area in the early 1980s, it ordered systematic cutting along roads and around resettlements to guard against ambushes. The army also built new penetration roads to outlying aldeas, as did the Christian Democrats in the late 1980s. Ambitious new roads are being built or planned for the early 1990s: to the Huehuetenango uplands to the west, La Perla and Barillas to the north, and Uspantán to the southeast. More often than not, the new routes pass along ridges and through gorges where old-growth forest still survives, prompting an extractive orgy by chainsaw operators and truck owners. But if recent events have accelerated deforestation, the pattern of land use indicates that the majority of the forest cover was gone before the violence. When INTA performed agronomic surveys of six fincas and aldeas in the early 1980s, it reported that only about 40 percent of the land was suitable for cultivation, and the majority of that only for certain perennials. Yet most of the land had already been deforested for growing maize, leaving behind steeply pitched fields and brush.

The fincas that took much of the best valley land are partly responsible for the destruction, by pushing Ixil cultivators up steep hillsides. But not commercial logging; until the recent advent of the chainsaw, the felling was done by campesinos swinging axes, who were usually too far from a road to sell the trunks. Only the most valuable wood was extracted, if that, leaving the rest to be burned and treeless slopes to plunge for miles. Even now, the charred cadavers of forest giants crisscross fields sprouting a few anemic cornstalks. At first I thought the presence of the guerrillas might serve to protect certain areas from deforestation. That failed to take into account the tens of thousands of refugees who, while living under EGP administration, clear-cut remote pine and cloud forest to plant enough maize to keep from starving. Some of the most extensive clear-cutting I saw is in a deep ravine on the way to the Finca La Perla, where thousands of Ixils used to shelter from army rampages. Most of the forest cover which survives near the three towns seems to be fenced off on larger properties, some owned by ladinos and others by well-off Ixils, but it is not likely to survive subdivision for Ixil farmers.

Lengthening journeys for firewood are a related sign of ecological distress. Twenty years ago Ixils walked half a kilometer or so for firewood, but now they are going five, six, or more. "Firewood used to be much closer, without the need to buy it," Nebaj's síndico told me. "People just picked it up wherever they found it. Ladino and some Indian owners cared; others didn't even care. Now they complain to the judge and there's a fine." In town the cost of a month's firewood has climbed past the price of bottled gas,[26] although the cost of setting up a gas range has prevented many from making the switch. In outlying aldeas where firewood is less scarce than in the town center, some people buy standing trees from owners as far as three hours round-trip from their houses.

Even with the terrible loss of life in the war, the Ixil homeland remains too crowded for subsistence maize agriculture. When I surveyed leaders and household heads in the town of Nebaj, they reported owning an average of less than two hectares each (see table 2.7 in chapter 2). At an average forty years of age, they also reported a mean of four living children. Even though Ixil families tend to restrict the inheritance of land to males, the average heir in these families will receive less than one hectare—far below the .6 hectares of arable land per family member that Mayan cultivators need for self-sufficiency in maize.[27] The cost of being landless is, moreover, high: when the daily wage around Nebaj was Q5 (about U.S. $1) a day in late 1990, a hundred pounds of maize cost Q40. If that kept a young family of five in food for ten days, according to a local estimate,[28] eight days of wage labor would be required just to buy the maize, with precious little to cover the cost of black beans, the main protein source, as well as other necessities like clothes, medicine, and school supplies. As most of the population was reduced to slivers of worn-out land, it was also being reduced to poverty even by traditional standards, let alone as measured by development models.

The dilemma raises an obvious question. If population growth is indeed generating impoverishment in Ixil country, how do Ixils perceive the situation? Do they perceive the number of children they have as a survival strategy, as much of the social science literature claims, or would they like to limit their fertility?

Ixil Attitudes Toward Family Size

At thirty-eight years of age, Pedro has six children and owns two-thirds of a hectare of land, which is why he extracts wood and goes to the coast to make a living. He denies that he has children to provide income but agrees they are important to provide for old age. Whether he will have more children is "according to the will of God," therefore he is not interested in family planning. When I ask how his six children are going to fare with just sixteen cuerdas of land, his answer is the campesino exclamation "Saber!" (who knows?).

Diego is twenty-five years old, has three children, and owns almost a hectare of land. Instead of going to the coast like many of his neighbors, Pablo buys lumber from local woodcutters and rents trucks to sell it in Guatemala City. Since exporting lumber to the capital is against the law, the business requires expensive negotiations with the authorities. Pablo also hopes to buy two cows with a loan from the government agricultural bank. When one of his children had to be hospitalized recently in Guatemala City, the clinic persuaded his wife to start taking birth control pills. The couple are supposed to go to the capital every month for a check-up but can't afford the trip, hence they have run out of pills. But Pablo says he wants to wait six years for his next child, then stop at four children whose medical care and education he can provide, instead of having ten children whom he cannot support.

*—Interviews with two evangelicals at the
partitioned Finca Chemalá, 1990*

So far the Guatemalan population shows little movement toward "modern" levels of fertility, that is, the demographic transition of falling rates associated with industrialization in Europe and the United States.[29] Despite rapid urbanization, in the late 1980s population growth was creeping upward to 3.2 percent a year.[30] Should Guatemalan women continue to have an average of 6.4 live births, according to the national family planning council, the 1990 population of 9.2 million will quadruple to 34.3 million in the first quarter of the next century. Even in the event of a rapid decrease in fertility, to an average of 2.52 live births per woman, according to the council's calculations, Guatemala's population will double to 19 million by 2025.[31]

Calculating the birth rate in Nebaj is complicated by our lack of a firm population baseline, but it is probably higher than the national average, in keeping with the tendency of rural, Indian, and unschooled women to produce more babies than their urban, ladino, and more educated counterparts. Normally, the number of live births is obtained from the civil register. This is a source that optimists consider accurate for all but the most short-lived infants.[32] But even if this is the case, calculations from the civil register in Ixil country have been complicated by the war, particularly the late registration of children born in the montaña.

To illustrate the problem, a government health survey shows the Nebaj birth rate ranging from a low of 34 births per thousand in 1981 (when reporting would have been low owing to the exodus of refugees) to 75 per thousand in 1984 (when latecomers returning from the montaña were registering).[33] For 1988, the 1,555 on-time birth registrations[34] suggest a high birth rate whose precise level depends on our estimate of the population under government control. If we suppose that only twenty-five thousand Nebajeños were under government control in 1988 (see table 8.8), the result is 62.2 births per thousand women. A middle assumption of twenty-nine thousand gives 53.6 births per thousand women, while thirty-three thousand Nebajeños under government control gives a birth rate of 47.1—still above very high national rates in the 41–43 range.

Perhaps because middle-class observers so often criticize the poor for producing too many children, social scientists have taken pains to explain the rationality of large families for peasants. "People are not poor because they have large families," Mahmood Mamdani concluded from his study of U.S.-financed birth control programs in India.

Table 8.8
*Base Population/Birth Rates per 1,000 Women in Nebaj
for 1,555 On-Time Registrations in 1988[1]*

Base Population	Birth Rate per 1,000 Women
25,000	62.2
27,000	57.6
29,000	53.6
31,000	50.2
33,000	47.1

SOURCE: Calculated by the author on the basis of data collected in the Nebaj civil registrar's office.

"Quite the contrary: they have large families because they are poor."[35] That is, peasants have large families because each child eventually produces more income (or survival advantage) than he or she costs. "However primitive the conditions under which they live," Alain de Janvry summarizes the maximization literature, most couples "are individually rational in adjusting the number of children they have to the economic, political, juridical and ideological conditions of their lives."[36] In Guatemala, studies of Tz'utujil Maya families on Lake Atitlán, by John Early and James Loucky, also point toward the utility of many children or "high fertility logic."[37]

Because maximization is still the prevailing explanation for high peasant fertility, I expected Ixils to acknowledge that they had lots of children to contribute to production. Ixil children indeed work from the age of seven or eight, especially to tend animals and haul heavy loads of firewood. But parents deny having large families for economic reasons, at least around town where I did most of my interviewing. No, Ixil women told me: children are just something that happens. Many refer to God's will, but they also complain that large numbers of children keep a family poor. As for men, they often say they want fewer children, citing the difficulty of providing food, and are quite aware of the consequences for land inheritance.[38] Men also usually deny that large families are intended to enhance family income, pointing out that maize does not reward additional labor inputs with higher production. As for taking a large family to the coast, meager pay and lowland illnesses make this an unconvincing investment. Instead, men told me, they had large families for "not thinking."

Ixils do not spontaneously identify family size as a problem the same way they do the need for reconstruction aid.[39] Only when I brought up the matter did Ixils acknowledge it, even if they then did so with eloquence and conviction. "For lack of orientation, we dedicate ourselves to manufacturing children," a tailor and father of six lamented. "When there were only two of us, and one child, life was better. There was money in my pocket. Now life is a struggle. I have repented of having so many children." The quasi-helpless attitude raises the question of whether, as maximization theorists contend, Ixil couples manage to stop having children at the point where they perceive that costs outweigh benefits. Perhaps Ixils are embarrassed to admit that the number of children they have is the result of calculation. But if we take them at their word—a denial of calculation, together with complaints about the burden of large families and explanation of their size in terms of God's will or a failure to think ahead—it suggests a non-maximization interpretation of high fertility.

In a study of southern Mexico, Debra Ann Schumann found that, contrary to Mamdani, the social context of decision making limits choice and blocks modification of natural fertility patterns. Among Tzeltal Maya immigrants to the lowland forests of Chiapas, she found no demonstrable effect of reproductive decision making on fertility, nor was demand for labor the most important variable affecting it. More important were religious ideology, public opinion, and the availability of family planning, with decision making coming out of a "preattentive" sphere.[40] The same factors seem to be at work in Ixil country, with Catholic sisters putting in their word on the subject. But even if they did not, many women would still regard one pregnancy after another as what God sends them. The majority of the population does not have ready access to modern birth control, and those who do tend to find that the available techniques—pills, intrauterine devices, prophylactics, rhythm—are not very acceptable or practical. Generally speaking, Ixils express fear of birth control, citing negative experiences (typically someone else's) with the government health center that provides it.

Obviously, if large families are economically rational for Ixils, they are not likely to lower their fertility. Nor is there much chance of reducing population growth, especially if it keeps couples so poor that they have no choice but to maximize the number of children who can be sent out to scrap for additional income. But if large families are not economically rational—if these are instead the result of "not thinking" (and not having an acceptable alternative)—then Ixils might well respond to new and improved forms of family planning. Under current circumstances, the interest of Ixils in large families is probably diverging like never before. Numerous progeny may still be actively desired by couples who live in outlying aldeas and perceive that they have enough land. Women who told me they wanted smaller families tended to have an unusual amount of schooling and be involved in commercial activities. Younger Ixils tend to be more interested in limiting the size of their families than older ones, apparently because they are receiving less land from their fathers, which forces them to struggle with larger subsistence shortfalls.[41]

Escaping the Crisis

How much do they pay for work in the United States?
—Popular question in Nebaj

At the start of my study, I hypothesized that the violence might ultimately benefit Ixil farmers by (1) helping to recover their grandparents' land from departing finca owners, and (2) improving the person/land ratio through the ghastly process of reducing the population. It is true that a significant share of the land surface owned by ladinos has been returned to the indigenous population.[42] It is also true that population loss has increased the amount of land per capita (see table 8.9). But I doubt Ixil farmers will derive any lasting benefit, for two reasons. First, as mentioned earlier, their high fertility will apparently recoup the losses of the war in the 1990s and double the population in the 2010s. Second, the result of finca partitions to date suggests that, even if all ladino holdings were returned to Ixil smallholders, their use of the land would soon exhaust it.

As we saw in the cases of Bichibalá, Santa Avelina, and Chemalá, many Ixils lack the resources to do anything with their land except extract dwindling maize harvests. They do not have enough land for

Table 8.9

Improvement in Land per Capita as a Result of the Violence

		Projected Land per Capita for 1989 Without the War		Estimated Actual Land per Capita in 1989	
	Area (km²)	Projected Census Population[1]	Hectares/ Person	Estimated Actual Population	Hectares/ Person
Nebaj	608	45,438	1.34	32,709	1.86
Chajul	1,524	38,672	3.94	19,423	7.85[2]
Cotzal	182	17,669	1.03	17,940	1.01
Ixil Triangle	2,314	101,779	2.27	70,072	3.30

1. Projected census population in 1989: Instituto Nacional de Estadística 1988:24. Estimated actual population in 1989: based on figures from the United Nations Development Program (UNDP)/Program for Refugees, Repatriates and Displaced Peoples (PRODERE), as corrected by the author (see notes to table 8.4).

2. Per the previous discussion in chapter 8, the improvement in Chajul's hectare/person ratio can be attributed to the way government statisticians calculated population increase, as can the failure of Cotzal's hectare/person ratio to increase. The global figure for the Ixil Triangle gives the best picture.

fallow periods, and the size of the average family dictates continued subdivision through inheritance to the point of landlessness. Worse, since much of the finca sector is already covered with the subsistence plots of colonos, putting the land in their own name does not increase what is available for subsistence.

Because land cannot be stretched like rubber, as Nebaj's síndico put it, one way Ixils could change their response to scarcity is by reducing the size of their families. As the preceding section indicates, Ixils are becoming more interested in doing so, even if their success to date has been limited. Another way Ixils can change their response to scarcity is how they make a living. As it turns out, the only towns in the western highlands resisting pauperization no longer depend on traditional subsistence agriculture. Instead, they have moved into commerce, small-scale coffee cultivation and other profitable cash crops.[43]

In this respect, at least, Ixils are taking longer strides than in family planning. No one advocates abandoning maize, but more Ixils are joining government extension agents in decrying it as a dead-end economic strategy. "All you see around here is maize, maize, maize!" a bilingual promoter cries. "One quintal per cuerda isn't good for anything! We live like pigs. What's needed instead are fruit orchards, apples produced by Israeli-style cooperatives." Fortunately, models are closer at hand than Israel. K'iche' Mayas to the south have already diversified their agriculture for home consumption and the market. Ixil interest in nonagricultural occupations also follows a K'iche' pattern, this one established centuries earlier, when population growth and ecological deterioration forced diversification into artisan trades and commerce. A critical factor, according to Thomas Veblen, was the degradation of a wide swathe of Totonicapán and southern Quiché by sheep grazing.[44] The Ixil area has yet to desertify like the dry, eroded landscape to the south, but its inhabitants are already casting about for alternative models. The movement toward reformed religion includes an obvious effort to change the way resources are invested, from community rituals to the improvement of self, family, and congregations that reinforce the new priorities.[45]

Even as many Ixils learn the language of salvation, exceedingly few have learned to talk ecology, that is, the language of preoccupation over resources that Western observers so often impute to indigenous peoples. My queries on this subject provided little ground for encouragement: the Ixil word for tree, *tze'*, translates literally as *palo* or stick, and it was hard to find anyone who would put in a good word for trees as anything but firewood, building material, or a quick source of cash. Rituals of propitiation still practiced by some Ixils, such as burning incense before cutting a tree, were not preventing forest cover from being razed.[46] Most of the population was so hard-pressed that it had no choice but to deforest even the kind of mountain slopes from which a cultivator can fall and break his neck. According to technicians starting reforestation projects, the best argument with Ixil farmers was not soil conservation, let alone concepts of the ecosphere. Instead, it was their need for firewood. As a result, reforestation programs pushed mainly non-native, rapid-growth tree species that would appeal to peasants because they could be harvested within a few years for burning. With ecological restoration a pipe dream, the only hope for what was left of old-growth forest was that new stands of trees for firewood would relieve some of the pressure on it.

Another language Ixils were learning faster than ecology was that of emigration—from outlying villages into the town center, to Guatemala City and, in their dreams, to the United States. This was not to be confused with seasonal movement to the plantations, the pattern that originated in the coercive methods of labor procurement we saw in chapter 2, then became "voluntary" as Ixils lost self-sufficiency in maize, and was still the most important form of economic migration in Ixil country. The new migration was, instead, the urge to move to a bigger and brighter place. It meant breaking with the peasant ecology of dispersed settlement which, paradoxically, seasonal movement to the plantations had helped maintain. From the point of view of subsistence maize agriculture, the most adaptive response to scarcity was to move out from the crowded town centers to outlying lands, hence the settlement of the Sumal ridge north of Nebaj from early in the century, and of Amajchel in the warm lands north of Chajul since the 1960s. This was why refugees with the most mouths to feed seemed the most eager to return to their outlying lands, even on the army's terms, because of the greater availability of land and firewood there.

Now for the first time, thousands of Ixils were turning their backs on subsistence maize agriculture to make a new kind of life. Some were virtually landless; others were still proprietors but no longer wanted to face the manifold pressures. Hence the Ixils around Sumal Chiquito who were starting to sell coffee-growing land to ladinos and well-off Ixils for low prices. In one case, a schoolteacher bought 110 cuerdas for the bargain price of Q10 each, that is, five hectares of valuable land for U.S. $300. The seller was fed up with being forced to live jammed together with his neighbors in a concentrated settlement and serve in the civil patrols. Although he barely knew how to sign his name, he was going to the capital to join a son living there.

Springing up around the adobe and tile urban cores of Nebaj, Chajul, and Cotzal were new rings of refugee housing, the color of fresh lumber, reaching higher up hillsides that used to be forested or down into ravines that used to be pasture. Despite acute shortages of firewood and agricultural land, life in the towns looked sufficiently favorable compared to the model villages that thousands of refugees clustered around them. The heavier demands by civil patrols out in the aldeas were one reason. The civil patrol in town required only guard duty once every two weeks, a Pulay woodcutter explained, as opposed to tramping through the mountains hunting for guerrillas. New urbanites also talked about the greater *vida* (life) and *movimiento* (movement) attracting them: town was more *alegre* (joyful or lively). With a push from insecure conditions out in the aldeas, these people were choosing water from a tap, electric light, and proximity to a road over the old ideal of proximity to their fields, even if it meant more dependence on wage labor for a living.

Even Ixils returning to their aldea preferred, if at all possible, to hold onto their refugee housing in town. The relief agencies tried to prevent it, not wanting to finance two shelters for each family. But dual residence is an ancient pattern in Mayan life: the house in town is used while serving in the civil-religious hierarchy, with the other out in the countryside for growing maize and raising animals. One place the tradition was reasserting itself was Las Violetas, the refugee camp in Nebaj that had become a new neighborhood. Refugees returning to the countryside were required to put up their houses for sale. But extended kin ties made it hard to tell exactly who was living where and the neighbor's committee looked the other way, permitting many households to realize the old ideal of a town and a country house, albeit in the form of wooden shacks. Las Violetas was full of Ixils from village backgrounds who were experimenting with new urban occupations and, despite their penurious circumstances, hoping to *superar* (get ahead).

Nebajeños going to Guatemala City were overwhelmingly young and without families, particularly young women working as domestic servants. When the latter returned for town fiestas, they were a suspect category, marked by the allure and stigma of urban experience. The attractions of urban life, including freedom from Ixil relatives, meant that a significant number of these women settled there. In the capital and regional centers there was also a growing number of students and professionals, unable to find jobs at home fitting their ambitions. An earlier wave left during the violence, often relatives of people who had been accused of collaborating with the guerrillas, with some still afraid to return.

The capital was not the ultimate destination in the minds of Nebajeños, however. That was reserved for the United States, a compelling standard of modernity and comfort for the entire country. As of the early 1990s, Guatemalans settling in the United States still tended to be ladinos from urban backgrounds. The Nebajeños there consisted of ladinos, a few K'iche's, and a single Ixil who married a North American at the height of the violence, was taken to northern Minnesota, and became so traumatized by the isolation that she returned to Guatemala. But word had spread, so that men in the most rustic settings could now be counted on to ask *"Hay chance en los Estados Unidos?"* Refugees fresh from the mountains, with very limited Spanish, asked if I could take them to the United States to work. Sweatshirts bore slogans like "Los Angeles, California" and (in English) "U.S.A.—I'm gonna win!"

Ixils told stories about gringos who showed up in airplanes offering work in the great country to the north. According to one version, the Ixils lost their chance when no one wanted to go. According to another, the gringo flew off to obtain the necessary papers but never returned. The Ixils closest to actually attempting the journey overland through Mexico were unusually bilingual and well educated: they either had pursued studies outside Nebaj or worked as labor contractors. Like the majority of Central American immigrants to the United States, I suspect, they were not victims of political persecution. Instead, they were economic migrants attracted by North American images of consumption. If Ixils do establish themselves in the United States, they will be only one of the myriad migration streams from ecologically degraded localities in the Third World seeking advancement by moving to the center of the world system.[47]

NINE

The Struggle to Rebuild
Civil Society in Nebaj

Xolcuay, Chajul, 1990

The luxury of relatively safe, open political opposition is both rare and recent. The vast majority of people have been and continue to be not citizens, but subjects. So long as we confine our conception of the political to activity that is openly declared we are driven to conclude that subordinate groups essentially lack a political life or that what political life they do have is restricted to those exceptional moments of popular explosion. To do so is to miss the immense political terrain that lies between quiescence and revolt and that, for better or worse, is the political environment of subject classes. It is to focus on the visible coastline of politics and miss the continent that lies beyond. —James C. Scott, 1990

WHEN outsiders look at Ixil country, they tend to see it in terms of a titanic political struggle between Left and Right. But for most Nebajeños, these are categories imposed by external forces on a situation they perceive rather differently. Class and ethnic divisions that seem obvious to outsiders are, for Nebajeños, crosscut by family and community ties. Because of their wealth of local knowledge, Nebajeños are intimately aware of the opacity and confusion of local politics, far more so than interpreters from afar. They are aware of subterfuges that went into the construction of how events were reported to the outside world. Their firsthand experience of army brutality is complemented by knowledge of how the guerrillas provoked it, and of EGP brutality as well. They have insights into the motives of assassins and victims, revolutionary militants and army informers, which never entered a human rights report but shape their judgment of what happened. What seem clear consequences of national and international developments to cosmopolitan observers are, for local people, wrapped in all the ambiguity of local life.

For outsiders interested above all in politics, it must be emphasized that, for Nebajeños, the whole category of *política* is associated with treachery and failure.[1] This includes the electoral apparatus, despite wishful interpretation of it as a sign of democracy, owing to the disjunction between what politicians offer prior to election and how they behave afterward. Few have favorable memories of any regime except Ríos Montt's, and of his mainly for saving the town from extermination. Older people are more likely to praise the law-and-order dictator Jorge Ubico (1931–44) than Guatemala's two reform governments (1944–54). In the late 1980s "Left" and "Right" were not labels used by most Nebajeños, nor did political rivals confront each other over ideology. Instead, they competed in terms of personality and patronage, with opposition parties decrying waste and corruption in the town hall and the DC warning that, if it was voted out of office, aid programs would be cut off. As a result, the space of hope to which reformist politicians appeal is hard to find.

Disenchantment is no surprise in view of the structural impasse facing Guatemalans, as incarnated by a powerful, violent ultra-Right that refuses to tolerate dissent. Three decades of insurgency have given the army an open-ended rationale for militarizing national life, relegating political parties, elections, and civil government to the status of a charade, albeit a lucrative one for politicians. So discredited is the political system that, according to John Watanabe, the most relevant political opposition is not between parties or candidates but between the community and the government, hence a "sovereign" community before the state.[2] This also helps explain the high regard for Ríos Montt, who many Guatemalans perceive to have come from outside the corrupting world of *política*, thrust aside the politicians, and cleaned up the government through sheer moral strength.

Disbelief in political solutions is what has made Guatemala such fertile ground for born-again religion. Only the transformation of enough individual sinners like you and me, evangelists tell their audiences, can possibly rescue Guatemala from evil. Take a popular story preachers tell across Latin America, of the *presidente* who exclaims how much better his government would work if everyone was an evangelical. As retailed to Nebajeños in 1988, by a ladino evangelist imported from the capital, the tale begins with a drug pusher and murderer who accepts Christ in prison, then becomes so well known as a faith healer that he is taken to the national palace.[3] "Mr. President, my general," the evangelist rants breathlessly, evoking the awesomeness of his commitment,

"I am an evangelical Christian!" "You are truly an evangelical," the presidente responds with corresponding awe. "If all my government consisted of evangelicals, I wouldn't have so many problems!" No matter that the supposed date of the meeting, 1974, points to a military president who was running death squads out of the national palace. The lesson the ladino evangelist pounded home with this story, the refrain he panted every few minutes, was "race or stature doesn't matter, the gospel is for everyone!"

Evangelical claims for the world-changing potential of moral commitment may not seem very credible. Still, the conflict of assumptions between evangelicals and most scholars is so obvious that it calls for us to look carefully at our own. Because of the long rivalry between Hispanic and Anglo colonialism, North American scholars want to banish the characteristic prejudices of Anglo moralism from their studies, hence have made an historical-structural view almost normative. The same historical-structural assumptions are shared by the majority of Latin American intellectuals, as illustrated by the common practice of addressing a contemporary issue by explaining the history of it, starting with the Spanish Conquest. This may be a cogent way of talking about Latin America, but it is also a very deterministic one. On the one hand, it implies that changes in direction are extremely constrained or impossible; on the other, paradoxically, it fuels élanist views of achieving change through revolutionary violence. Evangelicals are not immune to explaining the tragedy of Guatemala in terms of structure and history, but their religious assumptions provide a distinct source of hope. While most remain pessimistic about changing the country, they make much of the ability of individuals to change themselves, their families, and their immediate surroundings. Given the popularity of this "conversionist" or "revivalist" view of the possibilities open to Guatemalans, can any such changes be seen on the local level in Nebaj?

Certainly, espousing born-again salvation and political neutrality help Ixils distance themselves from political confrontation. But the value of these discourses is not just defensive: they also help Ixils construct more equitable social relations with ladinos. The preacher's refrain quoted above, "race or stature doesn't matter, the gospel is for everyone," is a standard evangelical teaching across Latin America, but its egalitarianism has special resonance in a place like Nebaj. From Colby and van den Berghe we have a detailed account of ladino domination in the town, a legacy Ixils remember and experience to this day. Given the blood debts of the violence and growing Ixil assertiveness, the result could easily be sharp and obvious ethnic tension. But such is not the case. While Ixils have not forgotten their bitter memories and some ladinos complain about *indios* who are becoming more competitive, ethnic tension seems to be abating.

The sense of community in post-massacre Nebaj is ambiguous: it requires condoning serious social inequities and war crimes. But it comes out of a preexisting language of moral obligation that the war may have reinforced, perhaps because Nebajeños view the violence as having come primarily from outside the municipio rather than welling up from local conflicts. It is the result of active effort by members of both ethnic groups, for whom reformed religion transcends ethnic distinctions, and for whom espousing political neutrality displaces blame for the killing onto external forces. This is a language of community that embraces both ethnic groups and is flexible enough to accommodate changes in the power relations between them.

Meanwhile, Ixils have been using institutions approved by Guatemala's counterinsurgency state to reopen political space in which to make their own decisions. This effort can be understood in terms of rebuilding civil society, a concept typically understood in opposition to the state. Defined by what it is not—not the state, not the economy, and not the family—civil society exists at the level of social institutions where participation is voluntary or sanctioned by tradition. Such institutions—saint societies, evangelical congregations, development committees—may be far from democratic or egalitarian. But they have a certain autonomy from the state and represent the rule of law or custom in the face of arbitrary power, making them a vehicle for local expression and control.

Because of the stark polarization of politics in Guatemala, it is easy to overlook the significance of nonconfrontational institutions that appear totally subordinate to the state, such as evangelical churches. This is why, in discussions of contemporary Guatemala, the term *popular organizations* usually refers to groups that are in active opposition to the state and being persecuted by it. The obvious example in Ixil country at the time of this writing were the communities of population in resistance (CPRs), the settlements of internal refugees being attacked by the army and defended by the guerrillas. However, this chapter will begin with forms of popular organization in the constricted parameters of Nebaj and how these contribute to rebuilding civil society. It concludes with the CPRs; the arrival of human rights discourse in Nebaj in the early 1990s; and the implications for how Ixils around the three towns have defended themselves from political violence.

The New Reformed Standard

I would go to mass, then to the marimba for liquor. I went to mass and it didn't do anything for me. Sure, Padre Javier preached against liquor, but we didn't pay attention, we were thinking of other things. I finally repented when I fell down and hurt myself. Lord, take away this liquor, take away this vice, I prayed. I prayed to the Lord and joined the evangelicals. Vice and the marimba were pleasurable to this flesh of mine. That's why the brethren prayed a lot with me. Take away this vice, Lord. The brethren kept on praying. In another fifteen or twenty days, I didn't think of liquor anymore. I didn't think of cigarettes anymore. I didn't think of the marimba anymore. Two or three months later, I asked the brethren to pray for me again. The Lord put my life in order, six years ago.
                                                    —*Former catechist, 1989*

Now I've accepted. What would other people think?
                            —*Evangelical convert explaining why she cannot*
                                          engage in prohibited conduct, 1989

Throughout the 1980s, Protestantism seemed to have the upper hand in Ixil country. In town, many of the young Ixils pursuing their education and dreaming of escaping subsistence agriculture were evangelicals. Out in the villages, the first response to my queries was sometimes that there were "few" Catholics and "many" evangelicals because the latter were so much more active and visible, even though they proved to be only a large minority. Evangelicals did dominate some aldeas: in 1986, based on a tabulation of 467 households in Salquil Grande, Andrés

Sobering up

Fajardo found that 44 percent were Protestant (with 25 percent Catholic Action, 30 percent costumbrista, and 2 percent split).[4] Three years later, the small aldea of Parramos Chiquito claimed to be almost entirely evangelical.

The influence of evangelical teaching on Catholic lay leaders was also telling.[5] Take the charismatic leader at the Finca La Perla who hauled out a large Bible, provided by the parish priest, and searched for proof texts like a fundamentalist, to justify his quest for personal righteousness. Like charismatics generally did in Chajul, he stressed his separation from other Catholics. "Catholic Action is always drinking and committing impure acts. But the Renewal does not smoke, drink, or dance except in the Holy Spirit." Ironically, a rival leader in Catholic Action sounded the same note. Clutching a Bible, this middle-aged catechist said he had stopped drinking nine years before. For the fifteen or twenty men most active in the local Catholic Action chapter, he continued, it would be a loss of prestige to drink heavily. As I admired a colorful pastiche of devotional images, he asked what I thought of them. It was just a question of what people had become used to, not of idolatry, he said defensively. The worship service he had just led was vaguely evangelical in style, and visits by a priest were rare. "If the Catholic Church still exists now that there are so many religions," he pondered, as if the proliferation of alternatives had cast doubt on his faith.

Protestantism was providing a new orientation for Catholic farmers facing land scarcity and being forced to diversify into new forms of craft and trade. It provided a behavioral code that, as Liliana Goldin and Brent Metz have pointed out, contradicted Mayan tradition but was widely considered useful and appropriate to the new situation. In particular, Protestantism encouraged a new sense of productive time in which folk Catholic traditions tied to the agricultural cycle come to seem wasteful.[6] Yet this new reformed standard was hardly confined to evangelicals, nor did it originate with them, at least in Ixil country. Thinking about one God, the figure of Christ, the Bible, and spiritual individualism was probably introduced to more of the population by Catholic priests and Catholic Action than by Protestants.[7] The charismatic renewal in the Ixcán (and ultimately Ixil country) was introduced by a North American priest of the Maryknoll order. Moreover, some of the most powerful impressions of Protestant hegemony date to a period of acute persecution of the Catholic Church. By the late 1980s, the Catholic pastoral structure was reasserting itself. Contrasts between drys and wets, reformed and unreformed cut across the Catholic/Protestant divide. What Protestants had, for the time being although not necessarily forever, was a more effective form of organization and leadership—that of the sect or schismatic church—for riding the new wave.

Usually observers regard ideological divisions in the Catholic Church as a sign of weakness. But in view of the contradictory demands by different constituencies, for a broad inclusive fellowship accommodating tradition on the one hand and for congregational-style discipline on the other, the availability of three kinds of Catholicism for a people undergoing rapid, traumatic change could also be considered a source of strength. Under the same ecclesiastical canopy, Ixils could worship the gods of their ancestors, experiment with a new kind of discipline (Catholic Action), and sample infusion by the Holy Spirit (charismatic renewal). They could waver and change their minds more than once, as converts often do, without crossing the public divide between Catholicism and Protestantism. Even the competition between Catholic Action and the charismatic renewal might be healthy, encouraging each to reach out to new people, so long as a priest could keep them together with traditionalists under the Catholic umbrella.

Catholic Action was something of a halfway house between tradition and the new reformed Christianity: while it led the break from the saint societies in the 1950s and 1960s, over the next two decades its criteria loosened, partly as a consequence of members returning to old ways and partly because priests wanted to stay on good terms with traditionalists. Unlike evangelical and charismatic groups, Catholic Action claimed to represent the whole community. Before the war, its *centros* or chapters seem to have been the core of modern social organization in most aldeas, even if the majority of villagers remained traditionalists. Then with a shove from the violence, Catholic Action disintegrated into competing groups of catechists, charismatics, and evangelicals. Absent the guiding hand of a Catholic priest, the reform impulse led to more rhetorical emphasis on the Bible, more emotional forms of worship, and a more obviously congregational form of organization.

When I asked Ixils what they thought of traditional practices, evangelicals averaged considerably less approval than traditionalists, catechists, or charismatics. But except for drinking, which the majority of Catholics joined in criticizing, evangelicals generally declined to condemn Ixil traditions such as consulting with Ixil priests and diviners, going to the marimba, and participating in cofradías. Instead, they displayed a tolerant, distancing attitude.[8] "I'm not thinking about them," one evangelical said of Ixil priests. "If that's their thing, let them continue. Why should I say whether it's good or bad? Only God knows, everyone has his own ideas." An evangelical pastor saw nothing wrong with participating in a theatrical production in which an Ixil priest rescues the town's beauty queen from an earth deity. "It's the culture of the town," he said of the saint societies. "If someone wants to do it, let them do it. For me no, because I have my own religion. Everyone is free." Another pastor living in Antigua was trying to reconstruct an Ixil version of the Mayan calendar, justifying his task on the grounds that, regardless of the calendar's religious associations, it is a technical and cultural achievement.

The problem of liquor is the most visible marker of reformed religion, as usually seems the case in Mesoamerican Indian communities. Nebaj has long been a town of drunks who eye their next shot with mixed emotions,[9] but abstaining from alcohol is in fashion like never before. Even cofradía heads were swearing sobriety for Easter processions, with a few vowing that, for fiestas, they would limit their drinking to ceremonial toasts and refuse to provide any further liquor. The unconscious still litter the streets in the wake of fiestas, but fewer than before. Some Nebajeños argue that drinking has declined because of the war and resulting poverty, but the means of inebriation have, if anything, become cheaper, owing to displacement of the officially taxed aguardiente by locally manufactured kuxa.[10] With kuxa always available to the poorest day laborer, drinking can prolong itself from a ritual occasion into a daily affair, and finding a way to stop can still be a matter of life and death.

Like traditionalists, evangelicals seek a feeling of human solidarity and transcendence in group rituals,[11] but they do so in a way that avoids the effects of heavy drinking. True to a longstanding paradox of Protestant revivalism, the emotion in a worship service encourages a more controlled life.[12] The members of evangelical congregations are disproportionately in their twenties to forties, couples with young children and heavy family responsibilities. What they have in common is, not a certain position in the Nebaj class structure, but the wish to husband their resources for what they call "the ordered life." "Some have land, others don't have land and have to go to the coast," a pastor explained. "But now we see where the money goes. Because if we are not evangelicals, we have to drink, they throw us into jail and we have to pay a fine. But now we control our lives."

The language of self-discipline in evangelical churches has tempted social scientists to look for Max Weber's "Protestant ethic" and the "spirit of capitalism." According to Weber, the doctrine of predestination left seventeenth-century Calvinists so anxious over whether they would go to heaven or hell that they compensated by throwing themselves into their "calling," an individual's pursuit of God's will as manifested by a life of abstinence, thrift, and productive investment.[13] Scholars recognize that the particulars of Weber's model never made the journey to Latin America: predestination fell by the wayside in the revivals of the eighteenth and nineteenth centuries. As a result, evangelicals do not dwell on the problem of whether or not they have been saved.

Still, it is not hard to find associations between Protestantism, thrift, and entrepreneurship in Guatemala. In the Kaqchikel Maya town of San Antonio Aguas Calientes, Sheldon Annis found that evangelicals were overrepresented in owning motor vehicles, commercializing local handweavings, and cash-cropping.[14] In the Lake Atitlán towns of San Juan and Panajachel, James Sexton found evidence that Protestants were wealthier than Catholics.[15] The question is how typical these correlations are. In research around Quezaltenango, Timothy Evans found that the equation between Protestantism and bourgeois status was occasional. While there was indeed a link between Protestantism, cash-cropping, and small-scale commerce in the K'iche' Maya town of Almolonga, it broke down next door in Cantel, where the owners of a well-known linen factory were Catholic whereas their workers tended to be evangelical.[16] From her surveys of the market system in the western highlands, Carol Smith concludes that, while an association between Protestantism and a new class of petty capitalists may exist in some towns, it does not in many others, where the same class of rising entrepreneur tends to be reformed Catholic or even traditionalist.[17]

In Nebaj, when Thomas Lengyel worked with Ixil language informants in the mid-1970s, he sensed that evangelicals and Catholic catechists had rather different value orientations. Both groups were interested in education, but catechists remained committed to agriculture while evangelicals wanted to leave Nebaj to study. Young evangelical leaders were more interested in emulating ladinos and operating in Spanish than their Catholic counterparts were, to the point of seeing ladino ways as morally superior. Catechists also wanted to be able to operate in Spanish, but for what Lengyel called tactical reasons, to defend themselves and their community. Catholic catechists were, despite their rejection of the saint societies, more oriented to the local culture and rooted in the community than evangelicals were.[18]

Fifteen years later, it is not hard to find young evangelicals who fit the image of the innovative, hardworking entrepreneur. When the Ministry of Development administered a questionnaire to refugees returning to their land, 14 percent of the evangelicals reported a nona-

Table 9.1

Religion and Nonagricultural Occupations in Nebaj

	% of Total Sample	Non-agricultural Skill (%)	Commerce (%)	Teaching (%)	Employee (%)	Agriculture/ Domestic (%)	Total No. of Cases
		(number of cases for each category is in parentheses)					
Evangelical	40.6	46.8 (22)	50.0 (20)	37.5 (24)	50 (3)	35.6 (37)	106
Catholic Action	17.2	12.8 (6)	12.5 (5)	26.6 (17)	33 (2)	14.4 (15)	45
Charismatic Renewal	3.8	4.3 (2)	7.5 (3)	1.6 (1)	—	3.8 (4)	10
No Religion	3.0	—	—	12.5 (8)	—	—	8
"Reformed" Total	64.8	63.9 (30)	70.0 (28)	78.2(50)	83.3 (5)	53.8 (56)	169
Traditionalists	35.2	36.2 (17)	30.0 (12)	21.9 (14)	16.7 (1)	46.2 (48)	92
Total	100.0	100 (47)	100 (40)	100 (64)	100 (6)	100 (104)	261

SOURCE: Author's survey, August–September 1989. The 261 cases are drawn from two samples: 98 households in Cantón Xemamatze and 163 leaders and entrepreneurs in the town center.

gricultural occupation, as opposed to only 9 percent of the Catholics.[19] But evangelicals do not dominate nonagricultural occupations, as can be seen in Table 9.1. Of the Ixils who responded to my survey, the 40.6 percent who said they were evangelicals were only slightly overrepresented in nonagricultural sectors. Of 47 people interviewed with an *arte* or skill (tailoring, carpentry, and so on) as their primary occupation, 46.8 percent were evangelical, as were 50 percent of the 40 people whose primary occupation was in commerce. In the category of schoolteachers and promoters, evangelicals were slightly underrepresented, with just 37.5 percent of the 64 schoolteachers and promoters.[20]

Even if we lump Catholic Action members, charismatics and 8 respondents who said they had no religion[21] together with evangelicals into a "reformed" category, the resulting 64.8 percent of Ixils surveyed are not wildly overrepresented among those involved in commerce (70 percent reformed) and teaching (78.2 percent reformed). Consequently, movement into nonagricultural occupations does not depend strongly on reformed religion. More successful Ixils include traditionalists as well as catechists, charismatics, and Protestants. Unlike San Antonio Aguas Calientes and Almolonga, where Protestantism was closely associated with a new entrepreneurial elite, the violence-driven evangelical boom in Nebaj was associated with a wider spectrum of the population.

The amount of land that Nebaj Catholics and Protestants report owning does not differ greatly.[22] For the Ministry of Development questionnaire mentioned above, 325 evangelical household heads claimed a higher average of cuerdas (86.6) than 771 Catholics did (71.7 cuerdas).[23] My own survey of 98 households in the urban cantón of Xemamatze showed that there, too, evangelicals came out ahead of Catholics in land ownership. But the differences were not large, and what was most striking was the shared poverty of both groups. Few had been evangelical for more than a decade, to be sure, and the upward mobility associated with Protestantism often requires a second generation. As for the language of abstinence and thrift used by evangelicals, the research of Cecilia Mariz on Brazilian shanty-town dwellers suggests that it merely accentuates a language of austerity common to the poor, especially women, as they struggle to support their families. The implication of Mariz's work, like Cornelia Flora's in

Colombia, is that the economic position of the majority of Latin American evangelicals is too marginal to produce saving and investment in new enterprises.[24] While evangelical discipline has obvious survival value, it is no panacea for structural constraints impoverishing an entire population.

From Costumbre to Gospel to Video

Right now we're thinking which word to take up, because we're sad and
don't have enough to eat. —Man from Janlay, 1989

Guatemala's Indian towns are famous for their fiestas, especially the annual celebration each holds to honor its patron saint. Mayan traditionalists and folklore-conscious ladinos say the celebrations are sadly deteriorated from former years. An occasion that used to revolve around the saint societies is now less focused, with different groups organizing their own events and no unifying symbol except the town itself. In Nebaj the most determined modernizers of the fiesta have been schoolteachers and bilingual promoters, especially Ixils. With most belonging to reformed religious groups, they do not wish to participate in the hard-drinking festivities surrounding the saints. Instead, they want to imitate the fiestas in more ladino towns like Santa Cruz del Quiché, hence new military-style marches, sporting events, cultural nights dedicated to poetry and oration, and the selection of a town queen.

In Cotzal and Chajul the cofradías seemed on the point of extinction in the late 1980s.[25] Saints remained in the same mayordomo's house year after year because he could not find a new sponsor to take charge of them. The few elders still serving as mayordomos were said to pay younger men to carry the saints in processions. The traditionalists of Nebaj also complained of increasing difficulty in recruiting new members for the cofradías. After Easter 1989, two saints were "late" or "pending"—still in the hands of last year's sponsors—because no one would take responsibility for the coming year. But in Nebaj, even threadbare traditionalists were displaying an impressive dedication to the saints. Some cofradía heads were men who would have been considered too poor for the office before the war; now they were going to the coast for up to four months to raise money for it. One of the lower-ranking saints, San Pedro, was served in 1988–89 by men who were nearly all from the refugee neighborhood of Las Violetas.

The most immediate threat to the cofradías of Nebaj was the vote-buying of the Christian Democrats. In the name of protecting the national heritage, politicians distributed a thousand quetzals to the head of every indigenous cofradía in the country for two years in a row. In Nebaj, the largesse made more people jealous than it gratified. Some elders warned that, when it ended, men would no longer be willing to sacrifice as they had before. In 1990 there was said to be a "strike" by junior mayordomos complaining that the senior mayordomos were not distributing the money equitably.

From fieldwork in another Mayan town, John Watanabe concluded that religious change is "an inconclusive praxis of inquiry, interpretation and doubt."[26] The same can be said of Ixil country where, in the quiet times between services, away from the noise of churches and fiestas, religious allegiances are in flux. Over years of turmoil, many Ixils have cut loose from traditional icons and the Catholic clergy but have yet to settle into a new faith. There are more Catholics than evangelicals, a village leader says with an air of uncertainty, his calculations complicated by the split between charismatics and catechists. "Those from here go there, and those from there come here, then they visit the evangelical church, next they leave it and return here."

Most of the refugees coming out of the mountains in the late 1980s said they were Catholic, having missed the wave of conversion in the government-controlled towns earlier in the decade. But some of them were also up in the air religiously. "Before I was a Catholic," explains a new arrival from Amajchel who used to be a catechist and lost his house to the army six times. "But now I don't know what religion I have. I haven't thought about it. In the mountains, I was thinking only that there exists one God, that he takes care of us, and that perhaps he's going to help."

Some Ixils say they have no religion at all. "I'm nothing, neither Catholic nor evangelical," Juana of Cotzal told me. "I belong to whatever it takes to eat." The "nothing" category includes a few highly schooled Ixils who say they are atheists. It also includes a few traditionalists who, bitter against the clergy for criticizing them, now simply deny being Catholic. When the association of evangelical pastors in Nebaj conducted a survey of orphans in 1986, 39 percent of the single parents or guardians said they were evangelical and 29 percent said they were Catholic. A full 33 percent said they were nothing,[27] perhaps to ingratiate themselves with evangelical surveyors who might soon distribute relief supplies. But the popularity of the response shows that it has become thinkable for many Ixils.[28]

When an outsider asks about religious identification on the village level, the first answer is often that Catholics and evangelicals are *iguales* —"equal" or "the same." Not only are they numerically equal, the implication goes, but the distinction between the two is unimportant to the village and its needs. For an anthropologist who had been led to expect a religious war in Ixil country, religion proved to be a surprisingly unemotional issue. For all but the most committed or bitter, generally leaders commenting on rivals, it was less a question of competing ideologies than of the survival value of converting to a nonalcoholic regime.

Born-again theology idealizes a crisis style of conversion, like St. Paul's on the road to Damascus. Some Ixil converts are certainly in crisis, particularly men battling alcoholism, and evangelical leaders seek to explain conversion in crisis terms.[29] Still, the standard phrasing of "I accepted the Lord" suggests the deliberative quality of religious identification in Ixil country. In a study of war widows in a Kaqchikel Maya town in Chimaltenango, Linda Green found herself obliged to distinguish between "conversion" and "identification." While widows enthusiastically identified with religious groups, their penchant for identifying with more than one at the same time suggests that conversion is too grandiose an interpretation.[30] Typical of peasants, Ixils rarely bother to conceal their pragmatic attitude toward religion, a point confirmed by the frequent complaint that wayward members joined a church for *interés* rather than *convicción*.

The closer one gets to born-again religion in Nebaj, the more tentative and disorganized it seems. For all the claims made for Protestant strength in the country at large, in Nebaj the evangelical churches were clearly in the doldrums in the late 1980s. More evangelicals were staying away from services than attending them, even as a larger percentage of Nebajeños claimed to be evangelicals. While the churches were still drawing new members, many older ones stopped coming, and enthusiasm was clearly ebbing. Local leaders explained the vacant benches in their temples as a consequence of the wartime boom. "From 1982 to 1986 there was a tremendous increase in all the evangelical churches," a ladino pastor told me. "But many arrived out of self-interest, to be together with others, as a form of protection. The evangelical church was like a refuge. This is why some of the churches do not have the attendance they used to. There are only a few who really have convictions."

Certainly, Ixils who joined evangelical churches because they were afraid for their lives were not likely to continue attending once the pressure was off.[31] But spiritual decline was also part of the rhythm of revivalism, as illustrated by the backsliders who threatened to outnumber the faithful. "Falling" is, of course, one of the great themes of evangelical discourse. In Nebaj it often occurs at the death of a loved one, when family and friends encourage evangelicals to apply the traditional painkiller of drinking. Another scenario is the hardship of migration to the coast. The result is a large category of men who have declared themselves evangélicos, then gone back to drinking and "for shame" no longer come to church.[32] "Falling," or accusations of same, is also a motive for the popular practice of jumping from church to church. Even in the respectable Church of God, a lay leader estimated that 40 percent of the members fall, with three-quarters of these returning to church life and a fourth abandoning it. The pastor of the poorer and more typical Monte Basán Church said that, of his members who fall, the majority do not return. Asking after personal ecclesiastical history was one of the failures of my survey: evangelicals were embarrassed to acknowledge how many different churches they had belonged to.

Laxity was particularly evident in some aldeas. According to a disgusted evangelical teacher assigned to Ojo de Agua, near Cotzal, a recent evangelical campaign had been attended by all the same people who had just flocked to a visiting priest. While the majority of the village had declared themselves evangelical, only a few did not drink. "Here there is no pastor, no leader, to tell people what the rule is," he told me, not long before falling spectacularly himself. "I've figured out that people here declare themselves evangelicals because they like to sing the hymns and clap. It is not to avoid liquor [that they convert] because, when there is a marimba, they all come to drink. What this village needs is someone who explains what it is that has to be done, what can't be done, someone who speaks the dialect [mainly K'iche' Maya]. When preachers come here, they preach in Spanish or Ixil, which the people do not understand well."

Church splits took a particular toll on evangelical faith. In the late 1970s and early 1980s, the defection of junior leaders from the Methodist Church produced groups that were more responsive to Ixil needs. But once the movement had differentiated into twenty-two groups by the late 1980s, church splits seemed to create more bitterness than new members. "The pastors do false things just like the priests," said a disillusioned member of the Spring of Eternal Life Church, which had just split into several factions over a construction project. "Some extract money from the people. Others extract money and chase women. When a problem is raised, the pastor just says that it's a lie, or envy from others. The people don't remain faithful; they think there is no God."

Even though many Guatemalans have been attracted to born-again religion, their enthusiasm may be fleeting or not passed to their children. A comparison with a nearby town, where Protestantism became established earlier, suggests the possible evolution in Nebaj. The Mayas of Sacapulas live in a dry eroded valley where agriculture is productive only in an irrigated strip along the Rio Negro. Because of rapid population growth, they have been migrating to the capital for much of this century. Many found work in the army or national police; now the more educated are becoming schoolteachers and civil servants. Evangelical growth came before the violence, at least in the town center, and especially among ambitious young people who now occupy influential positions.

By the late 1980s, however, the town's youth were no longer following their older siblings and parents into the churches. Many of the earlier generation of converts had left to pursue careers in the capital, leaving the town's congregations smaller than before. When I quoted the 1984 health census, that 33 percent of the family heads in town were evangelical, a disappointed pastor replied: "The majority of this town may have passed through the evangelical church, but where are they?" The ambience had changed, another leader explained. Through cable television, youth were becoming absorbed in worldliness and drugs. Jesus Christ had been very popular with the teenagers of this town in the 1970s; now their successors were more interested in rock music and videos. They were being converted to consumer capitalism as represented by the town's new satellite dish.[33] Where Protestantism still boomed was on the dry, scrubby ridges above town, in hard-scrabble aldeas that clustered around government schools and Church of God chapels. Here, evangelical leaders claimed, their members were outnumbering Catholics.

Already in Nebaj, a second generation was emerging in the evangelical churches, of adolescents who were more interested in acquiring sunglasses than imitating their parents. According to one such youth, who was already "fallen" due to drinking, Protestant as well as Catholic youth engaged in the same kind of behavior because of the influence of their friends. The more prosperous households were acquiring televisions and, by 1992, there were three video parlors on the plaza specializing in Rambo-style violence. Young Ixils were being bombarded with images of sex, status, speed, and mobility. Like so many millions of other Latin American youth, they were being taught to imitate urban consumption patterns far beyond any visible means of attainment.

The Ixil-Ladino Détente

My feelings were mixed when the Christian Democrats elected Don Chico as mayor of Nebaj in 1990. As a government health inspector known for his frequent trips to aldeas, he was well qualified for the job. But because Chico was a ladino and a Catholic, his victory contradicted my assertions of Ixil and evangelical ascendancy. On the day of his investiture, Chico wore the cotón, the ceremonial jacket of Ixil men. He grasped a staff of office dating to the time when Ixils ran the town by themselves. And he led a procession of the town council, all but one of whom were Ixils, into the marketplace. "This is indeed the new mayor," Nebajeños nodded approvingly, even those disenchanted with the Christian Democrats. The other reason to rue Chico's victory was the danger to his integrity, judg-

ing from the disgrace of his party's two previous mayors. But as soon as Chico had the chance to audit municipal finances, he called a town meeting. "I'm not going to cover up what the previous mayor did, it doesn't matter if they're from the DC," he announced, before sending the evidence to higher authorities. —*My visit to Nebaj in 1991*

I sensed more community between Ixils and ladinos than one might expect from Colby and van den Berghe's report of twenty years before. True, my predecessors were focusing on a system of ethnic inequality while my subject was how a town recovers from a bloodbath. I was predisposed to be impressed by any sign of peacemaking. Thomas Lengyel notes that Ixils are usually reluctant to voice their resentment of ladinos, at least in the company of outsiders.[34] Many ladinos are less guarded but might also censor themselves around a foreigner like myself. Still, even a semblance of ethnic harmony seemed no mean feat following a civil war in which mainly indigenous guerrillas had killed respected members of the ladino community, while the Guatemalan army had forced a mainly ladino civil patrol to execute Ixil suspects.

Guatemalans go to considerable trouble to achieve what they refer to as *tranquilidad*, *amabilidad*, or *cultura*, an air of polite affability associated with Hispanic formalism. While their social skills are impressive, the culture of politeness can also serve as a veneer for considerable resentment, distrust, and mendacity. Following a holocaust in which kin and neighbors become implicated on opposite sides of the killing, there is a great deal to paper over, and not just between two ethnic groups. Although the Nebaj civil patrol was imposed by the army, the killing during its early days was performed by Ixils as well as ladinos who therefore share responsibility for it. Even if we confine the problem to how Ixils and ladinos feel about each other, Nebajeños must come to terms with vengeance killings by the guerrillas as well as the army and many changes of fortune. They must deal with the departure of ladino patróns, the rise of some Ixils, the impoverishment of many others, and the insecurity of living in a war zone.

The reciprocal fears involved in this latest stage of tranquility-building were emphasized by an older bilingual promoter recalling the injustices of his youth. "Recently the ladinos have turned more humane and understanding. Before, they treated Ixils like animals.

They changed because the Ixil people advanced through education. This was a weapon to defend themselves. The ladinos could not commit more abuses. This change occurred mainly during the violence. Since the guerrillas were made up of Indians, the ladinos were afraid. Some were threatened, one or the other died."

There were also mutual interests in what I will call, for lack of a better term, *ethnic détente*. For ladinos, the utility of Ixil leadership was punctuated by political killing which gave them the compelling reason of personal safety for handing over authority. Ladinos also depend heavily on Ixil labor, while Ixils derive benefits from ladino negotiating skills with army officers and other authorities. Indeed, ladino insouciance toward military authority became an important model for the Ixil townspeople of Nebaj, as suggested by the greater conformity of their peers in the ladino-bereft Cotzal and Chajul.

Still, it might seem implausible that the violence could bring Ixils and ladinos together, especially if we view the revolutionary movement as an ethnic uprising. Ladinos sometimes paint it in those terms, as an indigenous uprising against themselves, and solidarity literature can leave the same impression. It is true that a large majority of the people who joined the revolutionary movement in the western highlands were Maya, but probably not much more than their share of the population. The Guerrilla Army of the Poor was essentially Marxist and class-oriented, as suggested by its name and the polemics with Mayan nationalists that continue to this day.[35]

When we look at who killed whom, ladino reformers were among the first targets of death squads, and more ladinos may have been killed by the army than by the guerrillas. In one well-known clan, three members owning land or a vehicle were killed by the EGP, but I learned of another three, less prominent men killed by the army. In 1989 a few relatives were said to still be in the mountains with the guerrillas. A member of another ladino family scattered through Cotzal and Nebaj said she lost two uncles and eight cousins, all to the army. The security forces were so indiscriminate that they have few apologists even among ladinos, including the social class we might think they were defending. Remaining finca owners do not commend the army for defending their property. Instead, they complain that it destroyed their property along with everyone else's.

As a result, despite certain killings with ethnic overtones, the violence did not pit Ixil and ladino blocs against each other. Instead, many members of both ethnic groups decided they were being placed in jeopardy by largely external forces.[36] Hence the stories of joint solidarity against killing whether by the army or the guerrillas.[37] Actually, such solidarity is nothing new because, even at the height of ladino control, moral obligation crossed ethnic lines. Today, Ixils and ladinos regularly condemn members of their own group for gross misbehavior toward members of the other. I heard ladinos criticize relatives for the way they acquired their land, and Ixil elders condemn guerrillas for killing ladino patróns who had treated them decently. To the issues posed by labor contracting Nebajeños of both ethnic groups bring a strong sense of morality, distinguishing between patróns who show concern for the welfare of their laborers and those who do not, between those who use force and those who do not, and between laborers who meet their obligations and those who do not.

Distinctions between good and bad patróns, or good and bad army officers, are easily recognizable as what James Scott calls "moral economy."[38] This is the expectation of unequal but mutual obligations between members of different social classes in a shared moral universe. Through the language of *la comunidad*, in circulation before the war and now omnipresent because of the need to rebuild, Nebajeños have invented a cross-ethnic sense of purpose that manifests itself through innumerable alliances. Village delegations go to ladino schoolteachers for help in applying to aid agencies. Small finca owners whose relatives were killed by the guerrillas reoccupy their property with the help of villagers who spent eight years with the guerrillas. Even before the violence, ladino and Ixil activists worked together in the same political parties,[39] if only because Ixils comprised a large majority of the voters. Cooperation was even more obvious in the late 1980s, as Ixils became more prominent in party leadership and the majority on each party's list of candidates.

If shared experiences help explain ethnic détente in Nebaj, so does a newly popular presentation of self among the subordinate ethnic group. Town Ixils said that ladino behavior had improved now that they were *capaces* (capable). They added that ladino behavior was least changed toward *humildes*, that is, older people and villagers who still display a great deal of deference. "It depends on the way one presents oneself," a bilingual promoter explained. "If you present yourself well, then you're well treated. But if you don't express yourself well in Spanish, they don't pay any attention, they treat you like a child."

The remark suggests the importance of Ixils who can deal with ladinos on equal terms and mediate relations between the two groups. Many (although far from all) Ixils in this category come out of government schools and mission training programs which, aside from imparting Spanish and literacy, encouraged the kinds of personal initiative acceptable to ladinos and the national power structure. Hence the ladino admission that Ixils are more capable than they used to be, an acknowledgment that they cannot be paternalized as before.

Ethnic equality is a common theme in evangelical preaching, encouraging a new fraternal discourse of "brothers" and "sisters" that redefines the old moral economy in more egalitarian terms across ethnic lines. In the case of the largest church before the war, the Methodists, the contradiction between egalitarian rhetoric and ladino control spun off a new generation of Ixil leaders, each with his own small congregation. Now that the ladino-controlled Methodist Church has been reduced to a shell, the most obvious meeting ground for ladinos and Ixils is the Full Gospel Church of God. The church in Nebaj is led by a man whose K'iche' parents came to the area forty years ago as market vendors. Like a few other K'iche' families in the Ixil towns, he and his brothers have moved up in the world, to the point of owning several small trucks. In church life, the brothers have been a bridge between the town's two main ethnic groups, as Indians but not Ixils, and as outsiders but not ladinos. Recently his leadership has attracted the kind of ladino teachers and store owners who used to be found in the Methodist Church.

In the town congregation, the Ixils tend to be young, city-directed people who are upwardly mobile or trying to be. Says a pastor from another church composed mainly of maize farmers: "In the Church of God all of them are promoters, pastors, different people who are fat. Up to three or four hundred quetzals a month (U.S. $100+) the pastors take in. Ladinos are there, too. Here there aren't any because everyone is from the aldeas, they come here with nothing." The bitterness in the remark suggests that, even if ethnic discrimination in Nebaj is abating, such is not the case with new kinds of inequality and resentment. While the majority of Church of God members in the town of Nebaj are Ixils, their language is rarely heard in services: at least in that context, they seem more interested in honing ladino-style social skills.[40]

In the Mam Maya towns of San Marcos and San Pedro Sacatepéquez, in a more developed part of the western highlands, John Hawkins suggests that "watching TV" is a clue to the decrease in ethnic tension since the mid-1970s, by providing a new status standard against which Indians and ladinos are measuring themselves. With the proliferation of mass media, Guatemalans may be increasingly defining their welfare in relation, not to each other, but to the imagery of a global consumer society. Hence a loss of interest in local ethnic rivalries, which are becoming less consequential in view of the golden world over the horizon in the United States.[41] No matter how high, remote, and cold the settlement, such hopes always preceded me in Ixil country.

Power Structure and Popular Organization Under Army Rule

No, there aren't groups of power anymore. Now we're all organized into committees.   *—Bilingual promoter, 1989*

Guatemala was widely regarded as a country where the security forces had suffocated dissent, except for the guerrillas roaming the mountains and a few brave human rights organizations. Yet congregational-style churches were providing new forms of expression, discipline, and suprafamilial authority. Opposition parties came together for every election. Even the Nebaj civil patrol seethed with resentment. While created by the army and performing a repressive function, its half-hearted interpretation of the army's strictures did much to bring Ixils together around the common desire to keep both soldiers and guerrillas off their backs. The result was space for reasserting civil society, as illustrated by the "municipal coup" of 1988. The army had imposed obvious limits on what could be said and done, but it also had vacated a sphere in which civilians were making their own decisions. The army did not visibly meddle in town politics and, when appealed to, was more likely to remain aloof than to intervene.

When I asked who dominated town affairs, Nebajeños could identify certain individuals with weight like the head of the civil patrol or the incumbent mayor. But no one was willing to name a social group or faction, such as the civil patrol, labor contractors, or bilingual promoters. The old power structure was gone in Nebaj, but nothing had really taken its place. Not the army, which was withdrawing from civic affairs and reconstruction, nor the civil patrol, which was slowly falling apart. Not the Christian Democrats, who were in danger of being thrown out of office. Nor the evangelical churches, despite their considerable gains.

Three of the four mayors appointed by Ríos Montt were evangelicals (the exception being the charismatic who was soon replaced in Chajul). So were two of the three mayors elected by the Christian Democrats in 1985. But after the two evangelical mayors proved corrupt, they were replaced by Catholics in the 1988 election, with only one evangelical mayor being elected that year, in Chajul. In the 1990 election, all three of the new mayors were Catholic. In terms of running for office, candidate lists suggested that evangelicals were somewhat underrepresented compared to their share of the population. The exception was Cotzal: here evangelicals were politically hyperactive, to the point of running so many competing candidates that almost none were elected, until young men from the influential Church of God put together a winning slate in 1990, albeit headed by a respected Catholic. One reason evangelicals were still shy of town hall was the impact of political rows on their congregations. In Cotzal, the mayor for 1986–88, his vice mayor and their incompetent paving contractor left the Church of God after being accused of enriching themselves, then started their own churches—each his own, for a total of three.

Traditionally, Ixil country was the kind of area that voted for the official party, as the only way to jockey favors from the capital. "The leaders here have been *gobernista*," a disgusted schoolteacher said of the ladino elite, although he might have been talking of the Ixil principals as well. "In the time of Estrada Cabrera, they were Cabreristas. When Ubico arrived, they belonged to the Liberal party of Ubico. When Ubico fell, they became Poncistas. All of a sudden Ponce fell, came the revolution of the twentieth of October [1944], and they became revolutionaries." Going with the winner still makes sense to Ixils: just before the runoff to the 1990 election, a Cotzaleño university student went to great length to demonstrate that everyone should vote for the likely victor, Jorge Serrano Elías, because the larger his margin in Ixil country, the more Ixils could claim from him.

Still, in the 1970s Ixil voters in Cotzal and Nebaj were increasingly willing to vote against the party in power, a tendency that the violence did not reverse. Although the Christian Democratic party's control of the three town halls was only reduced to two in 1988, and it held onto two in 1990, its percentage of the vote shrank dramatically. The reason it was not thrown out of office in all three towns was the fragmentation of the opposition, which invariably ran three or more competing slates, each headed by men who hoped their own party would win the national election and reward them accordingly.

Perhaps because of the rampant personalism of local politics, political parties did not visibly divide along ethnic or religious lines, with local observers rejecting my attempts to interpret them in that light.[42] Invariably Nebajeños told me they voted for a candidate based on his personal reputation, not his party, and regardless of his ethnicity as well. A generation before, in the time of Colby and van den Berghe, traditionalists affiliated with the Revolutionary party had faced catechists aligned with the Christian Democrats and a ladino elite that coalesced around the Democratic Institutional party.[43] But even before the violence, catechists and traditionalists found themselves in the same electoral coalition, and now ladinos and Ixils, evangelicals, catechists, and traditionalists were to be found in each party.[44]

In the 1970s Catholic missionaries and catechists hoped to create a new, more democratic form of local politics. Since the evangelical movement is led by some of the same men, might it carry the same aspirations? Like Catholic Action, evangelical churches represent a new form of independence from traditional cultural expectations. Just as the Catholic Action of the 1950s encouraged young men to disobey their elders, evangelical churches express a similar drive for independence by young men. In the mid-1970s, Lengyel noted the youth of Protestant leaders compared to the gerontocracy of the saint societies. What the reformed groups meant for young men was a chance to exercise leadership earlier in their lives and in novel ways. "You have the right to lead, you have the right to sing, you have the right to preach," a heavy drinker turned church supervisor told me.

Except when an unusually literate pastor was holding the stage, the central fixture of evangelical services was not the Bible but the microphone and sound system. I found one group that did not have walls to keep the wind out of its meetings but did have a proficient band armed with an amplifier. In local idiom, the single word *aparato* (for "apparatus") was sufficient to refer to the ritual necessity for a loudspeaker. As one person after another took their turn at the mike, they had the chance to express themselves in their own language, at high volume, and in a way that was not likely to be interpreted as a challenge to the army.

We have already seen how, despite the army's imposition of martial law, local power in Nebaj was not centralized by the violence. Guerrillas destroyed the prewar power structure; the army intervened to impose its own parameters, such as the civil patrol and a de facto death penalty for trading with the guerrillas; but between the two armies there was a vacuum of authority. Missionaries with long experience in Quiché believe that the violence has also created a vacuum in community spirit, by damaging traditional forms of solidarity.

According to a member of the Summer Institute of Linguistics, trust used to center on the immediate family and diminish as one moved outward to the extended family, village, and ethnic group, with ladinos considered free game for being cheated. Now that sense of solidarity has broken down, she believes, with one member of a family joining the guerrillas and another conscripted by the army. Padre Miguel lamented that even Catholics were less willing to volunteer for community tasks such as whitewashing the church; instead, they wanted to be paid. The erosion of community spirit could, of course, be interpreted as a growing sense of personal independence. It would be hard for Ixils to take advantage of new, competing sources of patronage without breaking to some degree with previous forms of solidarity.

Development agencies continue to promote Rochedale-style cooperatives and other group enterprises, even though the highlands are littered with the remains of such efforts. The two major co-ops in Ixil country before the war were associated with the Catholic Church and were hit so hard by the army that the one in Chajul disappeared. The other in Nebaj barely survived, but its troubles were not due solely to persecution. Co-op leaders stress how many of their members were killed, but most Nebajeños also blame dishonest administration. Since co-op expansion had been based on loans to members, the destruction of villages and hives wrecked repayment schedules. With the co-op in disarray, surviving leaders in the town center are said to have divided up the remaining funds.

At the same time that army death squads were hunting down co-op leaders suspected of subversion, the government was asserting jurisdiction over their organizations through its National Institute for Cooperatives (INACOP).[45] Headed by an army colonel, INACOP arrived in Nebaj at the height of the violence in 1980–81, but reading it only as an agency of surveillance does not account for the initiative displayed by some of the organizers, several of them local men whose politics put them at odds with the army's mayhem.

Still, not a great deal was accomplished. A co-op started by small-scale ladino coffee growers around 1980 soon lost its capital to the war and the personal investments of two members, leaving the enterprise with a discouraging debt. When the national coffee co-op FEDECOGUA refloated the operation in 1989, its crop-buying plan was subverted by a catastrophic fall in international prices, leaving the first Ixil members feeling cheated. As before the war, the more impressive operations in Ixil country still have ties to the Catholic Church, including the bee cooperative in Nebaj, which was refloated with a loan from the Inter-American Foundation, and a cooperative-style association in Chajul.

The three Ixil towns were full of talk about organizing new cooperatives. Two more finished the difficult bureaucratic process of obtaining legal recognition from INACOP in 1990. Unfortunately, the requirement that members buy a share (costing at least a month's wages) excluded the poorest Ixils, who also lacked the reserves needed to defer income for a group enterprise. More than one widows' project fell apart when the members, most being in dire necessity, insisted on dividing up the first earnings instead of maintaining the group's capital. Generally, cooperatives in Guatemala continued to have serious problems with their finances.[46] The expectation that management was corrupt extended to virtually anyone handling group funds, undermining the kind of trust needed to make a collective enterprise work.

Cooperatives failed so frequently that, despite the image of communal solidarity that appeals to foreigners, it had to be asked how much they really appealed to Mayan campesinos. "It's because people often prefer to work for themselves," a ladino INACOP organizer told me. "You see the same thing in every part of the republic. But if you ask foreign countries like the United States and Canada for support, the first thing they ask for is a proposal showing that the people are organized and working for the community. Therefore more co-ops get organized, even if only three or four people out of a hundred want them." If only as a hoped-for source of capital, cooperativism was far from dead in Ixil country. What lacked was not interest on the part of Ixils but financial follow-through by development agencies.

An even more widespread organizational form in Ixil country is the committee. The *comité pro-mejoramiento* (literally, "committee for improvement") dates from before the violence, as a vehicle for Catholic activists, bilingual promoters, and the town hall to solicit funds from foreign embassies and other donors. Under Ríos Montt, Summer Institute missionaries encouraged the formation of a *comité del pueblo*, including Catholics as well as evangelicals, to oversee the administration of relief supplies. With the return of civilian government after 1985, the Christian Democrats seized upon village committees as a patronage conduit. Hence, when the Cerezo administration launched a Ministry of Development, its promoters instigated development committees in every Ixil aldea, apart from which various nongovernmental organizations have organized still others to administer their own projects. To evade the 1985 constitution, even the army started referring to its civil patrols as "voluntary committees."

Closely associated with the committee is the figure of the *promotor*, usually an Ixil trained by a state or private agency as its local liaison. Although employed by a bureaucracy, the promoter is supposed to further the interests of the ethnic group, such that his or her personal interests come to depend on building it up as a constituency. The occupation of the last four mayors of Nebaj—three bilingual promoters and a health inspector—suggests how public employees have displaced Ixil principales and ladino finca owners as pivotal figures.[47] Obviously, their location as intermediaries with outside institutions has enabled them to build up new kinds of patronage networks.

The supplanting of gerontocratic principales by cooperatives, committees, and promoters might seem to have great democratic potential.

The new networks incorporate a fairly wide range of the community; are supposed to make their own decisions; and are intended to be entrepreneurial, in the sense of developing village projects to submit to outside agencies. They are extremely dependent on donors, however, as suggested by the language of supplication used to approach anyone who might have access to grants or loans. Yet it would be a mistake to dismiss them as only subordinate instruments of the state and international philanthropy. "Remind the authorities that there are still many needs here, like a road, health clinic, and village hall," the head of a well-armed civil patrol admonished dignitaries at a school inauguration, "and that they should not neglect us."

Civil Patrols and Civil Society

Why are you a civil patrol chief?

They came to my house, I didn't do anything! The only reason I'm chief is that the neighbors asked me.
          —*Nebaj civil patrol leader throwing his hands in the air, 1989*

The most paradoxical form of popular organization in the Ixil Triangle—so paradoxical that many observers would deny that it was a popular organization at all—was the civil patrol. In chapter 4 we saw how the patrols were imposed by the army after its previous network of surveillance and control, consisting of military commissioners, was shattered by the EGP. When the patrols began to disintegrate in Nebaj in the late 1980s, the army responded with thinly veiled threats of kidnapping. Listen to the following exchange with an army-appointed leader who, like others I met, was an Ixil with little enthusiasm for his job:

ANTHROPOLOGIST: Are the civil patrols necessary?

VILLAGER: It could happen again like the time before. The subversion could come into town again, just to talk, one doesn't know, and there could be kidnappings.

ANTHROPOLOGIST: Are the civil patrols obligatory?

VILLAGER: The government says no, but here it's obviously necessary to have them. So that the same thing doesn't happen again like it did before. Now [men] don't want to patrol because they see that the situation has calmed down.

ANTHROPOLOGIST: Are the army officers angry or are they giving up?

VILLAGER: They're angry. What they say is that if [men] don't want to patrol, if [the people] don't like the army and don't want to help it, the army will go to other towns. This happened in Chicamán, where the people didn't want to patrol, the army took away the rifles and left. Guerrillas showed up to talk and the army came back to kidnap the people who had talked with them—maybe three. This is what happened two years ago. This is what could happen again here.

Like this man, many Ixils felt that the civil patrols were an unfortunate necessity because they served as a buffer against the army as well as the guerrillas. Such support is so obviously the result of a coercive situation that acquiescence may be a better term. But support for the civil patrol was not the same as support for the army,[48] and it helped reconstruct civil society in at least two respects.

First, the civil patrol responded to a widespread desire for protection from the pressures of both sides in the violence. Indeed, after the Tz'utujil Mayas of Santiago Atitlán forced the army to leave their town and set up their own unarmed *ronda* (patrol), Ixils began to discuss setting up their own. Paralleling the sentiments of so many Ixils, the Atitecos not only denounced the army for hundreds of murders but also told the guerrillas to stay clear.

Second, the civil patrol set up a new pattern of mutual expectations between military officers and Ixils. If the latter demonstrated their loyalty to the army by patrolling, the army would "protect" them, that is, not treat them like guerrilla sympathizers. The new set of mutual responsibilities was far from equitable, but it became a bridge across the deadly distrust opened up by EGP attacks on the army. Gradually, it permitted Ixils to make appeals that army officers were obliged to heed, such as the argument from equity: if ladinos and Ixil government employees don't have to patrol, why do we have to? By the end of the 1980s, the army's rhetoric of campesino volunteers serving alongside their soldier brothers in defense of peace and liberty was being turned against it. The moral logic of the civil patrols had gone far enough to undermine them. Consider the following statement by an ex-patrol chief in 1991.

"Why should we patrol? As if we're paid? It's voluntary, no? Sure,

Civil patrollers at a school inauguration, 1989

the army officers are angry but it's the people who rule, no? The officers just order us around but don't do anything. The ones in charge just come and get angry: why aren't you patrolling, why aren't you looking for them in the mountains? But they don't go up there themselves, they just send the civil patrol. . . . We want peace, [the war] is an affair of the guerrillas and the soldiers, of the officers, they're the ones who get paid. Who knows why they're fighting: for land, for business deals, for politics? But it doesn't have anything to do with us. This is an affair for those who get paid. We're just here planting our maize and taking care of our animals, it's their affair, no?"

Ixils obviously felt divided over the patrols, with weariness and resentment of the burden competing with their continued fear of being compromised by the guerrillas and punished by the army. Yet a form of coercion had become a platform for subverting army demands, reasserting autonomy, and widening the space available for civil society.

The Communities of Population in Resistance

The Ixil people are the most valiant of our country but they were reined in by the military. Now we [of the CPRs] are like the remnant, but we are

going to lift up our fallen brothers. The wall of silence is collapsing, the
people are losing their fear and leaving behind their face of conformism.
The coming year will be different.
     —*Representative of the communities of population in resistance, 1992*

As dissidence ripened within the civil patrols, the Guatemalan National Revolutionary Union (URNG) was using its military presence to win recognition at the bargaining table. Next door in El Salvador, the Farabundo Marti National Liberation Front (FMLN) was able to negotiate an internationally verified peace settlement in 1992. But the Guatemalan guerrillas lacked the political punch of their Salvadoran allies. True, URNG fighters showed no sign of being defeated militarily. New fronts appeared near Guatemala City, to guarantee that guerrilla actions made the evening news. But the URNG had far less impact on the economy than its Salvadoran counterpart. As a result, the Guatemalan business establishment was not pushing the army to make concessions. Even after international pressure forced the army to acquiesce to negotiations under President Jorge Serrano Elías (1991–), the URNG's bargaining position was so weak that there was little sign of a settlement.

Another reason the URNG had little to offer was that its support among Mayan peasants seemed very limited. "Prolonged popular war" had been premised on organizing campesinos to support it, but the army's offensives had reduced such bases to a few zones of refuge. How much support the EGP had even there was open to question, as suggested by a shift in how the montaña communities were governed. What was reported to the outside world was the first general assembly of the communities of population in resistance (CPRs) in February 1990.[49] The revolutionary movement had never explained how it administered the people in the montaña, and the same hermetism surrounded the origins of the new governing structure.

According to ex-militants in Nebaj, the montaña communities were governed by a firm hierarchy of *dirección de frente, dirección regional,* and *dirección distrital* named from above, with local (neighborhood-level) committees that some of my sources said were named from above and that others said were chosen by the community. Refugees in Nebaj also described "area committees" whose position in the hierarchy was unclear. Apparently the area committees were like a judiciary, hearing and resolving disputes including appeals of the EGP hierarchy's decisions, but could also perform administrative tasks. Only the area committees appeared in CPR presentations, however, along with periodic assemblies of the population that justified the area committees' claim to be based on popular sovereignty. As for the EGP's role in organizing the montaña and its top-down system of authority, the CPRs made no reference to it, denying any relation with the guerrillas other than being defended by them. When I was able to interview a CPR delegate in 1992, he denied any knowledge of the EGP-appointed hierarchy that ex-combatants and political cadre in Nebaj had told me about.

With their first general assembly, the CPRs launched a drive to win national and international support by publicizing the army's attacks. Even if the montaña settlements were providing maize and recruits to the guerrillas, attacking them was a violation of international law as long as they were inhabited by unarmed civilians. As a result, the CPRs wanted recognition as a noncombatant, civilian population. They demanded that the army dismantle, not just its military siege of the area, but its bases, civil patrols, development poles, and model villages.

Contrary to the "between two fires" refrain around government-controlled towns, CPR leaders refused to assign any blame to the guerrillas or call for their corresponding withdrawal.[50] When the government's human rights procurator proposed a joint withdrawal from the area,[51] the first to reject it was not the army but the CPR leadership, which reiterated its demand for the army's unilateral withdrawal.[52] Despite the army's accusations that the CPRs were a guerrilla front, they picked up support from the Catholic Church, ecumenical Protestant groups, and the human rights movement. In the media and diplomatic circles, these bodies put the army on the defensive by denouncing its attacks on CPR settlements. Yet the army was not about to withdraw from Ixil country with the EGP at large, so what the CPR leadership achieved was favorable publicity, not the ceasefire its constituents yearned for.

The negotiating posture suggests that the CPR leadership was part of the same EGP hierarchy that had administered the Amajchel area since the early 1980s. So was the CPR structure just another front, the latest of the URNG's efforts to maintain the loyalty of internal refugees, hold onto them as a logistical base, and bolster its negotiating position? That was my suspicion. Then I talked with a CPR functionary who had just come to Nebaj to rejoin his family. According to Pedro (not his real name), the CPRs of the Sierra had "got rid of" (*sacaron*) the EGP's regional and district administrations in 1990–91. Why? "The people have gotten tired. [They said] 'you told us there would be a change this year but it did not turn out that way, and now we see that year after year there is no change. This is why we want to get connected with the [government procurator for] human rights to end this situation. . . .' What now prevails between the CPRs and guerrillas is distrust. [The people] no longer want to get involved in the movement because the guerrillas just have them bottled up (*detenido*), for political reasons."[53]

This version of events hardly seemed to fit the CPR bargaining position. Why would CPR leaders never breathe a word of criticism against the EGP if they had broken with it? According to a member of the humanitarian delegations who visited the CPRs in 1991–92, what held them together was a tremendous fear of the army, as reinforced by army offensives and a decade of political education. The depth of feeling against the Guatemalan government is suggested by an attempt to vaccinate CPR children in February 1992, by the International Red Cross. Access to humanitarian organizations had been one of the CPR's demands, in fact the only one that the government conceded. Following lengthy preparations, a Red Cross team was flown by helicopter to the CPR community of Vicabá, only to have the parents mount a sudden, furious protest against a government health promoter with the team. The CPR leadership had agreed to the presence of such a functionary, but the day before the visit a popular assembly—called by whom is unclear—decided that "we don't want anything to do with the government." Apparently the parents were afraid that the vaccines might be contaminated. The Red Cross team felt obliged to withdraw, leaving thousands of children without badly needed medical help.

The available evidence suggests a complex relation between the CPR leadership and the EGP. Judging from the latter's top-down command structure, which extended from military units to political cadre to the population, the area committees began as a concession to popular sovereignty. During the first years in the montaña, the EGP evidently succeeded in defining (and dominating) the area committees ideologically. These would have been under the same pressure from a war-weary population as the EGP's district- and regional-level committees, however. Then in 1990–91, the area committees apparently either led a revolt against the EGP command structure or pretended to, in order to channel discontent in a more acceptable direction.

During this same period, the Ho Chi Minh Front was building up its military forces in Ixil country. It is said to have added a third company and received an influx of recruits from elsewhere in thè western highlands. Unfortunately, as the guerrillas became more dependent on roadblocks for supplies, and more intent on disrupting the government's resettlement machine by blowing up electrical towers and burning trucks, they also seemed to be alienating the government-controlled population more than before. When guerrillas approached Cotzal on May 25, 1992, for example, townspeople are said to have shouted and lit torches to warn their neighbors. At the army-controlled resettlement of Amajchel, whose inhabitants had been with the CPRs until recently, the civil patrollers became sufficiently diligent that the guerrillas killed several of them around the start of 1992. When the civil patrollers managed to ambush a guerrilla, they are said to have torn his body to pieces.

The most obvious sign of alienation from the EGP was a June 21, 1992 rally against it in Chajul. Shortly before, guerrillas had burned one of the town's few trucks. The reason was that it had carried military supplies, the kind of job owners tried to avoid but accepted to stay on the army's good side. In reaction, some of the most affected Chajuleños asked the town hall to present a grievance to the government's procurator for human rights, an office of verification set up to respond to the demands of the international human rights community. As many as several thousand Ixils attended, as did the adjunct procurator César Alvarez Guadamuz, to hear denunciations of the insurgents.

There is no doubt the army was involved: in Guatemala City it offered to fly journalists to the event, which resembled "peace marches" it was organizing in other towns to play the human rights theme against the URNG. But when I interviewed Chajuleños a week later, there was no doubt that popular feelings were involved too. "The people go out to their fields, the guerrillas show up to pester them, 'sell me this, sell me that,' " an evangelical store owner told me. "Soldiers show up, it's pow-pow-pow, and the people run for their lives." "There's profound rejection of the guerrillas here," an ex-mayor claimed. "It's because of them that the people are shut up in the town. They can't work anymore because of [the guerrillas]. They can't trade anymore." From a solidarity point of view, a human rights protest against the guerrillas might seem perverse. But it was an example of how Ixils were incorporating the language of human rights into their struggle to create space for themselves between the army and the guerrillas.

Human Rights Comes to Nebaj

When the army prohibited contact with the guerrillas, when there were serious checks at the edge of town, by the people themselves who saw the falseness of the guerrillas, finally there was a bit of tranquility, finally [the people] could go out to the aldeas. Finally the economic means came in to support the family. But when [the people] stopped patrolling, the guerrillas began to bother again. People don't go out to patrol because they like to, only when [the guerrillas] cause a provocation, only to defend themselves. —Ex-mayor of Chajul, July 1992

When I visited Ixil country in 1992, the Catholic Church was commemorating its martyrs more openly than before. The parish priests led converging processions to the spot where Father José María Gran was murdered twelve years before. In Cotzal, Catholic Action was putting up the names of victims—220 and climbing—for the anniversary of the July 28, 1980, massacre in which more than 60 died. A new painting in the Catholic church showed Christ leading a march of demonstrators demanding their rights, against a background depicting scenes of conquest and oppression. In Nebaj, a new resettlement wanted to name itself after Javier Gurriarán, the parish priest before the violence.

The usual constraints were still at work: in 1990–91 two lay advisers of the Quiché diocese were murdered, apparently because Bishop Julio Cabrera was taking up the situation of the refugees in the montaña.[54] But the Quiché diocese was determined to show that it could not be intimidated, and a growing number of Ixils wanted their family members remembered in public, to make clear that the dead had not deserved their fate. "Before they were terrified, they remained in silence," a church worker told me. "Now they feel like it is something necessary. Perhaps because now the people take heart to say, 'they killed my papa.' They begin to feel that these people have not died, that they still live in the heart of the community."

The most surprising development in Nebaj was the new human rights office, attached to the government's Procurator for Human Rights. The procurator was set up by the 1985 constitution as a response to international concern over government abuses. As a "judge of con-science" or office of verification, it could only investigate and embar-rass, not prosecute except through the country's almost nonfunctional judicial system. The procurator also took care not to point a finger at high-ranking army officers. Indeed, its investigative staff was infiltrat-ed by the army's G-2 section. But the procurator did legitimize human rights as a topic of debate in the press, streets, and government, which was no small achievement in a society as repressed as Guatemala.

As for the new *auxiliatura* (aid office) in Nebaj, opened with funds from the government of Sweden, this was something very new. Despite all the human rights reports filed on the Ixil Triangle, no one had ever set up a public defender's office there. Such an institution was almost unthinkable given the power of the army, which regularly iden-tified human rights as a communist lure. When I spent a year in Nebaj in 1988–89, Ixils never used the term *human rights* in public. Even in pri-vate, Ixils usually associated it with *la subversión*, and several years later some of them still wanted nothing to do with it. "Why? We don't need it," a young evangelical told me. "It just means divisions, quarrels, dis-cussions, it's not good for anything." Yet in the meantime, human rights had become part of everyday vocabulary in town, and more often than not the term was being used approvingly.

"Everything now is 'human rights,' " the ladino head of the ambu-lance brigade complained. When his men were late in picking up a patient or when a schoolteacher disciplined a child, Ixils said their human rights had been violated. The most common kind of case brought to the procurator's office were reportedly land disputes, which fell outside its jurisdiction. But Nebajeños also credited the procurator with the sudden departure of the national police, after these were accused of demanding bribes and the mayor asked them to vacate their office in the town hall.

The most politically sensitive denunciations to the procurator were against the civil patrols in the aldeas. Now that the system in town was moribund, the contrast with the still-mandatory patrols in the country-side was plain to all. In response to one such complaint, from an unwilling Ixil patroller in Xecotz, the assistant procurator convened a meeting with army officers, civil patrol chiefs, and military commis-sioners in which he explained the law and an army captain agreed to cooperate. Aside from the man in Xecotz reportedly rescued, approxi-mately eleven of the fifty-seven or more aldeas in Nebaj by mid-1992 were no longer patrolling.

The nonpatrolling aldeas were all small, new resettlements set up by farmers who were moving out from the older model villages of Acul, Tzalbal, and Salquil Grande to live closer to their land. Instead of refus-ing to patrol, the new villages could simply fail to start doing so, in the kind of unobtrusive maneuver often preferred by peasants. In Canaquil, for example, the people were so divided over whether to begin patrolling or not that eventually the army-appointed patrol chief gave up trying to organize them. No meeting had been held on the matter, a quietly pleased Canaquilan claimed, nor were they ever visited by human rights organizers. "If we have guns from the army and the *can-ches* show up to take the guns away," he reasoned, "it means a problem with the army and we don't want the responsibility, we don't want to fight with anyone." Wasn't Canaquil afraid of the army? No, "because now there is peace, now there is liberty." And what would Canaquil do if the guerrillas came? "Who knows what will happen? If they show up to mess with us, the people will rise up with machetes or sticks."

In another of the new settlements, Batzsuchil, the patrol chief in nearby Tzalbal tried to force the inhabitants to continue serving in their old location. Following an altercation, the Batzsuchil abstainers went to the procurator's office in the department capital and won their case. Otherwise, however, the procurator seemed to have little to do with the new stage of dissent against the civil patrol. The Nebaj office was run by a ginger young lawyer who saw himself as a mediator rather than a defender of victims. His language was a model of the euphemism so many Guatemalans use to avoid problems with "them." According to the lawyer, the task of human rights in Nebaj was education, not just raising demands. Problems with the civil patrol he attributed to a lack of education on the part of overzealous Ixil patrol chiefs, not the army, whom he praised for its exemplary cooperation.

Indirectly, human rights organizations and the procurator's office could take credit for maintaining pressure on the Guatemalan army. But the decade of change we have traced in the Nebaj civil patrol—from originating as an army-imposed death squad, to acting as a buffer "between two fires," to slowly falling apart—was generated by the responses of Ixils rather than international bodies. The importance of local politics can be demonstrated in another way as well: as of June 1992, formal complaints about the civil patrol had come only from aldeas of Nebaj. None had come from the towns and aldeas of Cotzal and Chajul where there were so few ladinos to serve as a social buffer for Ixils to assert themselves.

Even in Nebaj, a large majority of aldeas continued to patrol. Aside from memories of army violence, they continued to feel jeopardized by guerrilla activity. "The human rights [*sic*] arrived [in Salquil Grande] maybe two years ago but the people don't believe it," an auxiliary mayor told me in 1992. "They said, `you don't have to patrol, it's voluntary.' How can we stop patrolling if we have to protect ourselves? There could be a death. If we do not patrol, they can show up again to cause problems. Without the protection of the civil patrol, there can be tricks (*engaños*)." So long as the URNG kept on a war footing to strengthen its bargaining position, its presence would keep the Ixil population "between two fires" and reinforce support for (or acquiescence in) the civil patrol system.

Perhaps it was because this equation was so entrenched that, as of mid-1992, the army was displaying a cautious attitude toward the new era of human rights discourse in Nebaj. Allowing the civil patrols to slack off, then calling them out to meet the latest incursion, was a way for the army to suggest that Ixils would have to patrol only as long as the guerrillas operated in their vicinity. In the country as a whole, the above-ground Left continued to be persecuted at accustomed levels, but around Nebaj the army accepted, at least in public, the procurator's explanation that the civil patrols were voluntary. Telling civil patrol chiefs that it could only be "responsible for" villages and men who patrolled was saved for less public occasions. The army also started releasing prisoners to the procurator and urged civilians with complaints against the guerrillas to take them to the same institution. While visiting Chajul, I saw the army release two Ixils who had been caught trying to sell red skirts to the guerrillas; in previous years, they would have been taken away to be killed.

The Public Secret and Human Rights

Before the war, on Good Friday, young Ixil men used to dress up like finca owners, in broad-brimmed hats, long floppy coats, spectacles, riding pants, and boots. Then, as the crucified Christ was carried out of the chapel, they would shoot firecrackers at a dummy of Judas hanging above the door. Since the height of the violence, the so-called enbutados *(booted ones) dress up as guerrillas. One Good Friday the ritual confused the army, which began to pursue a mock guerrilla and nearly shot him.*
—Author's interviews, Nebaj 1989

The only militant form of popular organization in Ixil country was beyond government control, in the montaña. We already have looked at the ambiguous relationship of the communities of population in resistance to the Guerrilla Army of the Poor. Now let us turn to the wider movement that the CPRs were joining in the early 1990s, the "popular organizations" or "popular movement." This was the unarmed wing of the Guatemalan Left, whom the army accused of being guerrilla fronts and persecuted accordingly. When I first saw the popular movement in action, during a protest of the Mutual Support Group (GAM) in 1987, it seemed anything but popular in the sense of having a large, visible following. Accompanied by foreign solidarity activists, a hundred or so protesters were approaching the annual Day of the Army parade in the capital. Turned back by massed police, the protesters marched instead to the presidential palace. Along the several miles of their route I did not see a single gesture of support. Not a single cheer, wave, or ripple of applause.

GAM was the organization of relatives of the "disappeared," that is, victims of government kidnappings. "Alive they took them," GAM demonstrators shouted, "alive we want them back." Almost as well known was the Runujel Junam Council of Ethnic Communities (CERJ),[55] which led the resistance to the civil patrols and demanded their abolition. CERJ had a larger visible constituency than GAM, particularly in southern Quiché where more and more men were refusing to serve in the civil patrols. Another popular organization was the Committee for Campesino Unity (CUC), famous for its role in leading plantation strikes in the late 1970s and joining the armed struggle. Now it was popping up again wherever Mayan peasants confronted large landowners and the state.

Unlike survivors of the violence around the three Ixil towns, or most Guatemalans for that matter, these organizations did not dissemble their feelings about government security forces. Instead, they denounced human rights violations in no uncertain terms. GAM modeled itself after an organization in Argentina, the Mothers of the Plaza de Mayo, which won the indictment of hundreds of military officers for kidnapping, torture, and murder in the late 1970s. But in Guatemala, the army showed no sign of losing power like its counterpart in Argentina. Year after year, members of the popular organizations continued to be kidnapped and killed. Yet their persecution attracted attention from foreign journalists, as well as financial support from solidarity and human rights organizations in the United States and Europe, and by the early 1990s the popular organizations were drawing more people than before. As a result, they were a significant source of pressure on the government and the army.

To that same regime, what the popular organizations had to say sounded very similar to what the guerrillas had to say. When I talked to CPR delegates in the capital in July 1992, they blamed the start of the violence exclusively on the army; refused to acknowledge any popular complaints against the guerrillas; and dismissed popular feeling against them around Nebaj as purely the result of military repression. Like the CPRs, other popular organizations focused their denunciations exclusively on the army. Only off the record did they sometimes criticize the URNG, for pursuing its own military priorities, leaving noncombatants to be massacred, and marginalizing the popular organizations in peace talks with the government.

Fronting for the guerrilla movement was not the only possible explanation for the ideological congruence of the popular organizations. Since at least some victims of government repression had been involved with the revolutionary movement, the same compatibility could result if the popular organizations were run by widows and kin of dead militants. Or perhaps they sounded like the guerrilla organizations simply because they were on the Left and shared the same experience of repression. Because of the threats they faced, in any case, the popular organizations were something like political sects. Standing out for their willingness to confront the security forces, they had a strong consciousness of themselves as groups apart with a special mission. With the same Manichean perspective as the foreign solidarity movement, they foresaw a dramatic transformation of society in which they would play a central role.

For Quiché Department, the agenda of the popular organizations included abolition of the civil patrols, withdrawal of the army, punishment of those guilty of human rights violations, and reparations for war damages. Given the inability of the Left to protect its supporters, such demands posed difficult questions for Mayan campesinos who usually choose less confrontational ways to defend themselves. Since many Ixils had aligned with the army to curtail its killing, they might perceive open challenges to it as a threat to themselves and their communities.

When large numbers of men began to refuse to patrol in southern Quiché several years before, the men who continued patrolling viewed abstainers as traitors and obeyed army orders to persecute them. Perhaps hardcore patrollers had lost members of their family to the guerrillas, or were deeply implicated in army killings, or wanted to use their authority to rob neighbors. Or perhaps they felt that patrolling was the only way to keep guerrillas and soldiers at bay. Such fears are suggested by the hostile reception patrollers gave human rights investigators in Parraxtut, a K'iche' Maya aldea of Sacapulas on the edge of Ixil country. Ten days before, on March 17, 1990, civil patrol leaders killed a member of a family refusing to serve and severely wounded another. When adjunct procurator César Alvarez Guadamuz arrived, together with CERJ president Amilcar Méndez, they were mobbed by machete-wielding patrollers and their women. It is likely that the villagers were instigated by the army, judging from similar incidents in southern Quiché, but a videotape of the incident also suggests that they felt genuinely threatened by human rights intervention in their aldea.[56]

That such feelings are widespread has been acknowledged by Mario Polanco, a representative of GAM. "Many join the patrols because they do not know that participation is not mandatory according to the constitution," Polanco told an interviewer in 1990. "But many others want to join. They have been subject to almost forty years of military indoctrination and are loyal to the army. They are also the majority of the Indian population. Maybe sixty, or even seventy percent of the indigenous population supports the military. The army has held rallies attended by over 10,000 people in which they burn effigies of GAM director Nineth de Garcia. Neither the GAM, the Committee for Campesino Unity (CUC) nor any other popular organization has ever been able to bring 10,000 Indians together for a protest.... The number of Indians who support the army greatly worries us."[57]

Polanco's assessment of Mayan support for the army might seem to contradict my own picture of Ixil neutralism, but little may differ except our respective vantage points. As a North American anthropologist, I tried to avoid strong political markings, enabling me to harvest Ixil rejection of both sides in the conflict. For a GAM organizer like Polanco, however, the association between human rights and the Left could easily mark him as a subversive and stir up an angry reaction, hence the perception that a majority of the population supports the army, which may be the case when they perceive another ill-conceived effort to organize them against the state.

The divided feelings of Ixils and like-minded Mayan campesinos should give the human rights movement pause. Because the army dominates the Guatemalan government and is responsible for continuing abuses, human rights organizers conceive of their struggle in terms of citizens demanding accountability from the state. But if my experience in the Ixil area is any guide, many rural-dwellers do not perceive themselves as victims only of state violence. Instead, they know they were hammered by the army only after being placed on the anvil by the guerrillas. Blaming both sides for their situation has led, in practice, to an alliance with the army which they do not wish to see upset by dissidents and outsiders.[58] What the Left regards as the result of repression is also the result of popular experience with the Left, followed by repudiation of it.

Obviously, Mayan opinion on issues of conformity, resistance, and political expediency is anything but united. Just because there is widespread repudiation of the armed Left among Mayas at present does not mean they will always reject a revolutionary program. A dramatic change in the configuration of power, such as occurred in Argentina when the military dictatorship disgraced itself in the Falklands War in 1982, could have a dramatic effect on what Ixils say in public. Presently, there is much knowledge of culpability that cannot be acted on because no one dares make the accusation in public. This is just one instance of a wider phenomenon Michael Taussig refers to as the "public secret," that is, what everyone knows but cannot talk about in public because of the prevailing distribution of power. Hence, the public secret is a way of remasking the truth in order to avoid confrontation and reprisal.[59]

From the point of view of human rights organizations, as well as survivors clamoring for justice, public silence is responsible for maintaining the impunity of officially protected killers. Over a period of years, silence can reshape memory, history, even notions of right and wrong, to the point that might makes right.[60] But in Nebaj, memory of army abuses is nurtured by the entire population, so that public silence does not mean forgetting what happened. At least some Nebajeños derive satisfaction from the death of notorious army informers, yet I detected no interest in systematic punishment of guilty parties, perhaps because such prosecutions would cast a far wider net than most Nebajeños would like to see.[61] Moreover, because the violence they experienced came from both directions, their assessments of responsibility do not point exclusively to the army. Indeed, one reason Nebajeños emphasize the external origin of the violence is probably exculpatory, to deflect blame from local men who committed crimes under duress.

Under these conditions, the demands of the popular organizations could stir up reactions that were not just orchestrated by the army. For example, what would be the result of a human rights campaign to prosecute army-conscripted civil patrollers for the murders they committed in 1982? With most men having served in the patrols, even a well-aimed indictment could easily be interpreted as a first step toward wider legal reprisals. While virtually all Ixils seem to feel they were wronged by the army, most also feel victimized by the way they were caught "between two fires." For people who continue to be trapped by the exigencies of armed conflict, the public secret is a way to suspend issues that cannot be resolved in favor of others more amenable to solution.

The public secret may also be the key to the relative calm in Nebaj. The army reestablished state authority not just by destroying the guerrilla network in town, but by spreading around responsibility for the killing. With the civil patrol extended to the entire male population, everyone became implicated in the new order. Bloodshed seems almost universal in legitimating social contracts, ranging from unranked band societies to the first state societies with their sacrificial victims buried around temples, to the impositions of the nation-state and the role of martyrs in revolutions. In contemporary Guatemala, the army's invocation of fallen soldiers and civil patrollers is sure to evoke the memory of others who were killed by the army. If we probe the symbolic basis of Guatemalans' struggle to maintain community on the local level and build it on the national level, the blood of all these victims is surely central.

TEN

Let the Dead Bury the Dead?

Ancestor crosses above the model village at Juil

I want to work on the coast and be free. It's more free. They [EGP fighters] are not free. They could die in an ambush.
—Ex-guerrilla in Nebaj, 1991

WORKING on the coast has long meant exploitation for the Mayas of Guatemala. Yet for the ex-guerrilla quoted above, the brutal but relatively well-paid job of cutting cane was preferable to revolutionary sacrifice. For several decades, peasant insurgencies like the one in which he fought have been the subject of considerable academic study. Scholars have debated the structural causes of rural insurgencies and the motives of insurgents, but usually they have assumed that such movements are popular, in the sense of attracting broad support from peasants. Yet my description of a war-weary population is nothing new, having become a standard finding of journalists and social researchers, many of them more sympathetic to the revolutionaries than to the governments.[1] If we give due weight to the commentaries of noncombatants, the popular character of peasant-based insurgencies is likely to be transitory. Once a population has been ravaged by war, what prevails is the hunger for stability, even on blatantly disfavorable terms. This puts scholars like myself who identify with the Left in an uncomfortable position. If subordinate groups usually do not want to pay the cost of defying dominant ones, where do we find a revolutionary subject to support in our work?

Perhaps this is why, in the 1980s, many of us showed such interest in probing subtle forms of "subversion" or "resistance."[2] Doubtless resistance is am important subject for research, but like the bygone "acculturation" paradigm it echoes,[3] this is an analytical category that projects quite an agenda into the lives of the people we study. Its siren song can be detected even in the work of James Scott, who has done so much to demystify the scholarly quest for the popular roots of revolution. His most recent work digs beneath the public transcript of amity between elites and subordinates, to the hidden reactions of subaltern groups. We might presume that, beneath the polite manners of subordinates, there always lurks a hidden transcript of rebellion that requires excavation by researchers.[4]

In a situation like that in Nebaj, the ambiguity of survivors requires more than a hunt for the hidden transcript. It is not just that expeditions to expose secrets can endanger survivors, by exposing them to retaliation from offended power holders. Or that we hardly serve the interests of subordinate groups by ferreting out their secrets for the benefit of whoever wishes to consume social research. Or that ambiguity provides a discursive vacuum into which it is easy to project a foreign agenda, whether of the counterinsurgency state or the insurrectionary Left. A deeper problem is that "resistance" often fails to focus on the kind of target scholars and activists deem appropriate, such as a dictatorship or plantation owners or the dominant ethnic group. For example, many Guatemalan Indians appear to see less in common between themselves and the guerrillas than between the guerrillas and the army, raising the question, who and what are they resisting?[5] Are Ixils resisting both the army and the guerrillas, or is their bitterness toward the guerrilla movement, their fear of being associated with it, a minor contradiction that will eventually work itself out?

A similar problem arises with how to evaluate a claim like neutralism, often the most popular rhetorical posture in armed confrontations. If claiming to be neutral is simply the public transcript, then it should be deconstructed to reveal the wellsprings of Ixil resistance, and essentially disregarded. The Left can rest assured that, deep down, poor people feel the way it always knows they have: repressed and escapist, perhaps, but still available to be raised to revolutionary consciousness, still ready to fight if the right conditions can be created. And so the revolutionary mission survives. But is it right to deconstruct neutralism in this way? Isn't the very act of doing so an invitation to political factions who, claiming to represent "the people" or "national security," wish to polarize the situation in which the poor struggle to survive? What if neutralism is less a disguise than a hard-won axiom of survival, around which Ixils are trying to reorganize their social identity and civil society?

A typical Ixil commentary like "this is their affair, not ours" suggests the functional complementarity of the two sides, how their particular forms of violence have justified and shaped each other. In the case of Guatemala, violence is produced by, not just the repressive policies of the Guatemalan state, but the particular forms of resistance that part of the Left has chosen. Both sides express a long tradition of resorting to arms to deal with the contradictions of republican life. Since the 1960s, a succession of guerrilla organizations have provided the army with a convenient rationale for militarizing the state. Some Guatemalans go so far as to claim that the army secretly supports the guerrillas to justify its domination of national life.

That many Ixils supported the Guerrilla Army of the Poor in the early 1980s is corroborated by the oft-repeated statement that we were *engañado* (deceived). Ixil experiences with plantation owners and labor contractors provided an audience for revolutionary appeals. It is harder to show that support for the guerrillas grew out of local social movements, let alone that substantial numbers of Ixils came to share the EGP's ideology. Certainly, Catholic organizations became targets for the security forces, in part because they had provided organizing opportunities for the guerrillas. But judging from how the guerrilla movement spread, what brought Ixils into it were army reprisals against EGP organizing, not the trajectories of local organizations before the guerrillas appeared. As the EGP extended its clandestine network, the army's reactions were sufficiently indiscriminate to produce more recruits than were eliminated. Pushed into the guerrilla movement were Ixils of almost every description, from catechists involved in cooperatives and commerce to very traditional maize farmers. Yet a similar spectrum of Nebajeños fell into line with the army as soon as the civil patrols and Ríos Montt began to rationalize the army's use of force.

This suggests that the proverbial revolutionary subject (as well as the counterrevolutionary one) grew out of how individuals, families, factions, and villages were caught up in the moves and countermoves of the two sides. Because the guerrillas were ineffective in defending their supporters, joining them carried an impossible cost for many Ixils. Given the overwhelming role of force and the transitory strength of the guerrilla movement, the term *popular* can be applied to the latter only in a limited sense. As of this writing (1992), an estimated twelve thousand Ixils—about 14 percent of the Ixil population according to my estimate in chapter 8—continue to live under EGP administration along with another eleven thousand people from other ethnic groups. Doubtless we could find cases of greater commitment to an insurgency. But the evident waxing and waning of support for such movements suggests that they have to be strictly delimited in terms of time to avoid essentializing them.

Authors depicting the insurgency as a popular movement usually point to ethnic feeling as its ultimate source. Yet the most sophisticated analyst of class and ethnic interaction in Guatemala, Carol Smith, found little evidence of ethnic mobilization for the revolutionary movement in the part of the western highlands she knows best, around Totonicapán. In Ixil country, which is supposed to have been a hearth of the guerrilla movement, the violence did not originate in ethnic confrontations, nor did it polarize the population ethnically. Even in Cotzal, where local men killed an owner of the Finca San Francisco at an early date, vengeance killing quickly became a contest between Ixil factions vying for control of the town hall. Nor is ladino discrimination against Indians necessary to explain why the army piled up as many bodies as it did. Thirteen years before, the army behaved the same way in eastern Guatemala, where most victims were ladinos.[6] Identifying the revolutionary movement with ethnic aspirations also ignores the many Ixils who decided they were betrayed by the guerrillas, a position voiced increasingly by Mayan intellectuals.

Certainly the guerrillas appealed to Ixil grievances against ladinos, but there is no sign that the grievances would have led to rebellion without the polarizing effect of guerrilla and army counterblows. To the contrary, there is considerable evidence that most Ixils would have preferred to stay out of the line of fire. In keeping with recent work on "passive resistance," the typical Ixil approach was and still is incrementalist, as expressed in the ubiquitous campesino phrase *poco a poco* (bit by bit). Before the violence, like Mayas elsewhere in the western highlands, Ixils were making gradual inroads on ladino monopolies in local government and commerce. The most prominent ladino families were already leaving Nebaj and the town hall was being taken over by Ixils, who were also moving into labor contracting, truck ownership, and the teaching profession. Counterinsurgency disrupted this process, then accelerated it. Once the Guatemalan army put its house in order under Ríos Montt, it appointed Ixil mayors and schoolteachers. It also replaced ladino military commissioners killed by the guerrillas with Ixils who comported themselves more carefully.

Even though the war ended ladino domination of Nebaj politics, the language of ethnic vindication has been mainly absent. This is interesting because, by the late 1980s, a Mayan cultural revival was in evidence in Guatemala. Led by literate, urban-connected professionals, Mayan organizations called for an end to cultural discrimination, won official approval for new alphabets over resistance from the Summer Institute of Linguistics, and demanded a place at the peace talks between the guerrillas and government.[7] New cultural organizations were emerging in Nebaj as well, to start libraries, promote literacy in Ixil, and preserve Ixil traditions. Yet when I visited in mid-1992, most Ixils were not aware of the campaigns to commemorate "the five hundred years"—the quincentenary of European colonization of the Americas—or to nominate their K'iche' neighbor Rigoberta Menchú for the Nobel Peace Prize. The new alphabets championed by Mayan organizations did not stir a town where there was relatively little interest in vernacular literacy in the first place.

What was most evident in Nebaj was ethnic bridge building, from political parties and civic committees to evangelical churches. Ethnic assertion was not the template of town politics, let alone an issue to be brandished in public. Perhaps this is due only to the exigencies of military occupation; certainly ethnicity figures in what Nebajeños mutter about each other. As Richard Adams reminds us, "One can perfectly well harbor antagonism against a category or class, e.g., "ladino," while accepting individual ladinos in various congenial roles."[8] But what should our scholarly priorities be? If our task is breaking through complacency and silence to reveal structural inequities, it may be crucial to establish in fine detail how different classes of people distrust and mistreat each other. But if this point is well established, as I believe it is, perhaps a more strategic task is to look at how people from ethnic groups with a past history of conflict are trying to overcome it. In this case, because of the Nebajeño decision to blame external forces for the violence, the relations between many Ixils and ladinos may actually have improved.

What I have chosen to call "ethnic détente" is being reinforced by the egalitarian preachments of reformed religion. Before the war, Ixil country was one of many places where the Catholic clergy enthusiastically organized cooperatives, village committees, and other participatory development projects. After being driven out by the Guatemalan army, the priests of the Guatemalan Church in Exile translated their experience into the Exodus language of liberation theology. Struggling to explain the sacrifice of fellow priests and lay catechists, they became convinced that their pastoral efforts had fostered a popular revolutionary movement. My alternative reading is that, while some catechists indeed joined the revolutionary movement, enough others aligned with the army that Catholic institutions in Ixil country may not have been the incubators of revolutionary sentiment which they seemed at the height of army repression.

The rapid growth of evangelical churches in Nebaj is correctly associated with persecution of the Catholic Church. Almost half the evangelical churches in town were founded or led (in 1988–89) by Catholic catechists. Some of these people turned evangelical before the violence, however. Judging from their testimony, two contradictions within the Catholic system were also responsible for the defections. One was dissatisfaction with dependence on the parish priest. The other was the inability of the Catholic Church to be both an inclusive body representing the entire Ixil community, including drinkers and abstainers, and a more exclusive, congregational body for Ixils seeking discipline and sobriety as they redefine their cultural tradition to face a situation of increasing land scarcity.

Hence, evangelical churches in Nebaj are the result of changes in Ixil ecology and culture, not just missionary work and political violence. Generally speaking, Ixil evangelicals are not highly sectarian or confrontational toward Ixil culture. Unlike evangelicals in some towns studied by anthropologists, they are not concentrated in distinct occupational niches, nor do they seem to be distinct from other religious groups in political terms. Instead, they are part of a broader-based reformation in Ixil society that began before evangelical churches had attained any size, which initially found expression in the Catholic Action movement, and now in Catholic charismaticism as well.

Members of the new religious movements break with Ixil tradition by turning their backs on the saints and Ixil priests, but politically their limited goals and avoidance of confrontation are in line with traditional Mayan practice.[9] The seeming conformism of evangelicals has hardly meant social or political stasis: over the last ten years Ixils have recaptured the town hall, the marketplace, and the business of labor contracting from ladinos and K'iche' Maya merchants. Catholic catechists, charismatics, and traditionalists have all been involved in these changes, not just evangelicals, but the discourse of the latter highlights the neutrality that Nebajeños under the army's control espouse. Their ability to reconstruct civil society in Nebaj, by setting up moral reciprocities with the military instead of directly challenging it, suggests how many Guatemalan Indians may continue to pursue their interests without recurring to the Left and the human rights movement.

Events in southern Quiché suggest that the human rights movement will get a mixed reception in Ixil country. Human rights discourse in Nebaj is already being encouraged by the Catholic Church and the procurator's office, but with considerably more circumspection than to be expected from the popular organizations operating in southern Quiché. Groups like GAM, CERJ, and CONAVIGUA are not just external agents, any more than the revolutionary movement was. Just as these organizations have in southern Quiché, they may find a constituency in Ixil country who, under national and international law, have every right to demand justice. But because legal justice is impossible under the current distribution of power in Guatemala, outsiders will take an active role in organizing the plaintiffs, defining their grievances, and giving local conflicts an international profile. Their straightforward approach to searching out and raising grievances is likely to draw a higher level of repression.

To survivors of a failed revolutionary movement, this kind of human rights activism may well arouse unsettling parallels. Just as the EGP played on class and ethnic tensions that Ixils had long finessed, the human rights movement uncovers and publicizes recent crimes of violence. In each case, the translation of subterraneously waged conflicts into the open brings swift retaliation against local people who cannot be protected.

The evangelical modus operandi is quite a contrast. If the evangelical revival in Latin America is a process of empowerment, it is proceeding by way of accepting (for now) the garrison states and dependent economies symbolized so graphically by contemporary Nebaj, not by protesting openly against them. While the human rights movement seeks to make oppressive situations explicit, evangelical churches resort to euphemization. They mystify rather than elucidate conflicts, by reducing all the injustices of history to the level of a personal moral struggle for each member. Because born-again religion euphemizes conflict, critics often assume that it has the power to "disappear" historical memory as efficiently as the Guatemalan security forces "disappear" opponents. As yet, there is no evidence for that in Nebaj. Instead, evangelical religion focuses on an individual's responsibility to change his or her personal behavior. Because it encourages collective religious effervescence and social reinforcement, the result is not social atomization. Instead, it is a new kind of social group.[10] In view of the ability of reformed religion to help participants change their lives in small but significant ways, is it possible that reformed religion at the grassroots could, gradually and cumulatively, reform an oppressive situation?

Evangelical growth in Nebaj is so recent, and on such uncertain institutional foundations, that it hardly provides a basis for speculation, let alone conclusions. But a conversionist movement does help participants change their daily practices, their social relations with others, and how they socialize their children. The success of some Ixils in equalizing their relations with local ladinos, chiefly through schooling, sobriety, and learning ladino codes, suggests the kind of contribution that reformed religion is making. If power is based on inequality, then power at the national level can be understood as the accumulation of inequalities at the local level. Lessening inequality at the local level should eventually have an impact on how power is exercised at the national level. Unfortunately, ethnic egalitarianism is hardly the only force at work. Among others is a population which is growing so rapidly that, together with ecological deterioration, it may not permit anything but pauperization for most Ixils. Now that Nebaj is filled with agencies for helping war victims, it is a town learning to live off the emergency of its hinterland.

Reinterpreting how Ixils experienced the violence may have wider relevance. Since the Vietnam War, a substantial literature has grown up explaining revolutionary insurgencies in terms of popular aspirations. In the case of Ixil country, widely presumed to have been a revolutionary stronghold in the early 1980s, I have argued that revolution came from outside, with less reference to Ixil experience and aspirations than has often been assumed, and that the local population became involved mainly because of the polarizing effect of guerrilla actions and government reprisals. If violence came from outside Ixil country, instead of welling up from within, it helps explain the paradox of a local situation that seems to be on the mend despite a national situation that, thanks to the power of the Guatemalan army and the persistence of the URNG, continues to be ruled by death squads.

The Ixil experience also suggests that it is time to question the academic priority of excavating "resistance." There is no lack of resistance to be found in Ixil country, but what I am questioning is how central it is to Ixils. What about the ethic of forbearance enunciated by traditionalists like the Ixil priest Shas K'ow, the born-again Christian discourse of careful neutrality, and the evident ability of Ixils and ladinos to wage peace in the midst of war? I am also questioning what it is that Nebajeños resist. If we take what Nebajeños say at face value, they are resisting not just the Guatemalan army, a national security state, dependent capitalism and colonialism but violence itself, in this case, the mimetic contest in which Right and Left, counterinsurgent and insurgent, try to remake an entire society in their own starkly polarized images. In a world where violence is proliferating, and where political conflict is often waged along ethnic lines, it is good to find a town where members of two opposed ethnic groups have made common cause against strife.

Notes

Las Violetas, on the outskirts of Nebaj, 1989

Preface

1. Gleijeses 1985:21.

1. La Situación

1. North American archaeologists (Smith and Kidder 1951:78) date the Early Classic tombs they excavated in Nebaj to A.D. 600–1000.

2. For an account of Ixil calendar divining, see Colby and Colby 1981.

3. Rolando Paiz Masselli, director of the National Reconstruction Committee in 1982–83, estimated that 80 percent of the population in El Quiché, Huehuetenango, Chimaltenango, and Alta Verapaz—more than 1.3 million people—were forced to leave their homes. According to Masselli, about 70 percent of the displaced returned home under Ríos Montt's amnesty (1982–85) (AVANCSO 1990:11, 19).

4. Black 1984:81.

5. At least seven writers (Marnham 1985; Sheehan 1989; Daniels 1990; McGuire 1991; Wright 1991; Canby 1992; Perera 1993) have included journeys to Nebaj in their books.

6. Following our departure, in December 1989 and January–February 1990, two men and one of their sons living near the town center were killed in army-style nocturnal executions. One victim was said to have declared that the civil patrols were unconstitutional; another lived on the edge of town and was said to be trading with the guerrillas.

7. Ixil women have become the cover girls of the Central American War. Their iconography appears in such works as Simon 1987, Manz 1988, and Carmack 1988, as well as in countless solidarity publications and postcards. The most published photographers include Jean-Marie Simon, Patricia Goudvis, Derrill Bazzy, and Gianni Vecchiato.

8. Tanner 1988. Two associates visiting Nebaj told me the U.S. embassy had been very helpful in paying Jody Duncan's medical bills. She was not the only foreigner to meet her fate in Ixil country. In 1979 three backpackers ignored warnings against walking to Cotzal, only to be robbed and dispatched with bullets through the head, perhaps by local men armed by the Guerrilla Army of the Poor. One of the tourists survived. In 1985 two North Americans were ambushed and executed by civil patrollers from the ladino settlement of Llano Grande, just west of Ixil territory. Again, the motive seems to have been robbery. Despite these mishaps, most tourists seemed to lead a charmed existence.

This is especially striking in view of the speculation caused by their incautious behavior. Fortunately, none of the three armed groups seemed to hold them accountable to normal standards in a war zone. When I asked an army captain whether he considered it safe to walk to Sumal Grande, he replied that gringos might be able to do it, but not him or anyone else in army uniform. The guerrillas were reported to have broken off the ambush of a truck as soon as they spotted a gringo riding in the back.

9. According to the 1880 census, Cotzal had 66 literates in a population of 2,825 while Nebaj had less than half as many literates (31) in a population more than twice as large (5,945). Seventy-four students were enrolled in school at Cotzal but only 24 in Nebaj. While Cotzal had a total of 120 artisans (mainly weavers), Nebaj had just 7 (figures courtesy of Pierre van den Berghe).

10. In accordance with the new orthography of the Academy of Mayan Languages of Guatemala, this work changes the spelling of Mayan language groups as follows: Quiché becomes K'iche', Cakchiquel becomes Kaqchikel, Kanjobal becomes Q'anjob'al, Kekchi' becomes Q'eqchi', Tzutujil becomes Tz'utujil, and Aguacatec becomes Akateko.

11. A coordinating group that, since 1982, has included the Guerrilla Army of the Poor (EGP), the Organization of the People in Arms (ORPA), the Rebel Armed Forces (FAR), and a faction of the Guatemalan Labor party (PGT).

12. Burgos-Debray 1983. It would be hard to exaggerate the influence of *I, Rigoberta Menchú*, which has become the single most popular personal testimony from Latin America in recent years. The book has aroused considerable interest in multicultural and feminist studies as well as anthropology, seems to be moving toward canonical status, and catapulted the author to a Nobel Peace Prize in 1992. For a sample of the growing critical literature on the work, see the essays in the Summer and Fall 1991 issues of *Latin American Perspectives*, especially by Doris Sommer and Marc Zimmerman.

13. Skocpol 1982:353.

14. Wolf 1969:291; Paige 1983.

15. Popkin 1979; Scott 1976; Paige 1975. My purpose here is only to question the premise that participation in a revolutionary movement reflects popular aspirations, not to deal with the theories themselves. Jeffrey Paige (1983:731–33) is the only one of these theorists to address Guatemala, when it was at the height of the violence (and confusion) of the early 1980s. He concludes that Mayan peasants joined the revolutionary movement because they were being rapidly proletarianized by land monopolists, a position based on misconceptions prevalent in the early 1980s that I will address in chapter 3.

16. Popkin 1979:262.

17. Scott 1976; Popkin 1979; Skocpol 1982:365.

18. In the case of Guatemala, Richard Adams (Newbold 1957) also found a

lack of ideological commitment when he interviewed communist-allied peasant leaders who were arrested following the overthrow of the Arbenz administration in 1954.

19. Migdal 1974:211–12, 228, 247–48.

20. From Q'anjob'als in neighboring Santa Eulalia, Huehuetenango, Shelton Davis (1988:26) heard the parallel expression "between two thorns." Roland Ebel (1988:188) noted the same perception of the violence in the Mam town of San Juan Ostuncalco, as do the diaries of Ignacio Bizarro Ujpán, a Tz'utujil of Lake Atitlán (Sexton 1992:41–43).

21. Wickham-Crowley 1990.

22. Compare Earle 1991:798, Smith 1992:32, and van den Berghe 1990:262–63, 280–81.

23. Scott 1990.

24. Compare Berryman's (1991:104) description of a parish in the western highlands where four or five thousand people were killed, and returning Catholic Church workers who "found people surprisingly willing to talk about the violence. In fact, la violencia was a common reference point in their conversation. They . . . would remark 'they treated us worse than dogs,' referring to how the army acted toward those it suspected of guerrilla ties. As soon as discussion moved toward any sort of organization, however, they would resist: 'Oh, this is like the meetings they used to have at night,' " in reference to how guerrillas organized the population.

25. If Ixils simply damned the guerrillas, their statements would be easy to explain as a rhetorical posture to please the army. But when they criticize the army in the same breath, despite the manifest power of the army over their lives, it becomes apparent that they are not simply saying what the army wants them to say.

26. For an explanation of this situation, see the section on the Communities of Population in Resistance in chapter 9.

27. Americas Watch 1989. Runujel Junam means "everyone is equal" in K'iche' Maya. In CERJ's first three years of existence, fifteen members disappeared or were murdered (Hockstader 1991).

28. Loucky and Carlsen 1991.

29. Thanks to Jo-Marie Burt for reminding me of this concept at an opportune moment.

30. McCreery, forthcoming. According to Robert Bocock, as quoted by McCreery, civil society consists of "other organizations in a social formation which are neither part of the processes of material production in the economy, nor part of state-funded organizations, but which are relatively long-lasting institutions supported and run by people outside of the other two major spheres. A major component of civil society so defined would be religious institutions and organizations." For a collection of articles on the concept of civil

society in contemporary political philosophy, mainly in the European context, see Keane 1988.

2. Ixils and Ladinos

1. Excerpts from text recorded by Stephen Elliott in Ilom and translated by Thomas Lengyel, in Lengyel 1987:339–80. "Diego Chavez" is a pseudonym for an Ixil elder.

2. Smith 1990a:85.

3. Colby and van den Berghe 1969:64–69.

4. This was a widespread trend as modern export agriculture spread through the Third World in the nineteenth and twentieth centuries. For parallels in neighboring countries, see Durham 1979:42 on the expansion of coffee in El Salvador and Wasserstrom 1983:113–16 on the Soconusco region of Chiapas, Mexico.

5. McCreery, forthcoming.

6. McCreery, forthcoming.

7. McCreery, forthcoming. For an essay focusing on the mandamientos, see McCreery 1986. For the impact of early-twentieth-century mandamientos on the Kaqchikel Maya town of San Andrés Semetabaj, see Warren 1978:145–8.

8. Lincoln 1945:61.

9. Burkitt 1930:58.

10. McCreery 1990:108–12; 1991, 9:18–19.

11. While Nebajeños have long referred to the leading colonists as *españoles* (Lincoln 1945:64), these may have included fewer peninsular-born Spaniards than fair-skinned Guatemalans accepting *español* as an honorific.

12. McCreery, forthcoming.

13. McCreery, forthcoming.

14. McCreery, forthcoming.

15. Burkitt 1930:57–58.

16. Lincoln 1945:75–76.

17. In 1913 Burkitt (1930:52) encountered Pedro Brol as a sugar cane grower but, by 1939, Lincoln (1945:64) refers to him as a coffee grower, suggesting that finca owners like him moved into coffee during the 1920s boom.

18. Colby and Colby 1981:32–33.

19. Elliott 1989:7–8; personal communication, May 2, 1990. The 180 caballerías that Cotzal lost to private titles is not much greater than the 150 lost by Chajul, the difference being that Cotzal lost a larger percentage (45 percent as opposed to 5 percent) of its smaller land base. For a detailed account of Liberal land titling in the neighboring municipio of Santa Eulalia, Huehuetenango, see Davis 1970.

20. Compare McCreery, forthcoming.

21. Elliott 1989:6; McCreery, personal communication, April 10, 1989.

22. Elliott 1989:10–11. Ironies never cease in such stories. Gordillo went bankrupt a few years after winning the decision. According to an old ladino opponent in Chajul, the reason was all the money he had spent to buy the court, although the onset of the Great Depression doubtless played a role. His property returned to the bank holding the mortgage. When the dictator Ubico offered to return the land to the Ixils if they would pay off the debt, the elders of Ilom refused, on grounds that they should not have to pay for what was rightfully theirs. Eventually, the land was purchased—or rather, a modest down payment was made—by Luis Arenas, the so-called Tiger of the Ixcán whose assassination by the guerrillas in 1975 is considered the start of the violence in Ixil country.

23. Compare McCreery, forthcoming.

24. Per the chart of land measures in Appendix 1, 1 caballería equals 45.374 hectares.

25. *El Imparcial*, July 1, 1924, as quoted by McCreery, forthcoming.

26. Lincoln 1945:61–62.

27. Compare Davis (1970:36–37) on the Q'anjob'al municipio of Santa Eulalia.

28. Lincoln 1945:9, 74, 88.

29. Lincoln 1945:78.

30. Colby and van den Berghe 1969:77, 122.

31. Calculated from the 1950 census (as provided by Nachtigall 1978:46–50), in which the town center's total population was 3,480. According to the 1973 census, in which ladinos declined to 7.9 percent of the municipio's total population, they now comprised 26.1 percent of the town center's population of 4,151.

32. Lengyel 1987:55.

33. While Arbenz is remembered as a martyr for democracy, he was forced to defend himself from the Right through strong-arm tactics of his own. These may have included the murder of his rival, the more popular, conservative and possibly coup-minded Colonel Francisco Arana. For the evidence against Arbenz, see Rosenthal 1962.

34. Colby and van den Berghe 1969:110–11.

35. For an illustration of how small-town ladino society produces agrarian populists, see the autobiography of Padre Andrés Girón, an agitator for land reform in the 1980s, in Cambranes 1986:37–135.

36. Handy 1990:173.

37. Méndez Montenegro 1960:719–21.

38. Elliott 1989:11–13.

39. For an explanation of how land reform alienated army officers, see the work of Jim Handy (particularly 1990:178), who has produced the most sophisticated analysis of the tensions surrounding the agrarian reform.

40. Anderson 1983:109–20.

41. For a review of the literature on cofradías in Mesoamerica, see Greenberg 1981:1–22 and Chance 1990. According to Chance's (1990:39) review of the literature, civil functions were added to the religious hierarchies of the cofradías at a rather late date, in the nineteenth century. Civil offices have also been the first part of cargo systems to disintegrate in the twentieth century, owing to the reorganization of local government and the introduction of political parties.

42. According to Colby and van den Berghe (1969:122–24), the civil side of the civil-religious hierarchy was quite alive in the Nebaj of the 1960s even though the town hall was controlled by ladinos. At an annual meeting in October, the Ixil principales assembled to choose, not just the holders of various religious offices, but the indigenous members of the town council. Hence, the civil-religious hierarchy in Nebaj was able to adapt to changes in the Guatemalan political system. By the late 1980s, town officials still collaborated with traditional religious authorities in ceremonies such as the blessing of the *varas* (staffs of office) when auxiliary mayors change in January. But the principales no longer chose any party's political candidates.

43. For portraits of Catholic Action and its conflicts with traditionalists, see Falla 1978 on the K'iche' town of San Antonio Ilotenango, Warren 1978 on the Kaqchikel town of San Andrés Semetabaj, and Brintnall 1979a on the Akateko town of Aguacatán.

44. Padre Gaspar's idea of salvation was doubtless more sacramental than evangelical (Lincoln 1945:12). As far as Ixil traditionalists were concerned, they and their beloved costumbre represented true Catholicism.

45. Colby and Colby provide the most in-depth account of Ixil prayer-making and divining, although two Methodist missionaries (Lawrence and Morris 1969) have provided a useful summary of these and related Ixil traditions.

46. Lovell 1990:10.

47. Unfortunately, I could not find statistical data on slope and soil type for Ixil country, preventing an estimate of how much land is actually available for Mayan farming practices.

48. Collier 1975:76–78.

49. Hinshaw (1975:55) points out that the cost of faithfully contributing to an evangelical church year after year would not be much less, and could even exceed, the more episodic but larger expenditures for serving a saint. Significantly, Nebaj pastors complain that many of their members do not contribute, suggesting that reformed religion can indeed be cheaper.

50. Among the Akateko Mayas who have an even stronger pattern of ancestor worship and gerontocracy, the Catholic Action movement was motivated
by such a rupture between fathers and sons. In Aguacatán, the introduction of
a lucrative cash crop—irrigated garlic—helped sons break with their fathers
after receiving only part of their inheritance of land (Brintnall 1979a).

51. Colby and Colby 1981:44–45.

52. Pierre van den Berghe to author, August 1, 1987, as corroborated by
Palomino 1972:65.

53. Nachtigall 1978:200, 328.

54. Nachtigall 1978:329–30. Achilles Palomino (1972:57) reported the same
regulation.

55. Compare Flavio Rojas Lima 1988:144, 180, who found a similar trend in
the K'iche' town of San Pedro Jocopilas.

56. John Watanabe (1984:208–12) reports the same tension in the Catholic
Action movement of Santiago Chimaltenango, a Mam town in Huehuetenango. Catechists felt considerable animus against traditionalist celebrations, particularly the drunkenness these involved. But if catechists attacked costumbre
too vigorously in the name of orthodox Catholicism, traditionalists might
become so alienated that they turned evangelical. Yet, if catechists failed to condemn costumbre, they opened themselves up to charges of laxity, encouraging
frustrated Catholic puritans to turn evangelical.

57. Adams et al. 1972; Wasserstrom 1975.

58. Colby and van den Berghe 1969:124–26. Catechist support for the PID in
1966 was not unusual judging from reports of the same alliance in San Antonio
Ilotenango, in southern Quiché (Falla 1980:462–63), and San Juan Ostuncalco,
Quezaltenango (Ebel 1988:175). Flavio Rojas Lima (1988:139) reports an
alliance between Catholic Action and PID in coalition with the National Liberation Movement a decade later in San Pedro Jocopilas, Quiché. These cases
suggest how local factionalism could give catechists a trajectory contradicting
outsiders' assumptions about their interests.

59. Wolf 1969:282.

60. Smith 1974.

61. Smith 1987a:11.

62. Lincoln 1945:67–69; Colby and van den Berghe 1969:76.

3. The Violence Comes to Ixil Country

1. "La Toma de Nebaj" 1982:39 versus Fox 1982:660.

2. "La Toma de Nebaj" 1982:40.

3. "La Toma de Nebaj" 1982:40.

4. International Work Group on Indigenous Affairs 1978; Chernow 1979.

5. Democratic Front Against Repression 1980.

6. Fernández Fernández 1988.

7. For the influence of consciousness-raising and liberation theology, see Lernoux 1980 and Berryman 1984.

8. Davis and Hodson 1982:35.

9. Smith 1984a:219–20; Smith 1987a:1.

10. Payeras 1983:68. For another informative account, of the prehistory of the EGP, see Debray 1975.

11. Melville 1983:25.

12. On the Catholic colonies, see Simon 1989:39, 65–71, and Manz 1988a and 1988b. On government colonization projects, see Dennis et al. 1988. For the most complete account of the destruction of the Ixcán colonies, see Falla 1992.

13. The penumbra of rumor and fear surrounding the EGP's arrival has been described by an ex-Maryknoll missionary who wrote a dissertation on the Ixcán projects. "The concept of a guerrilla was largely enigmatic to the Maya," writes James Morrissey. "For some, it was a mythical figure indistinguishable from numerous other beings who populated the fantasy world of their more traditional elders. Others understood that a guerrilla was an unconventional and surreptitious warrior, but his origins, affiliation, location, and cause were unknown. They were assumed to be bad, and the thought that one might encounter them inspired fear. Back in 1969, rumors had filtered into Ixcán Grande telling of their theft of food and other belongings from the isolated poor families in the vicinity of San Luis Ixcán. The fact that the Guatemalan military fought them whenever they surfaced reinforced the notion that they were the 'enemy.' The Maya of the Ixcán clearly wanted nothing to do with them. The few who spoke of them did so with an air of foreboding which suggested that they knew of something they preferred not to talk about. For three years they remained a vague background theme in the Ixcán, making people a bit nervous but not enough to keep them from going about their business" (Morrissey 1987:14–15).

14. Payeras 1983:51. The testimony of the only persisting recruit, a ladino settler, was published in the EGP's *Informador Guerrillero*, no. 10 (June 16, 1982).

15. Handy 1984:234. A *foco* is a point of concentration.

16. Payeras 1983:36. Judging from Black 1984:79, this was the Rebel Armed Forces, which tried to open up a front in the same general area where the EGP would be more successful.

17. Gillespie 1983:493.

18. Black 1984:85–87.

19. This is not the same Finca San Francisco, in Nentón, Huehuetenango, where the Guatemalan army killed 302 men, women, and children on July 17, 1982 (Falla 1983b).

20. Lincoln 1945:66.

21. Especially when opposed by Indians, titling community land was suffi-

ciently "complicated and expensive" (McCreery, forthcoming) that the amount Cotzal lost to finca owners suggests active complicity by town leaders.

22. Elliott 1989:12.

23. The change in policy was, according to a member of the Brol family, motivated by the ease with which quinceneros could clandestinely supplement their own budding harvests with the finca's.

24. Payeras (1983:62) dates Sajíc's kidnapping to 1972.

25. Black 1984:79.

26. Compare Payeras (1983:67–68), who makes little reference to guerrilla finances but describes how they make the mistake of "financing the real or supposed needs of our new compañeros, thus generating material self-interest."

27. An anonymous Catholic priest quoted by Frank and Wheaton (1984:42) claims that the merchants, two in number, "were sent from their community, following a Catholic Action meeting."

28. Payeras (1983:90–91) gives a date of October 1978.

29. Payeras 1983:72–76.

30. Elliott 1989:11.

31. Schlesinger and Kinzer 1982:127.

32. This point is obscured by Payeras's emphasis on debt peonage, a labor procurement technique that Arenas may have used to recruit Q'eqchi' laborers for another venture to the north, the Finca San Luis Ixcán. The most dire accounts of how Arenas treated his laborers seem to have originated in the more difficult conditions at San Luis Ixcán, not at La Perla. For a more sympathetic account of Luis Arenas, see Daniels 1990:176–210.

33. Payeras 1983:76.

34. It would have been hard for the guerrillas to address the workers "in their own language" (Payeras 1983:76) because at least three were being spoken—Ixil, Q'anjob'al, and Spanish—in the latter of which the visitors addressed those workers who did not run away at the gunfire. According to the rather different version that reached James Morrissey (1987:16–17), the guerrillas "held clandestine meetings with people who worked on the ranch. They tried, unsuccessfully, to get the people to agree to murder Arenas. The workers were terrified at the thought of the repercussions of such an action, yet they were just as terrified of the guerrillas. They agreed not to reveal the presence of the guerrillas if they mingled with the workers and tried to perform the deed themselves."

35. According to Payeras (1983:85), Fonseca was fingered by an informer. According to a Nebaj version, he was arrested after showing off a weapon. According to still another, he got into a fight with another youth, which led to the discovery of the grenade and pistol he was carrying.

36. Payeras 1983:84–87.

37. Falla 1978.

38. Payeras 1983:65–66.

39. Interview in the refugee camp at the Nebaj air strip, November 21, 1982.

40. This point is made in an Oxfam America report (Davis and Hodson 1982), which found that Indians joined guerrilla organizations not out of ideological commitment but to protect themselves.

41. "Report on Violence in Northern Quiché" 1980:1–2.

42. "Report on Violence in Northern Quiché" 1980:3.

43. "Report on Violence in Northern Quiché" 1980:3, 5.

44. In 1966 Colby and van den Berghe (1969:82) were told that Catholic Action had about a thousand members in Chajul, eight hundred in Cotzal, and three hundred in Nebaj. In 1973 Nachtigall (1978:332) was told that Catholic Action had about fifteen hundred members in Chajul, with a thousand in Cotzal and Nebaj.

45. Local interviews, 1988–89; "Report on Violence in Northern Quiché" 1980:4.

46. "Report on Violence in Northern Quiché" 1980:4.

47. "Another Massacre in Guatemala: An Eyewitness Account of What Happened in Nebaj, Quiché, on March 3, 1980," a one-page typed document. Also, "Testimony of the Peasants of Nebaj for the Federation of Guatemalan Workers, Guatemala City," a three-page typed document signed by The Committee of Peasants of Nebaj.

48. Davis and Hodson 1982:49. Contrary to the local testimony I was able to gather, the army claimed to have responded to gunfire from the crowd ("Seis muertos y 8 heridos en Nebaj, Quiché," *Diario El Gráfico*, March 4, 1980).

49. Two thousand to three thousand are army and guerrilla estimates, respectively, quoted by Wickham-Crowley (1990:208).

50. Coffin 1981:16.

51. Author's interviews, November 1982.

52. Morrissey 1987:17.

53. A manual produced by the U.S. Central Intelligence Agency for the war in Nicaragua (Tayacán 1984:33) advises how to create political martyrs by "taking the demonstrators to a confrontation with the authorities, in order to bring about uprisings or shootings, which will cause the death of one or more persons, who would become the martyrs, a situation that should be made use of immediately against the regime, in order to create greater conflicts."

54. Payeras 1983:71.

55. Morrissey 1978:663–67. Morrissey's "Don Guillermo" is probably the Guillermo Monzón whom *Informador Guerrillero* (no. 10 [June 16, 1982]) describes as the "chief of military commissioners of the zone" who was executed on May 28, 1975. The cooperative members were seized in July (Davis and Hodson 1982:47).

56. Morrissey 1987:17.

57. Paige 1983:733.

58. Schwartz (1990:277–78) provides a balanced account of land concentration in the Petén, in a needed corrective to overreliance on solidarity viewpoints. An example of the latter is Timothy Wickham-Crowley's (1992:223, 236) confusion of the Ixil Triangle with the Northern Transversal Strip.

59. James Morrissey (1978) describes heated conflict among Maryknoll priests over how many smallholders the mission would permit to settle in its Ixcán projects, with clients of one project director squaring off against clients of the next.

60. Land redistribution is recommended in a 1980–81 army planning document (Cifuentes H. 1982:45, 49) in the depths of the Lucas García regime, although the National Institute for Agrarian Transformation (INTA) had already begun to acquire and distribute several fincas in Cotzal in the late 1970s (see chap. 8). A comparative case of land distribution in the midst of counterinsurgency is the INTA colonization project at Playa Grande, Ixcán. It began in 1979, was disrupted by a guerrilla offensive in 1981 and army massacres in 1982, but has continued to grow under tight army control (Dennis et al. 1988; also Manz 1988a, 1988b; Simon 1989; and Guatemalan Church in Exile 1989a).

61. Smith 1984:219; Smith 1990b.

62. My summary of events in La Estancia is indebted to the reconstruction of Robert Carmack (1988:47–55). Another valuable source is Guatemalan Church in Exile 1982:40–50, with Arias 1990 providing a helpful description of the political context.

63. Compare Smith 1987b:269 and Smith 1990b:15–16.

64. Smith 1990a:228.

65. Arias 1990.

66. For a Quiché youth's trajectory from Catholic Action to CUC to the EGP, see Simon 1987:128.

67. See the proceedings of the Russell Tribunal (Jonas et al. 1984) for the testimony of Pablo Ceto, a student from Nebaj whose activities seem to have centered on southern Quiché rather than the Ixil area.

68. Authors applying the term *base communities* to Nebaj (Frank and Wheaton 1984:41–43; Arias 1990:247) draw on a fascinating document ("Sebastián Guzmán: Principal de principales" n.d.), that justifies one of the EGP's most controversial executions in Nebaj. The ten-page typescript has been attributed to Padre Javier, the parish priest who joined the revolutionary movement after his order was forced to leave Quiché in 1980. It accuses the town's leading principal—that is, the most powerful elder in the traditional religious hierarchy—of giving the army death lists of catechists and cooperative organizers who were impeding his business as a labor contractor. If the accusation is true, the violence in Nebaj grew directly out of the conflict

between traditionalists and catechists, as the latter became identified with the consciousness-raising efforts of the Catholic Church. Religious conflict would assume class overtones as the head of the saint societies, who is also a labor contractor and power broker, retaliates against catechists struggling to end the community's dependence on plantation exploiters. Betrayed by their traditional leader, according to the document, the people flock to the Guerrilla Army of the Poor and demand his *ajusticiamiento*.

It is not hard to see why the EGP considered Sebastián Guzmán an enemy. His enemies would have included the aldeas of Xoloché and Tzalbal, against whom he won a land dispute; catechists who had collided with him in politics; and debtors who had taken his wage advances, then failed to show up for work and suffered punitive measures. When I asked Nebajeños about him in 1988–89, his reputation was mixed, like that of any important principal. But no one classified him with other local politicians who gave the army death lists. Why the guerrillas assassinated him during a religious procession remains a mystery to Nebajeños. Some refer to a prodigal son who supposedly joined the guerrillas; others point to his labor contracting and the fact that many Ixils owed him money. Unaware of the EGP manifesto claiming responsibility, some Nebajeños believe he was killed by the army.

Significantly, the indictment of Guzmán glosses over the reconstellation of political forces in Nebaj before the violence. When reformers won the Nebaj town hall in the 1976 election, their coalition included good-government ladinos, Sebastián Guzmán's traditionalists, and Christian Democratic catechists who—if the manifesto is to be believed—were simultaneously being betrayed to the army by Guzmán. The alliance fell apart before the 1980 election, but the victims of the first kidnappings included at least two prominent members of Guzmán's own political party, which the army also happened to be repressing next door in Cotzal. The document's reference to his great enemy as the "Christian base communities" is doubtless a reference to Catholic Action and its village chapters, which Ixils refer to as *centros* (centers).

69. Instead, many Ixils dismissed these kidnappings as the result of *errores* (errors) by the victims. The implication is that the victims were guilty of helping guerrillas whom most Ixils regarded as foreign and dangerous. Jean-Marie Simon (1987:107) quotes various statements illustrating the prevailing mentality of distrust and noninvolvement.

70. Smith 1990:265; Handy 1989:192.

71. Any discussion of Indian rebellion requires careful attention to how the subject has been "constructed" by our predominantly nonindigenous sources (Handy 1989; Adams 1990). In a comparative study of Mayan revolts across the border in Mexico, Victoria Bricker (1981) found that they tended to begin in the imagination of anxious ladino colonizers, whose overreactions to religious movements were what set off the violence. Mayan rebelliousness has also been

exaggerated by intellectuals seeking precedents for contemporary guerrilla warfare. One example is Guatemala's Nobel Prize-winning novelist Miguel Angel Asturias, whose *Men of Corn* (1949) begins with an Indian resistance fighter named Gaspar Ilom, apparently after the aldea of Chajul by that name, and possibly after a Chajuleño who led the fight to save it from the Finca La Perla. The historical Gaspar Ijom was a fighter in courts and government offices, not a bush rebel, but when the novelist's son Rodrigo Asturias organized the Organization of the People in Arms (ORPA) in the 1970s, he chose as his nom-de-guerre Gaspar Ilom.

72. McCreery 1990.

73. Wasserstrom 1975.

74. Smith 1992.

75. Falla 1978.

76. By way of exception, a solidarity author makes the point clearly in "La Toma de Nebaj" (1982), a detailed account of the EGP's January 21, 1979, occupation of Nebaj that was published in Paris. While triumphalistic in tone, the author specifies the tit-for-tat nature of the army response to EGP actions from the assassination of Luis Arenas onward.

4. The Civil Patrols, Ríos Montt, and the Defeat of the EGP

1. Author's interview, December 21, 1982.

2. Wickham-Crowley (1992:290) argues that it is only this kind of "mafiacracy" (or more technically, "praetorian patrimonialism")—like the Batista regime in Cuba and the Somozas in Nicaragua—that is vulnerable to a revolutionary movement in contemporary Latin America.

3. "Sebastián Guzmán: Principal de principales" n.d.

4. Wickham-Crowley 1990:225–30.

5. Coffin 1981:6, 8, 17.

6. This account is based on Michael Christian's (1982) diary of a December 1981 visit to Nebaj plus the author's interviews in 1988–89.

7. Nyrop 1984:215 dates the civil patrols to a September 1981 order from Benedicto Lucas García.

8. Americas Watch 1986:26.

9. Cifuentes H. 1982:47, 49–53. Americas Watch 1984:71 traces the idea of the civil patrols to Mario Sandoval Alarcón in 1970.

10. This is an abridged version of a much longer testimony that was presented to the author as a tape recording. In December 1982, the mayor of Cotzal dated the formation of the civil patrol to January 25.

11. Author's interview, Nebaj, November 1982.

12. The total number of persons killed in this manner ranged from a dozen to sixty, according to different estimates by Chajuleños.

13. This is the date as identified in Christian 1982; a Nebajeño relying on his memory seven years later identified it as December 12.

14. Anfuso and Sczepanski 1983.

15. Handy 1984:265–72.

16. AVANCSO 1990:19.

17. Americas Watch 1983, 1984; Amnesty International 1987.

18. Strangely, the massacres at Ilom and Estrella Polar are well established in local testimony but, like other major massacres at Bipulay (Nebaj), Xecax (Nebaj), and Chisis (Cotzal), never appeared in human rights reports, as if survivors were beyond the network of the Catholic and revolutionary groups gathering information. The Committee for Campesino Unity reported the massacre of "the entire population" of Chel, Juá, and Amajchel on April 3–5, along with the massacre of thirty-five at Covadonga (CGUP 1983:57). Local sources describe the number of people killed at Covadonga as thirty-five to forty-five, at Ilom as eighty-five to ninety, at Estrella Polar as ninety-six, and at Chel of the same magnitude or higher. This would bring the dead to three hundred or more, not including the massacres at Juá and Amajchel.

19. Nairn 1983:17 plus author's interviews, 1988–89. The hooded prisoner was a local youth who subsequently served in the army, returned to civilian life, and in February 1990 was killed while serving in the civil patrol, an end that some Nebajeños considered his just desserts.

20. Author's interview, La Pista refugee camp, November 22, 1982.

21. A civil patrol leader I interviewed in late 1982 blamed the lieutenant colonel for the death of ninety-seven people including his own father.

22. Reportedly a nom-de-guerre for Otto Pérez Molina, a highly regarded young officer who subsequently was promoted to important staff positions in the defense ministry and presidential palace.

23. "Informa RR. PP. del Ejército: Comandante Alvaro, de Guerrilla, pereció en acción en Chacalté," *El Grafico*, June 16, 1982. This news story gives figures of both 100 and 112 for the number killed. CGUP 1983:66 reports 120 killed.

24. An Amnesty International briefing (1982:viii) attributes the deaths to unknown men who attacked the village. The EGP's *Informador Guerrillero* (no. 19 [1983], p. 4) took credit for a *combate* in which the guerrillas caused fourteen casualties that same month in Chajul, without specifying a date.

25. While the army communique in *El Grafico* cited above dates both the Batzul and Chichel massacres to May 18, Amnesty International (1982:viii) dates the Batzul incident to on or about May 19.

26. "Hechos," two-page typescript dated May 5, 1980.

27. When Ixils under government control use the indefinite *they* to assign responsibility for killing, further acquaintance usually reveals that they are referring to government security forces. When Ixils blame guerrillas, on the

other hand, they do not hesitate to say so. Where Ixils seem genuinely uncertain is in regard to individual homicides for which witnesses are lacking.

28. *Informador Guerrillero*, no. 10 (June 16, 1982), p. 2.

29. The most well-known case, the Ixil grandson of a well-known finca owner, was executed by the EGP around 1983. There is much disagreement and speculation about his actual deeds, but his name is associated (perhaps wrongly) with the assassination of three Ixil bilingual promoters, an Ixil teacher, an Ixil town councilman, and a well-known Ixil Catholic leader. The list includes one of his own brothers and a brother-in-law whom the army pressured to speak out against him, which may be the only reason some consider him responsible for their deaths. Nebajeños generally agree that he met his end after organizing the robbery of cattle and coffee for personal profit, not for the alleged homicides in 1981–82.

Perhaps the most detailed solidarity interpretation of the violence in English, *Indian Guatemala: Path to Liberation* (Frank and Wheaton 1984:76), acknowledges that "even before people were organized into civil defense patrols, there were some violent clashes between Indians who supported the resistance and those who now sided with the army. Indeed, there were even a few atrocities committed by certain EGP units against groups of Indians whom they believed were collaborating with the army. Nevertheless, there was no comparison between these isolated incidents—stemming from errors and interethnic conflicts—and the genocide being perpetrated by the army."

30. Typical of the confusion surrounding such events, the crime was also attributed to Mobile Military Police operating out of the Finca San Francisco.

31. For a typical assessment, see Gillespie 1983.

32. Thanks to Richard Wilson for making these points in a letter. Corroborating them is the testimony of one of the EGP's first recruits in the Ixcán, a ladino woman, published in *Compañero* 1982:27–30. For an account of the war among the Q'eqchi' to the east in Alta Verapaz, where catechists are said to have been the first to join the guerrillas, see Wilson 1991:38.

33. According to a surprisingly low army estimate dating from early 1981 or 1980 (Cifuentes H. 1982:31), one hundred or fewer EGP leaders and political cadre had recruited about twelve hundred people.

34. Interviews in Campamento Nueva Vida (the refugee camp at the Nebaj air strip), November 21–22, 1982.

35. "Parte de guerra," January 1982. The toll for December 22 included two army guides in Chajul, three reactionaries in the Finca Estrella, three reactionaries and four thieves "who robbed the population when it evacuated according to an emergency plan" at Bisiquichum, and three army collaborators in Juá, all the latter being villages of Chajul along a route to the Ixcán. The date makes it possible that these killings were a reaction to the start of the civil patrol.

36. Wickham-Crowley 1990:215–17, 225. In other words, without the kind of judicial proceeding recognized by international law, guerrillas execute non-combatants suspected of helping the other side.

37. Simon 1989:54.

38. Smith 1990a:266.

39. *Informador Guerrillero*, no. 19 (1983), p. 4.

40. Counting whether more people were in the montaña or under army control is complicated by the even harder to quantify category of people who left for the coast or larger towns.

41. Quoted in AVANCSO 1990:22. The government health centers counted only 27,078 people during 1983–84, but these figures do not include a number of aldeas in Chajul and Cotzal that were under army control. Shortly before the army's 1987 offensive against Sumal, the health centers counted 49,619 people under government administration.

42. The only one to appear in human rights reports seems to have been Cocop (April 16, 1981), in reaction to an EGP ambush (Coffin 1981:13, 19–20; Davis and Hodson 1982:50). The massacre at Bipulay is described in the epigraph on page 121. It followed the EGP's July 28, 1980, attack on the army barracks at Cotzal.

43. Another display of support for the army were the "Ixil companies" it organized in the three towns, each consisting of 100 to 120 Ixil youths. Unlike other army units, the Ixil companies spoke the same language as the indigenous population and also knew the terrain. While some members had previously been conscripted into regular army units, others were volunteers. According to a volunteer who joined at the age of fourteen: "I became disillusioned, because for two years this town was nearly abandoned. It was half empty. Practically the majority of the people went off with *la subversión*. And the guerrillas went after my father"—a labor contractor whom they tried to kill. The EGP's ransacking of the household also left an impression on the youth, who rose to sergeant and was offered the chance to become an officer.

44. Falla 1983a:37–41.

45. Falla 1983a:39.

46. Falla 1983a:40.

47. Author's interviews in Campamento Nueva Vida, the refugee camp at the Nebaj air strip, November 21–22, 1982.

48. Thanks to Orin Starn for this observation.

49. Payeras 1987.

50. Frank and Wheaton 1984:100

51. EGP fronts included the Marco Antonio Yon Sosa to the east in Verapaz; the Augusto C. Sandino in southern Quiché, Sololá, and Chimaltenango; the Luis Turcios Lima on the south coast; the 13th of November in the Oriente; and

the Otto René Castillo in the capital (*Informador Guerrillero*, no. 8 [May 16, 1982]).

52. See Berryman 1991:68 and the letter from Arturo Arias published in *Report on Guatemala* (Oakland, California), Summer 1991, pp. 12–13.

53. "Como en Vietnam, nos preparamos para lo peor," *Informador Guerrillero*, no. 18 (December 1982), p. 10.

54. Compare the following account of what happened in eastern Guatemala in the 1960s: "Many were the campesinos who, between the sword and the wall, turned against the guerrillas and reproached them . . . for bringing down on they themselves and their families the anger of the repression, while the guerrillas always had the possibility of fleeing. It is a fact that civilian collaborators and peasants tied to their land suffered more from the terror than the guerrillas themselves." The author is Regis Debray (1975:298–99), the well-known theorist of the guerrilla foco, in collaboration with Ricardo Ramírez, founder of the Guerrilla Army of the Poor.

5. From Montaña to Model Village

1. But geography cannot be the only reason, because the remaining refugees with the EGP in the Ixcán are close to the border and could cross it.

2. Ministerio de Defensa Nacional 1985.

3. On October 30, 1988, a motor vehicle carrying three members of the army's G-2 section blundered into an EGP roadblock between Río Azul and Pulay. When an unarmed (and inebriated) civil patroller tried to pick up the gun of one of the fallen soldiers, he too was killed. On January 23, 1989, between four and twelve soldiers were killed when the EGP ambushed an army truck on the road between Chajul and Juil.

4. Guatemalan Church in Exile 1990:14–15. The month was December 1989.

5. Americas Watch 1984, 1986, 1989; *Central America Report* 1990.

6. Shelton Davis (1988:28) and John Watanabe (1992:182) found similar mixed feelings about the civil patrol in Huehuetenango.

7. A drunken ex-guerrilla walks into a Nebaj fiesta for the Day of the Patroller with a pistol stuck in his belt. After patrollers confront him, he wounds two people. When the incident is reported to army headquarters, who should walk in out of breath and flop down but the assailant, who proves to be a member of the local G-2 unit, the army's intelligence and death squad branch. "Because I'm a Christian," a captain tells the patrollers, "I'm not going to take him prisoner, just dismiss him from the service," despite which the assailant continues to be seen around town. The captain pays Q50 and Q75 to the two men who were wounded, the equivalent of U.S. $18 and U.S. $25, which is hardly justice but suggests how the civil patrol has helped Ixils stand up to abuses by the army.

8. The estimate is from a representative of the communities of population in resistance whom I interviewed in Guatemala City in July 1992.

9. AVANCSO (1990:48) compiled higher estimates of refugee flows from army and Catholic sources, as follows:

1985	1,800
1986	5–600
1987	3–5,000
1988	3–4,000
Total	8,300–11,400

In early 1991, the CPRs of the Sierra said that eight thousand of their people had been captured in recent years (*Siglo XXI*, March 4, 1991, pp. 24–25) while an army colonel said that in 1988–89 the army brought in approximately nine thousand persons who were subsequently attended by the Special Commission for Aid to Refugees (CEAR) (as quoted in *Siglo XXI*, approximately March 7, 1991, p. 7, reproduced in "Dossiere" 1991). Despite the agreement between these estimates, I think they are too high. In 1988, Mac Chapin (1988:12) was told that "a minimum of 2,000–3,000 people were processed in Nebaj during the initial months of the offensive," with another 558 refugees arriving in March, April, and May 1988. When CEAR/Nebaj showed me its records later that year, these listed 2,386 new arrivals from January to November 1988. After early 1989 the flow of refugees slowed considerably, to the point that CEAR rarely housed more than a hundred at a time, which remained the case when I visited in July 1991. Hence my belief that the actual number of refugees brought down to Nebaj from mid-1987 to mid-1991 is closer to 5,000–6,000 than 8,000–11,000.

10. Records of the Special Commission for Aid to Refugees (CEAR) in Nebaj show that, of 766 refugees released between May and November 1988, 549 (72 percent) said they were going to resettle in Nebaj or its aldeas, 119 (16 percent) in Chajul, 89 (12 percent) in Cotzal, and 9 (1 percent) elsewhere. Judging from the last reliable national census in the Ixil area (1964), Nebajeños comprise less than half the Ixil population.

11. The Guatemalan Church in Exile (1989a:23) distinguishes between "refugees" organized in zones of refuge (administered by the EGP) and "displaced" persons who live beyond these zones as well as army control.

12. "We continued in the mistaken practice of putting the new organization under the authority of their own leaders," Payeras (1983:68) wrote of the first contacts with highland Indian villages in 1974, "although their ways of thinking blocked the expansion of the war. But we soon realized . . . that the most resolute and politically aware among them should be its leaders."

13. I heard of at least five other cases in Nebaj besides that of Sebastián Guzmán. They included:

- Felipe Raimundo of aldea Ixtupil, along with two sons Miguel and Jacinto, around 1980;
- José Brito of Santa Marta, in 1980;
- Juan Sánchez and his son Andrés Sánchez, both of them principales of Sacsihuán and Santa Marta, in 1983 after the aldeas were destroyed and the people were living in the montaña;
- Francisco Cedillo, dragged away from his house in Janlay on May 8, 1981.

14. Because of the sensitivity of the question, I did not always ask refugees whether the guerrillas had killed members of the civilian population. When asked, a few said they did not know of such cases, but the majority said they did. From January 1989 interviews in Nebaj:

- the wife of an EGP functionary, the latter still in the mountains, says that the guerrillas have always killed "ears";
- a pastor's assistant and survivor of the army massacre at Chel describes how, in January 1983, the guerrillas killed a Methodist pastor named Jacinto López, after accusing him of planning a mass surrender of refugees—like the Church of God pastor had in Salquil Grande a few months before. "They have killed many, like fifty," he estimates, for common crimes as well as security offenses;
- a man from Sumal Chiquito whose father and brother were killed by the army, and who also lost a wife and a baby to respiratory illnesses in the montaña, says the guerrillas killed his sister in 1984 because of the calumny that she talked too much with soldiers. "When someone committed an offense, [the guerrillas] always killed him/her. There was no jail. When [people] did not want to help with tasks, or when they wanted to surrender to the army. Also robberies, but only big ones, and only the second time."

15. AVANCSO 1990:53.

16. For a graphic account of refugee conditions in Nebaj during this time, see Chapin 1988.

17. The following year another epidemic at the CEAR camp—this time, measles—took the lives of some fifteen adults and children.

18. Author's interviews December 1990 and July 1991. María Tiu Tojín's disappearance is mentioned in Washington Office on Latin America 1991:5.

19. As Pierre van den Berghe (1990:284) points out, the model villages of the Ixil Triangle may bear a closer resemblance to the world's first concentration camps, in the Anglo-Boer War of 1899–1902. The British coined the term after burning Boer homesteads and interning noncombatants to pursue their counterinsurgency war against Boer irregulars. "As for the euphemism," van den Berghe explains, "the Nazis gave it such a bad name in the 1940s that the British

had to invent the 'model village' in their war against the Kikuyu of Kenya in the early 1950s."

20. The twelve more or less "model" villages included Acul, Tzalbal, Salquil Grande, La Pista, Río Azul, Pulay, Xolcuay, Juil, Ojo de Agua, San Felipe Chenlá, Bichibalá, and Santa Avelina. Another five aldeas (Ilom, Chel, Juá, Xoncá, and Xix) had begun to rebuild on the concentrated model by 1985 but seem to have received almost no assistance, a situation that also faced campesinos nucleating around several small fincas (Las Amelias, Nueva America, Santa Delfina) that were never destroyed. Hence, there were about twenty resettlement sites as of the end of 1985; another sixty as of the end of 1990; and another ten to fifteen as of mid-1992.

21. In 1989 I was told about a man living in the Sumal zone of refuge who supposedly slipped back and forth to the coast, but if this occurred it was rare. The EGP policy of discouraging the civilians under its control from going to Nebaj had the effect of cutting them off from seasonal movement out of the area.

22. The U.S. Agency for International Development (USAID) denied that it was supporting the army's pacification program, but Guatemalan officials said that subsidies from USAID and the United Nations were crucial. These arrived in the form of food-for-work donations, roofing material, and other forms of support for government agencies working in the Triangle (Barry and Preusch 1984:1, 4). I met a former Peace Corps volunteer who said he was hired by USAID to observe how its donations were being used.

23. 1990 census of Nebaj aldeas, Committee for National Reconstruction.

24. Author's interview, Nebaj army headquarters, February 6, 1989.

6. The Holy Ghost in Northern Quiché

1. The general's own brother, Bishop Mario Ríos Montt of Escuintla, shared this preoccupation (Simons 1982:116). For more detail on the Summer Institute, the Church of the Word, and evangelical missions, see Stoll 1982 and 1990.

2. For more detailed accounts of how the army persecuted the Catholic Church during this period, see Guatemala Information Center n.d., Berryman 1984, and Bermúdez 1986. CEP 1981, Mondragón 1983, and Chea 1988 also contain useful details.

3. Solidarity accounts such as Frank and Wheaton 1984:46–50 and " Martirio y Lucha en Guatemala" 1983 suggest the Catholic origin of CUC but refrain from specifying that certain priests were organizers. The most detailed testimony is from Luis Pellecer, a Jesuit who was kidnapped by the Guatemalan army in 1981 and brought back to light four months later to testify against the guerrilla movement (Senate Subcommittee on Security and Terrorism 1984:226–51). Although Pellecer was clearly influenced by the conspiracy theo-

ries of his captors, his account suggests the same alliance between the Catholic Left and the revolutionary movement that other Catholic clergy acknowledge off-the-record.

4. Fernando Hoyos was a Jesuit from Spain who helped organize CUC and escaped an army kidnapping in 1977. He resigned from the Jesuits to join the EGP, became part of a combat unit, and died in an ambush on July 13, 1982, near Ixil country, in Chojzu, Santa Eulalia, Huehuetenango (Guatemalan Church in Exile 1983b:10–11). The EGP named one of its columns in the Ho Chi Minh Front after him. Enrique Corral Alonso was another Jesuit who, in the course of leaving the priesthood, moved from popular organizing to the EGP (Senate Subcommittee on Security and Terrorism 1984:239). Andrés Lanz of the Sacred Heart reportedly ran the EGP's clandestine radio network, was captured by the army around 1983, and is presumed dead (author's interview, 1991). Donald McKenna was an Irishman variously described as a Jesuit (by Luis Pellecer, in Senate Subcommittee on Security and Terrorism 1984:239) and as a diocesan priest. He served briefly as parish priest of Zacualpa before joining an EGP combat unit as a chaplain or commander (for a 1981 interview, see Mondragón 1983:64–67). In the late 1980s McKenna lived in Nicaragua.

5. Frank and Wheaton 1984:69.

6. Melville and Melville 1971a:260–74.

7. None of the returned refugees or ex-combatants I asked would admit to having seen a priest in the mountain refuges of Ixil country, perhaps because the journey from Mexico is so long and dangerous.

8. As evidence that Javier was a subversive, various ladinos cited his habit of dressing in work clothes rather than clerical garb, carrying a hunting piece on trips to villages, and using profanity.

9. Lernoux 1989:5–7 citing Bermúdez 1986. Also CEP 1981:135–36.

10. From two Nebaj ladinos who were born in the 1920s. A Church of God history (Waldrop n.d.:4, 6) refers to Pullin's claim of a flourishing church in Nebaj in the 1930s.

11. Lawrence and Morris 1969:49 and Elliott 1983.

12. Colby and van den Berghe 1969:102

13. In the Mam Maya town of San Juan Ostuncalco, Scotchmer (1991a:226) also found that catechists were a significant source of Protestant leadership. For the K'iche' Maya town of Almolonga, Goldin and Metz (1991:337) report that many Protestants converted from orthodox rather than traditional Catholicism, "as if the former were a stage towards Protestantism."

14. The process accelerated in the early 1980s when the ladino-controlled church in Nebaj joined a new nationally run denomination in revolt against North American missionaries. The move backfired, with most of the remaining Ixil members withdrawing to a more cohesive Ixil-speaking congregation that affiliated with the North American mission.

15. Lawrence and Morris 1969:51.

16. Lengyel 1979:85.

17. Cifuentes H. 1982:29.

18. Guatemalan Church in Exile 1983a:5.

19. These figures are from the government health centers. Other surveys corroborate them. When evangelical pastors compiled a list of 1,815 Nebaj orphans in 1986–87, 39 percent of their single parents or guardians described the household as evangelical. According to a 1987–88 resettlement questionnaire by the Ministry of Development, 29 percent of 1,283 household heads said they were evangelicals. The figures for particular aldeas ranged from a low of 8 percent (for Parramos Grande) to a high of 47 percent (for the neighboring aldea of Parramos Chiquito). When I surveyed the urban Nebaj cantón of Xemamatze in 1989, 42.9 percent of ninety-eight households described themselves as evangelical.

20. Survey by Ministry of Development.

21. Of ninety-eight household heads surveyed.

22. One of the two largest denominations in Quiché Department, the Primitive Methodists, went from fifty-two churches in 1978 to twenty-five in 1983. According to the official who gave this figure to Virginia Burnett (1986:219–21), fifteen hundred of ninety-five hundred adult members died. Of the denomination's thirty-five pastors, ten were killed from 1980 to 1982, including three by the army under Ríos Montt. The far larger Full Gospel Church of God, which in 1991 claimed more than sixteen hundred congregations, reports that approximately fifty of its pastors have been assassinated since 1976 (personal communication from Full Gospel Church of God missionary).

23. Coffin 1981:8.

24. Pentecostal gains have forced theologically opposed churches to imitate their practices while trying to hold the line on doctrine, a strategy that fails to prevent weakly led outlying congregations from defecting to more dynamic pentecostal leaders. In a backward area like Nebaj, where pastors define propriety on the basis of prohibitions picked up during their scanty training, one point of separation for Nebaj Methodists was the prohibition against playing guitars in services, with aficionados departing for a more permissive pentecostal church. Another was the precise mode of baptism by immersion, in a tub inside the chapel or in a river, with the literal-minded insisting that because the Bible describes the ritual in a river, they too had to be baptized in a river. Only after losing most of their following did the Methodists offer Nebajeños the riverine option.

25. Watanabe (1990:199) describes a parallel case in Santiago Chimaltenango, Huehuetenango, where a catechist and DC activist was appointed mayor by Ríos Montt and became an evangelical pastor.

26. Scotchmer 1991a:136–39.

27. In my survey of ninety-eight household heads in Cantón Xemamatze, only 24.5 percent said they could read. According to local health centers, in 1984 the literacy rate was 25 percent in Nebaj, 32 percent in Cotzal, and 28 percent in Chajul. Before the violence, the Catholic Church estimated that the adult literacy rate in Quiché Department was 8 percent (Lengyel 1987:224).

28. This is two hundred more than reported by Nachtigall (1978:332) for 1973.

29. Cf. Evans 1990:108, 308.

30. June Nash (1960:49) found that the K'iche' Maya town of Cantel was about one-quarter Protestant in 1953–54. According to Benjamin Paul (1987:1), the Tz'utujil town of San Pedro La Laguna on Lake Atitlán was already 35–40 percent Protestant in 1970. The Western Akatekos were 22 percent Protestant by 1972 according to Douglas Brintnall (1979a:137). When Sheldon Annis (1987:76) did a survey of the Kaqchikel town of San Antonio Aguas Calientes in the mid-1970s, 20 percent of his sample identified themselves as Protestant. The Wycliffe Bible Translators (Williams 1987:2) reports that one-third of the Chuj Maya identified themselves as evangelical by 1970.

31. For more on this argument, see Stoll 1990:24–41.

32. See the publications of the Guatemalan Church in Exile, as well as Frank and Wheaton 1984.

33. For an influential analysis of why North American pentecostals became so conservative, see Anderson 1979.

34. See the papers by Elizabeth Brusco, John Burdick, and Kenneth Coleman in Burnett and Stoll, 1993.

35. Johannesen 1988:558.

36. The same association with new levels of economic integration can be made with the Catholic Action movement which, in Quiché at least, preceded the evangelical boom. This becomes apparent in Ricardo Falla's study of Catholic Action in San Antonio Ilotenango, a town in southern Quiché where a land-strapped population was turning to commerce. Falla (1980:190) learned that K'iche' Maya catechists were interpreting the power of the new monotheistic God preached by Spanish priests in terms of the traditional concept of *suerte* (personal fortune). But while suerte used to refer to a locally territorialized conception of the divine, such as the saints in the parish church and the earth-lords in the surrounding hills, now was manifesting itself in the global play of market forces. Catholic Action set itself against traditional religious strictures, but its own referents were suitably vague. It could be a religion of accumulation—during Falla's time, catechists dominated the new commercial economy in San Antonio—or it could be a religion of political confrontation, as encouraged by CUC organizers in the nearby aldea of La Estancia.

37. Evans 1990:102.

7. The Ixil Recovery of Nebaj

1. Americas Watch 1984:87–103; Kreuger and Enge 1985; Simon 1987; Chapin 1988; Manz 1988a; Washington Office on Latin America 1988; Guatemalan Church in Exile 1989a.

2. Even before the violence the army wanted to cultivate indigenous leadership, at least rhetorically. General Romeo Lucas García "spoke of professionals among the Indians as a sign that the race is lifting itself out of stagnation" (Falla 1978).

3. Smith 1984a:210–19.

4. Earle 1982:183. See also Watanabe 1981; Smith 1987a:11; Robert Carmack's essay on Santa Cruz del Quiché and Roland Ebel's essay on San Juan Ostuncalco, both in Carmack 1988; Ehlers 1990; Warren n.d.

5. Colby and van den Berghe 1969:111.

6. The most recent figure is from November 1984 when the Nebaj health center reported that 14 percent of the population under government control was ladino. Since the 15,188 people counted that year included rural dwellers, who are more heavily Ixil than townspeople, the actual ladino percentage in town was probably higher. According to the 1973 census (Dirección General de Estadística 1973), 26.1 percent of Nebaj's urban population (1,084 out of 4,151) was ladino. The 2,122 ladinos counted eleven years later were only 45 less than the 2,167 for the municipio as a whole in 1973, suggesting the stability of the ladino presence in Nebaj.

7. Colby and van den Berghe 1969:108.

8. Nachtigall 1978:142.

9. McCreery, forthcoming.

10. McCreery, forthcoming.

11. McCreery, forthcoming.

12. Cited in Nachtigall 1978:142.

13. "La Toma de Nebaj" 1982:37.

14. Compare Smith 1990a:278 on "community sentiment" as a powerful influence on wealthy and professional Mayas.

15. Author's interviews in Nebaj, July 1989, when U.S. $1 was equal to Q3. I was surprised at the low level of remuneration and wondered if contractors were minimizing their actual earnings, but one after another sketched the same picture.

16. The program included a few ladinos inherited from the Escuela de Castellanización before 1980.

17. Two of the promoters said to have been killed by the EGP were cases of personal vengeance for the death of an Ixil teacher with whom they had been drinking and whom they possibly murdered. The murder of the third promoter is also attributed to personal vengeance.

18. Lengyel 1987:80–81.

19. Lengyel 1987:80–81.

20. Adams 1976:288–93; Brintnall 1979b:647–49. Colby and van den Berghe (1969:90–93) discuss "passing" and the adoption of ladino traits in the Ixil area.

21. Thanks to Nebaj education supervisor Jorge Pérez Guevara for these figures. Thirty of the ninety-one teachers were women.

22. The enrollment figures for 1979 and March 1988 are courtesy of Nebaj education supervisor Jorge Pérez Guevara. Bilingual enrollment, list of April 14, 1989, is courtesy of Prof. Jacinto Brol Ramírez, bilingual supervisor in Nebaj.

23. The rest went to two new center-right parties, the Union of the National Center and the Democratic Party for National Cooperation (Tribunal Supremo Electoral, *Memoria* for the 1985 election).

24. Wolf 1956:1072–76; cf. Davis 1970:151–52.

25. Chea 1988. "They want to get the juice out of the guayava" is, according to popular wisdom in Guatemala, the goal of any political party. Partly as a result of decades of repression, parties are chronically incapable of articulating basic issues. Instead, they are rapidly shifting coalitions dedicated to electing kingpins and obtaining appointments. All too often, the victors and their appointees steal whatever they can, on the grounds that their predecessors did so and they would be foolish not to follow suit.

26. "Whenever something is built, there is a robbery," Nebajeños say. They are referring to the "commissions," or kickbacks, that contractors provide officials, a practice that leaves abandoned, half-finished projects in its wake.

27. Fagen and Tuohy 1972:20.

28. Watanabe 1984:181–85.

29. Tribunal Supremo Electoral, *Memoria: Elección de Corporaciones Municipales*, 1988.

30. Figures courtesy of Programa de Asistencia a Viudas y Huérfanos Menores, Víctimas de la Violencia, Secretaria Específica de Asuntos Políticos, Presidencia de la República, Guatemala City.

31. Author's notes, August 6, 1989.

8. Ecological Crisis in Ixil Country

1. The local labor market could still not absorb all the Ixils looking for work during slack periods in the agricultural cycle, hence the continued pressure to go to the south coast or Alta Verapaz.

2. Since the town hall has not succeeded in enforcing a small head tax on labor contractors for each person they sign up, no authority counts the number of people going to plantations for wage labor. The estimates I obtained from contractors were so partial and contradictory that I gave up the attempt. In

1966, when labor contracting was controlled by a smaller group of men, Colby and van den Berghe found someone with enough confidence to estimate that approximately 2,000 people left the area every month on labor contracts, from a population of 45,000. If we apply the same percentage to a presumed population of 70,000 in 1989, the result is 3,111 people leaving the area every month, or 37,332 monthly labor contracts per year. If seasonal migration has increased, as villagers claim, the actual figure would be higher.

3. Coffee is the only possible competitor with wage labor. If the Finca San Francisco (eighteen thousand quintales in 1989), Finca La Perla (six thousand quintales in 1988), other fincas, and smallholders produced thirty thousand quintales (hundred-pound weights) of coffee beans in a good year, a favorable world-market price of a hundred dollars per quintal would provide an income of U.S. $3 million. Much of this never reaches Ixil country, however, because it goes for loan repayments, commissions, inputs, and owner profits in the capital.

On the basis of estimates from labor contractors, Colby and van den Berghe (1969:131) calculate that in 1966 two thousand agricultural laborers, mainly young men, left the Ixil area each month, with an equal number returning. That would be 4.44 percent of the population. If we assume that 4.44 percent of a population of 70,000 was leaving every month in 1989, that would be 3,111 laborers per month, times twelve months, for a total of 37,332 work-months per year. If each laborer brings home an average of U.S. $35 per month, that would represent U.S. $1.306,620 per year. Given the damage the coffee sector sustained during the violence, labor exports probably bring more income to Ixil country than coffee does.

4. The Gini Index is a measure based on farm size and the amount of land, where zero equals absolute equity and one hundred equals complete concentration.

5. Hough et al. 1982:1–2, 7.

6. Melville and Melville 1971b; Jonas 1991; Frank and Wheaton 1984.

7. Lincoln 1945.

8. Lovell 1990:10 and 1992:1.

9. Horst 1967; Davis 1970; Smith 1977; Veblen 1978. For the comparative case of the Mayan highlands of Chiapas, see Collier 1975.

10. Dirección General de Estadística 1968:177–79; Dirección General de Estadística 1982:255–56.

11. De Janvry 1982:91.

12. The 1983–84 health count is 27,078, excluding a few outlying aldeas of Cotzal and Chajul. If we consider the earlier date of late 1982 and refugees who had yet to filter back, 25,000 is a reasonable estimate for the population under government control.

13. The local health center's 1983 figures for Cotzal show well over half the population (3,000+ of 5,530) under the age of twenty.

14. "Viudas y Huérfanos, Departamento de El Quiché," list provided courtesy of the Programa de Asistencia a Viudas y Huérfanos Menores, Victimas de la Violencia (PAVYH), Secretaria Específica de Asuntos Políticos, Presidencia de la República. When I showed the breakdown to the men who do the local health survey in Nebaj, they objected that the count was inflated. It certainly included some "natural" widows attracted by the occasional handouts intended exclusively for war widows. Even higher figures come from local aid administrators, such as the 1,200 widows and 4,000 orphans that an evangelical pastor claimed for Cotzal (as opposed to the 590 widows and 1,005 orphans counted by PAVYH). In Chajul a government functionary claimed there were 645 widows and 1,425 orphans (as opposed to the 502 widows and 783 orphans counted by PAVYH).

15. See Washington Office on Latin America 1988 and Perera 1993.

16. As corrected by the author (see table 8.3, n. 2).

17. Author's interview with CPR delegation in the capital, July 13, 1992.

18. Including the seventy thousand people under government control and the seventeen thousand people in the CPRs of the Sierra, but not the five thousand Ixils presumed to be in diaspora.

19. Calculated from Instituto Nacional de Estadística 1988:24.

20. Rossdeutscher 1991; Levitsky and Lapp 1992. In Costa Rica, solidarista associations now represent more workers than labor unions do.

21. An INTA official attributed the expropriation to a tax on idle lands that soon mounts to confiscatory levels. None of the heavily cultivated Ixil properties had actually been idle according to the legal definition, he said. Instead, they were given up by the Herreras to keep more valuable property elsewhere.

22. The five are:

- Finca Chemalá (Nebaj), financed by North American Presbyterians for the aldea of La Pista;
- Finca Las Vigas (Nebaj), financed by the Guatemala-based Emmanuel Mission for the aldea of Xeo;
- Agro Aldea (Chajul), financed by the evangelical Agros Foundation for the Jesus Saves and Heals Church;
- Finca Los Angeles (Cotzal), financed by the Agros Foundation for evangelicals; and
- Finca La Victoria, financed by the United Nations Development Program for the aldea of Sumal Chiquito. The Catholic diocese of Quiché has financed a sixth land purchase, for Las Violetas on the outskirts of Nebaj, but for refugee housing rather than agriculture.

23. Ehrlich and Ehrlich 1990:58–59.

24. Colby and van den Berghe 1969:31.

25. One-fifth quintal per cuerda is the equivalent of 3.3 bushels per acre, or 7.9 bushels per hectare. The average yield for maize in the United States is about twenty-five times as high (calculated from Nachtigall 1978:102–4 and Stadelman 1940:133).

26. In 1989, a *tarea* of firewood cost 25 quetzals (about U.S. $8) and might supply a house for a month. A bottle of gas cost Q8.50, probably lasted longer, but had to be purchased in the department capital.

27. Stadelman 1940:105. This is a study of maize cultivation in villages of similar ecology in neighboring Huehuetenango Department. Although it dates to before the era of chemical fertilizers, most Ixil farmers continue to get by without such inputs, whose long-term contribution to boosting productivity is open to question.

28. The source, a co-op organizer, estimated that the average member of an Ixil family consumes two pounds of maize a day. Two generations earlier, Stadelman (1940:93) reported the average adult's consumption of maize in Huehuetenango as two pounds a day.

29. For a bibliography of the ample research on population in Guatemala, see Arias de Blois 1978 and 1983.

30. Jorge Arias de Blois, quoted in *Crónica* October 6, 1989, p. 15.

31. Arias de Blois 1986:19–21. John Early (1982a:65) calculates that, at the 3.2 percent annual increase in 1975–76, the country's population will double every 21.5 years.

32. Pessimists include a French doctor working for Refugee Children of the World in Nebaj. She estimated that 23 percent of births were not being registered. To the extent that births are not recorded, the actual effect on population growth could be negated by the high rate of child mortality.

33. Diagnóstico de Salud, Nebaj Health Center, November 1984.

34. For 1988, the 1,939 registrations at the Nebaj town hall included 384 children who were born before 1987, leaving 1,555 who were born in 1987–88. For the 1,555 figure to represent current births in 1988, we must also assume that the same proportion of 1987 births not reported until 1988 is held over from the 1988 birth season for reporting in 1989.

35. Mamdani 1972.

36. De Janvry 1982:89.

37. Early 1982b:179–80; Loucky 1988:321–51. Loucky (1978) detected larger families in a Tz'utujil Maya town where children are put to work manufacturing rope, suggesting that parents are having more children to add to family income. Looking at the costs and benefits of high fertility in terms of the life-cycle, the costs accrue most heavily in an individual's child-bearing years, with benefits accruing later in life as one's children become income producers.

Hence, maximization arguments for "high fertility logic" should be scrutinized for possible bias in favor of elders, that is, an assumption that the interests of elders are normative for the entire society.

38. In my survey, 238 heads of Ixil households reported an average of 5.36 offspring, three-quarters of whom had survived to date, leaving an average of 4.02 children per household. Even though the reproductive careers of many of the surveyed parents were not over, and more siblings were on the way, male children already stood to inherit only half the land of their fathers.

39. As in the K'iche' Maya town of San Antonio Ilotenango, where Ricardo Falla (1980:23–25) learned that the inhabitants regarded religious conflict as a more important problem than the population growth he had planned to study. However, a fertility study of a Kaqchikel town in Chimaltenango a few years later found that most Indians thought their town and ethnic group was growing too fast (Glittenberg 1976, as quoted by Early 1982a:72).

40. Schumann 1982, courtesy of James Loucky for copies of his notes.

41. I have not reported the results of my survey because it was not correctly designed to assess Ixil attitudes toward fertility. But it suggests an association between Ixils having more schooling and wanting only "a few" children, while Ixils without schooling are more likely to say they want as many children as God sends them. Ixils who want a few children also report more than three-quarters (.77) of their school-age children in school, while Ixils who respond in terms of "God's will" say that little more than half (.52) their children are in school. There is also an association between youth and wanting only "a few" children, the average age of these respondents in my sample being 36.23, while those who answer in terms of God's will average 40.46 and those who say they want "many children" average 53 years of age.

The survey asked, "In your opinion, is it better for a man and his woman to have many children or is it better to have few?" Unfortunately, the survey did not ask respondents to specify how many children they meant by "many" or "few." But when my associate Sarah Gates added this question, the answer of four "many" respondents averaged 7.8 children, while the answer of eleven "few" respondents averaged 4.18.

42. Any estimate of how much land is returning to smallholders would have to be hedged with many qualifications. Instead, let me summarize the "ethnic shift in ownership" column of tables 8.5, 8.6, and 8.7 as follows:

- four cases of INTA administering the transfer of ladino-owned fincas (95 caballerías) to aldeas, two of which (Villa Hortencia I and II) include many K'iche's as well as Ixils.
- one case of a finca selling off peripheral land (87 caballerías, the majority in neighboring Uspantán rather than Ixil country) to its multiethnic permanent work force;

- five cases of church donors financing the purchase of ladino-owned fincas for Ixil farmers (10 caballerías), in one case primarily for house sites rather than agriculture.
- one case of a United Nations agency buying a ladino-owned finca for Ixil farmers (3–4 caballerías);
- two cases in which groups of Ixils (in one of the cases including ladinos) have bought individual parcels from small ladino-owned fincas;
- two cases in which individual Ixils have bought small fincas from ladinos, in one case through the same debt mechanism with which ladinos used to deprive Ixils of land;
- two cases in which Ixils were selling coffee-growing land (totaling 2.2 caballerías) to ladinos, a phenomenon that table 8.5 underreports because it includes only larger properties, even though a number of Ixil small-holders have also been selling coffee land to ladinos;
- one active title dispute (more than 4 caballerías) between a ladino family and an aldea, the latter inhabited by Q'anjob'al Mayas rather than Ixils, in which the Nebaj town hall was supporting the villagers;
- nine sales by ladinos to ladinos (26 or more caballerías), the purchasers in three of the cases (totaling 4.5 or more caballerías) being a son or in-laws;
- sixteen properties (totaling 50.5 caballerías) that have not changed hands, three of which (totaling 7.5 caballerías) were for sale at last report in 1991–92.
- one property (totaling 80 caballerías) that has not changed hands but in which permanent workers will supposedly be sold 40 percent ownership; and
- one property (7 caballerías) sold to the army for a military base.

43. For example, Aguacatán (Brintnall 1979a), Santiago Chimaltenango (Watanabe 1984:23–25), and San Pedro La Laguna (Paul 1988). For the sharpest portrait of socioeconomic differentiation between towns that are becoming commercial centers and others that have become impoverished hinterlands, see W. Smith 1977.

44. Veblen 1978:430.

45. The most sophisticated neo-Weberian analysis of Protestantism in Latin America to date is Martin 1990, although Annis 1987 provides a case study from the western Guatemalan highlands.

46. For a description of *saqb'icil* (dawn ceremonies) to propitiate the earth for extracting food and trees, see Colby and Colby 1981:40–42, who provide an origin story told by the baalbastix Shas Ko'w: "There appeared the trees, we appeared ourselves, there appeared our tortilla, there appeared our atole, there appeared our beans, there appeared our squash, there appeared our chayote. All those things appeared in the world. But only the holy earth gave them to us. For that reason, there is an obligation. For that reason we say prayers to our

maizefield. For that reason we give offering because the earth gives us food. That is the benefit of the candle. That is the benefit of the incense." Dawn ceremonies are held by families, cofradías, and even the town government but by the late 1980s were becoming less frequent.

In connection with his own acts of tree-clearing, the elderly Shas Ko'w (1895–1976) told the Colbys (1981:123): "I do a cuerda of work, happily clearing land, and I say, 'All that is my work.' Well, those are many souls; it's a cuerda of souls that I've killed because I've cut the trees. Perhaps there was a small animal. Perhaps there was a little snake. Perhaps there was a little bird. Lord, have mercy, perhaps it was his roosting place. Perhaps it was its nest and I moved it. I cut the trunk, the tree disappeared, the bird disappeared because it fled, it no longer stayed in the tree. All for the offense of my stomach. But that's what *pom* (incense) is for. That's what the candle is for. That's what Our Father left us instructed about. I honor God. I sprinkle my pom, I place my candle on the ground before the Earth. That's all that lies in my power. That's all that I can do." Contrary to essentialist images of indigenous culture, Shas Ko'w and his sacerdotal ethics may not be any more representative of Ixil society than Mother Teresa's are of our own.

47. For an account of the Q'anjob'al Mayas from Huehuetenango Department who have gone to the United States in large numbers, see Burns 1989.

9. The Struggle to Rebuild Civil Society in Nebaj

1. "For *política* all these people died" is a refrain in Cotzal, where many blame the war on local *políticos* for taking their personal rivalries to the army or the guerrillas.

2. Watanabe 1990:194–5.

3. President Carlos Arana Osorio, per Handy 1984:168.

4. Fajardo 1987:72.

5. In the K'iché Maya town of Almolonga, Quezaltenango, Goldin and Metz (1991:333, 335–6) found "a significant proportion of self-identified Catholics [who] have essentially converted to Protestantism, if not formally then ideologically." Since Goldin and Metz do not refer to the history of reform Catholicism in Almolonga, these "Protestant" Catholics or "invisible converts" are probably similar to Catholic Action in Ixil country. Goldin and Metz estimate that, while 48 percent of the town is Protestant, another 12 percent of the population shares the new reform ideology, that is, about 23 percent of Catholics.

6. Goldin and Metz 1991:329. For a more detailed contrast between the traditional and reformed modes of production, see Annis 1987.

7. In the Tz'utujil Maya town of Santiago Atitlán, where a large minority of the population joined evangelical churches during the violence of the 1980s, Robert Carlsen (personal communication, 1990) believes that an even larger

fraction of the population joined the Catholic Church—that is, defected from the town's traditional religious system to a more orthodox Catholicism.

8. I did not focus on ideological differences between Ixils who uphold tradition and those who have joined new religions, but an observation made by John Watanabe (1984:229) of the Mam Maya town of Santiago Chimaltenango, Huehuetenango, rings true: "Beyond these few restrictions . . . [catechists and evangelical] converts remain outwardly indistinguishable from other Chimaltecos. The new religions wear lightly in normal day-to-day affairs, and as in the past, the dictates of *naab'l*, one's 'soul' or moral 'normality,' continue to gauge acceptable Chimalteco behavior." Goldin and Metz (1991:336) detect "few significant ideological differences" between Catholics and Protestants in the K'iche' Maya town of Almolonga.

9. The most thorough research on drinking in a Mesoamerican Indian community, by Michael Kearney (1970:134–35), suggests that ambivalence over the effects of alcohol is widespread and predates the arrival of Protestantism.

10. This is another unintended consequence of the revolutionary movement, owing to its success in chasing the treasury police out of town after a long history of persecuting distillers for bribes, then murdering people in the early stages of the violence. The army has no interest in enforcing revenue laws, viewing the manufacture of kuxa as a useful diversion in a population that showed a capacity for guerrilla warfare. Free of the treasury police and their protection rackets, the kuxa industry flourishes behind the scenes. Distillers offer their product at one-fourth or one-fifth the cost of the taxed aguardiente imported from Quezaltenango, so that the bars that sell the latter had, by 1989, dwindled to a dozen.

11. Kearney 1970:141.

12. E. P. Thompson (1966:365–70) captured this paradox in a description of early nineteenth-century Methodists in England, in the course of arguing that middle-class Methodist ministers were subordinating lower-class members to the requirements of factory labor.

13. Weber 1958:95–154.

14. Annis 1987:98–105.

15. Sexton 1978:288, 292.

16. Evans 1990:90–100, 301–6. A more detailed portrait of the Protestants of Almolonga is provided by Goldin and Metz 1991.

17. Smith 1989:351–52. Ricardo Falla (1980) provided the best ethnography of this phenomenon, with his study of the commercially oriented Catholic Action movement of San Antonio Ilotenango, Quiché, in the 1960s and 1970s.

18. Lengyel 1987:69, 262.

19. The 1987–88 sample consisted of 971 male household heads applying to the Ministry of Development for aid. I lumped 130 "costumbristas" (traditionalists) and 548 "Catholics" into a single Catholic category because the one to

four proportion is far removed from the actual proportion of traditionalists to catechists.

20. While my interviewers and I surveyed every Ixil teacher and promoter we could locate, the sixty-four we interviewed did not comprise the entire class of Ixil teachers and promoters, nor did they comprise a randomly chosen sample. The same is true of the people we interviewed with a skill as their primary occupation, as well as the forty people involved in commerce: because I asked my interviewers to seek individuals who had performed a leadership or entrepreneurial role, our sample was not randomly chosen.

21. Each of the eight had a teaching degree.

22. When Lengyel (1979:85–86) interviewed his informants in the mid-1970s, Protestants reported owning far less than the Catholic average of 168 cuerdas and showed a much higher involvement in nonagricultural occupations. But as Lengyel noted, his sample of Protestants consisted of just seven households. Nor did these include evangelicals from Vicalamá who he knew owned more land than the men in his sample did. Other early evangelicals who migrated out to Amajchel probably held little land around Nebaj, but their interest in colonization suggests their interest in agriculture.

23. Again, I lumped together 155 "costumbrista" and 616 "Catholic" household heads because the one to four proportion does not reflect the actual proportion of traditionalists to catechists.

24. Mariz 1989a, 1989b; Flora 1976:321.

25. The sad state of the cofradías in Cotzal and Chajul suggests that Rojas Lima's (1988:214) observation about their stability under repression cannot be generalized. Of San Pedro Jocopilas in southern Quiché, Rojas Lima writes that the cofradías "find themselves in a position of greater stability . . . [than catechists]; this is due in part . . . to the more conservative character of these groups and their ability to . . . mediate a situation of subordination." Perhaps if charismatic and evangelical groups had not been available to absorb catechists, these would have taken refuge in religious tradition.

26. Watanabe 1984:227.

27. Asociación de Pastores Ixiles Evangélicos.

28. Compare John Watanabe's (1984:213) findings in Santiago Chimaltenango, in Huehuetenango, where many traditionalists say they live *sin religión*.

29. The usual path for Ixils is, according to an evangelical lay leader, "the completely defeated life . . . a life defeated by vices and family problems. They reach the edge of the abyss and realize that the Bible condemns sorcerers, diviners, witches, prostitutes, liars, adulterers, fornicators, all the evil which men do, all the works of the flesh." It is usually the men who take the first step in joining a church, he added. Seventy percent have problems with alcohol, he estimated, with domestic conflicts, lack of communication with spouses, and disillusion being the other main problems. Susan Harding (1987) has described

religious conversion as a way of learning to tell a story about it, suggesting how converts can combine instrumental action with emotional experience through the reconstruction of memory.

30. Green 1991.

31. Census figures from the K'iche' Maya municipality of Cunén suggest the impact of *la situación* on religious identification. Although Cunén escaped the devastation that befell its Ixil neighbors, 29 percent of the population was identifying itself as evangelical according to a 1983 health census of the town center, with 9 percent describing themselves as "other," and only 62 percent as Catholic. Five years later, just 21 percent of the town center's population identified itself as evangelical with "other" diminishing to 4 percent and Catholics climbing to 75 percent—a difference of 13 percent returning to identify with the Catholic Church. (Source: Diagnóstico Integral de Salud, Area Urbana de Cunén, Quiché, November 1983, Centro de Salud; and Diagnóstico Integral de Salud, Centro de Salud, Cunén, Quiché, 1988, with additional figures provided courtesy of health inspector Rodrigo Castillo.)

32. Judging from Robert Hinshaw's (1975:56) long-term study of the Kaqchikel Maya town of Panajachel, the ability of evangelical churches to keep men away from alcohol in the long term is open to question.

33. Compare Timothy Evans (1990:246), on the long-established Full Gospel Church of God in San Francisco El Alto, Totonicapán, which also seemed to be experiencing a high rate of nominalism. "I don't like the old folk's ways," one inactive evangelical youth told Evans. "I'd rather go to the disco."

34. Lengyel 1987:77.

35. Arias 1985; Smith 1992.

36. Obviously, Nebajeños might exaggerate the foreignness of the two sides in order to exonerate kin and neighbors who participated in homicides. In the case of the army, troops were usually from other parts of the country except for the Ixil companies described in chapter 4. As for guerrilla combatants, a majority have been Ixils, but their units seem to operate in sufficient isolation from the civilian population, even in the montaña, that most are not personally known.

37. Compare Roland Ebel's (1988:189) account of how the Mam (and ladino) town of San Juan Ostuncalco responded to the violence: "Municipal improvement seemed to have become something of a surrogate for the factional social and political activity that had only served to open up the community to the threat of reprisal or intervention from radicals of either the Left or the Right. Paradoxically, an era of trouble became something of an 'era of good feelings.' "

38. Scott 1976:3.

39. This being customary in the western highlands, compare Roland Ebel's (1988) essay on San Juan Ostuncalco, Quezaltenango.

40. Of this and similar churches in San Juan Ostuncalco, David Scotchmer (1991a:151–52) writes: "Although the church may be made up primarily of Indians, the leadership, organization, worship, and interaction will follow a distinctively Ladino church style. In essence, most of the churches listed under Type Four [pentecostal/missionary/national/Indian] could just as easily be listed under Type Three [pentecostal/missionary/national/ladino] were it not for their largely Indian membership. What this suggests is that many Indians may see their religious conversion as part of a larger process of acculturation to the dominant culture. At the very least, Indian membership within Ladino-dominated churches represents a safe social space in which Indians and Ladinos may relate with a minimum of suspicion, hostility, or competition. It may also open up avenues for Indians into the Ladino world from which they are otherwise cut off because of their Indianness."

41. John Hawkins, personal communication at Latin American Studies Association, Washington, D.C., April 4, 1991.

42. An exception was the Christian Democratic party in Chajul, led by Catholic charismatics, who also took care to integrate their slate with candidates from other religious groups.

43. Colby and van den Berghe 1969:124–26, plus author's interviews.

44. Compare Ebel 1988:189–91: "It appears that the growing religious pluralism in San Juan Ostuncalco continues to reduce the historic political tensions and factionalism in the town." In San Juan, a Mam community in Quezaltenango that largely escaped the violence, its religious groups took care to attend one another's services in 1980–81, to prevent the army and guerrillas from taking advantage of religious divisions.

45. Chea 1988:5.

46. A representative of the government agricultural bank claimed that co-ops are always the farthest behind in their payments compared to other borrowers. "They take longer to put together than to fall apart," he observed.

47. This is not the case in Cotzal and Chajul, where only one of the nine mayors since June 1982 has been a *promotor* and most have been older men oriented to agriculture. Virtually all the new government agencies in Ixil country are headquartered in Nebaj, and about half the bilingual promoters in Chajul and Cotzal are Nebajeños.

48. Compare Watanabe 1992:182.

49. Guatemalan Church in Exile 1990. The assembly included only the montaña settlements in the sierra around Amajchel, not those in the Ixcán, which apparently followed suit with their own general assembly.

50. When the government's human rights procurator visited Amajchel in February 1991, CPR representatives blamed only the army for their situation, even though interviews with other montaña dwellers at the encounter revealed the same critique of both army and EGP that I heard from refugees in Nebaj.

From people in the crowd, the procurator taped demands such as "the two armed parties should leave" and "the two armed parties should have a discussion and stop doing us damage" (*Siglo XXI*, between March 6 and March 15, 1991, p. 7, reproduced in "Dossiere" 1991). As did a reporter: "The army and the guerrillas should retire because they're the ones who look for trouble" (*Cronica*, March 8, 1991, p. 20).

51. *Siglo XXI*, March 11, 1991, p. 3.

52. *Siglo XXI*, March 14, 1991. The CPR leadership was reiterating the position set out in a communique published in *Siglo XXI* on March 4 (reproduced in "Dossiere" 1991).

53. Author's interviews, July 1992.

54. Myrna Mack Chang, an anthropologist publicizing the situation of internal refugees, was knifed to death leaving her office in the capital on September 11, 1990. Julio Quevedo Quezada, an agronomist working for the Catholic agency Caritas, was shot to death in front of his family in Santa Cruz del Quiché on July 15, 1991. Because of protests by the Catholic Church and the human rights movement, the Myrna Mack murder became a major test case and was traced to high-ranking army officers.

55. Runujel Junam means "Everyone is Equal" in K'iche' Maya. For an account of CERJ's first year, see Americas Watch 1989.

56. I obtained a copy of the untitled, unedited videotape from the government's Procurador de Derechos Humanos in the capital. *Central America Report* (1990) and Jones (1990:53) also describe the case.

57. Council on Hemispheric Affairs 1990.

58. Compare James Scott's (1990:86, 89) point that, ordinarily, subordinates have a vested interest in avoiding explicit displays of insubordination so as not to provoke tighter control measures.

59. From a talk given at the University of California-Berkeley, on February 13, 1992.

60. As suggested by George Collier's (1987:216–17) historical ethnography of a Spanish village where family members of socialists massacred during the Spanish Civil War had come to accept Franco-era propaganda vilifying the socialist movement.

61. What Nebajeños consider most reprehensible is the denunciation of personal enemies to the army as supposed subversives, yet at least a few informers who caused the death of many people in this way live in town unmolested. Since the country lacks an effective judiciary, Guatemalans do not ordinarily expect to obtain redress through the criminal justice system. As for personal vengeance, Nebajeños exhibit relatively little interest. It is possible that a new style of personal justice is emerging, however, through hired killers. In 1989–91 there were grenade and firearm attacks on at least three Nebajeños—the head of the civil patrol, a discredited ex-mayor, and an unscrupulous legal inter-

preter. My sources did not attribute the attacks to the army or the guerrillas; particularly in the case of the ex-mayor and the legal interpreter, more than a few Nebajeños felt that the victims of the attacks deserved them. Homicide was relatively rare in Ixil country before the war, certainly more so than in the capital and in the ladino-populated eastern part of the country.

10. Let the Dead Bury the Dead?

1. For the neighboring case of El Salvador, we have opinion surveys coordinated by the Jesuit sociologist Ignacio Martin-Baró shortly before his murder by the Salvadoran army. Seventy-three percent of a national sample denied that a Christian could in good conscience support guerrilla warfare. Only 24 percent of the campesinos surveyed and 19 percent of poor urban dwellers believed that a good Christian could support guerrillas, although 17 percent in each of the two latter categories said they were unsure of the answer (from Berryman 1991:112). For like-minded accounts, see Anderson and Anderson (1988) on five war zones around the world, Kriger 1991 on Zimbabwe, and Finnegan 1992 on Mozambique.

2. Lila Abu-Lughod (1990) and Jean and John Comaroff (1991) survey the literature on resistance.

3. Brown 1991.

4. Scott 1990.

5. Thanks to Norman Stoltzoff for help with this point.

6. For a summary of events in eastern Guatemala, see Wickham-Crowley 1990:207–10.

7. Smith 1992:32.

8. Personal communication, April 23, 1992.

9. Smith 1992.

10. Cf. Goldin and Metz 1991:334.

Bibliography

Abu-Lughod, Lila. 1990 "The Romance of Resistance: Tracing Transformations of Power Through Bedouin Women." *American Ethnologist* 17(1): 41–55.

Adams, Richard N. 1970. *Crucifixion by Power: Essays on Guatemalan National Social Structure, 1944–1966.* Austin: University of Texas Press.

—— 1976. *Cultural Surveys of Panama-Nicaragua-Guatemala-El Salvador-Honduras.* Detroit: Blaine Ethridge. [1st edition 1957]

—— 1990. "Ethnic Images and Strategies in 1944." In C. Smith, ed., *Guatemalan Indians and the State, 1540 to 1988*, pp. 141–62. Austin: University of Texas Press.

Adams, Richard N., Ruben E. Reina, Roland H. Ebel, June Nash, Miles Richardson, and Barbara Bode. 1972 (1957). *Community, Culture, and National Change.* Publication no. 24, pp. 1–54. New Orleans: Middle American Research Institute, Tulane University.

Americas Watch. 1983. *Creating a Desolation and Calling It Peace.*

—— 1984. *Guatemala: A Nation of Prisoners.*

—— 1986. *Civil Patrols in Guatemala.*

—— 1989. *Persecuting Human Rights Monitors: The CERJ in Guatemala.*

Amnesty International. 1981. "Guatemala: A Government Program of Political Murder." *New York Review of Books*, March 19, pp. 38–40.

———— 1982. "Guatemala: Massive Extrajudicial Executions in Rural Areas Under the Government of General Efraín Ríos Montt." Special briefing, July.

———— 1987. *Guatemala: The Human Rights Record.*

Anderson, Benedict. 1983. *Imagined Communities: Reflections on the Origin and Spread of Nationalism.* London: Verso.

Anderson, Jon Lee and Scott Anderson. 1988. *War Zones.* New York: Dodd, Mead.

Anderson, Robert Mapes. 1979. *Vision of the Disinherited: The Making of Modern Pentecostalism.* New York: Oxford University Press.

Anfuso, Joseph and David Sczepanski. 1983. *He Gives, He Takes Away.* Eureka, Calif.: Radiance Publications (republished as *Servant or Dictator?*).

Annis, Sheldon. 1987. *God and Production in a Guatemalan Town.* Austin: University of Texas Press.

APROFAM (Asociación Pro-Bienestar de la Familia de Guatemala). 1988. "Seminario Población, Recursos Naturales y Medio Ambiente," Guatemala City.

Arias, Arturo. 1985. "El Movimiento Indígena en Guatemala, 1970–83." In Daniel Camacho, ed., *Movimientos Populares en Centroamérica*, pp. 63–119. Costa Rica: Ciudad Universitario Rodrigo Facio.

———— 1990 "Changing Indian Identity: Guatemala's Violent Transition to Modernity." In C. Smith, ed., *Guatemalan Indians and the State, 1540 to 1988*, pp. 230–57. Austin: University of Texas Press.

Arias de Blois, Jorge. 1978. *Demografía Guatemalteca, 1960–76: Una bibliografía anotada.* Guatemala: Universidad del Valle.

———— 1983. *Demografía Guatemalteca, 1960–76: Una bibliografía anotada* (primer suplemento 1977–79). Guatemala: Universidad del Valle.

———— 1986. "La Educación y las Tendencias Demográficas: Impactos Mutuos." Guatemala: Asociación Pro-Bienestar de la Familia de Guatemala.

Asturias, Miguel Angel. 1967. *El Señor Presidente.* New York: Atheneum.

———— 1975. *Men of Maize.* Delacorte Press/Seymour Lawrence.

AVANCSO (Asociación para el Avance de las Ciencias Sociales en Guatemala). 1990. "Política Institucional hacia el Desplazado Interno en Guatemala." Cuadernos de Investigación No. 6. Guatemala City.

Barry, Tom and Deb Preusch. 1984. "The Pacification of Guatemala: The Role of U.S. Economic Aid." *Resource Center Bulletin* (November): 1–4.

Bermúdez, Fernando. 1986. *Death and Resurrection in Guatemala.* Maryknoll, N.Y.: Orbis Books.

Berryman, Phillip. 1984. *The Religious Roots of Rebellion: Christians in Central American Revolutions.* Maryknoll, N.Y.: Orbis Books.

———— 1991. "Churches in Conflict." Unpublished book manuscript.

Black, George, with Milton Jamail and Norma Stoltz Chinchilla. 1984. *Garrison Guatemala.* London: Zed Press.

Bricker, Victoria Reifler. 1981. *Indian Christ, Indian King*. Austin: University of Texas Press.

Brintnall, Douglas E. 1979a. *Revolt Against the Dead: The Modernization of a Mayan Community in the Highlands of Guatemala*. New York: Gordon and Breach.

———— 1979b. "Race Relations in the Southeastern Highlands of Mesoamerica." *American Ethnologist* 6(4): 638–52.

British Parliamentary Human Rights Group. 1984. *Bitter and Cruel: Report of a Mission to Guatemala*, October.

Brown, Michael. 1991. "Beyond Resistance: A Comparative Study of Utopian Renewal in Amazonia." *Ethnohistory* 38(4): 388–413.

Burgos-Debray, Elisabeth, ed. 1983. *I, Rigoberta Menchú*. London: Verso.

Burkitt, Robert. 1930. "Explorations in the Highlands of Western Guatemala." *Museum Journal* (Philadelphia: University of Pennsylvania) 21(1): 41–72.

Burnett, Virginia Garrard. 1986. "A History of Protestantism in Guatemala." Ph.D. dissertation, Tulane University.

Burnett, Virginia Garrard and David Stoll, eds. 1993. *Rethinking Protestantism in Latin America*. Philadelphia: Temple University Press.

Burns, Allan F. 1989. "Internal and External Identity Among Kanjobal Mayan Refugees in Florida." In Nancie L. Gonzalez and Carolyn S. McCommon, eds., *Conflict, Migration, and the Expression of Ethnicity*, pp. 46–59. Boulder: Westview Press.

Cambranes, J. C. 1986. *Agrarismo en Guatemala*. Guatemala: Serviprensa Centroamericana.

Canby, Peter. 1992. *The Heart of the Sky: Travels Among the Maya*. New York: HarperCollins.

Carlsen, Robert S. 1992. "Of Bullets, Bibles, and Bokunabs: What in the World Is Going On at Santiago Atitlán?" Ph.D. dissertation, University of Colorado.

Carmack, Robert M., ed. 1988. *Harvest of Violence: Guatemala's Indians in the Counterinsurgency War*. Norman: University of Oklahoma Press.

Central America Report. 1990. "Above the law? Civil patrols in Guatemala," *Central America Report* 17, no. 18 (May 18). Four-page special report.

CEP (Centro de Estudios y Publicaciones). 1981. *Morir y Despertar en Guatemala*. Lima, Peru.

CGUP (Comité Guatemalteco de Unidad Patriótica). 1983. *Alto al Genocidio de un Pueblo en Lucha*.

Chance, John K. 1990. "Changes in Twentieth-Century Mesoamerican Cargo Systems." In Lynn Stephen and James Dow, eds., *Class, Politics, and Popular Religion in Mexico and Central America*, pp. 27–42. Volume 10, Society for Latin American Anthropology Publication Series. Washington, D.C: American Anthropological Association.

Chapin, Mac. 1988. "Counterinsurgency and the Development Pole Strategy in Guatemala." *Cultural Survival Quarterly* 12(3): 11–17.

Chea, José Luis. 1988. *Guatemala: La Cruz Fragmentada.* San José, Costa Rica: Editorial DEI.

Chernow, Ron. 1979. "The Strange Death of Bill Woods: Did He Fly Too Far in the Zone of the Generals?" *Mother Jones* (May): 32–42.

Christian, Michael. 1982. "Guatemala Diary." *The Community Voice* (Bend, Oregon) (February): 7–8.

Cifuentes H., Juan Fernando. 1982. "Apreciación de Asuntos Civiles para el área Ixil." *Revista Militar* (September–December): 26–72 (dates to early 1980 or 1981).

Coffin, Mark B. 1981. "Nebaj, Guatemala: Many My Lai's." Twenty-three-page typescript.

Colby, Benjamin N. 1976. "The Anomalous Ixil—Bypassed by the Postclassic?" *American Antiquity* 41, no. 1: 74–80.

Colby, Benjamin and Lore Colby. 1981. *The Daykeeper: The Life and Discourse of an Ixil Diviner.* Cambridge, Mass.: Harvard University Press.

Colby, Benjamin N. and Pierre L. van den Berghe. 1969. *Ixil Country: A Plural Society in Highland Guatemala.* Berkeley: University of California Press.

Collier, George A. 1975. *Fields of the Tzotzil: The Ecological Bases of Tradition in Highland Chiapas.* Austin: University of Texas Press.

——— 1987 *Socialists of Rural Andalusia: Unacknowledged Revolutionaries of the Second Republic.* Stanford, Calif.: Stanford University Press.

Comaroff, Jean and John. 1991. *Of Revelation and Revolution: Christianity, Colonialism, and Consciousness in South Africa.* Vol. 1. Chicago: University of Chicago Press.

Compañero. 1982. "Testimonio: María Lupe, mujer parcelaria de la selva." *Compañero* (Guerrilla Army of the Poor) 5: 27–30.

Council on Hemispheric Affairs. 1990. "Profile: Mario Polanco, 'You Are the Assassins.' " *COHA's Washington Report on the Hemisphere* (August 22): 2.

Daniels, Anthony. 1990. *"Sweet Waist of America": Journeys Around Guatemala.* London: Hutchinson.

Davis, Shelton Harold. 1970. "Land of Our Ancestors: A Study of Land Tenure and Inheritance in the Highlands of Guatemala." Ph.D. dissertation, Harvard University.

——— 1985. "Civil Patrols—Armed Peace in Northern Huehuetenango." *Cultural Survival Quarterly* 9(4): 38–39.

——— 1988. "Introduction: Sowing the Seeds of Violence." In Robert M. Carmack, ed., *Harvest of Violence*, pp. 3–36. Norman: University of Oklahoma Press.

Davis, Shelton H. and Julie Hodson. 1982. *Witnesses to Political Violence in*

Guatemala: The Suppression of a Rural Development Movement. Impact Audit 2. Boston: Oxfam America.

DeBray, Regis (in collaboration with Ricardo Ramírez). 1975. "Guatemala." In R. Debray, *Las Pruebas de Fuego*, pp. 249–324. Mexico, D.F.: Siglo Veintiuno Editores, S.A.

De Janvry, Alain. 1982. *The Agrarian Question and Reformism in Latin America.* Baltimore: Johns Hopkins Press.

Democratic Front Against Repression. 1980 "Report on the Spanish Embassy Massacre in Guatemala." Eleven-page typescript.

Dennis, Philip A., Gary S. Elbow, and Peter L. Heller. 1988. "Development Under Fire: The Playa Grande Colonization Project in Guatemala." *Human Organization* 47, no. 1: 69–76.

Diener, Paul. 1978. "The Tears of St. Anthony: Ritual and Revolution in Eastern Guatemala." *Latin American Perspectives* 5, no. 3: 92–116.

Dirección General de Estadística. 1968. *Censo Agropecuario 1964.* Tomo 1. Ministerio de Economía.

—— 1973. *Censo de 1973, Lugares Poblados.*

—— 1979. *Guatemala: Población Estimada por Departamentos y Municipios, Años 1974–1985.*

—— 1981. *Censo 1981, Lugares Poblados.*

—— 1982. *III Censo Nacional Agropecuario, 1979.* Vol. I, Tomo I. Ministerio de Economía.

"Dossier: Aparecimiento Público de las Comunidades de Población en Resistencia (CPR) de la Sierra." 1991.

Durham, William H. 1979. *Scarcity and Survival in Central America: Ecological Origins of the Soccer War.* Stanford: Stanford University Press.

Earle, Duncan MacLean. 1982. "Changes in Ethnic Population Proportions in the Quiché Basin: A Case of Reconquest." In R. Carmack, J. Early, and C. Lutz, eds., *Historical Demography of Highland Guatemala*, pp. 183–88. Albany: Institute of Mesoamerican Studies, State University of New York.

—— 1991. "Measuring the Maya Disconnection: Violence and Development in Guatemala." *American Ethnologist* 18, no. 4: 793–98.

Early, John D. 1982a. *The Demographic Structure and Evolution of a Peasant System: The Guatemalan Population*, Boca Raton: University Presses of Florida.

—— 1982b. "Some Demographic Characteristics of Peasant Systems: The Guatemalan Case." In John Early and Christopher Lutz, eds., *The Historical Demography of Highland Guatemala*, pp. 169–81. Publication no. 6, Institute for Mesoamerican Studies. Albany: State University of New York.

Ebel, Roland. 1988. "When Indians Take Power: Conflict and Consensus in San Juan Ostuncalco." In R. Carmack, ed., *Harvest of Violence*, pp. 174–91. Norman: University of Oklahoma Press.

Ehlers, Tracy Bachrach. 1990. *Silent Looms: Women and Production in a Guatemalan Town*. Boulder: Westview Press.

Ehrlich, Paul R. and Anne H. 1990. *The Population Explosion*. New York: Simon and Schuster.

Elliott, Elaine D. 1989. "A History of Land Tenure in the Ixil Triangle." Unpublished paper.

———— 1990. "The Men of Corn: Ixil Land History in Ilom." Unpublished paper.

Elliott, Ray, with Mary Jo Stockdale. 1983. "The Odyssey of Cu'." *In Other Words* (Huntington Beach, Calif.: Wycliffe Bible Translators) 9, no. 5: 2–3.

Evans, Timothy Edward. 1990. "Religious Conversion in Quetzaltenango, Guatemala." Ph.D. dissertation, University of Pittsburgh.

Fagen, Richard R. and William S. Tuohy. 1972. *Politics and Privilege in a Mexican City*. Stanford, Calif.: Stanford University Press.

Fajardo, Andrés. 1987. "From the Volcano: Protestant Conversion Among the Ixil-Maya of Highland Guatemala." Honors thesis, Harvard College.

Falla, Ricardo. 1978. "El Movimiento Indígena." *Estudios Centroamericanos* 356–57 (June–July): 439–61. San Salvador: Universidad Centroamericana José Simeon Canas.

———— 1980. *Quiché Rebelde: Estudio de un Movimiento de Conversión Religioso, Rebelde a las Creencias Tradicionales, en San Antonio Ilotenango, Quiché (1948–70)*. Guatemala City: Editorial Universitaria de Guatemala.

———— 1983a. "El Hambre y Otras Privaciones Inducidas por el Ejército de Guatemala sobre la Población Civil." *Iglesia Guatemalteca en el Exilio*, September.

———— 1983b. "Masacre de la Finca San Francisco, Huehuetenango, Guatemala." Documento 1. Copenhagen: International Work Group for Indigenous Affairs.

———— 1992. *Masacres de la selva: Ixcán, Guatemala (1975–1982)*. Guatemala City: Editorial Universitaria.

Fernández Fernández, José Manuel. 1988. "El Comité de Unidad Campesina: Origen y Desarrollo. " Cuaderno 2. Guatemala: Centro de Estudios Rurales Centroamericanos.

Figueroa Ibarra, Carlos. 1976. *El Proletariado Rural en el Agro Guatemalteco*. Guatemala: Universidad de San Carlos.

Finnegan, William. 1992. *Mozambique: A Complicated War*. Berkeley: University of California Press.

Flora, Cornelia Butler. 1976. *Protestantism in Colombia: Baptism by Fire and Spirit*. London: Associated University Press.

Fox, Donald T. 1982. "Nebaj and the Future of Guatemala." *Christian Century* (June 2): 658–62.

Frank, Luisa and Philip Wheaton. 1984. *Indian Guatemala: Path to Liberation.* Washington, D.C.: Ecumenical Program for Interamerican Communication and Action (EPICA).

Gillespie, Richard. 1983. "Anatomy of the Guatemalan Guerrilla." *Communist Affairs* 2 (October): 490–97.

Gleijeses, Piero. 1983. "Guatemala: Crisis and Response." In Richard R. Fagen and Olga Pellicer, eds., *The Future of Central America: Policy Choices for the U.S. and Mexico*, pp.187–212. Stanford, Calif.: Stanford University Press.

———— 1985. "The Guatemalan Silence." *New Republic* (June 10): 20–23.

Glittenberg, Jo Ann Kropp. 1976. "A Comparative Study of Fertility in Highland Guatemala." Ph.D. dissertation, University of Colorado.

Goldin, Liliana R. and Brent Metz. 1991. "An Expression of Cultural Change: Invisible Converts to Protestantism Among Highland Guatemala Mayas." *Ethnology* 30, no. 4: 325–38.

Green, Linda. 1991. "Social Chaos, Moral Order, and Protestant Evangelicals." Paper presented to the American Anthropological Association, November 20–24, Chicago.

Greenberg, James B. 1981. *Santiago's Sword: Chatino Peasant Religion and Economics.* Berkeley: University of California Press.

Guatemala Information Center. n.d. "Genocide in El Quiché: A Testimonial of the Persecuted Church." Popular Histories No. 1.

Guatemalan Church in Exile. 1982. "Martirio y Lucha en Guatemala." *Iglesia Guatemalteca en el Exilio* (December).

———— 1983a. "La Santa Contrainsurgencia." *Iglesia Guatemalteca en el Exilio* (January).

———— 1983b. "Fernando Hoyos, ¡¡Presente!!" *Iglesia Guatemalteca en el Exilio* (July).

———— 1984. "Un Nuevo Estilo de Vida: Los Polos de Desarrollo," *Iglesia Guatemalteca en el Exilio* (September–October).

———— 1989a. *Guatemala: Security, Development, and Democracy.*

———— 1989b. " 'Offensive of the People'; Campesino Against Campesino," July. Booklet.

———— 1990. "Official Documents of the Communities of Population in Resistance of the Sierra, El Quiché, Guatemala."

Handy, Jim. 1984. *Gift of the Devil: A History of Guatemala.* Toronto: Between the Lines Press.

———— 1989. "A Sea of Indians: Ethnic Conflict and the Guatemalan Revolution, 1944–1952." *The Americas: A Quarterly Review of Inter-American History* (October): 189–204.

———— 1990. "The Corporate Community, Campesino Organizations, and

Agrarian Reform: 1950–1954." In C. Smith, ed., *Guatemalan Indians and the State, 1540 to 1988*, pp. 163–82. Austin: University of Texas Press.

Harding, Susan. 1987. "Convicted by the Holy Spirit: The Rhetoric of Fundamental Baptist Conversion." *American Ethnologist* 14: 167–81.

Hinshaw, Robert E. 1975. *Panajachel: A Guatemalan Town in Thirty-Year Perspective*. Pittsburgh: University of Pittsburgh Press.

Hockstader, Lee. 1991. "Village Becomes Cockpit of Guatemalan Human Rights Struggle." *Washington Post*, May 24, p. A38.

Horst, Oscar H. 1967. "The Specter of Death in a Guatemalan Highland Community," *The Geographical Review* 57, no. 2: 151–67.

Hough, Richard et al. 1982. *Land and Labor in Guatemala: An Assessment*. Report for U.S. Agency for International Development. Guatemala City: Ediciones Papiro.

Informador Guerrillero. 1982. "Quiché: La guerra se profundiza." *Informador Guerrillero* 10: 1–3.

——— 1982. "Los inicios de la organización en el Ixcán." *Informador Guerrillero* 10: 3–4.

——— 1983. "Como en Viet Nam, nos preparamos para lo peor." *Informador Guerrillero* 18: 8–10.

Instituto Nacional de Estadística. 1988. *Guatemala: Población Estimada por Departamentos y Municipios*. Guatemala City.

International Work Group on Indigenous Affairs. 1978. "The Massacre at Panzós." Document 33. Copenhagen.

Johannesen, Stanley. 1988. "The Holy Ghost in Sunset Park." *Historical Reflections* 15, no. 3: 543–77.

Jonas, Susanne. 1991. *The Battle for Guatemala: Rebels, Death Squads, and U.S. Power*. Boulder: Westview Press.

Jonas, Susanne, Ed McCaughan, and Elizabeth Sunderland Martinez, eds. 1984. *Guatemala: Tyranny on Trial*. Testimony of the Permanent People's Tribunal. Synthesis Publications.

Jones, Lynne. 1990. "Murder in Guatemala." *New Left Review* 182: 53–61.

Keane, John, ed. 1988. *Civil Society and the State: New European Perspectives*. London: Verso.

Kearney, Michael. 1970. "Drunkenness and Religious Conversion in a Mexican Village." *Quarterly Journal of Studies on Alcohol* 31: 132–52.

Kincaid, A. Douglas. 1987. "Peasants into Rebels: Community and Class in Rural El Salvador." *Comparative Studies in Society and History* 29: 466–94.

Kipp, Rita Smith. 1991. "A Practice Approach to Conversion as a Change of Identity." Paper presented to the American Anthropological Association, November 21–24, Chicago.

Koizumi, Junji. 1981. "Symbol and Context: A Study of Self and Action in a Guatemalan Culture." Ph.D. dissertation, Stanford University.

Kreuger, Chris and Kjell Enge. 1985. *Security and Development Conditions in the Guatemalan Highlands*. Washington, D.C.: Washington Office on Latin America.

Kriger, Norma. 1991. "Popular Struggles in Zimbabwe's War of National Liberation." In Preben Kaarsholm, ed., *Cultural Struggle and Development in Southern Africa*, pp. 125–48. Harare: Academic Books.

La Farge, Oliver. 1947. *Santa Eulalia: The Religion of a Cuchumatán Indian Town*. Chicago: University of Chicago Press.

"La Toma de Nebaj." 1982. *Polémica* (January–February): 37–43.

Lawrence, Donald P. and Gale L. Morris. 1969. "The Religion of the Ixil Maya, Past and Present." Thesis for the School of Theology of the Primitive Methodist Church of America.

Lengyel, Thomas E. 1979. "Religious Factionalism and Social Diversity in a Mayan Community." *Wisconsin Sociologist* 16: 81–89.

―――― 1987. "The Cultural Organization of Language in a Mayan Community." Ph.D. dissertation, University of Chicago.

Lernoux, Penny. 1980. *The Cry of the People*. New York: Doubleday.

――――. 1989. *People of God: The Struggle for World Catholicism*. New York: Viking.

Levitsky, Steve and Tony Lapp. 1992. "Solidarismo and Organized Labor." *Hemisphere* 4, no. 2: 26–30.

Lincoln, Jackson Steward. 1945. "An Ethnological Study on the Ixil Indians of the Guatemala Highlands." Microfilm Collection of Manuscripts on Middle American Cultural Anthropology No. 1, University of Chicago Library.

Loucky, James. 1978. "Production and the Patterning of Social Relations and Values in Two Guatemalan Villages." *American Ethnologist* 6: 702–22.

―――― 1988 "Children's Work and Family Survival in Highland Guatemala." Ph.D. dissertation, University of California-Los Angeles.

Loucky, James and Robert Carlsen. 1991. "Massacre in Santiago Atitlán." *Cultural Survival Quarterly* 15, no. 3: 65–70.

Lovell, W. George. 1985a. *Conquest and Survival in Colonial Guatemala: A Historical Geography of the Cuchumatán Highlands, 1500–1821*. Montreal: McGill-Queen's University Press.

―――― 1985b. "From Conquest to Counterinsurgency." *Cultural Survival Quarterly* 9, no. 2: 46–49.

―――― 1988. "Surviving Conquest: The Maya of Guatemala in Historical Perspective." *Latin American Research Review* 23, no. 2: 25–57.

―――― 1990. "Maya Survival in Ixil Country, Guatemala." *Cultural Survival Quarterly* 14, no. 4: 10–12.

―――― 1992. "Conquest and Population: Maya Demography in Historical Perspective." Paper prepared for Latin American Studies Association, Los Angeles, California, September 23–26.

Mamdani, Mahmood. 1972. *The Myth of Population Control: Family, Caste, and Class in an Indian Village*. New York: Monthly Review Press.

Manz, Beatriz. 1988a. *Refugees of a Hidden War: The Aftermath of Counterinsurgency in Guatemala*. Albany: State University of New York.

———— 1988b. "The Transformation of La Esperanza, an Ixcán Village." In R. Carmack, ed., *Harvest of Violence*, pp. 70–89. Norman: University of Oklahoma Press.

Mariz, Cecilia Loreto. 1989a. "Religion and Coping with Poverty in Brazil." Ph.D. dissertation, Boston University.

———— 1989b. "The Brazilian Pentecostals' Economic Values." Paper presented to the Latin American Studies Association, Miami.

Marnham, Patrick. 1985. *So Far from God: A Journey to Central America*. New York: Penguin.

Martin, David. 1990. *Tongues of Fire: The Explosion of Protestantism in Latin America*. Oxford: Basil Blackwell.

"Martirio y Lucha en Guatemala: Testimonio de la comunidad de La Estancia (El Quiché)." 1983. *Shupihui* (Iquitos, Peru: Centro de Estudios Teológicos de la Amazonia) 8, no. 25–26: 64–79.

McCreery, David. 1976. "Coffee and Class: The Structure of Development in Liberal Guatemala." *Hispanic American Historical Review* 56: 438–60.

———— 1986. " 'An Odious Feudalism:' Mandamiento Labor and Commercial Agriculture in Guatemala, 1858–1920." *Latin American Perspectives* 13, no. 1: 99–117.

———— 1990. "State Power, Indigenous Communities, and Land in Nineteenth-Century Guatemala, 1820–1920." In C. Smith, ed., *Guatemalan Indians and the State, 1540 to 1988*, pp. 96–115. Austin: University of Texas Press.

———— n.d. "Rural Guatemala, 1760–1940." Stanford, Calif.: Stanford University Press, forthcoming.

McGuire, Stryker. 1991. *Streets Without Names*. New York: Atlantic Monthly Press.

Melville, Thomas R. 1983. "The Catholic Church in Guatemala, 1944–1982." *Cultural Survival Quarterly* 7, no. 1: 23–27.

Melville, Thomas R. and Marjorie Melville. 1971a. *Whose Heaven, Whose Earth?* New York: Knopf.

———— 1971b. *Guatemala: The Politics of Land Ownership*. New York: Free Press.

Mendez Montenegro, Julio Cesar. 1960. "444 Años de Legislación Agraria, 1513–1957." *Revista de la Facultad de Ciencias Jurídicas y Sociales de Guatemala* 6: 9–12.

Migdal, Joel. 1974. *Peasants, Politics, and Revolution*. Princeton: Princeton University Press.

Ministerio de Defensa Nacional. 1985. *Polos de Desarrollo: Filosofía Desarrollista*. Guatemala: Editorial del Ejército.

Mondragón, Rafael. 1983. *De Indios y Cristianos en Guatemala*. Mexico, D.F: COPEC/CECOPE.

Moore, Alexander. 1989. "Symbolic Imperatives for a Democratic Peace in Guatemala." In Nancie L. Gonzalez and Carolyn S. McCommon, eds., *Conflict, Migration, and the Expression of Ethnicity*, pp. 28–45. Boulder: Westview Press.

Morrissey, James Arthur. 1978. "A Missionary Directed Resettlement Project Among the Highland Maya of Western Guatemala." Ph.D. dissertation, Stanford University.

―――― 1987. "The Ixcán: Guatemala's Crucible for Change." Unpublished paper.

Nachtigall, Horst. 1978. *Die Ixil: Maya-Indianer in Guatemala*. Berlin: Dietrich Reimer Verlag.

Nairn, Allan. 1983. "The Guns of Guatemala." *New Republic* (April 11): 17–21.

Nash, June. 1960. "Protestantism in an Indian Village in the Western Highlands of Guatemala." *Alpha Kappa Deltan* (Winter): 49–53.

Newbold, Stokes. 1957. "Receptivity to Communist-fomented Agitation in Rural Guatemala." *Economic Development and Cultural Change* 5, no. 4: 338–60.

Nyrop, Richard F., ed. 1984. *Guatemala: A Country Study*. Area Handbook Series. Washington, D.C.: American University.

Paige, Jeffrey. 1975. *Agrarian Revolution: Social Movements and Export Agriculture in the Underdeveloped World*. New York: Free Press.

―――― 1983. "Social Theory and Peasant Revolution in Vietnam and Guatemala." *Theory and Society* 12, no. 6: 699–737.

Painter, James. 1987. *Guatemala: False Hope, False Freedom*. London: Latin America Bureau.

Palomino, Achilles. 1972. "Patrones Matrimoniales entre Los Ixiles de Chajul." *Guatemala Indígena* 7, no. 1–2: 5–159.

Paul, Benjamin D. 1987. "Fifty Years of Religious Change in San Pedro La Laguna, a Mayan Community in Highland Guatemala." Paper presented to the American Anthropological Association, Chicago, November 18–22.

―――― 1988. "Entrepreneurs and Economic Inequality in San Pedro La Laguna, Guatemala: A Hundred Years of History." Paper presented to the Latin American Studies Association, New Orleans, March 17–19.

Payeras, Mario. 1983. *Days of the Jungle: The Testimony of a Guatemalan Guerrillero, 1972–76*. New York: Monthly Review Press.

―――― 1987. *El Trueno en la Ciudad: Episodios de la Lucha Armada Urbana de 1981 en Guatemala*. Mexico City: Juan Pablos.

Perera, Victor. 1993. *Unfinished Conquest: The Guatemalan Tragedy*. Berkeley: University of California Press.

Popkin, Samuel L. 1979. *The Rational Peasant: The Political Economy of Rural Society in Vietnam*. Berkeley: University of California Press.

Proceso. 1980. "El Pueblo Indígena Reconoció su Rostro y Recuperó su Sangre." *Proceso* (Mexico, D.F.) 202 (September 15): 32–33.

"Report on Violence in Northern Quiché, Guatemala, by a Parish Priest, August 1979 to January 1980." 1980. Five-page typescript.

Richards, Michael. 1985. "Cosmopolitan World View and Counterinsurgency in Guatemala." *Anthropological Quarterly* 58, no. 3: 90–107.

Ríos Montt, Jose Efraín. 1982. *Mensajes del Presidente de la República.* Secretaría de Relaciones Públicas de la Presidencia.

Rojas Lima, Flavio. 1988. *La Cofradía: Reducto Cultural Indígena.* Guatemala: Seminario de Integración Social Guatemalteca.

Rosenthal, Mario. 1962. *Guatemala: The Story of an Emergent Latin American Democracy.* New York: Twayne Publishers.

Rossdeutscher, Daniele. 1991. "Solidarismo Challenges the Labor Movement." *Report on Guatemala* 11, no. 4: 8–11.

Schlesinger, Stephen and Stephen Kinzer. 1982. *Bitter Fruit: The Untold Story of the American Coup in Guatemala.* London: Sinclaire Brown.

Schumann, Debra Ann. 1982. "Fertility and Economic Strategy in a Southern Mexican Ejido." Ph.D. dissertation, Southern Methodist University.

Schwartz, Norman B. 1987. "Colonization of Northern Guatemala: The Petén." *Journal of Anthropological Research* 43, no. 2: 163–83.

———— 1990. *Forest Society: A Social History of Petén, Guatemala.* Philadelphia: University of Pennsylvania Press.

Scotchmer, David G. 1986. "Convergency of the Gods: Comparing Traditional Maya and Christian Maya Cosmologies." In Gary Gossen, ed., *Symbol and Meaning Beyond the Closed Community*, pp. 197–226. Albany: Institute of Mesoamerican Studies, State University of New York.

———— 1991a. "Symbols of Salvation: Interpreting Highland Maya Protestantism in Context." Ph.D. dissertation, State University of New York at Albany.

———— 1991b. "Pastors, Preachers, or Prophets? Cultural Conflict and Continuity in Maya Protestant Leadership." Draft paper prepared for the American Anthropological Association, Chicago.

Scott, James C. 1976. *The Moral Economy of the Peasant: Rebellion and Subsistence in Southeast Asia.* New Haven: Yale University Press.

———— 1985. "Everyday Forms of Peasant Resistance." *Journal of Peasant Studies* 13, no. 2: 5–35.

———— 1986. *Weapons of the Weak: Everyday Forms of Peasant Resistance.* New Haven: Yale University Press.

———— 1990. *Domination and the Arts of Resistance: Hidden Transcripts.* New Haven: Yale University Press.

"Sebastián Guzmán: Principal de principales." n.d. Ten-page typescript, c. 1982.

Senate Subcommittee on Security and Terrorism. 1984. "Marxism and Christianity in Revolutionary Central America, Hearings, October 18–19, 1983." Judiciary Committee, U.S. Senate. Washington, D.C.: U.S. Government Printing Office.

Sexton, James D. 1978. "Protestantism and Modernization in Two Guatemalan Towns." *American Ethnologist* 5, no. 2: 280–302.

————— 1992. *Ignacio: The Diary of a Maya Indian of Guatemala.* Philadelphia: University of Pennsylvania Press.

Sheehan, Edward R. 1989. *Agony in the Garden.* Boston: Houghton-Mifflin.

Simons, Marlise. 1982. "Latin America's New Gospel." *New York Times Magazine,* November 7, pp. 45–47, 112–20.

Skocpol, Theda. 1979. *States and Social Revolutions.* Cambridge: Cambridge University Press.

————— 1982. "What Makes Peasants Revolutionary?" *Comparative Politics* 14, no. 3: 351–75.

Simon, Jean-Marie. 1987. *Guatemala: Eternal Spring, Eternal Tyranny.* New York: Norton.

Simon, Joel. 1989. "The Rise and Fall of Guatemala's Ixcàn Cooperatives, 1965–89." Master's thesis, Latin American Studies, Stanford University.

Simon, Joel and Beatriz Manz. 1992. "Representation, Organization, and Human Rights Among Guatemalan Refugees in Mexico—1980–92." *Harvard Human Rights Journal* 5: 95–135.

Simonelli, Jeanne M. 1986. *Two Boys, A Girl, and Enough!* Boulder: Westview Press.

Smith, A. Ledyard and Alfred V. Kidder. 1951. *Excavations at Nebaj, Guatemala.* Publication 594. Washington, D.C.: Carnegie Institution of Washington.

Smith, Carol A. 1974. "Causes and Consequences of Central-Place Types in Western Guatemala." In C. Smith, ed., *Economic Systems,* vol. 1 of *Regional Analysis.* New York: Academic Press.

————— 1978. "Beyond Dependency Theory: National and Regional Patterns of Underdevelopment in Guatemala." *American Ethnologist* 5, no. 2: 574–617.

————— 1984a. "Local History in Global Context: Social and Economic Transitions in Western Guatemala." *Comparative Studies in Society and History* 26, no. 2: 193–228.

————— 1984b. "Does a Commodity Economy Enrich the Few While Ruining the Masses? Differentiation Among Petty Commodity Producers in Guatemala." *Journal of Peasant Studies* 11, no. 3: 60–95.

————— 1987a. "Economic Reorganization as a Continuation of War: Military Impact on the Western Highlands of Guatemala." Unpublished paper.

————— 1987b. "Culture and Community: The Language of Class in Guatemala." In Mike Davis, Manning Marable, Fred Pfeil, and Michael Sprinker, eds., *The Year Left 2: An American Socialist Yearbook.* London: Verso.

———— 1989. Review of *God and Production in a Guatemalan Town* by Sheldon Annis. *Man* 24, no. 2: 351–52.

———— 1990a. *Guatemalan Indians and the State, 1540 to 1988*. Austin: University of Texas Press.

———— 1990b. "The Militarization of Civil Society in Guatemala: Economic Reorganization as a Continuation of War." *Latin American Perspectives* 17, no. 4: 8–41.

———— 1992. "Maya Nationalism." *Report on the Americas* 25, no. 3: 29–33.

Smith, Waldemar. 1977. *The Fiesta System and Economic Change*. New York: Columbia University Press.

Stadelman, Raymond. 1940. *Maize Cultivation in Northwestern Guatemala*. Contributions to American Anthropology and History, no. 33. Washington, D.C.: Carnegie Institution of Washington.

Stoll, David. 1982. *Fishers of Men or Founders of Empire? The Wycliffe Bible Translators in Latin America*. London: Zed Press.

———— 1990. *Is Latin America Turning Protestant?* Berkeley: University of California Press.

Tanner, Morgan. 1988. "Winning Hearts & Mayans: Guatemalan Special Forces Gut Marxist Insurgency." *Soldier of Fortune* (November): 45–51+.

Tayacán. 1984. "Psychological Operations in Guerrilla Warfare." Translated by Congressional Research Service, Language Services, October 15.

Thompson, E. P. 1966. *The Making of the English Working Class*. New York: Vintage.

Tribunal Suprema Electoral. 1985. *Memoria*.

———— 1988. *Memoria: Elección de Corporaciones Municipales*.

Van den Berghe, Pierre. 1990. *State Violence and Ethnicity*. University Press of Colorado.

Veblen, Thomas T. 1976. "The Urgent Need for Forest Conservation in Highland Guatemala." *Biological Conservation* 9: 141–54.

———— 1978. "Forest Preservation in the Western Highlands of Guatemala." *The Geographical Review* 68, no. 4: 417–34.

Waldrop, Richard E. n.d. "Sinopsis Histórica de la Iglesia de Dios Evangélico Completo: Cincuentenario 1932–1982, República de Guatemala." Fifteen-page typescript.

Warren, Kay B. 1978. *The Symbolism of Subordination: Indian Identity in a Guatemalan Town*. Austin: University of Texas Press.

———— n.d. "Interpreting La Violencia in Guatemala: The Many Shapes of Mayan Silence and Resistance in the 1970s and 1980s." In K. B. Warren, ed., *Confronting Violence: Cultural and Political Analyses of National Conflicts*. Forthcoming.

Washington Office on Latin America. 1988. *Who Pays the Price? The Cost of War in the Guatemalan Highlands*.

———— 1991. "Guatemala: A Test Case for Human Rights Policy in the Post-Cold War Era." March 12.

Wasserstrom, Robert. 1975. "Revolution in Guatemala: Peasants and Politics Under the Arbenz Government." *Comparative Studies in Society and History* 17(4): 433–78.

———— 1983. *Class and Society in Central Chiapas.* Berkeley: University of California Press.

Watanabe, John M. 1981. "Cambios Económicos en Santiago Chimaltenango, Guatemala." *Mesoamerica* (Antigua Guatemala) 2(2): 20–41.

———— 1984. "We Who Are Here: The Cultural Conventions of Ethnic Identity in a Guatemalan Indian Village, 1937–80." Ph.D. dissertation, Harvard University.

———— 1990. "Enduring Yet Ineffable Community in the Western Periphery of Guatemala." In C. Smith, ed., *Guatemalan Indians and the State, 1540 to 1988,* pp. 183–204. Austin: University of Texas Press.

———— 1992. *Maya Saints and Souls in a Changing World.* Austin: University of Texas Press.

Weber, Max. 1958. *The Protestant Ethic and the Spirit of Capitalism.* New York: Scribner's.

Wickham-Crowley, Timothy P. 1990. "Terror and Guerrilla Warfare in Latin America, 1956–70." *Comparative Studies in Society and History* 32, no. 2: 201–37.

———— 1991. *Exploring Revolution: Essays on Latin American Insurgency and Revolutionary Theory.* Armonk, N.Y.: M. E. Sharpe.

———— 1992. *Guerrillas and Revolution in Latin America.* Princeton: Princeton University Press.

Williams, Ken. 1987. "A Church That Continues." *In Other Words* (Huntington Beach, Calif.: Wycliffe Bible Translators) 13, no. 3: 1–2.

Wilson, Richard. 1991. "Machine Guns and Mountain Spirits: The Cultural Effects of State Repression Among the Q'eqchi' of Guatemala." *Critique of Anthropology* 11, no. 1: 33–61.

Wolf, Eric. 1956. "Aspects of Group Relations in a Complex Society: Mexico." *American Anthropologist* 58: 1065–78.

———— 1969. *Peasant Wars of the Twentieth Century.* New York: Harper Torchbooks.

———— 1982. *Europe and the People Without History.* Berkeley: University of California Press.

Wood, Elisabeth J. 1991. "Civil War and Reconstruction: The Repopulation of Tenancingo, El Salvador." Paper presented to the Latin American Studies Association, Washington, D.C., April.

Wright, Ronald. 1991. *Time and the Maya.* New York: Holt.

Index